CIVILITY AND SOCIETY
IN WESTERN EUROPE

CIVILITY AND SOCIETY IN WESTERN EUROPE, 1300–1600

Marvin B. Becker

INDIANA
UNIVERSITY
PRESS

Bloomington and Indianapolis

Manufactured in the United States of America

Library of Congress Cataloging-in-Publication Data

Becker, Marvin B.
Civility and society in western
Europe, 1300–1600.
Includes index.
1. England—Civilization—16th century. 2. England—
Civilization—Medieval period, 1066–1485. 3. Tuscany
(Italy)—Civilization. 4. Renaissance. 5. Civilization,
Medieval. 6. Europe—Civilization—16th century.
7. Europe—Social conditions—16th century. I. Title.
DA320.B4 1988   942   87-46252
ISBN 0-253-31118-7
92 91 90 89 88 1 2 3 4 5

To Betty, the guiding spirit.

"We work in the dark—we do what we can—we give what we have. Our doubt is our passion, and our passion is our task."
—*The Notebooks of Henry James*

"All life therefore comes back to the question of our speech, the medium through which we communicate with each other; for all life comes back to the question of our relations with each other . . . the way we say a thing, or fail to say it, fail to learn to say it, has an importance in life that is impossible to overstate—a far-reaching importance, as the very hinge of the relation of man to man."
—Henry James's speech to the graduating class of Bryn Mawr College in June of 1905

"Without . . . civil society man could not by any possibility arrive at the perfection of which his nature is capable, not even make a remote and faint approach to it. . . . He who gave our nature to be perfected by our virtue, willed also the necessary means of its perfection—He willed therefore the state—He willed its connexion with the source and original archetype of all perfection."
—Edmund Burke, *Reflections on the Revolution in France*

CONTENTS

Acknowledgments

Research for this study was facilitated by grants from the Penrose Fund of The American Philosophical Society and the Rackham Graduate School of The University of Michigan. I wish to thank them for their generous support.

M.B.B.

Introduction

The theme of this book is the shift in cultural forms and values in selected regions of Europe (for our purposes, Tuscany and England) during the period from the late thirteenth to the sixteenth century. This was a time when literati and artists worked, consciously and unconsciously, to detach themselves from the trammels of an archaic and communal culture formerly considered normative. This detachment had significant consequences for the grammar of the arts and idiom of the vernacular. At the basic level of language it worked to augment the semantic range of key words, calling into question the epistemological insufficiencies of an archaic lexicon. Tensions, contradictions, and ambiguities were not only manifested in the lives of poets and artists, but in their esthetic choices as well. Often these conflicts served as a spur, and even when individual figures oscillated or backtracked, they did so with an appreciation for agonistic patterns of experience and rhetorical strategies that made plausible their own irresolution. In so doing they not only coined a vocabulary but also searched out new forms. Rhetorical tactics promoted arguments on both sides of a question so that literati were frequently required to colonize that middle zone between a heroic honor culture on the one side and a more problematic civil society on the other. A miniaturizing or reduction of the demands of an archaic civilization, with its strict definition of loyalty, lineage, honor, and fate, was evident in the novelistic impulse toward the commingling of social codes. In the novella, the dialogue, and the Petrarchan sonnet, discourse was open to the intervention of opposite points of view with the reader being reminded of social and moral alternatives. Literary and artistic challenges to the highly textured and concrete presentation of social life, whereby human arrangements were made visible through attention to display, ostentation, conviviality, and the many forms of hospitality and courtesy, made possible the emergence of new conceptions of comportment, taste, and social engagement. Movement away from the task of fostering ancient solidarities by portraying the conspicuous show of wealth and emotion can first be perceived in the civilization of the city-states of north and central Italy in the late thirteenth and early fourteenth centuries. Here we discover the beginnings of the transformation of a vocabulary of courtesy and fidelity into the more subdued and less heroic idiom of civility. Ancient constraints were being relaxed, and the register of meaning of lineage followed suit. Family became more privatized, loyalties centered on the state, and local society in subject communities conformed increasingly to new norms generated by capital cities such as Milan, Genoa, Venice, and Florence. These norms were no longer so exclusively predicated on fidelity and service or lineage and lordship as had been the case in the not too distant past. In the thirteenth century it was still possible for town chroniclers to write the histories of north and central Italy by explicating conflict between the mighty clans. With the fourteenth century, however, the chronicles of urban life were no longer lent coherence by the competition for power and prestige among the great houses. One is aware that new civic actors were now commanding a higher order of literary, if not political, appreciation. In Florence such personalities as Giano della Bella and Salvestro de' Medici exercised a fatal fascination on their contemporaries in part because their political style threatened communal consensus.[1]

Modes of writing and thinking, limited in an earlier time to university circles of clerics, physicians, lawyers, and notaries, were now being democratized, that is, rendered middlebrow. This civic culture was fit for a laity practicing commerce and banking and educated in the vernacular at town school and counting house. The most successful of their number were well represented in the governments of the cities of north and central Italy: typical of this group was the Florentine man of commerce Giovanni Villani, perhaps the most gifted Italian chronicler of his age. He was himself the beneficiary of a commercial and vernacular education open to the vulgarization of the leading ideas of his time, as well as of the classical past. Businessman and officeholder, he yet found time to be concerned with cultural affairs and literary achievements. He offers us a striking eulogy of his fellow citizen, the poet and polymath Dante Alighieri. Commending his many notable accomplishments in eloquent prose and polished poetry, as well as his vigorous—if somewhat tarnished—participation in the high politics of the city, Villani goes on to observe that:

> This man was a great scholar in almost every branch of learning, albeit he was a layman; he was a great poet and philosopher, and a perfect rhetorician alike in prose and verse, a very noble orator in public speaking, supreme in rhyme, with the most polished and beautiful style which in our language ever was up to his time and beyond it.[2]

That Dante was a *laico* (layman), and that he was exceptional for his interests and extraordinary competence in poetry and philosophy, as well as his high skills in rhetoric, was to Villani singular and memorable. This Dante, because he was so learned, albeit not a cleric, was somewhat haughty, standng in isolation from his fellow citizens. Yet another eulogy by Villani, this time of Brunetto Latini (Dante's literary mentor), singled out this public man and literary arbiter whom Dante celebrated for teaching that art (rhetoric) enabling men to render themselves eternal:

> In the said year 1294 there died in Florence a worthy citizen whose name was Messer Brunetto Latini, who was a great philosopher and a perfect master in rhetoric, understanding both how to speak well and how to write well. And he it was who commented upon Cicero's *Rhetoric* and made the good and useful book called the *Tesoro* and the *Tesoretto* and the key to the *Tesoro* and other books in philosophy, and about the vices and virtues. And he was the rhetorician *(dittatore)* of our commune. He was a worldly man, but we have made mention of him because it was he who was the beginner and master in refining *(digrossare)* the Florentines and in teaching them how to speak well and how to guide and govern our republic according to political science *(la politica)*.[3]

Digrossare is itself an inelegant word, but it does reach toward a new social construct, as if seeking to fill a void. Latini was acclaimed because he had initiated those arts most essential for civilizing a community. A century later, the word *digrossare* appeared barbarous and archaic—applicable to such primitive communities as the Germanic tribes of Tacitus. Alberti spoke of dedicating oneself to civil concerns with eloquence and grace, not *rozzo* or *inepto*. (*Digrossare* was derived from the Latin *rudis,* and hence, the Italian *rozzo*.) Also in that century, Florentine literati would not have been singled out, as was Dante, for being exceptionally learned, though laic. Furthermore, these literati would surely not be reckoned uncomfortable when conversing with ordinary citizens; similarly, they would not be characterized as being "somewhat worldly"—the moral tag fixed on Latini by Giovanni Villani. A more critical issue, however, was the status of literati in the political life of Florence: in the generation of Latini and Dante, literary men regularly fell victim to the factious and ideological politics of the times. Neither Dante nor Latini were exceptional for having suffered the bitter fruits of exile. A century later Leonardo Bruni Aretino, in the proem to his *Ad Petrum Histrum Dialogue,* spoke of the ruin of his native city Arezzo in his youth and the security, comfort, and enjoyment he found in the civil life of Florence: a new paradigm of civil society was in process of creation.[4]

In the fourteenth century the word *digrossare* was applied only to those newly come into the arena of Florentine public life. The chronicler Giovanni Villani spoke of these *novi cives* as having no knowledge of the *bisogni civili* (civil needs). In the Trecento it was the opinion of literati and chroniclers that instruction must be given to these newcomers in order that they be reduced "ad civilem disciplinam" (to civil discipline). The first significant Tuscan corpus of writing on civil comportment was done by the judge and man of law Francesco da Barberino (d. 1348). In Filippo Villani's biography of this poet and prosateur, special commendation was bestowed on Barberino for offering women instruction in modest comportment. So effective was his literary style that the rules of conduct he promulgated could easily be retained in the memory. The judge appeared to be more successful in instructing women than in educating those recently entering the city *ad civilem disciplinem*. Civilizing them signified inducing them to embrace a battery of virtues associated with being "companionable." Rules of comportment were essentially those of courtesy, liberality, decorum, and compassion. In the opinion of Filippo Villani, Barberino was overly optimistic in expecting these *novi cives* to embrace the norms of *cortesia*: not for nothing was Filippo Villani the lecturer on Dante at the Florentine *Studio*. This poet's diatribe against newcomers ("men of sudden gains"), whose insolence was matched only by their newly acquired wealth, resonated through Trecento literature treating civil comportment.[5]

The legacy of Dante's generation coupled rude invective against the immigrant with a magisterial and abstract view of *la vita civile*. Inferior to the contemplative life, yet the civil order was worthy of high regard: the end and final purpose of *la umana civilitade* was *la vita felice*. Aristotle's *Ethics* was perhaps the greatest single influence on the social thought of Latini and Dante, and this work reinforced the conception that the goal of the civil order was the maintenance of *universalis civilitatem*. In this way Aristotle's ideal of *eudaimonia,* as presented in the *Ethics,* could be successfully pursued. This "happiness" became with Dante a most joyful beatitude. *La vita felice,* being the end and purpose of civil order, evoked the image of happiness hovering between this world and the eternal felicity of the world of the saints. The joy and pleasures of the "beatitude of this world" were possible in the City of Man because humans had a natural tendency to strive for the Good. In Dante's case this preoccupation with "earthly happiness" was to lead him down the primrose path toward heterodoxy.[6]

In Tuscany during the late thirteenth and early fourteenth centuries (at the height of the demographic expansion), we observe a sturdy intellectual enterprise consisting of a series of vernacular manuals, social allegory, and prose fiction recommending *bel parlar* (correct and pleasing speech) and good manners to city folk. These works also contain intensive instruction with appropriate annotations on ethical and civil matters. Examples and rules were generated for everything from dress and table manners to civic oratory and witty conversation. Especially significant were the collections of didactic tales representing the comportment of those cognizant of the ways of *belle cortesia, belli risposi, belle valentie,* and *belli amori.* In the fourteenth century these writings served the practical and prosaic objective of initiating *rudes* to the norms of *onestade* and *cortesia.* This middle-brow culture was responsible for the first flowering of the Italian novella, as well as the popularization of tales of ancient knights and the flowers (wisdom) of ancient philosophy. The title of one of these works is itself all-encompassing: *Fiori e vita di filosofi e d'altri savi e d'imperadori.* The vocabulary of these handbooks of courteous comportment and speech was freighted with language intended to bind the moral and physical into a consummate unity. A hedonistic concept of beauty *(bellezza)* fused the esthetic with the moral, thus securing the tie between *onestade* and *cortesia.* Bellezza was regularly invoked to elevate and dignify ordinary actions and gestures. Despite pessimism and bleak judgment concerning the prospects for refining *(digrossare)* the comportment and political behavior of *novi cives,* manuals, allegories, and fictions (the *novellino*) continued to advertise the spiritual benefits of liberality and the appropriateness of the exchange of love, service, and gift. (It might be added that the cultural circumstances in Tuscany during the late thirteenth and early fourteenth centuries were rather like those of England in the fifteenth century—a country we shall be visiting shortly. There the literary base was broadened and the demand for information on the part of English gentry, merchants, and men of law led to a spate of didactic and moralizing writings in the vernacular. (This point is made to suggest that many of the cultural developments we shall be discussing surfaced in the south of Europe a century or so before they became visible in far-off England.)[7]

To return to Tuscany, the literary impulses working toward didacticism were also evident in loftier literary forms. Aristotelian philosophic and discursive ethics were interpreted to endorse confident assertions concerning man's essential nature as a civil animal whose principal objective was making himself useful to others—this despite a scrupulous regard for a historical record of civic disarray and social injustice. Major figures from Latini to Dante and Marsiglio of Padua suffered bitter exile at the hands of fellow townsmen but still retained a certain confidence in the natural inclination of humans toward associative life. Similarly, a battery of literati who also felt the sting of outrageous political fortune continued to remain confident in the power of rhetoric: this discipline, if effectively practiced, could persuade townsmen to pursue the common good. Moreover, the dismal narrative of urban politics, with its factions and civil wars, did not baffle this trusting impulse. Logical and idealistic solutions were proposed to cure the thousand natural ills of communal society. Basic books of instruction in the art of governing were grounded in a lofty view of a science of rhetoric teaching "a ben parlare e governare" cities and people. Latini's *Tesor,* originally written in French and translated immediately into Italian, contained those proud words. Proof of popularity was vouchsafed: today there are seventy or more surviving manuscripts of the *Tesor.* The rhetorical mode was itself normative, and the government of cities was defined as "the most noble and high science and the most noble duty on earth, according to that which Aristotle proved in his book."[8]

At the level of theory there was a grandeur to much political and social speculation. Global remedies were offered to pressing public issues, and these solutions involved a recall to apostolic poverty, a return to the pristine purity of the primitive church, or the radical realization of the ideals of charity and fraternal love. Often the best thinkers were compelled to take sides in the bitter contest between popes and emperors in which the *plenitudo potestatis* of the Holy Father was pitted against the Roman pedigree of a divinely anointed emperor. The split between the followers of Saint Francis on the issue of apostolic poverty implicated a most original political thinker: William of Ockham tells us that he was unhappy and reluctant, but felt compelled at the urging of the Franciscan minister general to undertake an investigation of the decretals of John XXII. His stark conclusion was that this pope, who had acted against the radical wing of the Franciscans, was tainted with heresy, as was evidenced by his decretals. Heresy, the legitimacy of private property and wealth, the right ordering of the world, that is, Guelf versus Ghibelline—these issues promoted inquiry and debate as ambitious as it was heroic and rigorous. But there was change in the wind, and perhaps one can avoid the cliché "fourteenth-century crisis" when characterizing mutations, at least for Tuscany. Over the course of this century, Tuscan wills and pious benefactions indicate that there was a decline in legacies to the papal *camera,* the Angevin cause, and for purposes of crusading. Generalized bequests to Christ's poor gave way to more particularized forms of charity, especially to Tuscan foundations and hospitals. A marked shift away from benefactions to Christendom and toward distinctly regional and local institutions was clearly in process. Finally, a more ascetic, rigorous, and heroic laic piety was domesticated in favor of less dramatic forms. Withal, we have a fuller expression of the claims of the ego of donor and testator, and this worked against the more anonymous and abstract charitable impulse of an earlier time.9

The humanist dialogues and treatises of the fifteenth century were responsive to these impulses: less heroic, less imperious, less prone to search for global solutions, they contributed little to abstract and systematic political and social thought or to ecclesiology. A view of history was projected less hospitable to conceptions of the pristine purity of the early church or of an ideal society sustained by the radical dismantling of existing economic arrangements. Indeed the converse was often true, and in the humanist dialogue we observe that verisimilitude was lent to arguments defending clerical wealth and secular riches. The heroic code of asceticism and self-denial did not enjoy a privileged position with those literati intent upon dramatizing the claims of a *civilis societas.* Similarly, the ideological requirements of the old parties (Guelf and Ghibelline) were becoming less credible. Petrarch, notwithstanding his appeals to the emperor Charles IV, knew very well that the restoration of a universal monarchy was not a prospect to be realized. In his *De remediis utriusque fortunae,* he has the figure of Ratio (Reason) contest Spes (Hope), with the victory going to the former, who demonstrates how remote is the possibility of restoring imperial power over a warring pestilence-ridden and discordant Europe. No longer is the relationship between temporal and spiritual authority a lively issue to be fervently contested. Issues once vivid and troublesome receded, not because they were resolved, but because it was recognized that they were not amenable to theoretical solution. Problems were not dismissed so much as they were scaled down. The humanist dialogue was characterized by its reluctance to search for closure. Petrarch's *Secretum* displaced the examination of Christian conscience from its traditional clerical context to the domain of private conversation. The dialogue between the author and his spiritual mentor, Saint Augustine, has all the artistry of conversation; further, the exchange occurs in the presence of an allegorical figure, Veritas. Truth, like a "silent judge," presides over the debate: the irony at work is that the debate achieves neither stable clarification nor serenity nor final truth. Despite the presence of the presiding judge, neither the tormented writer nor the careful reader arrives at any ultimate understanding of those crucial questions pertaining to the high Christian matters of immortality and salvation. Conflicting fear and attraction clash and illuminate one another in a dialogue woven very like a tapestry.

Interest in the relationship between temporal and spiritual authority, and the intangible hierarchy of the orders—concerns once so productive of original social and political thought—tended to languish. In its stead we have discourse and dialogue treating the alleged superiority of those living according to vows over and against the dignity of the laic condition. Was the former state more worthy in the sight of God if living in the world outside the religious orders is more demanding? Issues were not dismissed so much as they were made problematic: questions pertaining to the legitimacy of wealth or the spiritual efficacy of poverty were discussed in pro and contra fashion. If answers were forthcoming, their implementation was restricted and solutions localized rather than advanced as a global remedy for the sins of human-kind. No longer do we have proposals for the reorganization of Christian society predicated upon implementation of broad concepts of charity. Discussions about the religious orders were frequently reduced to such quotidian matters as whether the mendicants were being hypocritical in preaching contempt for wealth. Humanist writings were neither as rigorous nor as philosophical as their scholastic forebears. Resolution of matters once fiercely debated and subject to logical analysis were now treated philologically, historically, and, most significantly of all, rhetorically. One thinks of Lorenzo Valla's declamation on the validity and authenticity of the Donation of Constantine or of Bruni's comparative analysis of contemporary legal customs or of Poggio's historical disquisition on differences among French, German, English, and Italian nobility. From Padua, a civic center second only to Florence, came the genre of *epideixis*. The revival of this classical rhetoric of praise and blame, to which the humanist Pier Paolo Vergerio the Elder contributed so much, served to provide historical context for the individual. When praising or blaming, it was vital to refer to external circumstance, thereby fixing the subject in historical perspective.[10]

When the word "civil" was intoned in fifteenth-century Tuscany, it was often used as an adjective to modify the word *conversation*. If one compares Giovanni Villani's account of the solitary Dante, who was learned, albeit not a cleric, with Bruni's eulogy of the poet, who conducted his studies not in quiet isolation but in an atmosphere of civil and urbane conversation, one comes to appreciate something of the dimension of change. Laic literary folk were no longer regarded as marginal and isolated; moreover, they were lauded for their active engagement with public life. Civil conversation itself was a prime mark of civility and a ready synonym for urbanity. Civilized discourse favored a nontechnical vocabulary remote from the narrow profes-sionalization of the medical man, lawyer, or scholastic. Relying on rhetoric rather than Aristotelian demonstration or apodictic logic, the advantage was given to argu-ment on both sides instead of debate to decision.[11]

When Baldassare Castiglione composed *The Book of the Courtier* in the early sixteenth century, he distinguished between those forms of knowledge which in no way contributed to the human ability to live together in a city or to know how to conduct oneself morally from, what he called, "la sapienza civile." "Artificial knowledge" derived from Minerva or Vulcan was itself distinctly inferior to that *sapienza* enabling individuals to live *civile*—that is, in society. If the word *civile* stood with *conversazione,* then the word *tirannico* stood in bold antithesis; in fact, the *vita tirannica* was stamped as the most appropriate antonym to urbanity in all its forms. The victory of civility—at least for Florence—had come as a consequence of the deployment of the resources of a territorial state against the privileges, immunities, and liberties of overmighty magnates and nobles with their retinues and armies of retainers. Nobles and magnates disavowed kinsmen, gave up coat-of-arms, distancing themselves from competitive and violent forms of behavior, once the mainstay of an honor code. When Machiavelli assessed those crucial historical changes occurring in Trecento Florence, he put the taming of nobility at the top of the list: the loss of martial virtue and military valor was costly for the defense of the republic against enemies.

La vita civile* stood opposite to the tyrannical life with its deep psychic investment in blood, kinship, and lineage. The politics of civil life was much more dependent upon patronage, clientage, fluid alliance, and the play of interest. Also, the *vita civile* was disapproving of conspicuous courtesy, overwhelming hospitality and that largess calculated to generate networks of influence. The good citizen, no matter how mighty, must avoid the shadow of the *tiranno.* This signified shunning civil violence and blood feud, in favor of voting in the council halls and exercising moderation in entertainment and family rituals. The distinction was made between *spesa civilissima* and the gaudy lifestyle of the past. Civil expenditures moderated and even released the individual from obligation both economic and psychic. No longer was it imperative to pay damages for the derelictions of one's kin or retainers. Ancient collective forms of liability were relaxed in business as well as in private life. A civil lifestyle impinged on the manner in which one mingled with social inferiors. A sense of measure governed activities, from choosing items of attire to selecting language appropriate for public address. A paradigm of a civil society characterized by measure and control, as well as by separation of private from public concerns, was projected in the new literature. Self-cultivation and self-conscious role-playing on the part of its leading members was matched by an inward-personal, as opposed to an outward-personal orientation.

The urban centers of north and central Italy were the first to put at risk the values of lordship, lineage, service, and social bonding through gift, hospitality, ceremony, and ostentation. In these urban communities archaic and feudal practices did not disappear, but they were no longer structurally vital for grounding political arrangements. Political values became depersonalized; administration turned professional and education more formal and structured. Social relations grew more problematic as communal and archaic protocol receded. Refinement of manners became an independent value as the culture split from the spontaneous and natural. Communal rituals were themselves professionalized and public drama was privatized. In these and many other ways urban customs and consciousness relaxed their hold on ancient solidarities. The traditional ethos had inspired and directed the reciprocal ties lending coherence to time-honored social arrangements. Rich and poor, high and low had cohabited a broad and inclusive social organism held together by oaths, pledges, bonds, processes of reparation and atonement, as well as personal communion.

In the early fourteenth century it was no longer possible to chronicle the political life of Florence by featuring contests of great lineages for power. The movement away from primary ties of obligation can be discerned in the decline of the role of government as peacemaker. The last legislative efforts of the commune to secure urban peace by arranging marriage alliances between warring clans or exacting the exchange of the kiss-of-peace from factious clans occurred during the first decades of this century. No longer do we find expressions of communal solidarity among Guelf consorts who swear to come to the aid of their fellows in case of feud or vendetta. The once-proud tower societies were fragmented into infinitesimal shares of one thirty-second or one sixty-fourth. An Alberti writing in the early 1340s looks back to the first years of the thirteenth century with nostalgia: his ancestors lived then under one roof, commanded a battle tower, fought together, and occupied a common grave. In life as in death they were united in spirit and devoted to one another. Writing in the 1370s, a Medici decried the fact that his house no longer was able to command the loyalty of kith and kin. What was formulaic in an earlier time was a corporate ethos expressed in the following oath: "If any one of us is offended, we are all outraged."[12]

To suggest that families and individuals were advantaged and disadvantaged by the decline of ancient solidarities is perhaps to trivialize the historical problem and miss the direction of change. Certainly, setting up an easy equation with benefits on one side and losses on the other ignores the fact that the winds of social change blew hard. Although no ready defeat of tradition was imminent, still, novelties were in prospect. Economic, social, and political arrangements were not securely grounded in the corporate world of the guild or in the honorific fraternity of a nobility. In Quattrocento Tuscany and other urbanized regions of Italy, the authority of the *arti* (guilds) was restricted. Further, the decline of extended notions of responsibility and unlimited liability encouraged looser and more ambiguous ties in business and social life.

Ethical codes of solidarity, reciprocity, and obligation inspired preferences in taste calling for a direct relationship between representation and reality. The pedagogy of rhetorical instruction was radically transformed. In the early thirteenth century the *ars dictaminis* (art of letter writing) taught that it was essential to be exquisitely sensitive to the requirements of social hierarchy. The critical issue to be determined by the writer was his relationship to the addressee. Appreciation of hierarchy (feudal and ecclesiastical) was essential in a world where the author was eager, above all, to stroke the harp of language in such a fashion as to gain the benevolence of the recipient. Furthermore, the level of style was a function of the relative place of the correspondent in the social order. The letter itself possessed a ritualistic quality derived from strict adherence to a limited number of rules. It should be noted that the maxims of rhetoric valid for letter writing also had application for oratory. By the fourteenth century, however, the precepts were significantly modified. One key feature of this change was the attempt to construct a more limited model of elegance. (In this matter there are parallels between painting and the rhetorical arts.) A new category of men was introduced into the galaxy of addressees; these were individuals "distinguished by some *habitus* (quality)," whose prestige did not depend on their place in a hierarchy. Attention was devoted to the psychological state of the addressee; this concern was in part prompted by a careful reading of Cicero's topics.[13]

In communal politics, ritual had been an indispensable element in building public order. Ceremonies of peacemaking and citizen reconciliation were elaborate and frequent public occasions. Peace pacts and settlement of feuds were also regularly documented in the protocols of Tuscan notaries over the thirteenth century. The values of courtesy and gentility generated those reciprocal exchanges essential for the conduct of public life: the obligation of hospitality and casual charity was universalized. The lexicon of politics featured the natural inclination of man to be companionable. Privacy was regarded with suspicion whereas gregariousness and spontaneity were treasured. The notion of society as *fellowship* was a by-product of these promiscuous impulses. The community was secured by networks of charity, love, and service. Just as oath-taking and the proffering of surety acted to mandate economic and social ties, so conspicuous display of wealth and emotion generated social credit. In Florence, in the fourteenth century, the political mechanisms whereby a guild patriciate had led and controlled the commune faltered, unable to sustain the financial and administrative burdens of a newly formed territorial state. By the same token, magnates and nobles had had opportunities to exercise political power, and they were even less adequate to the task of enacting any reliable program. Tuscan humanists in the early Quattrocento offered a version of political life abstract in character which accented the Roman virtues of an active citizen body willing to serve in the militia of the republic and participate in deliberations of government councils. This active citizenry was also to interact socially and, at least in theory, was to accept the ideal of equality before the law. Public honor and public duty were to take precedence over private allegiances. This version of "buon vivere civile" was ill-equipped to respond to administrative and technical problems of a regional state caught up in costly and endemic warfare. Contradictory demands for specialized knowledge, diplomatic skill, and continuity of leadership vied with requirements for widespread citizen participation and the revival of austere Roman virtues. Whether one leans toward the one model or the other, the fact remains that a conception of civil society distanced from that of an archaic and communal world was in place. The scaffolding and foundation of this civil society was not erected from the routine of courtesy, good manners, friendliness, or mutuality. Furthermore, definitions of a traditional social vocabulary of such key words as *nobility, glory, honor* and *fate* underwent semantic amplification. That they were predicated on blood, lineage, self-assertiveness, and steadfastness was a matter of debate and an issue that was systematically considered as problematic. The heroic values of chivalry were domesticated and the need for "good arms" was paired with that of "good letters."

In the north of Europe, such a version of civil society, not lent cohesion through ties of affinity, displays of prowess, wealth or exchange of service and courtesy, was difficult to project. In fact, this model would only become normative a century or so after its appearance in the city-states of north and central Italy. A political society distanced from an honor community required the erosion of ancient solidarities. Honor must itself be fixed to new moorings. An ethos of noble behavior less competitive and violent than that vouchsafed in Shakespeare's *Troilus and Cressida* (III, iii, 53–60) would be necessary:

> Take the instant way;
> For honour travels in a strait so narrow
> Where one but goes abreast. Keep then the path,
> For emulation hath a thousand sons
> That one by one pursue. If you give way,
> Or hedge aside from the direct forthright,
> Like to an ent'red tide, they all rush by,
> And leave you hindmost . . .

In England, the Northern European country we shall be considering, the nobles, in K. B. McFarlane's judgment, had, after 1487, become "more self-effacing, less sure of their mission to coerce incompetent or high-handed rulers,—congenitally wary, convinced of the benefits of passive obedience." McFarlane detects a chastised, indeed, even craven mood among the older English nobility of the late fifteenth century. Meanwhile, the increase in the numbers and influence of gentry had worked to weaken their dependence and loosen their affinity with this nobility. Writing just before this time (the 1460s), Chief Justice John Fortescue had contended that ". . . there is scarcely a man learned in the laws to be found in the realm, who . . . is not sprung of noble lineage. So they care more for their nobility and the preservation of their honor than others of like estate." A half century later the same case could not be made. A wider public arena required recruitment from the various orders for service to the crown. Political change favored importation of humanist pedagogy and development of a vernacular literature willing to dramatize, if not to champion, intellectual and social options remote from the traditional education of the great aristocratic households and court. The same humanists and vernacular literati constituted the first systematic critique of archaic lifestyles with their emphasis on indiscriminate hospitality, casual charity, and honorific violence. Again, as in Italy, we observe that this criticism had the effect of challenging ancient forms of social bonding. Also we notice that the Italian development predated that of England by better than a century in distancing itself from an honor community.[14]

The cumulative effect of the criticism of a lifestyle rooted in archaic rituals, customs, and practices was to expose traditional forms of bonding operating through exchange of courtesies and services. A conception of society very different from an earlier time was now discernable. Yet the word *discernable* can only be invoked with a certain caution. The present work carries the imprint of "tilt," and of course the word has a chivalric meaning: therefore, if one speaks of the "tilt toward civility," one must not denigrate the attraction and compelling force of the traditional ethos. Laic literature, both vernacular and Latin, tended to gain cachet by rendering problematic the traditional and the new. The deep texture and abiding power of these writings rests in their quintessential fairness, allowing authors to dramatize opposed options for conducting social exchange. Of course this essential objectivity was itself encouraged by the fact that the alternatives could reasonably be valorized; neither position was without historical justification when considered as a base for grounding social arrangements. That this exploration required varied rhetorical strategies and that it placed pressure on language to extend its semantic field is surely not unexpected. The conduct of literary argument and debate called for that measure of poise and tact essential for tolerating disjunction. Perhaps a comparison of Montaigne's views pertaining to the claims of honor with those of an earlier commentator might prove useful. The author of the widely circulated English *Boke of St. Albans* (late fifteenth century) monumentalized the lifestyle of the nobility, equating the high art of hawking and mysteries of hunting with the arcane and lofty armorial science. Even when fishing, one's gentility and honorific reputation was at risk. When discussing the piscatorial art, it advised gentlemen to use "an angle," for they must not fish in the vulgar way: "And also it is not too laborious ne soo dishonest to fysshe in this wyse as it is with nettes and other engynes which crafty men do use for theyr daily increase of goods."[15]

A century later, Montaigne, in his essay "Cowardice, Mother of Cruelty" (*Essays,* II, 27), wrote about a close friend who, having learned fencing in Italy and become renowned as a grand master, still chose in his quarrels only those weapons depriving him of any means of advantage over his adversary. This expert swordsman and duelist wished to advertise the fact that his victory over an opponent was not to be attributed to his skill but rather to his valor. Does not, mused Montaigne, the honor of combat consist "in the jealousy of courage, not of craft." Reflecting on the past, the author confides to his reader that, though it is no longer so, in his childhood "the nobility avoided the reputation of good fencers as insulting, and learned it furtively, as a cunning trade, derogating from true and natural valor." At this juncture Montaigne quotes Torquato Tasso, the Italian poet, who perhaps did as much as any sixteenth-century writer to reveal the problematics of the values of an honor community:

> To dodge, parry, withdraw, they do not seek;
> Nor does skill in their combat play a part;
> Their blows are not feints, now full, now oblique,
> Fury and rage forbid the use of art.
> Hear how their swords clash with a horrid shriek;
> Their feet stand fast, and never move apart.
> Their hands keep moving, though their feet remain,
> And not a thrust or slash is made in vain.[16]

One appreciates the literary vitality of both Montaigne and Tasso enabling them to dramatize a falling away from the code of prowess without offering easy remedy. Unlike the anonymous author of the *Boke of St. Albans,* the Frenchman and the Italian recognized that there was no ready analogy to the proposition that gentlemen should catch fish with hooks, avoiding the crafty setting of nets. Tasso was painfully aware of the psychic cost exacted for satisfying the excessive claims of honor. His *Aminta* stood worlds apart from that pedestrian crowd of pastoral dramas well forgotten. His poetry celebrated the play of the natural, the instinctive and passionate not yet crushed by conventional morality or the requirements of honor. He offered a full exploration of the many facets of love, lending exquisite narrative form to the confusion of youthful passion with its engaging shyness and delicacy of feeling. Implicit was the comparison of this love over and against the stylized exchanges of courtly love. Of course, such innocent sentiments must give way to the battering of lust, and finally, to the cynical disillusionment of the mature, who know only too well how fleeting and useless is virginal modesty.

Something of the same problematic view of human behavior informed Italian manuals of comportment, of which *The Book of the Courtier* was perhaps the most exemplary and influential. Castiglione's tone was cordial, almost serene, and some-times nostalgic, as he reviewed the variety of human behavior and plurality of motives of a recent past without offering any easy precepts or absolute pedagogical instruction for proper social comportment. No set of rules or prescriptions could eradicate human vanity or overcome the fracture between private and public morality. Manner books were no longer preoccupied with introducing "new men" to *la vita civile (digrossare)* or persuading a reprobate nobility to abstain from the profligate way of chivalry and violence of *la vita tirannica.* Instead, they endeavored to project the image of a society as an artificial construct existing for its own sake. This was not a society brought into being through humankind's sociability, gregariousness, charity, hospitality, or the exchange of courtesies. Nor was this a society sustained by networks of allegiances and the play of a heroic ethos. Distanced from a "community of honor," it prized modesty and decorum more than ceremony and extravagance. Emphasis was on those very arts that made one pleasing to others. Monumental obligations were not to be dramatized. In fact, the opposite was true: the difficult was to be made to look easy. Respect for limits and social convention elevated decorum and grace to the sublime. Society was no longer the foundation on which were secured the various orders and estates or the scaffolding for the ascent of nobility. The elegiac views of Nietzsche on the taming of this aristocracy are revealing:

> The essential thing, however, in a good and healthy aristocracy is that it should *not* regard itself as a function either of the kingship or the commonwealth, but as the *significance* and highest justification thereof—that it should therefore accept with a good conscience the sacrifice of a legion of individuals, who, *for its sake*, must be suppressed and reduced to imperfect men, to slaves and instruments. Its fundamental belief must be precisely that society is *not* allowed to exist for its own sake, but only as a foundation and scaffolding, by means of which a select class of beings may be able to elevate themselves to their higher duties, and in general to a higher *existence*.[17]

Torquato Tasso's words are lyrical in comparison with Nietzsche's. Moreover, they show the brighter side of the historical coin, and for our purposes, though less grandiose, are equally memorable: "*La civiltà* is an *arte* and of all the *arti* the one most noble and the one no one can disdain to obey." When Castiglione referred to Prometheus's theft of fire from the gods, he described it as the benefiting of men with "artificial *sapienza*." enabling humans to live and endure. As we have noted, such *artificiosa* knowledge was markedly different from *sapienza civili*. The latter was of course a higher form of understanding, allowing humans to assemble together in cities and live *moralmente*. Guicciardini was to complain, on a much more mundane level, that living together in society was no easy task: "There is nothing more difficult *nel vivere civile* than arranging suitable marriages for one's daughters." Difficult or easy life might be in civil society, yet humans were generally advantaged: architects could be more certain that their buildings would endure; poets that their works would be read; and artists that their creations would continue to be viewed. The Florentine Bernardo Davanzati, a keen commentator on economy and society, observed that with a people possessing a *cultura civile* exchange is no longer a matter of simple barter; all products of nature and of the arts are enjoyed through *commerzio umano*. Civil life was no longer defined in opposition to the contemplative life, nor was it something inculcated by disciplining the new citizens. Likewise, it was not a by-product of "good customs" or being "companionable" or being "charitable" or being "convivial." Not created by favors, gifts, or courtesies, society had become an abstraction with a life of its own. A world of obligation had been somewhat trivialized, so that *ommagio* (homage) was now a mark of respect rather than a solemn and ceremonially engaged commitment. The word *anachronism* made its first appearance in Tuscany in the sixteenth century. A hundred years later it was to become current to the north, in England.

CIVILITY AND SOCIETY
IN WESTERN EUROPE

ONE

The Tilt toward Civility and the Winds of Change

To embark upon a venture into essay writing concerning the almost glacial-like victory of the mores of civility in Western Europe from the fourteenth through the seventeenth century is to explore the painfully slow surrender or, better still, evacuation, of great expanses of quotidian social behavior. It is also to engage in an exploration of the gradual and erratic shifts in the sense of society. Indeed, it was not until the eighteenth century that the term "society" lost most of its active and immediate sense. So advanced a thinker as David Hume used the term in a variety of ways: in his *Enquiry Concerning the Principles of Morals* (1751), he employs the term both with its ancient meaning, "company of his fellows," and the more modern notion, "system of common life." The newer usage does outnumber the archaic by some 110 instances to 25. Society was losing its old sense of what we might characterize as "face-to-face" relationships in favor of a more abstract conception of society as a "system of common life."[1] At critical points in Hume's argument the intermediate use of the term surfaces so that the meaning can be located somewhere between the immediacy of company and fellowship and the more formal notion of society as a distant object. Yet, despite his appreciation for the ambiguities, Hume presents a clear representation of the more modern conceptualization. Not only is the active and immediate sense of old being shunned, but Hume uses the alternative word "company" very much as we would:

> As the mutual shocks in *society*, and the oppositions of interest and self-love, have constrained mankind to establish the laws of justice . . . in like manner, the eternal contrarieties, in *company*, of men's pride and self-conceit, have introduced the rules of *Good Manners* or *Politeness* . . . (*Enquiry*, VIII, 211)[2]

For society to be regarded as competitive, distant, and abstract, and therefore bereft of active fellowship and traditional sociability, signified that sacred bonds, obligation, and mutuality were to be put in the background—thus miniaturized. New definitions of sociability and civility induced anxiety, and attendant warning signals were emitted. To relinquish even the most

1

modest rituals of conviviality and fellowship could ultimately lead to the unraveling of sacred ties and duties essential for the well-being and spiritual health of community. An event of no great pith and moment in the annals of time occurred in 1573. Perhaps a brief consideration of it will alert us to the sense of alarm at the neglect of appreciation for traditional social rites. In that year the Venetian inquisitors rendered unfavorable judgment upon a splendid painting by Paolo Veronese intended to commemorate the Last Supper. The inquisitors maintained that the portrayal of this sacred moment was unacceptable for several good reasons, among these Veronese's rendition of an apostle preparing to partake of his food with a fork. Perhaps the artist became flustered at the charge, but, in any case, he deepened his own problem by countering that the implement was not a fork but a toothpick. (Parenthetically, one might recall the many arguments linking the rise of the use of the fork at table with the onset of the new etiquette of civility.) In the end, the subject of the painting was transferred from the house of the Last Supper to a feast held in the House of Levi. Why such a fuss? Those table manners which interdicted immediate access to a single cup or dish were nothing short of a monstrous innovation. One must understand how vital the rites of commensality were. To transform the Last Supper into a civil exercise or, better still, an exercise in civility, was to challenge an identity between the social and spiritual.[3]

1

One is alerted to the bitter controversies initiated in sixteenth-century England concerning the decline of hospitality and "old country ways" in favor of more limited and civil conceptions of proper housekeeping. Whole tracts and dialogues were composed in which direct confrontation was featured between the largess of extended generosity over and against the parsimony of civil conduct. At this point it might be well to offer some general view of just what these obligations involved. Sensitive to a fault, sixteenth-century moralists monitored the withdrawal of obligation from community with a scrupulous and sustained rigor. Aristocracies were especially excoriated for the failure to fulfill customary responsibilities, that is, the solidarities of honor involving lordship, kinship, and friendship. Excerpts from a long letter of Ulrich von Hutten to the humanist Willibald Pirckheimer in October, 1518, warned the knight's urban patron against harboring a too glossy picture of castles and noble life therein:

> Do not envy me my life as compared to yours. Such is the lot of the knight that even though my patrimony were ample and adequate for my support, nevertheless here are the disturbances which give me no quiet. We live in fields, forests, and fortresses. Those by whose labors we exist are poverty-stricken peasants, to whom we lease our fields, vineyards, pastures, and

woods. The return is exceedingly sparse in proportion to the labor expended. Nevertheless the utmost effort is put forth that it may be bountiful and plentiful, for we must be diligent stewards. I must attach myself to some prince in the hope of protection. Otherwise every one will look upon me as fair plunder. But even if I do make such an attachment hope is beclouded by danger and daily anxiety. If I go away from home I am in peril lest I fall in with those who are at war or feud with my overlord, no matter who he is, and for that reason fall upon me and carry me away. If fortune is adverse, the half of my estates will be forfeit as ransom. Where I looked for protection I was ensnared. We cannot go unarmed beyond two yokes of land. On that account we must have a large equipage of horses, arms, and followers, and all at great expense. We cannot visit a neighboring village or go hunting or fishing save in iron.

Then there are frequently quarrels between our retainers and others, and scarcely a day passes but some squabble is referred to us which we must compose as discreetly as possible, for if I push my claim too uncompromisingly war arises, but if I am too yielding I am immediately the subject of extortion. One concession unlooses a clamor of demands. And among whom does all this take place? Not among strangers, my friend, but among neighbors, relatives, and those of the same household, even brothers.[4]

For the rest, Von Hutten does not stint on the delights or pleasures of rural living but does reckon their cost with unsentimental precision. Particularly frightening are the prospects if the harvest fails, for then must ensue "dire poverty, unrest, and turbulence." Indeed, one finds extensive evidence lamenting the high toll exacted by neighborhood, church, monarchy, retainers, and servants from those who would exercise "good lordship." One can traverse the many regions of social experience, from the excessive claims of clientage, courtesy, and indiscriminate charity to the disadvantaged requirements of enforced solidarity and joint ownership of property, always discovering the press of mutuality. Honor called for competitive assertiveness. One can also enter the shadowy territory generated by those supernatural consequences devolving on the individual from the sins and trespasses of kinsmen, friends, neighbors, and fellow countrymen. These and numerous other liabilities, both penal and fiscal, filled out the social landscape of duty and obligation. The burden of archaic, heroic values and code of chivalry was not light. To characterize the tilt of European society away from ancient solidarities toward very different forms of civility is to cross many different emotional boundaries rooted in time-honored obligations moving in the direction of looser social arrangements and bonds. In 1565, Saint Carlo Borromeo of Milan to all intents and purposes abolished the sacrament as a social ritual by inventing the confessional box. A barrier was erected between sinner and priest that could only be crossed by disembodied murmurings. It was now impossible for the priest to lay hands upon the head of the penitent as a token of his reconciliation to his neighbors and his God. Surely this was not the end Borromeo had in mind, but the effect was to diminish the impact of a quintessential rite of reconciliation.[5]

If one were to trace the language of religious conciliation, obligation, and mutuality, one would be confronted with abundant evidence of historical change. These linguistic migrations have been judged by Michel Foucault and a battery of followers to be evidence, or at least to be symptomatic, of archaeological shifts in the ways of the mind. Do linguistic shifts parallel those evidences of change in social and spiritual life over these centuries? This is of course the bedrock question. Between 1400 and 1700, words such as *communion, charity, conversion, spiritual friendship,* and *restitution* (among others) had assumed new meanings. So too did other terms such as *penance, satisfaction,* and, even, *religion.* Of course the very idea of society and civility had altered, and this in turn worked to transform the vocabulary of spiritual obligation and sacred ties. Comparable transformation can be discerned in the vocabulary of penal and economic obligation where mutual liabilities were lessened. Of interest is the fact that the word for *savings* first lost its pejorative meaning of *hoarding* in Italy in the fifteenth century. In sixteenth- and seventeenth-century France, the term *wadium,* once used for gift exchange between warriors to indicate a pledge, now assumed a double meaning of personal and moral obligation on the one hand and interest payment on the other. The Latin *wadium* had become the French *gage.* The word *credit* also took on a two-sided meaning, both economic and moral. In both French and English the meaning of *pay* had, in the year 1400, carried the charge of creating a relationship: making peace, providing satisfaction, or repairing damaged ties with God were among its more common usages. Two centuries or so later the word lost most of its relational value in favor of the simpler designation of handing over money for goods or services.[6]

The lexicon of politics also underwent a metamorphosis with terms such as *policy, politic,* and *political* acquiring new meanings in the England of the sixteenth and seventeenth centuries. Now this language was descriptive of political affairs, political principles, or political opinions. In matters of election, a process of calculation would vie with one of social distinctions. In an earlier time the likelihood of politics signifying systematic thought on the art of government was chiefly the work of clerical university circles and metropolitan lawyers. The conduct of internal affairs of state and the "ins" and "outs" was the preoccupation of those doing the work of government or of others pressing their interests. The change was toward a fuller description of attitudes and actions, as well as a willingness to recognize the disjunction between private interest and the public good. A favorable sense of privacy was first evident in the England of the sixteenth century and was significantly amplified by literati in the following century. The privatization of emotion and its withdrawal from a semipublic world where honor and reputation were acquired by those who passionately assumed obligation was to receive unprecedented dramatic and philosophic attention. The literature of an earlier time conveyed the image of a feudal society so compacted of small units and so granulous that any individual seeking to disengage himself from the narrow, omnipresent, and abundant conviviality was likely to be regarded as a hero or rebel. One who withdrew from this society might not be deliberately seeking to do evil, but by his very act of isolation he was making himself vulnerable to the Enemy: so it was with the literary portrayal of the criminal and the heretic.[7]

That there was a significant change in attitude toward poverty, violence, crime, and the most fundamental familial arrangements has been confirmed with scholarly regularity by the past three generations of researchers. The scholarship of the present generation is certainly bearing adequate witness. Furthermore, these transformations influenced more than language and ideology; they also worked to modify—sometimes dramatically—the bedrock of human behavior. From the thirteenth to the sixteenth century in England crimes against persons declined whereas crimes against property increased. Crimes of an earlier time were more likely to be directed against outsiders, whereas in a later day, violence against immediate family members was on the rise. The decline of the homicide rate from the thirteenth to the sixteenth and seventeenth centuries was roughly 50 percent. A few further instances may serve to illustrate behavioral changes: an investigation of British ducal families over the fourteenth and fifteenth centuries indicates that even among this privileged order, 36 percent of males and 29 percent of females died before the age of five. For those males attaining the age of 15, nearly one-half (46 percent) met with a violent end: three hundred years later the figure had fallen to a mere 4 percent. Such a statistic suggests how relevant was the domestication of the European nobility. This is a theme I shall return to presently, but surely it betokens a trend toward a new lifestyle. The second example pertains to deathbed confessions, for which we have ample—even overwhelming—documentation. The content of wills demonstrates that in the critical matter of bestowing pardons for offenses committed by others against oneself or in seeking pardons for offenses committed against others, testators were at first more generally insistent upon reparation. Only gradually, over the three centuries from the fifteenth to eighteenth, was there a decline in the requirement that the heirs make restitution or reparation.[8]

The will was the prime instrument by which obligation was discharged. The preamble to a last testament of an English gentleman from the county of Kent expressed that solemn duty of all good Christians: "entendyng . . . not to departe out of this lyfe intestate make and ordeyne this my present Testament of my mevigle goodes the which oure lord god hath lent me." The first clause included in many wills often went like this: *Volo primo et principaliter quod debita mea plenarie sint soluta.* To die with debts unpaid was judged to be a misuse of the wealth entrusted to the individual by God. Not to provide for payment of debts was nothing short of theft and was certain to be punished in the hereafter. The Middle English doggerel verse of *Gentleness and Nobility* made this grim point most effectively:

> Yet some wyll suffer hys dettes unpayd tobe
> And dye and leopard hys soule rather than he
> Wyll any of hys landes mynysh and empayre
> That shuld after hys deth come to hys heyre[9]

In the centuries between 1400 and 1700—give or take a few decades—we observe a decline in the claims of extended sociability, reciprocity, and mutuality. Perhaps a sentence or two from Chaucer's English translation of Boethius's *De Consolatione Philosophiae* will evoke something of the spirit of social thought of the earlier time:

> . . . al this accordaunce of thynges is bounde with love, that governeth erthe and see, and hath also commandement to the hevene. . . . This love halt togidres peples joyned with an holy boond, . . . and love enditeth lawes to trewe felawes. (bk.II, metrum 8)

We see that Boethius's "sodales" is rendered by Chaucer as "trewe felawes." Dante, from whom Chaucer gained so much, made explicit the necessary connection between love and justice in the *Monarchia*:

> Just as greed, though it be never so little, clouds to some extent the disposition of justice, so does charity or right love sharpen and brighten it. . . . Greed, scorning the intrinsic significance of man, seeks other things; but charity, scorning all other things, seeks God and man, and consequently the good of man. And since, amongst the other blessings of man, living in peace is the chief . . . and justice is the chiefest and mightiest accomplisher of this, therefore charity will chiefly give vigour to justice; and the stronger she is, the more.[10]

Of course Dante's indebtedness to Saint Thomas Aquinas is clear. When the Dominican noted the benefits of just rule over and against tyranny, he remarked that "there is nothing on this earth to be preferred but true friendship," and "fear makes a weak foundation." Aquinas, following the Latin translation of Aristotle's *Politics*, averred that man is by nature a social animal, and living in a community "enables man to achieve a plenitude of life, not merely to exist, but to live fully, with all that is necessary to well-being." One can return to John of Salisbury and his *Policraticus* (1159) and observe how deep were the roots of political and social life in the soil of mutuality and helpfulness:

> Then and then only will the health of the commonwealth be sound and flourishing when the higher members shield the lower, and the lower respond faithfully and fully in like measure to the just demands of their superiors, so that each and all are as it were members one of another by a

sort of reciprocity, and each regards his own interest as best served by that
which he knows to be most advantageous for the others.[11]

2

̣̣ted by a vocabulary of moral
tionnelles (relational values)
transitional centuries (1400–
of sociability through charity
seriously challenged, first by
town governments and their
ligious reformers encouraged
e old church maintaining that
sential scaffolding—even skel-
th century, civic programs had
ents throughout the north of
ouragement of almsgiving were
charity were championed. The
ips in which the beggar prayed

ereby humanists and reformers
ty governing social relations for
to society at large. Indeed, the
inadvertently, contribute to the
ould be regarded by Calvin as
ars who hypocritically preached
of saints and martyrs as heroic
e favorable social consequences
of the humanists. The emotive
of anger and envy received full
vas symptomatic of a society in
d a franker literary acknowledg-
ng in the Italian vernacular of the
o the depth of concern. Importa-
the vocabulary of late sixteenth-
gh the agency of John Florio, the
e best English-Italian dictionary.
ook hold, so too the term *society*,
oward new significance. Again, as
n only in Latin, the new meaning
ion denoting fellowship, compan-
ionship, reciprocity, benevolence, and mutual benefaction. So, too, the definition of the term *state* was losing something of its concrete meaning of
command over men and material things. Thomas Starkey, Tudor humanist

and great admirer of the Republic of Venice, may well have been the first—or at least one of the first—to use the word *state* with its more modern connotation. Parenthetically, it might be noted that, apart from Western Europe, the word for society does not appear in the classical vocabulary of Indo-European institutions. Instead, the concept is evidenced in a different fashion. "In particular one recognizes it under the name of realm *(rouaume):* the limits of society coincide with a certain power, which is the power of the king."[13]

Now to the question of how a more abstract notion of social relationships evolved. The new view must first be distinguished from its forebear—that which obtained in what Emmanuel Le Roy Ladurie called a culture "de la promiscuité." Unlike traditional conceptions, this was a society distanced from its members and delimited from other collectivities. It exercised new claims while advancing new responsibilities. I would alert you to what I would consider the structural base of this transformation. Iconographic documentation of the older world is ample for charting the language of colors, symbols, and devices for registering fidelity and allegiance. Codified representations of crowds, with figures grouped in heraldic patterns, were commonplace. Lay chivalric orders, religious confraternities, clubs, and societies, through costume and emblem, delivered clear messages of affinity. Indeed, if one reads in the sprawling literature of the thirteenth and early fourteenth centuries on social organization and the social ethic, one finds a repetitious, detailed, and sometimes analytical view of the obligations of the various vocational callings, professions, and estates. Sin was perceived principally as lodging in defective human relationships and stunted sympathies. From John of Salisbury's *Policraticus* to the *Summa* of Saint Thomas Aquinas to the manuals of the confessors, as well as canon lawyers and writers on penance, we witness the mapping of an exact typology of society based upon an ethic of solidarity. This mode of affirmation and criticism contributed to a literary growth industry featuring the estates satire prominent throughout Northern Europe in the fourteenth and fifteenth centuries. An abstract conception of society separate from its various orders and collectivities was virtually nonexistent in the north of Europe. Political and social theory were solemnly preoccupied with duties and obligations rather than with rights.

In England, vernacular writings were so extensively devoted to the theme of obligation that modern scholars have classified a substantial part of this legacy as the "literature of complaint." A case can be made for the fact that political and social writings in the fourteenth and fifteenth centuries were almost frozen in their obsessive preoccupation with the failure of the estates and orders to fulfill their ascribed roles. The Tudor historian G. R. Elton has taken a bleak view of fifteenth-century English thought, arguing that only the Continental Renaissance could jolt literature from its sterile social analysis. English political thinkers from More, Elyot, and Starkey onward required the stimulus of Continental writings to set them to work. Poetry was mired in the debased leavings of a trivialized Chaucerian tradition. The top poets were required to attend school in France and Italy. Even at its best, Wyatt's rendition of the sonnets of Petrarch were often slavish and seldom stately and sweet.

The new history had its beginnings in the ancients and that embattled Italian import, Polydore Vergil. So, too, English biblical scholarship derived from the Italian humanists via the later-day continentals, Erasmus, Budé and Scaliger. The importance of Italian jurists for English civil law can no longer be slighted. The customs of England were inadequate for conducting commercial relations and diplomacy. One does not have to accept without qualification Elton's overview, yet his comments are both cautionary and salubrious. Most probably, the crisis in institutional authority was favorable to the sentiment that the experience of antiquity might be an exemplary model to be followed by those in public life. Thus were certain feelings of discomfort and ambiguity overcome. Classical Latin literature provided a version of the *familia* anchored in the notion of privacy. Roman writers polemicized against ties between the domestic and political. Italian humanists favored the Roman model, which served to clear public space of family networks, alliances, parties, and factions. Thus the individual would be more obedient to public authority and less responsive to the claims of kinsmen and honorific bodies.[14]

The very apposite passage from Cicero's *On the Laws,* quoted by Petrarch in a somewhat patronizing fashion but with rare political insight in his epistolary tract "How a Ruler Ought to Govern His State," deserves to be cited. This work, addressed to Francesco da Carrara the Younger, Lord of Padua, belongs to the genre of the "Mirror of Princes" but occupies very different ground from that of such tracts as *On Kingship* by Saint Thomas Aquinas and Giles of Rome's *On the Governance of Princes.* Drawing heavily on Roman political experience, Petrarch understood the classical message pertaining to the changing mores and character of an aristocracy:

> For it is not so mischievous that men of high position do evil—though this evil is bad enough in itself—as it is that these men have so many imitators. For if you will turn your thoughts back to history, you will see that the character of our most prominent men has been reproduced in the whole state; whatever change took place in the lives of the prominent men has also taken place in the whole people. And we can be much more confident of the soundness of this than of what so pleased our beloved Plato. He thought that the characteristics of a nation could be changed by changing the character of its music. But I believe that a transformation takes place in a nation's character when the habits and mode of living of its aristocracy are changed. For this reason, men of the upper class who do wrong are especially dangerous to the state, because they not only indulge in vicious practices themselves, but also infect the whole commonwealth with their

vices, and not only because they are corrupt, but also because they corrupt others, and do more harm by their bad example than by their sin.[15]

In the fifteenth century, over much of Northern Europe, we have officials who directed both affairs of state and the household of the prince. But almost everywhere, with the exception of the German principalities, the court was fragmented and complex administrative forms were in the making. The word *secretarius* had signified close friend and confidant of the prince; gradually it acquired the meaning of someone doing administrative work of a professional quality. In England, by the late fifteenth century, we witness the beginnings of government, not by royal household alone, but by something approximating civilian service. Surely this was cumulative and slow in arriving, but it was readily identifiable under Henry VIII and Thomas Cromwell. Cromwell's achievement depended less on constitutional engineering and more on local patronage networks, with a steady stream of reliable information and the exercise of control over the commissioners of peace. Yet, unlike Cardinal Wolsey, he did not attempt to monopolize the business of the king; instead he encouraged formality in the conduct of royal affairs and the regular attendance of government counselors.

During this generation and the one just preceding it, the fruits of laic and secular education had come to harvest. These two conditions—civilian service and laic and secular education—replicated those of the regional states of north and central Italy in the thirteenth and early fourteenth centuries and were the precondition for much that followed throughout Europe. In England the fifteenth century had been the locale for much increased provision for education, but little significant change in substance and kind took place. By Italian humanist standards, the lay folk of England were hopelessly old-fashioned and untrained in politics and giving counsel. During the first two generations, Tudor England was the scene for importing Continental ideas concerning the education of nobility and gentry for public life. Starkey, admirer of the Republic of Venice and early user of the term *state* in its newer sense, was but one of a band of Continent-trained humanists who condemned the extravagant, wasteful, and violent style of the nobility. They and their quarrelsome retainers and idle household servants were naught but parasites preying on the commonwealth. In the next generation civic objectives were deepened and enhanced with a sense of history. Continental humanist scholarship not only took root but there was now a lively reciprocity. Supports and bridges were erected between the latest results of these studies (antiquarian, geographic, linguistic, and so on) and a community of gentlemen increasingly patriotic and civic-minded.[16]

Again, the domestication of nobility had been the principal experience of the thirteenth- and early fourteenth-century Italian communes. Out of this experience emerged an abundant and sprawling literature in which the benefits of civic tranquility were extolled. Beyond this, the new literature transvalued claims of an older world of loyalties and obligations by granting sympathetic access to a system of beliefs seemingly distant from contempo-

rary experience. By reconstructing the history of antiquity, humanists, artists, and literati made plausible very different models of virtue and conduct.
One thinks of the humanist-inspired iconography of Saint Jerome, who
embodied Church Father and the cult of scholarship in his single figure. Of
course that veritable legion of civic saints fathered by the sculptor Donatello
still stands in city center to remind Florentine citizens of their sacred civic
duties. The antique conception of body, illuminated by the senses, inspires
deeds testifying to spiritual renewal. Conversion was no longer a distant
quest—an arduous pilgrimage of the wayfaring man—to the antipodes. Few
realms of comportment or social experience were secure from the intrusion
of classical models, whether this involved the intimacies of the country villa
or the public ceremony of the festival. The pulpit was opened to classical
forms of oratory. Ideas of courtesy and chivalric display were rivaled by new
conceptions of the *vita civile*. As we have seen, even the status of saints was
not immune: no longer were they so certain to be portrayed as friends and
benefactors to the devout; rather, they were now cast as heroic figures
suitable for public wonder and civic imitation. Serious political writers
questioned whether social bonds could be effectively secured by the sacred
ties of charity and spiritual reconciliation. Polemical and satirical attacks
were both directed against ideas of fraternalism and the natural impulse
toward associative life. The neoclassical ideal of republicanism with its
balanced constitution and independent arms-bearing citizenry took shape in
Florence from the time of Bruni and Matteo Palmieri to Machiavelli.[17]

These soundings or, better still, literary rumblings were not unrelated to
the social experience of north Italian urban elites. Judging from last wills and
pious benefactions, it would be fair to suggest that reconciliation and restitution of ill-got gains peaked somewhere between the 1330s and 1340s in
Florence. More generalized concerns for society were evidenced in the new
civic philanthropy so prevalent in Tuscany and other parts of north and
central Italy in the fifteenth century. The sense of obligation came to be
expressed more in terms of the general needs of community rather than those
of an individual seeking to repair damaged social ties. Finally, there was a
sharp decline in large-scale benefactions inspired by panic and the need for
sudden reparation. With this in mind, it can be suggested that the conception
of philanthropy as an abstract and rational system of benevolence was fur-
thered. So too were the more specialized and professionalized institutions
designated for the care of the poor, the sick, the infirm, and the aged.
Florentine chancellors and humanists such as Leonardo Bruni Aretino and
Poggio Bracciolini adduced arguments, examples, and evidence—both historical and psychological—to legitimate or, at least, naturalize acquisitive
impulse on the grounds that it worked to confer general benefits on the
community. In 1427, Stefano Porcaro, the Captain of the People of the
Republic of Florence, celebrated the virtues of wealth in a public oration:

> Whence are our houses and palaces procured . . .? From riches! Whence
> come our clothes . . .? Whence the meals for us and our children? From

riches! Whence the means to educate our children and make them virtuous
. . .? From riches . . . these consecrated churches with their decorations,
the walls, the towers, the defences . . . your palaces and dwellings, the
most noble buildings, the bridges, the streets, with what have you built
them, whence do you obtain the means of preserving them, if not from
riches?[18]

Civic humanists distanced themselves from their forebears Petrarch and
Boccaccio, and were less responsive to the austerity of ancient stoicism and
the scriptural promptings of the Franciscan ideal of poverty. Taking inspiration from the Aristotelian view that material goods were to be regarded as
necessary aids to the pursuit of moral life, they sanctioned the acquisition of
wealth to the extent that it enabled the citizenry to lead lives of virtue
fulfilling civic duties. Nothing inherently evil could be attributed to the
acquisition of wealth, so long as it was put to good purpose. Furthermore,
without wealth and mercantile activity cities would lack dignity and splendor; worse yet, the full faith and credit of the Republic would suffer irrepara-
ble damage. Humanist rhetorical exercises impuned the motives of friars,
judging them to be hypocritical. Further, these mendicants preached contempt for wealth and disrespect for property, thus sowing the seeds of
sedition. Better some collective provision—perhaps civic in nature—for
those unable to work. Almsgiving and begging were much diminished in this
projection of civic values.

The humanist dialogue was entirely appropriate for ventilating views on
such barbed and prickly topics as the spiritual worth of voluntary poverty,
the social utility of wealth, and the alleged hypocrisy of the mendicants. Civil
conversation modeled on the colloquial Ciceronian dialogue, with its imitation of everyday speech and appreciation for the impromptu gesture, allowed
for criticism of society without claiming to have the final word on tense
issues. The informality of the setting and the flexibility of linguistic protocol
removed discussion from an academic or ecclesiastical domain where the
rigors of debate led to proof or disproof. With the dialogue it was possible to
investigate the values of society and spiritual life avoiding any easy didacticism or intellectual closure. Poggio Bracciolini, author of one of the more
effective compositions of this genre treating these very matters *(On Avarice)*,
explained in a letter of December, 1442, his affection for the form by para-
phrasing Cicero's *Academia,* 2. 3. 7: "For in a debate the truth will be elicited
from both sides." This literary genre was to prove durable, becoming one of
the most successful cultural exports to the north of Europe in the sixteenth
century.[19]

Movement toward civil society was evidenced in the new classically
inspired historiography of Bruni, Poggio, Machiavelli, and Guicciardini,
which appropriated ancient rhetorical strategies to distance itself from recounting blood feuds and foregrounding conspiratorial theory as a mode of
political reasoning. Indeed, we witness a loosening of strict social obligation

with the decline of the vendetta, *wergeld,* compurgation, and composition. Families such as the Velluti regarded the pursuit of revenge by distant kinsmen as dangerous both to life and patrimony. Efforts by the lawyer Donato Velluti to settle family quarrels through tactics of informal arbitration were seldom successful. The claims of blood and honor calling for revenge were not dismissed but were now less likely to evade the catchment of those institutions presumably initiated to regulate them. Florentine diaries, memorials, and books of counsel made prudence, not duty, their North Star. Again it is worth noting that the incidence of magnate violence and crime peaked in the 1340s and 1350s, suggesting that the exercise of civic restraint was not without impact. Results of recent research have suggested that by the late thirteenth century the Florentine nobility was much more likely to depend upon—even rely upon—communal institutions instead of kinfolk for the implementation of testaments and other judicial acts. By the close of the fourteenth and beginning of the fifteenth century, kinship ties among the nobles had become increasingly voluntary.[20]

Such attitudes can be generalized: many in Florentine society were advantaged by the strengthening of public institutions and more abstract forms of justice—particularly the *gente nuova* or new citizens. Vital to the interests of both magnates and merchants (the two were far from being mutually exclusive) was the limiting of collective liability, both penal and fiscal. The erosion of an ethic of solidarity and a tilt toward an ethic of civility was already apparent in the writings of the first generation of Florentine civic humanists in the last quarter of the fourteenth century. Coluccio Salutati not only wrote against but also spoke in the General Council of his natal city (Buggiano) against the barbarous practice of perpetual leasing, whereby those assuming a lease on land obligated themselves and their heirs to work that holding and pay rent in perpetuity. Likewise, he opposed the barbarous customs of taking reprisal against merchants and exacting criminal obligation from sons for the derelictions of their father. He was to carry these principles so far as to reduce the liability of dentists for bad extractions, and Jews for the Crucifixion. The advantage of moving away from surety, oaths, and bonds was sometimes matched by discomforting insights characterizing society as governed by the claims of ego and play of interests.[21]

3

We can achieve a certain insight into the historical psychology of the period by considering the repudiation of the once so authoritative doctrine of Atonement pronounced by Saint Anselm, whereby satisfaction of God's honor and compensation for human sin were absolute requirements. Payment of debt must be adequate to turn away the vengeance of God. Of course, divine wrath was turned away by Christ, the Son of God, whose passion and death made restitution for the sin of Adam. A sense of dependence upon the omnipotent divine will, superhuman patience, extreme devotion to Christ's passion, an unquenchable fervor for penitence, and a desire to return to God through suffering were marks of sanctity and features of lay piety. Traditional monastic ideals and customs were democratized and extended into laic life, but without the restraints of monastic discipline. The heroic and often restless preoccupation with spiritual perfection characteristic of lay piety and the unquiet heart (to use a phrase from Augustine's *Confessions*) was inspired by an Augustinian theological vision. But when this vision was popularized in sermons and devotional tracts, the saint's moderation, his trust in the goodness of God, and the sacramental character of life were often disregarded in favor of a harsh call to penance. Vernacular literature in the early Tuscan *volgare,* including sermons of Saint Augustine and other patristic writings, seldom duplicated the theological subtlety of the Church Fathers. Instead, they were shrill in their insistence upon payment, atonement, restitution, and penance. Vernacular sermons of the early fourteenth century, Tuscan devotional tracts, and of course the letters of Saint Catherine of Siena were vivid in the representation of Christ's blood as "largess" *(largità).* [22]

The humanists of the fifteenth century came to understand these matters somewhat differently. John the Baptist had not preached to the Jews to do penance or perform penitential acts: satisfaction, reparation, or restitution were not at issue, but rather what was required was a change of mind and heart. These humanists addressed, for the most part, an upper-class audience relatively leisured, literate, and familiar with a wide range of devotional writings. The idea of satisfaction for sin, whether by Christ or the believer, was regarded by humanists, in their more optimistic moments, as detracting from human dignity and was believed to be "uncivilized." What was essential were the interworkings of the sacraments; abstinence and fasting were difficult to square with the mores of civility. The erudite were in substantial agreement as to the deprivation of the Christian household of its penitential role whereby it had rendered satisfaction for sin. Initiation into the "True Faith" was achieved through instructing the young, not through ritual and symbolic act. In this widening laic perspective a life of withdrawal was no more holy than a life of civic responsibility. Already in late fourteenth century the humanist Coluccio Salutati had asked the rhetorical question as to whether Abraham, with his wives and children, had led a life less pleasing in the sight of God than the solitary ascetic. In an epistle to Pellegrino Zambeccari, chancellor of Bologna, a man given to rapid alteration of fancies of love and flights of asceticism (at the moment Pellegrino was contemplating dedicating his life to monasticism), Salutati wrote:

> Do not imagine, Pellegrino, that one can seek perfection by fleeing from the crowd, shunning the sight of everything beautiful and locking oneself up in a monastery or a hermitage. Do you really believe that God prefers a solitary, inactive Paul to a creative Abraham? Do you not think that God looked with greater pleasure upon Jacob and his twelve sons, two wives

and large herds than upon the two Macarii, upon Theophilus and upon Hilarion? In an attempt to run away from the earth, you may well tumble down from heaven to earth. But I, while I am busily engaged on earthly things, can always raise my heart from earth to heaven. As long as you are serving, as long as you are striving for your family, children, relatives, friends, and for the fatherland which comprises them all, you cannot help lifting your heart heavenwards and thus please God.[23]

Penitential or compensatory behavior aimed at reconciliation between man and God, and restoration of amicable social relations. The business of Christian life revolved around the routine of such conciliatory behavior. Principal saints of the fifteenth century were often the friends of God who demonstrated their sanctity by persuading enemies to make restitution and repair the sacred bonds with their earthly neighbors, thus reconciling themselves to their "Heavenly Father." The key critique picked up by Erasmus from the Italian humanists was that these methods of satisfaction and reparation were uncivilized, if not barbaric. Sinfulness was not to be perceived as a visible and social problem. If we grant that religion is the extension of human relationships beyond the boundaries of mere human society, then the question to be answered might be phrased thusly: What were the structural essentials of human relationships that encouraged two differing religious versions?

If we remain with the version traditional since the time of Anselm, that sin required some objective restitution, then we may ask, what were the essential ingredients in the field of social arrangements encouraging such a view? Parenthetically, it might be noted that Anselm's rule of satisfaction was readily translated into the doctrine of purgatory, with the living of the later Middle Ages hard at work to facilitate the felicitous transit of the dead into the next world. Again, a survey of early vernacular Tuscan devotional writings (one might remember that the greater number of *volgare* manuscripts of this genre surviving for the thirteenth and fourteenth centuries in Italy were Tuscan) indicates how strict and highly specified were the battery of ties and spiritual allegiances. Much of the literature in translation from which laity were to be instructed and gain spiritual nourishment had, in the first instance, been written for cloistered nuns and monks. Furthermore, the *volgare* utilized an archaic vocabulary of rewards, gifts, and countergifts when representing spiritual debts and spiritual promises of heavenly felicity. This was an idiom soon to be seriously challenged in the Latin writings of the humanists who were to feature a much more restrained and recondite language when discussing individual salvation and immortality of the soul. About the ample literature concerning saints' lives, humanist scholarship was generally cautious. Deceiving the populace for their own good and offering false lures and promises of eternal reward was nothing short of lying, and to boot it was artless. The purpose of this most popular literary form was to instruct, edify, and reform, not to offer false prospects of assistance. In the fine arts too we observe that the romanticism of the late Middle Ages, with its intense commiseration for the suffering of the Son of God—a pathos which fueled popular piety—was challenged by the more formalistic and decorous esthetic of the humanists.[24]

4

In discussing social arrangements in the north of Europe (particularly England), we observe the putting into place of a complex system of obligations and social credit earned through service and deference in the twelfth and thirteenth centuries. Building upon this with many subtle variations, we have the emergent structure of a contract or indenture system characterized for the England of the fourteenth and fifteenth centuries by modern historians as "bastard feudalism," whereby the crown and the magnates were able to secure an abundant supply of client gentlemen. Continuing with ever greater energy and elaboration, we recognize a lordly and courtly culture expanding and establishing its warrant for power through magnificent display, ostentation, and patronage. Relationships were cemented by hospitality, entertainment, and annuities for praiseworthy service. The Fleming Philippe de Commynes, writing in his French chronicle, characterized King Edward IV of England's chamberlain, William Lord Hastings, as "a man of great sense, virtue, and authority." Both of Philippe's masters, Charles of Burgundy and Louis XI of France, made rich gifts and pensions to the chamberlain. The shrewd Louis invested the tidy sum of 2,000 crowns to win Hastings's good will.[25]

Great households maintained their military authority, and social ties were objectified and concretized by gifts, pensions, honors, and offices. In fifteenth-century England, royal succession was ensured by bloody military conquest, not through parliamentary legitimation. Fees and material benefits in the form of financial bonds and livery were required as proof of adequate motivating circumstance; the world of gift and countergift was always near at hand, being realized in symbol and ritual as well as quotidian agreement. At the close of the fourteenth century, Richard II was retaining knights with esquires to fill local offices, secure provincial allegiances, and work in parliament for royal advantage. On the Continent annual pensions in the form of *fief rentes* or *fief de bourse* secured service in addition to furthering the ends of diplomacy. In Burgundy the gradual advance of the parvenu duchy in the late fourteenth and fifteenth centuries was much dependent on the purchase of vassals and lords, the retaining of knights and esquires, and the magnificence of the court. The Order of the Golden Fleece was emblematic of the extension of Burgundy as a political entity. In Scotland bonds of manrent, and later, of maintenance, were drawn up to ensure mutual obligation between lairds and burgh offices on the one side and dependents on the other. Bonds of service, or manrent, strengthened the kindred by conferring honorary membership on outsiders who then were afforded protection in return for personal service. Stripping of honor, defamation, and eternal infamy were the excruciating costs of betrayal. Affinities, alliances, bonds of friendship, and the creation of *compagnons et alliés*—these and a host of other pledges of mutuality made release from the nexus of obligation no easy matter. Indeed, literary discourse for portraying the soldier and soldiering without sanction of religious, moral, or social duty was either devoted to exploring the infinite recesses of the infidelity and deceitfulness of the human heart or demonstrating, vividly, the crass materialism of knight, squire, and sergeant who harbored but a single thought: ". . . when will the paymaster come?"[26]

Charters and accounts of agreement were secured in a procrustean bed of traditional formulas. A study of political display and entertainment reveals that the field of social rites was expanding exponentially. Orders of chivalry were closely related to the English indenture and the need for powerful friends and allies. On the increase were the numbers of knights and esquires retained for life. The bond of chivalry carried a heavy freight of protocol defining with extravagant precision the courtesies one knight owed another. Empathy and an easy cosmopolitanism were ideally to make geographic and psychic frontiers between knights imprecise. Indeed, the teachings of civility were themselves limited and most often were prescriptions for obedience to a single code pertaining to a nobility. Royal policy was intended, overwhelmingly, not to disrupt prevailing social arrangements, but to make the feudal world operate according to its own morality and assumptions. The purpose of the Order of the Star was to revitalize the French chivalric ethos after the debacle of Crecy.

The king of England did not call parliament to hobble the royal will. Parliament was not an assembly of the estates of the realm, nor was it the expression of the political ethos and authority of the nation. The modern term *institution* is much too precise a word for describing the parliaments and colloquia of the thirteenth and fourteenth centuries. Often these were occasions for high ceremony and regal display. Similarly, words such as *civil servants* and *bureaucrats* are certainly anachronistic. Only gradually did officials receive appointments for their competence and dare to boast about it. This was a society lent structure through lineage, patronage, affinities, liveries, maintenance, retinues, clientage, money fiefs, pensions, and the like. This is not to underestimate the mercantile interests in fourteenth- and fifteenth-century Continental Europe, but to suggest that they operated in a world where the nobility was very likely to impose its point of view. In England there was no well-defined city interest, and the crown was pushed by nobles into continuous adventures. Even in the seventeenth century, merchant groups tended to be more royalist and Tory than parliamentarian and Whig. In Flanders political loyalties of nobles determined the course of local history, no matter how much local characteristics of nobility varied from one region to another. Relations between feudal magnates in England were as important in fact as they were in the contemporary chronicles. A hundred men were obliged by indenture to William Lord of Hastings, and they with their retainers were the nucleus of the three thousand he commanded at the Battle of Barnet in 1471. The commercial value of land counted for much less than the fact that both status and political power were bound up with its possession. In the last resort, what was critical was the ability to raise a force of men from one's own estate. Even as late as the English Civil War, a commander like the marquis of Newcastle went into battle captaining a force principally composed of his own tenants.[27]

The emotional appeal of service, even in a domestic capacity, should not be slighted. Even the mighty Henry II of England was not immune from its attraction, authorizing his administrator, Hugh Cleer, to write a treatise claiming for him the hereditary right to the seneschalship of King Louis's French court. This right conferred on Henry, in addition to jurisdictional prerogatives, the privilege of cutting the French king's bread. From the thirteenth through the fourteenth, fifteenth, and even sixteenth century, great princes and kings gained glory as often in the banquet halls as in the battlefield. Wise distribution of royal favors was a sure mark of good kingship and could still factionalism at court. Ostentation and public display were of course sound political investments. Prayers and bequests put the recipient under obligation; so too faith was demonstrated by outward signs. English artistic idiom in both the figurative arts and architecture was linear and decorative. The arts of the period in the north of Europe offer glamorous testimony to the mandating of social relationships through ritual and enchantment. Under Charles the Bold of Burgundy (a duchy of recent political formation, and considered *nouveau* by the older European powers), herculean and successful efforts were made to initiate a romantic, cultural revival of chivalry. By strict adherence to knightly custom and chivalric code, this parvenu state sought to acquire political legitimacy.[28]

Chivalric literature and the statutes of the numerous chivalric orders newly founded in the fourteenth and fifteenth centuries spoke conspicuously to the singular significance of the manner of accomplishment rather than of the thing accomplished—glory rather than results. Yet, although the influence of the chivalric romance and epic, with their accent on the ludic element, must not be slighted, secular orders of chivalry from the time of Alfonso XI (1330), with the institution of the Order of the Sash in Castille, to the last of the orders (that of Saint Michael by Louis XI in 1469) did have political and military aims. As B.-A. Pocquet du Haut-Jussé wrote of another famous order,

> . . . the creation of the Order of the Golden Fleece by Philip the Good (1429) was also designed, beneath the worldly trappings that adorned it, to secure for the duke a devoted band of lords who were not his vassals. It had no connection with the old enfeoffed pensions; it was the flowering of an

entirely different practice, that of using sealed bonds, which since the fourteenth century lords had exchanged between themselves and by which they allied themselves and promised mutual aid on the very fringe of the feudal hierarchy.[29]

A cosmopolitan nobility whose lives touched so many people was constantly creating indentures, obligations, emotional mortgages—in a word, "chits." The boundaries between public and private were porous for the male noble. Not surprisingly, the very definition of society proved to be synonymous with casual almsgiving, gregariousness, largess, revelry, and hospitality. Wealth was profoundly social. Closure was a threat to the idea of easy sociability essential for the nurture of complex networks of relationship and, most of all, the ready circulation of property. The rites of fraternity were the central arch of courtly education. Youths were instructed to imitate the martial deeds of their patrons (the new fathers) in their passage into an artificial family of noble warriors. Their apprenticeship completed, the youths received their arms in a group structured very like a family. Indeed, the very synonyms for the term *society* were those of fellowship and companionship. Sociability was exalted in prose and poetry as the mark of a virtuous sovereign. Deception and lies were, however, necessary in order to protect honor and avoid scandal. Courtly love, which stimulated the desire for personal autonomy, invariably did so at the expense of the bonds of community: this *amour* sowed a whirlwind of confusion and discord. The first rules imposed on the lovers were the solemn obligation of discretion and secrecy. In a spate of manuals and handbooks, from that of the Chevalier de la Tour Landry's *Livre pour enseignement de se filles* (1370–71) to the *Chastoiement des dames* by Robert of Blois and the *Menagier de Paris*, burgher and noble women were counseled, nay, even warned, as to the risks of dishonor if acts of courtesy were liable to misinterpretation by lascivious and insensitive males.[30]

When the bonds of fellowship failed, spiritual and political regression set in, with the court becoming a theater of intrigue. The poets of chivalry and Arthur's Round Table portrayed such a regression as leaving only the primitive ties of blood and kinship as mainstays. Revenge was not a passion but an obligation, and one gained honor by loving *well*. It was precisely this world of heroic duty, reciprocity, mutuality, surety, bonds, indentures, and bastard feudalism that was in the process of being downsized. Even the term "civility" was virtually synonymous with courtesy and applied to the debonair and courtly among nobles. With the more humble, *civility* most often implied neighborliness. The manorial courts promoted "love days" during which contentious members of the village could settle disputes. Good godparenting required villagers to do much more than name the child; ideally, godparents should assume responsibility for the physical and spiritual well-being of the young child. Parish guilds, youth guilds, religious confraternities, parish charities, and co-parenting formed mutually beneficial ties within the community. Middling and well-to-do villagers relied upon neighbors for pledging and a host of other favors—legal and economic.

The marks of civilized behavior among the nobility were located in the glamor of good lordship and the burdens of indiscriminate charity and what has been characterized as "the old country ways." Villagers called on lay and ecclesiastical lords for assistance, and the distribution of alms and food were routine. The trencher, serving as a plate upon which the rich man ate his meal, was made of an inferior quality of bread. After the repast this bread was collected and bestowed on the poor along with the bits of meat and gravy that had seeped in. To return to earlier comments concerning the ethos of solidarity, the field of religious experience was rich with the fructifying seed of atonement and spiritual reparation. It would be easy to discover parallels between lordly and village behavior, with the emphasis on pledging, "love days," and indiscriminate charity and the cycle of the Christian year, the drama of the liturgy, and the incidence of carnival and festival. Finally, the belief that God had sent His only Son to earth to redeem men with His precious blood had ample confirmation in the quotidian experience of a society where kinship, penal liability, and the need to offer satisfaction for crime were at the center of social change.[31]

The court records of Ghent in the county of Flanders (the second largest city north of the Alps in the fourteenth century) disclose how vital to the body politic and social was the primordial cement of pledge, surety, bond-posting, ritual atonement, and compensation for crime and insult. In the absence of compelling public authority and civic tribunals, this intricate network of mutualities offered the best prospect for maintenance of urban order. Individuals were required to give satisfaction for crimes, often being sent on a distant pilgrimage to do reparation. Kinsmen purged themselves as innocent parties in the solemn presence of the victim's clan in order to be liberated from penalty. Rules for the division of the blood price *(Maagzaen)* were complex and detailed. Kindred were entitled to reparation for injuries suffered by a relative. In certain instances the clan might be likened to a peace association, while in others it was a tool for vengeance. The various factions had uniforms or colors by which retainers were identified. If a culprit made unfounded accusations, thereby uttering impure words, he might be forced to undergo ritual purification by taking part in a religious procession or pilgrimage. The principle of family solidarity and collective liability worked so that when one renounced a kinsman's debt, he also forfeited the prospect of inheriting from the estate. Flanders was of course among the most highly urbanized territories in Northern Europe during the fourteenth, fifteenth, and sixteenth centuries. Yet its juridical practices and customs were not so remote from such frontier regions as Wales, where blood money was preferred for settlement of grievances and blood feuds over the cumbersome machinery of the law. Better to repair damaged relationships with reparations of blood money. In sixteenth-century Wales and distant Ireland, fear of personal vengeance prevented kinsmen of principals to a dispute from attending church. In Scotland mechanisms for reconciliation were built into the bonds of manrent, with the requirement of counsel designed to lead to arbitration of disagreements. Private and tribal justice, with its traditional formulas of settlement, were matched in these border regions of Europe by archaic rituals of humiliation intended to shame the guilty.[32]

5

As we have observed, beginning with the Italian humanists of the fifteenth century and continuing with Erasmus in the sixteenth century, dissatisfaction mounted among literati with ideas of atonement, reparation, and restitution. Such behavior was increasingly to be perceived as barbarous and uncivilized. Excessive display of lamentation and emotion were to be replaced by adopting more decorous exequies and dignified rituals. In Italy notarial and juridical training was closely linked with the early history of humanism. The study of Roman legal practice under the early Empire, with its distaste for reprisal and blood liability, had a significant impact. In Petrarch we see a strong affinity to the classical ideal of moral self-sufficiency. This ideal encouraged the withdrawal of emotion from a world of collective responsibility. Petrarch would release himself from such generalized moral obligation by pleading his own inadequacies with a certain sense of serious irony. He judged himself to be more in need of help than the many others. In *De vita solitaria* he was to write, "I could wish to have everybody or at least as many as possible to gain salvation with me but in the end what do you expect me to say? It is enough for me, yea, a cause of great happiness, if I do not perish myself." For Petrarch, *otium* was a type of studious leisure made possible by a disengagement. This disengagement was no heroic gesture or ascetic renunciation but bore the mark of the Ciceronian ideal of *libertas*—a power over one's life. At the same time imperfections of the human condition were not to be transcended. The idea of privacy was naturalized by an insistence on one's own frailties and inconsistencies. The ideal of celibacy was defended, but despite its Christian tonality the objective was not the monastic one of self-sacrifice, but rather, the goal was self-understanding. Finally, the conception of privacy would, in subsequent centuries, achieve the favorable connotation of lack of accountability moving beyond the notion of solitude to one of dignified withdrawal.[33]

The conception of rendering visible satisfaction as an essential for the pacification of one's neighbors and their ultimate reconciliation with God was considered entirely remote from the true meaning and spirit of the gospels. The classical construction of Romans 5:3 of the phrase "non poenitebit nobis fidei nostrae" will be rendered "we will not be ashamed of our faith." This classical sense moves away from the translation "we will not repent of our faith." Similarly, Romans 5:12, traditionally viewed as the text essential for proving the doctrine of Original Sin, was interpreted both in Italian vernacular writings and in the humanist scholarship of Erasmus so that the progeny of Adam sinned not by inheritance, but through imitation of him. It has been effectively argued by scholars of the present generation that the Ten Commandments came to rival the seven deadly sins, and that the fraternity of the brotherhood was being challenged by the paternity and fatherhood of God. At the same time it can be argued that changes in the marketplace and law courts were less favorable to collective responsibility and even to ideals of neighborliness. These changes worked closer to the limits of moral responsibility, approaching freer conceptions of exchange and social relations. The vocabulary of exchange, both material and spiritual, was undergoing a series of displacements. *Compensation, satisfaction, restitution, penance,* and *payment* were losing something of their literal quality. No longer were they so likely to create a subtext of relations between man and man, and man and God. Were these specific migrations and transformations of meaning part of a larger process accompanying a tilt toward civility? To set in place a durable vocabulary whereby exchange was conceived of as benefiting both parties, yet not producing unlimited or extended liability, was a sure signal of this transition. A language of moral terms was being strengthened by being impregnated with individual rather than relational morality.[34]

An archaic vocabulary had sought for unity of the physical, the spiritual, and the social. In matters religious the integrity of the English writers' attitudes toward the relationship of physical and spiritual realities is a mark of the vernacular idiom. But this vocabulary was relaxing something of its hold. The word *gentillesse,* so frequently invoked in Middle English writings as a bridge between the spiritual and social, would, in coming times, lose pride of place. Words such as *meed* and *hire,* signifying reward and payment for both material and spiritual transactions, were losing something of their currency by the sixteenth century. So too do we find limitations being imposed upon such favored words as *largess, courtesy,* and *hospitality.* These words denoting custom and practice essential for the right ordering of community and workings of good lordship were now the focus of protracted literary debate. If one studies the reception of humanist and literary importations from Italy into the north of Europe, one is struck by the extent to which both language and genre were shaped by new conceptions of civility and public life. Consolidating their prestige on a cultural plane neither clerical nor narrowly professional, humanists moved from ecclesiastical or academic domains where linguistic practice was subordinated either to metaphysical speculation or immediate commercial gain. The impulse was toward the oratorical rather than the textual as they exploited the resources of classical Latin aiming to influence, through eloquence, an audience neither markedly professional nor theological.[35]

6

In fourteenth- and fifteenth-century England there had been a large and sturdy literature of complaint directed against the political and social wrongs of the times. Criticism of the royal household—the center of government—was chronic, revealing the persistent antagonisms between court and country. This dissatisfaction was a significant element in so many of the political controversies raging through the later Middle Ages until 1485. The taste for magnificence, splendor, and royal patronage was both grounds for strong rule and a flash point for disaffection and even rebellion. Literary accounts of these matters and reflections on their significance did not, however, redefine relationships between private good and public advantage, nor did they search out new values and ideals for the conduct of public life. The essential remedies involved activating the traditional vocabulary designed to make social bonds palpable and concrete. The exception was of course to be found in spiritual writings framed to reinforce a social ethos through the mechanism of *caritas* and Christian love.[36]

Thomas More, exemplary of that first generation of classically minded Englishmen, with exquisite irony undermined the vocabulary of public glory and honor, conspicuous display, and magnanimity in his *Utopia*. These manifestations of chivalry and largess contributed not to the durability of the social order, but rather to its moral and political degradation. Unlike his literary forebears, More did not find any ready remedy or easy target for invective. Blame could not be smugly heaped on the shoulders of bad counselors to the king. Clearly, a dialogue such as the *Utopia*, conducted in Latin, permitted the author a greater distance from the ethics of the world he desired to challenge, while at the same time the Latin limited his audience. Further, the vernacular and the medieval Latin were replete with terms reflecting a social order sanctioned by analogies and correspondences between things spiritual and material. The copiousness of Ciceronian Latin permitted commentators on politics, history, and society to portray a more ambiguous social reality; at the same time, Ciceronian Latin, with its confident array of clauses encased in architecturally crafted periodic sentences, gave the author a sense of control. More austere and decorous, the classical Latin worked back into the English prose, allowing for a degree of analysis hitherto exceedingly rare.[37]

Certainly the new rhetoric exerted a fatal fascination on literati, pedagogues, and some theologians. Often it was prized as an instrument for demystification capable of revealing to the reader that traditional rituals were no more than rhetorical tropes. This discipline of discourse highlighted the art of the probable. Securely linked to politics by Aristotle, it was of course concerned with the here and now *(hic et nunc)*. Beyond traditional measure, it was now elevated to the status of instruction in creation of the linkage of a civil society whose appropriate aims were those suitable finalities of peace and the common good. Movement toward a civil society strengthened the literary impulse to highlight the density and even the ambiguity of human interrelationships. The importation of a host of Italian courtesy books and manuals of courtly behavior is evidence of the felt need for exploring the nuances of social negotiation. In many fields, from literary criticism to art theory to drama theory, do we find a new openness to strategies of artifice and illusionism. Sir Philip Sidney's definition of poetry, in his *Defense of Poetry* (1595), owed much to Italian humanist and Aristotelian definition of poetry and is perhaps too well known to cite. Ben Jonson's definition, although close to Sidney's, is more markedly classical and worth quoting:

> A Poet is . . . a Maker, or a fainer; His Art, an Art of imitation or faining; expressing the life of man to fit measure, numbers, and harmony, according to *Aristotle:* from the word, which signifies to make or fayne. Hence, hee is called a Poet, not hee which writeth in measure only; but that fayneth and formeth a fable, and writes things like the Truth. For the fable and fiction is (as it were) the forme and Soule of any poetical works, or *Poeme*.[38]

The reception of the theory of drama is perhaps most telling, since it was in the theater that this age was to invest its best talent and energy. Ideas from Giambattista Giraldi Cinthio and Battista Guarini revolutionized the possibilities of the tragic form, permitting attention to be focused on the problematics of social cohesion. Dramaturgy used thick description to create a network of motives so that the outcome of the play was not one for which any single character was exclusively responsible. French drama was disciplined by the importation of classical ideals of dignity, decorum, and reasonableness. Dramatists worked tirelessly to display the innumerable facets of honor: an aristocratic society was sent to school where models from antiquity were being compelled to cope with the changing ambiguities of that sometimes virtue. Often the message was that the inner mechanism of pride must be bound to the promise of public regard.

In prose literature the ambiguities of fame and public opinion might be dismissed at first blush as mere folly only to be acknowledged, perhaps grudgingly, as having high public worth. John Florio's translation of the operative passage in Montaigne's *Essays* (II, 17) reads: "If this false-fond opinion doe notwithstanding serve and stead a commonwealth to hold men in their duties." In varying degrees numerous authors (Fulke Greville, Samuel Daniel, and Francis Bacon) expressed this problematic view. Opinion, even as pejoratively designated as "the breath of the vulgar," could inspire virtuous actions which conferred benefits on the civil order. Disagreement there might be as to its positive contribution to the ethical tone of public life, yet few would deny Florio's translation from Montaigne: "Opinion is a powerful bold and unmeasurable party." One recalls that array of advice of the humanists in the first part of the century. Sir Thomas Elyot, lawyer, diplomat, admirer of Erasmus, friend of Thomas More, and reader of Italian and Latin texts on civic comportment, reminded magistrates to be "openly published" and refrain from the attractions of private life. His *The Boke Named The Governour* (1531) extolled the virtues of public life and would educate the public man. Thomas Starkey, court humanist and admirer of things Venetian, in his *A Dialogue between Pole and Lupset,* analyzing the sources of social disorder, opined that the cause was that "wyse and polytyke men" did "flye from offyce and authoryte." Those preferring quiet and private pleasure, not using their talents for public good, "dowth manyfest wrong to hys cuntrey and frendys, and ys playn vniust and ful of iniquyte." An answer proffered confidently by the Tudor humanist asserted that "lytyle avayleth vertue that is not publyschyd abrode."39

In Thomas Wilson's influential *Rhetorique* (1557), complex allegorizing is rejected in favor of "plain [intelligible] opening" of the text. In both Erasmus and the English educator John Colet, the accent was on the pastoral value of the literal interpretation of the Bible. Not preoccupied with the spiritual sense, Erasmus would remove technical uncertainties and textual corruptions so that the message of Christ would come through clearly to the contemporary reader. For Erasmus and Colet the biblical word was an act—the oration of good—intended to move an audience to follow the Christian way of life. Erasmus associated allegorizing with dialectic. His allegiance to the oratorical tradition of the Italian humanists and their classical forebears was not equivocal. Recalling his first years of study and the significance of being *liberaliter educatum,* he wrote in the *Declamatio:*

> The most miserable time of my youth was when [we] boys were flayed by 'modi significandi' . . . and at the same time were taught nothing but to speak poorly. Truly, the teachers obscured grammar by introducing dialectical and metaphysical difficulties so that they would not appear to be teaching childish things.

The task of the exegete or translator was to enhance the clarity of divine speech, and therefore heighten its impact on the human will. Lorenzo Valla's influence was evident and compelling with Erasmus and, in turn, with John Colet and the model education soon to be imitated throughout England after being installed at St. Paul's. Erasmus had read Valla's *Adnotationes* in *Novum Testamentum* (ca. 1455) and was to publish it in 1504–5. Earlier, in the 1490s, his linguistic sensitivities had been informed by Valla's *Elegantiarum Linguae Latinae Libri VI.* The allegorical sense, once found imminent in the Bible, was now perceived through rhetorical method as a form of *eloqutio* used tropologically by the divine orator to enhance and make effective his message.40

Of course an appetite for the allegorical and didactic was still powerful. Yet when Henry VIII arose impatiently and "departed to his chamber" during the performance of a morality acted by the king's own players, he was making a gesture emblematic of a desire to experience drama as a mirror of society rather than as a medium for the transposition of sermons from the pulpit or abstract debates from the classroom. Serious questioning of the dramatic effectiveness of literature as a cautionary tale was to become fashionable. Henry Howard, earl of Surrey (ca. 1517–47), friend of Wyatt and first among poets open to humanist influence, when translating the fourth book of Virgil's *Aeneid,* was much indebted to Gawin Douglas's translation, using the Scotch poet's work as a crib. But the influence of the Italian poets and critics prompted Surrey to imitate Virgil's style and sense, while discarding Douglas's compelling passion for moralizing. Literati were now more likely to question the value of history and poetry as a repository for emblematic patterns or easily replicable moral lessons. The homiletic tradition was regularly introduced into the theater of Christopher Marlowe's generation only to be undermined. Drama was coarsening its techniques: characters were shedding something of their abstraction to be converted into recognizable social types. The old interlude plays, with their personified virtues and vices and open moralizing, were increasingly thought unfashionable. As Samuel Taylor Coleridge was to observe, stage figures were being individualized by attention to manner and mode of speech rather than by evocation of intellectual differences. Satire and epigram, by imitating Roman models, served as a sensitive register of contemporary manners. In narrative poetry the allegorical and moralistic were rivaled by the frank sensuality of the Ovidian romance, as well as by the taste for versified politics and history.[41]

Edmund Spenser, like other leading poets of his generation, aimed to achieve the lofty Horatian purpose of civilizing mankind through learning and literature. The humanist strategy of psychologizing by portraying internal conflict rather than deeds of arms shifted the locus of virtue from the tilting yard and battlefield to the human psyche. In a letter to Sir Walter Raleigh, appended to books 1–3 of the *Faerie Queene,* he wrote, "the general end . . . of all the books is to fashion a gentleman or noble person in virtuous or gentle disciplines." Spenser's friend and fellow literateur, Gabriel Harvey, wrote the following as a tribute to the author of the *Faerie Queene:*

> Petrarch was a delicate man and with an elegant iugement graciously confined Loue within the limits of Honour; Witt within the boundes of Discretion; eloquence within the termes of Civility: as not many yeares sithence an Inglishe Petrarch did.[42]

An education and style of life was lent literary representation which did much to disvalue heroic ways and archaic lifestyles. New rhetorical strategies imported from the Continent were favored by poets and proseteurs such as Sir Philip Sidney, whose literary tact was everywhere in evidence. He would not endorse any narrow moral judgment on the frailties of wormish mankind; nor would he confront the reader with truths overly solemnized. He would only go so far as to counsel living with imperfections, recognizing one's own weaknesses, and forgiving them in others. His *Old Arcadia* offers a portrayal of that ever-widening landscape between the idealized pretentiousness of individuals and their self-interest. His work often carried the heavy charge of political advice to ruler and courtier. In his *Apology for Poetry,* Sidney celebrated the potential of the courtier for learning, seeing his actions artfully made to conform to the processes of nature. In *Astrophel and Stella,* Sidney's sly and subtle wit was always on the brink of casting into doubt, albeit most tenderly, the heroic and romance values he praised. Sidney harbored the burdensome suspicion that princes compensated their subjects for the loss of precious liberty by a round of spectacles and courtly festivities. Self-consciousness concerning the social utility of political ritual was a mark of Tudor writings. Thomas Cranmer had baldly championed such ceremony "as a commodity . . . for a good order and quietness," while Sir Thomas Elyot defended it because "we be men and not angels, wherefore we know nothing but by outward signification."[43]

Sidney was known to have translated the first two books of Aristotle's *Rhetoric.* Markedly different from the moralistic conception of the role of rhetoric as quintessential for instruction in political virtue commonly found in the writings of Cicero and Quintillian, Sidney took a pragmatic, even skeptical, view of the ethical benefits of the art of persuasion. John Hoskins (1566–1638), lawyer and wit, friend and critic of the best writers of his generation, believed that Sidney had gone to school, not in Aristotle's moral writings but in his *Rhetoric,* and this—via Machiavelli:

> The perfect expressing of all qualities is learned out of Aristotle's ten books of moral philosophy: but because, as Machiavel saith, perfect virtue or perfect vice is not seen in our time, which altogether is humorous and spurting, therefore the understanding of Aristotle's Rhetoric is the directest means of skill to describe, to move, to appease, or to prevent any motion whatsoever.[44]

7

The new literature operated at a more prosaic and modest level, importing from the Continent humanist criticism against the harsh claims of honor and exorbitant ways of chivalry. Humanist texts psychologized, extending the range of meaning and ambiguity of key words such as *benevolence, beneficence,* and *liberality.* Drawing from Cicero's *De oratore,* the conventional figure of the knight was metamorphosized into that novel creation, the courtier, so readily appropriated by fashionable Spanish, French, and English authors of the sixteenth century. The gamesmanship of the amateur, so esthetically stylized by Castiglione, was favored over the ruthless competitiveness of the warrior professional. Humanists of Erasmus's generation condemned the literature of chivalry with its "bold baudy and open manslaughter." In the English translation of Juan Luis Vives' *Office and Duetie of an Husband,* it was argued that these writings harmed men and women making them "wylye and crafty kindling and stirring up covetousness" and "inflaming beastly and filthy desire." The English humanist and school-master Roger Ascham (1516–68) concurred in this judgment, excoriating Sir Thomas Mallory's *Le Morte Darthur* in a scathing phrase: ". . . in which book those be counted the noblest knights that do kill most men without any quarrel and commit foulest adulteries by subtle shifts. . . ." Thomas More's bitter invective against wasteful extravagance and violence of knights, their tourneys, ceremonies, and feastings was but the most illustrious instance of the new literature aiming to extend the boundaries of civility to encompass high gentry and nobles.[45]

The writings of the first generation of humanistically minded Englishmen such as Sir Thomas Elyot, Richard Morison, Thomas Starkey, Richard Pace, Roger Ascham, and others associated learning, literacy, and the social graces of dancing and the arts with the desirable ends of policy, civility, and justice. This was one of the privileged moments in the history of culture, and it can be argued that a band of writers, diplomats, government counselors, and lawyers—humanistically inclined—averred, in unequivocal terms, that unless nobles and high gentry relaxed their old country ways in favor of a more civil lifestyle, they were likely to lose political influence and be replaced by lesser men, that is, their social inferiors. They must be prepared to give good counsel to the crown and good service to the realm. The theme of good counsel itself was repeatedly dramatized in the theater. The first of the Tudor dramas to achieve high literary status in the eyes of sophisticated contemporaries was *Gorboduc* by Thomas Norton and Thomas Sackville. The moral of the play pointed to the terrible dangers to the kingdom when bad advice was rendered to the king. It is interesting to note that Sackville, who was the cousin of Queen Elizabeth I, relinquished his role as a writer soon after completing *Gorboduc* in favor of assuming the office of minister to the queen. If one follows the progress of this type of drama, so favored by Elizabethan playwrights, one observes how a simplified version of political advice gives way to a more problematic model. The same conclusion can be drawn from the prose literature of the times, where counseling becomes an intricate and demanding art.[46]

Civilizing values, advertised in humanist dialogues and treatises on education and manners, called for gentry and nobles to relinquish old country ways, the extravagances of chivalry, and even the more heroic demands of a warrior ethic. These judgments tended to be more a reflection of the sentiments of clerical and middling folk than of rural magnates and great potentates. The limitation of older styles of tuition were buttressed by complaints concerning the narrow horizons of nobility and gentry:

> The entire virtue and perfection of the gentleman, your lordship, does not consist in correctly spurring a horse, handling a lance, sitting straight in one's armor, using every kind of weapon, behaving modestly among ladies,

or in the pursuit of love, for there is another of the exercises attributed to the gentleman.

Not just one exercise, but many others should be added to skills in "marciall feates": fencing, tennis, swimming, wrestling, and other sports, along with "more than indifferentlys well seene in learnings, in the Latin and Greeke tungues." All of this contributed to the civil conversation and civil behavior of the courtier and gentleman. In England and on the Continent (particularly France) we observe that rhetorical training and discipline of children and adolescents through grammatical exercises and moral precepts was, in the sixteenth century, distinguished from any adult program of *imitatio,* word play, musical accomplishment, and linguistic virtuosity. Rhetorical pedagogy was relegated to the early years, while rhetorical craft was demonstrated in the mature by self-fashioning, diction, grace of manner, and lingustic agility. This adult purchase on erudition and ethical discrimination was nourished by the earlier exercises in secular schools and universities in the domains of etymology and ear for synonyms and antonyms. An aptitude for speaking and writing on either side of a question and the realization of plenitude (copiousness) in discourse were nurtured by continued reading and practice in writing. The adult would reveal his civility and refinement through the registry of esthetic judgments and intellectual nimbleness. In the first part of the sixteenth century, when humanistic influence was strongest, English poetry tended to employ language more measured than in any other historical moment.[47]

The well-born Florentine man-of-the-world, of the church, of letters— Giovanni della Casa—composed his *Galateo* between 1551 and 1555. Translated into French in 1562 under the title of *Galacée ou la maniere et fisson comme le gentilhomme se doit gouverner en toute compagnia,* and soon thereafter into Spanish, German, and English, it became one of a triad of classical Italian handbooks on manners, along with Guazzo and Castiglione. In the following century the three books were recommended by the Englishman Richard Lassels, a professional guide for young gentlemen doing the Grand Tour. In his *The Voyage of Italy,* where the three manuals are cited, he makes this marginal reference:

> As for their [the Italians'] manners, they are most commendable. They have taught them in their books, they practise them in their actions, and they have spread them abroad over all Europe, which owes its civility unto the Italians, as well as its religion.

There were those in England who, according to Shakespeare's *Richard II,* did indeed listen to the

> Report of fashions in proud Italy,
> Whose manners still our tardy apish nation
> Limps after in base imitation.

Sometimes such Englishmen were figures of fun; sometimes of menace. Roger Ascham, tutor of Princess Elizabeth, spoke of "fonde books . . . sold in every shop in London, commended by honest titles the sooner to corrupt honest manners." But even this notorious detractor of Italian fashions welcomed Sir Thomas Hoby's translation of Castiglione's *Courtier* as worthy of instructing the young. Educated in Padua, the diplomat Hoby would have his courtier "wise and well seene in discourses upon states." Had Ascham lived but a few years longer, he would most probably have commended Robert Peterson's translation of Della Casa's *Galateo.*[48]

This work by Peterson, a member of Lincolns Inn, from the anonymous French version of 1576, was praised as "grave," / "Eke wise and good, for civil folke to have." At the outset, both Peterson and Della Casa present a tactful, literary appraisal of urbane and civilized comportment far distanced from the heroic code of a recent past:

> An albeit Liberalitie, or magnanimitie, of themselves beare a greater praise, then, to be a well taught or manored man: yet perchaunce, the courteous behaviour and entertainment with good maners and words, helpe no lesse, him that hath them: then the high minde and courage, advaunceth him in whome they be. For these be such things as a man shall neede alwayes at all hands to use, because a man must necessarily be familiar with men at all times, & ever have talk & communication with them: But justice, fortitude, and the other greater, and more noble vertues, are seldome put in uze. Neither is ye liberall and noble minded man, caused every hower to doe bountifull things: for to use it often, cannot any man beare the charge, by any meanes. And these valiant men y^t be so full of highe minde and courage: are very seldome driven to trye their valour & vertue by their deeds. Then as muche as these last, doe passe those first, in greatnes (as it were) & in weight: so much do the other surmount these in number, & often occasion to use them.[49]

Comparable evidence for the expression of equally poised and cautionary social views exists in abundance for the Continent in the sixteenth century. Manuals of instruction, as well as imaginative literature, allied themselves with a more civic and public purpose, while at the same time registering misgivings concerning chivalric education and the pursuit of heroic ambition to the detriment of the minor diplomacies so essential to civil life. Della Casa made the provocative but so commonsensical observation that in the round of daily life few opportunities existed for fighting Circassian tigers and African lions.

Of course a grander vision of the prospects of public life was to be found in the many humanist tracts, biographies, and scholarly treatises aiming to reconstruct the military and political experience of antiquity. Moving away from ideals of reckless individual courage and the world of single combat with the warrior's selfish passion for booty, humanist writings often revived ancient prescriptions for discipline and organized military structure. Veneration for the wisdom of the ancients made the Roman conception of the relationship between "good arms" and "good laws" a favorite theme. Furthermore, the classical manifestations of citizen patriotism and soldierly training were diffused throughout Europe. Machiavelli's *Art of War* was a culmination of discourse on the relationship between political and military organization of society begun in Florence a hundred years earlier by humanistically trained admirers of the antique. The *Art of War* was a literary success, and in the sixteenth-century translations it appeared in English, French, German, and Latin: there were twenty-one editions of this provocative humanist dialogue.[50]

8

The first usage of the word "humanist," mentioned in the *Oxford English Dictionary,* is attributed to the English diplomat and Continental traveler Fynes Moryson: "The Humanist I mean him that affects knowledge of state affaires, Histories (etc.)." You may remember that it was Moryson who heaped scorn upon the vile practices of an archaic society with its predilection for wasteful hospitality, casual ways, and armies of servants. His blunt remarks, echoing the opinion of many of his contemporaries, summed up the final outcome of open hospitality: ". . . our greatest expense and in the casting out of excrement." Well-traveled Englishmen held practical reservations concerning traditional features of "good lordship" and "open hospitality." The importation of educational programs and rhetorical practices of Continental humanists bore a heavy cargo of civic purpose directed at tempering the extravagant and violent behavior of an obstreperous noble class and turning young gentlemen toward service to the state. The writing of history was traditionally seen as a literary activity in itself. Now, through its study, "a yonge gentilman shal be taught to note and marke nat only the ordre and elegancie in declaration of the historie, but also the occasion of the warres, the counsailes and preparations of either part . . . the fortune and successe of the holle affaires." Montaigne defined a new "fourth estate" who were "in charge of laws." Possessing "the sovereign authority of goods and lives," this estate was not only separate from the *noblesse,* but also obeyed a different ethic from the nobility, motivated as they were by "justice" instead of "honor." Richard Taverner, in his *Garden of Wisdom* (1539), gave the sage advice that any man eager to be conversant in public affairs must ". . . fashion himself to the manners of men."[51]

The language of chivalry was being divested of its aureate diction and its ties to an archaic culture based upon the exchange of favors, gifts, and services. The confident flow of colorful talk was checked, as were other easy transactions between lover and maid. In the poetry of Sir Thomas Wyatt, lover and lady face each other as equals in negotiations. They are accomplished in the business: sometimes entering into partnerships and sometimes remaining rivals. As autonomous human beings they are just as likely to be portrayed as behaving aggressively as they are of being depicted as acting as morally responsible individuals.

> If it be yea, I shalbe fayne;
> If it be nay, frendes as before;
> Ye shall an othre man obtain,
> And I myn owne and yours no more.

The contradiction between, on the one side, the idea of the fair lady's grace which, like the Deity's, cannot be earned and therefore should be freely given, was opposed on the other by the speaker's conviction that his fidelity should receive its due, that is, its hire. The lexical conventions of courtly love were no longer secured in customary, tenurial relationships:

> If fansy would favour
> As my deserving shall,
> My love, my paramour,
> Should love me best of all.
> But if I cannot attain
> The grace that I desire,
> Then may I well complain
> My service and my hiere.

The relationship between lady and servitor was closer to that of the indenture of bastard feudalism than to the vassalage of courtly love.[52]

Edmund Spenser's *Faerie Queene* took inspiration from Ariosto's *Orlando Furioso*. The English poet was to distance himself from the conventions of medieval romance, drawing attention to his own poetic ingenuity and self-consciously appropriating a chivalric idiom. Indeed, the vocabulary for expressing traditional forms of behavior was acquiring flexibility and a new dimension. One can trace such words as *grace* and perceive how the archaic meaning of material favor (gift and countergift) was being augmented and was achieving an esthetic quality. In Middle English the word *gracious* had been used most often in conjunction with a reward or gift. Now it was applied more frequently to a style of comportment. In literature tribute was paid to "Petrarchs Thuscan gracefulnesse" as lending esthetic value to language. Chivalric fictions were transformed into metaphors. For example, the language of chivalry alluding to the tournament became impressionistic rather than systematic. Meanwhile, the register of interpretation of such key words as *honor* was more shaded and nuanced. The semipublic character of the language of love, which had been traditionally permeated with a vocabulary of feudal service and obligation, now underwent revision. The literary representation of this passion tended to be gradually privatized and separated from the domain of solemn duty. Love was portrayed as engaging the intellect and intelligence as well as the senses. The imagery of vassalage and idiom of courtly love were rivaled by a language of commerce. Romeo's lines to Juliet register something of this new diction of adventuring for commodities:

> I am no pilot; yet wert thou so far
> As that vast shore wash't with the farthest sea
> I should adventure for such merchandise (2. 2. 82–84.)

The marketplace and world of exchange provided an arsenal of images of profit and loss. The figurative language of commerce and of the exploration of recently discovered far-flung continents with their untold riches informed and inflated the Marlovian world of heroic ambition. Shakespeare's sonnets offered a word-hoard of terms pertaining to economic activity from contract to usury, from profit to loss, from thrift to spendthrift. New money, social climbing, courtly corruption, and the city peopled with sharpers, rogues, and conney-catchers testified to the debasing of honor and severing of social ties. Money and lust were often the solvents of social bonding in the ever more plentiful fiction of Elizabethan times. The fields of charity, friendship, warm fires, and hospitality were miniaturized. In poetry the word-stock of vassalage and courtly love was rivaled by the idiom of commerce and accounting, with gold and silver displacing coral and rose.[53]

In the Elizabethan theater the dynamics of love were presented through the depiction of individuals exercising free choice. Rigid codes of propriety, exaggerated conceptions of family honor, and the jealousy of husbands and fathers was often ample dramatic ground for sympathizing with unconventional female behavior. Chaucer's explicitly religious frame of reference in his *Troilus and Criseyde* is omitted by Shakespeare, who leaves his characters in the "disorder of mortality." Hamlet does not question the duty of revenge, but the ideal certainly does not fire him. The theme of duty and deeds of blood was itself being psychologized as dramaturgy worked to distinguish the claims of self from obligation to kin. Here we find the beginnings of a lexicon for portraying privacy. Solitariness was being transposed into solitude. In an age of clan and clientele, the duel of honor in which gentlemen fought for reputation, was portrayed by the scholar and antiquarian William Camden as an integral part of the civilizing process. The duel of honor had, in the seasoned historical judgment of Camden, superseded the "killing affrays" of the fifteenth century. (It might be remembered that Camden was the revered teacher of that superbly classically trained poet and playwright, Ben Jonson.) Later, when Blaise Pascal condemned dueling, it was not for its deadly outcome, but for the elaborate courtesies surrounding the ritual.[54]

9

In an earlier time, remaining outside the *mouvance* had already lost its mark of distinction. The term "vassal," once of little social consequence, had become a word of praise. In the *Song of Roland,* French barons were addressed: "Baron fraceis vos estes bons vassals." The *chansons de geste* had the tenacious purpose of celebrating virtues displayed in the interests of a lord. The emotional appeal of service—even of the domestic role in the lord's household—was widely advertised in chivalric poetry. Ceremonies of welcome and salutation informed the manners and vocabulary of splendid courts seeking to attract and hold important men in royal service. The word *isolate* came into French much later, having been borrowed from the Italian. In turn it was to be borrowed by the English from the French *isolé.* At first the meaning "like an island" had been employed as an architectural term having the geographical significance of separateness or disconnection. Soon, however, it would be applied to those at court having no retinue and being without obligations or human bonds. He might be surrounded by relatives or other human beings, but they were not essential to him: in a word, he was detached and, as it were, *isolate.* This meaning gained strength, testifying over the centuries to the decline of networks of fixed social and religious obligation. One must also consider evidence from that abundant literature satirizing and parodying courtly conduct and affectation.[55]

The word *cortigiana,* first recorded in late fifteenth-century Italy, was a euphemism for a rather high-class prostitute. Edward Blount's 1607 English translation of Lorenzo Ducci's courtier treatise under the title of *Ars Aulica: or the Courtiers Arte* was dedicated to Ben Jonson's patrons, the earl of Pembroke and his brother. This was perhaps the most psychologically troubling, as well as the most esthetically wrought work of this genre. The spirit of Jonson's finest historical drama *Sejanus* shares Ducci's dark preoccupation with the maneuverings and dissimulation of a Tacitean courtly politics. The aim of the courtier's will, under all circumstances, seeks to realize his own narrow advantage. This and other manuals of conduct were almost subversive in their distrust of the efficacy of heroic conventions, codes, and ceremonies. Possibly the sense of self—the social construction of personality—may have been enhanced by the loss of confidence in courtly ideals and archaic rituals. Deep misgivings about pageantry and studied courtesies could lead to serious concern for inward promptings. A sense of self-worth might make a man feel superior to ordinary obligation. Of course an esthetics of behavior was encouraged by manner books such as those of Giovanni della Casa and Castiglione, since vice was not branded as sinful, merely portrayed as ugly. This diagnosis called for the remedies of charm and grace. Speakers in the dialogues did not experience feelings of guilt, and the social world in which they moved was not haunted by spiritual anxieties. The literary tactics were those of informality and inclusion, with acknowledgment, often melancholy, of the transitoriness of human creations. Yet this sense of impermanence did not undermine the energy of a Castiglione, who was able to realize a heroic enterprise: he shaped a language capable of absorbing and transmitting rules and usages minted in social commerce and cultural exchange. This integrating literary hybridism allowed for cultural pluralism. Conversation united individuals in a common search for personal enrichment through cultivation of nontechnical language habits. The very fact of impermanence served to heighten the beauty of a rich and pluralistic identity fructified by the patient exploration of cultural variety. Deep spiritual malaise was psychologized and transmogrified into a beguiling, if not ennobling, melancholy.[56]

Meanwhile, *The Courtier* and other handbooks of comportment were finding lively competition from a wide variety of writings devoted to fashioning a gentleman for participation in a larger society. The very word *fashion* assumed a new range of meanings, including those pertaining to artifice and dissembling. This time, however, the connotations were highly ambiguous, serving the need for flexibility of character and delicate social negotiation. Saint Augustine's powerful admonition, "Hands off yourself. Try to build up yourself and you build a ruin," had become remote. So, too, had the advice of the twelfth-century English cleric and courtier Walter Map, who, in his *Courtier's Trifles*, when cataloguing the horrendous vanities and vices of the court of Henry II, exhorted his readers to maintain their own virtues in this nest of thieves and prideful men through secret devotion to the Holy Trinity. Instead, in the sixteenth century we notice a growing appreciation for the pastoral world of domestic and unheroic virtues as respite from the tensions of courtly life. One harbors the vision of a pretty shepherdess as consolation in place of a sacred image. This is an interior landscape removed from comedy and tragedy. The anticourtly bias was now directed toward shallowness and dilettantism, with the judgment that elegant tactics were inappropriate for a gentleman acting in society at large. Italian imports, such as Torquato Tasso's *Aminta,* presented ideals of simplicity and lack of artificiality as freeing the individual from the demands of harsh law—particularly the law of honor. Civil and honest behavior transcended any narrow notions of politeness or courtly tact. To this end the translation of Stefano Guazzo's *Civile Conversation* (1581) served to extend the debate into a more ample public space. Meanwhile, an ethos of urbanity informed poetic writings with a tonality both civilized and polite.[57]

1 0

From the first ducal courts in Quattrocento Italy, at Ferrara, Mantua, Milan, and Urbino, the authority of recently established *condottieri* (military commanders) rulers was legitimated by veneration and patronage of letters and eloquence rather than by skill at arms. Institutionalization of the Florentine Academy in 1542 enhanced the reputation of the Medici for connoisseurship and erudition, linking the literati and artists of Tuscany to the ducal house. In their advocacy of the "new learning," humanistically minded reformers were highly suspicious of an old-fashioned nobility devoted to an archaic lifestyle of revels, good housekeeping, studied courtesies, honorific violence, and casual charity. These time-honored acts surely created networks of obligation serving to anchor the chains of loyalty. Of course these allegiances and linkages could also be the source of chronic disorder and insistent factionalism. Not infrequently, these ties among friends, retainers, and kinsmen baffled the efforts of the crown to extend the influence of personal monarchy. The humanist Guillaume Budé, in his *L'institution du prince,* contended that royal authority was vested in the French king alone, and that while the aristocracy should of right hold their privileges, they had no share in royal authority. In the France of the early seventeenth century, Cardinal Richelieu's attempts to tame a congenitally insubordinate nobility led not only to plans for establishing new colleges, but also to the founding of the French Academy. Here we have evidence of an explicit, albeit optimistic, acknowledgment of the power of language, the superiority of eloquence and reason over and against naked force.[58]

Jean Bodin (1530–96), when writing of the illustrious accomplishments of Francis I, noted: "As soon as [the king] began to love literature from which his ancestors had turned away, immediately the nobles followed suit." It should be recalled that in the 1520s, Budé persuaded King Francis to found the Bibliotheque Royale, and, in 1530, the Collège de France. "Good letters" as an "instrument of virtue" was a literary commonplace. The heroic virtues of Rome and a new age of Augustus would make the obedience of nobles an instinctive response. So great was the magnetic, magical force of the classical world with its emphasis on the strict correlation between good arms and good laws! Classical authors were read with an almost pious regard for the virtues of discipline. Transformation of the heroic code was at the center of dramatic interest for the French classical theater from Alexander Hardy to Corneille. With Senecan tragedy as a model, the French playwright demonstrated the limitations of the Senecan hero, as the character's need for self-realization worked against his need for restraint. Increasingly, this tragic figure became aware of those forces over which he had no control. A relationship between discipline and the sense of theater existed, with the audience called upon to imagine itself different from what it was. The psychology by which anger and vengeance could be transformed into something that might legitimately be characterized as generosity was a topic of almost infinite dramatic investigation. No easy problem this, since this generosity was marked by grandeur far distant from anything resembling humility and, in fact, a higher stage in what the literary scholar Paul Bénichou termed "la religion de l'orgueil."

In England the humanist goals were perhaps more modestly set forth in a letter of June 15, 1531, to Thomas Starkey by Edmund Harvel: "To make all the land know *quam sit humaniter vivendum,* help to take out all barbarous custom and bring the realm to an antique form of good living." In the same year, Elyot's *Boke Named the Governour,* that courtesy book—a guide to a gentleman's education—appeared with its dedication to Henry VIII. It was to go through eight editions before 1580, and its author was rewarded by the king with an appointment to the court of Emperor Charles V. Elyot complained in the book that "to a great gentleman it is a notable reproach to be well learned and to be called a great clerk." In the next generation, the foremost humanist educator, Roger Ascham, broadened, adding urgency to the call for reformation of the courtier and his manners. A typical passage displaying the force of his rhetoric runs:

> Take heed, therefore, you great ones in the Court, yea though ye be the greatest of all, take heed what you do, take heed how you live. For as you great ones use to do, so all mean men love to do. You be indeed makers or marrers of all men's manners within the realm. For though God hath placed you to be chief in making laws, to bear greatest authority, to command all others: yet God doth order that all your laws, all your authority, all your commandments do not half so much with mean men, as doth your manner of living.

Ascham had been tutor to Princess Elizabeth, as well as King Edward VI's Latin secretary (a post he continued to fill under the Catholic Queen Mary), and his summons to the well-born to amend their style of life had some authority. *The Schoolmaster,* published posthumously in 1580, was replete with diatribes against an education in chivalric texts in which "those be counted the noblest knights that do kill men without any quarrel and commit foulest adulteries by subtlest shifts." By the end of the century that *enfant terrible* of literature, Thomas Nashe, whose satire, mock encomia, and short fictions did so much to subvert humanist rhetorical theory, would yet endorse—at least in his more solemn moments—the Ciceronian *paideia:* "Our learning ought to be our lives amendment and the fruites of our private study ought to appear in our publique behaviour."[59]

Again, Fynes Moryson (1566–1630), that sober, factual, reliable, and rather unimaginative recorder of European mores, habits, and customs (mind-bogglingly detailed), provides us with a less literary, more concrete version of these times of change. Concluding that England had on the whole been much benefited by the decline of "good lordship" and the rising tide of civility, he wrote that "in our age wherein we have better learned each man to live of his owne and great men keepe not troopes of idle servants . . . the English are become very industrious and skillful in manuall arts." This judgment was shared by leading political and literary contemporaries such as Raleigh and Gilbert. A very different response, esthetic rather than practical, came in the arts with the importation of the courtly masque from Medicean Florence. Here we witness the elaborate representation of the dependence of a civilized nobility on the monarchy. Ideas borrowed by Ben Jonson and forms borrowed by his collaborator Inigo Jones from Italian entertainments celebrated aristocratic dignity, while at the same time calling upon nobles to renounce their insane quest for glory and their prickly defense of honor. Instead, the nobility were exhorted to pursue the practical arts and submit to the discipline of peace. Jonson had characterized poetry as an art disposing men "to all civil Offices of Society . . . the absolute Mistress of manners . . . which leads on and guides us by the hand to action with a ravishing delight and incredible Sweetness." Inigo Jones was just as sanguine concerning the social utility of architecture, contending, for example, that the ancient Romans had erected Stonehenge so that its ordered proportions would civilize the rude and barbaric Britons. In his masque designs he often used classical buildings as emblems for social and political concord. The harmonies of music and poetry in the masque were symbolic of a kingdom at peace, where service to the crown replaced the false glory once gained from reckless chivalric pursuits and the killing fray of the tourney.[60]

1 1

Humanism, energetically and sometimes rudely, intruded itself into that realm of residues of archaic values and allegiances, first in the fourteenth-century Italian city-states. The quickening of public life and creation of civic institutions permitted the dismantling of many ancient liabilities and responsibilities. Throughout the rest of Europe the pace of the development of civil institutions and public administration was much slower. A complex of feudal relationships only gradually gave way to civic ties as the crown secured loyalty and service in return for personal privilege. Haltingly, ties of vassalage were perceived as less effective; the crown was required to communicate and negotiate with interest groups well defined and self-aware. However, by 1500, there were no more than 5,000 officeholders and 3,000 subordinates in all of France to enforce the royal will. This signified that there was but one royal official for every 60 square kilometers or one for 3,000 inhabitants. For Florence, with a population in 1427 of a quarter million or so throughout all its domains and territories, there were at least 400 to 500 notaries working for the various governments over the course of their political tenure. Only in highly integrated territorial states such as Venice and Florence was it possible to establish complex systems for tax assessment and collection. In addition to the notaries, there were 25 civil lawyers, a battery of magistrates, and some 2,000 elected or appointed officeholders. France had territorial jurisdiction over lands five times more extensive than that of Tuscany. The king's notaries and secretaries numbered about 120. If one compares this figure with that of a single commune such as Bologna, one finds that at the end of the fourteenth century, 280 notaries served the government.[61]

Yet this must not obscure the fact that change was at work in the north of Europe in the fourteenth and fifteenth centuries. The king of France and duke of Burgundy granted public servants special safe conduct and letters of recommendation, making them answerable only to the highest courts in the realm. The status of these officials was gradually elevated through the practice of granting fiscal and legal privileges. Movement toward administrative monarchy was accompanied by an increase in the appointment of lay rather than clerical civil servants. In France the university graduates often forgot their ecclesiastical status after the mid-fourteenth century. The grip of the ruler was strengthened. In England, from the time of Edward III on, civil servants received some legal education. When Thomas More replaced Cardinal Wolsey, he was the first lord chancellor to have studied at the Inns of Court, and with his tenure was initiated a line of lawyer chancellors who brought this training to that high post. A most telling statistic for England concerns the working group of justices of peace in six subject counties: in 1562, two-thirds of the justices had never been enrolled in universities or Inns of Court. By 1636, although the number of these justices had doubled, only 16 percent lacked a formal education. By then, too, there appears to have been a quickening of local interest in county elections in England, suggesting that the rural electorate was far from passive and deferential. In the case of France, Francis I created many offices, and while it is true that many of these were sold to raise revenue, the Venetian ambassador's report of 1546 should not be taken lightly: ". . . offices are infinite in number and grow daily . . . half of which would suffice." In the next century, under Louis XIV, the number of royal officials had increased some eleven times over what it had been in 1500.[62]

In an earlier time, serving the public weal and being served by it was in itself a source of complaint both in England and France. At the close of the fifteenth century, William of Worcester, a contemporary of John Paston, lamented that many a son of a knight had abandoned the road to glory, taking the path of wealth through advocacy and the Inns of Court. His lament for the decline of chivalry and its proud tuition concluded on the harsh note that these men of law were "more esteemed among all estates than he who spent 30 or 40 years of his days in great jeopardy in your ancestors conquests and wars." This bleak view, easily duplicated in many another fifteenth-century commentator, stands in pessimistic relief against the optimistic rhetoric of Continental and English humanists who not only celebrated service to the state, but also singled out chivalric romance and epic as the worst nurture for aspiring youths soon to be dedicated to the virtues of public service. The humanistically trained Thomas Cromwell, who was well traveled in Europe, had studied in Italy, and was now minister to the crown, perceived that the machinery of state could be utilized systematically to effect change in society. In Spain and France this signified making war ever more efficiently. In England the reverse was true, as warmaking became less efficient. But, as if to compensate, new patterns of duties were imposed upon courts and institutions in order to improve royal and local government.[63]

Cromwell's authority was as personal as that of Wolsey or Henry VIII, but the political alterations he sponsored diminished the subsequent impact of personality on the formation of governmental policy. In the meetings of the council he did not, as his mentor Wolsey had done, monopolize the giving of advice to the crown. He also appears to have been much more devoted to attending to matters procedural. This included regular attendance of a specific and well-defined body of councilors who were, for the most part, officeholders. They met at court or Westminster, where maintenance of formal records of business conducted became part of an established order which survived the fall of Cromwell in 1540. Furthermore, the royal court had a humanist intelligensia united, in the main, in support of Henry VIII's new order. This "Padua-London coterie" did heavy and effective propaganda work for the crown. Their Italian training in the classics and in Machiavelli stood them well. Thomas Cromwell's 1535 injunctions to the University of Cambridge provided for the reading of the Greek text of Aristotle, the humanist writings of Agricola, Melancthon, and Trapenzuntius in place of Duns Scotus and the other scholastics. This was high tribute to the value of the new pedagogy. Set in place, these reforms resulted in creation of the Regius Chair, to which the Ciceronian humanist Sir John Cheke acceded in 1540.[64]

12

In the sixteenth century the new pedagogy was broadcast as a cure for the ills of society. A humanist commonplace, nurtured by the Ciceronian rhetorical tradition, ventured harsh judgment on the ineptitude of the logically and dialectically trained mind when confronting the realities of public affairs. Beyond that, scholasticism stood condemned—however unfairly—as irrelevant to the pursuit of worthy goals of the active life. Polemicists were insistent about the "frivolous labyrinth" into which the science of dialectics must lead; "curious definitions" and "subtle distinctions" advantaged neither the literary nor the civic arts. Humanist education would have logic as an adjunct to rhetoric rather than philosophy. Erasmus had written that "it is not by learning rules that we acquire the power of speaking a language but by daily intercourse with those accustomed to express themselves with exactness and refinement and by the copious reading of the best authors." His *De duplici verborum ac rerum* of 1512 was a standard text for Latin rhetoric and composition, going through 100 editions before 1600. The royal grammar, based on the work of Erasmus, Colet, and Lyly, and prescribed for English grammar schools until 1604, had runs of 10,000 copies at a time when 1,200 or so was the norm. From the first, rhetorical works written in England (the 1530s) advertised the value of the skills and discipline imparted, most particularly for those in law and public life. Landed gentry, an order not in the vanguard of educational progress, perceived the social advantages of educating sons in the classics and the vocational benefits of attending the Inns of Court. The promise of the new education, as advanced in these texts, was delivered in real coin: relevant points were frequently illustrated by legal examples and political questions. The concept of rhetoric as the cultivation of "distinguished writing" and an aureate style was challenged by a Ciceronian commitment to rhetoric as effective preparation for civil life. Thomas Wilson, author of a most successful Tudor rhetorical handbook, was memorialized by Gabriel Harvey, the scholar and literary man, late in the sixteenth century, for his writings which were as "the dailie bread of our common pleaders & discoursers." Wilson went beyond the standard critique of the rhetorical poetics and tricky stylistics of an earlier time, mocking "the fine courtier [who] will talke nothing but Chaucer." Of other benighted and pretentious orators, he writes that they

> will bee so fine and so poeticall withall, that to their seeming there shall not stande one hair a misse, and yet euery body els shall thinks them meeter for a Ladies chamber, then for an earnest matter in any open assemblie.

A "Ladies chamber" was in fact exactly the locale for medieval allegories to place the figure of Truth. In *Court of Sapyence,* rhetoric is an exquisite Dame worshiped passionately by elegant courtiers. With Wilson, rhetoric is Ciceronian and male, doing the world's business in courts, council halls, and parliaments. By the time of Sidney, Spenser, Shakespeare, and Marlowe, the study of rhetoric occupied pupils of English grammar schools for fully four years.[65]

From Henry VIII himself, or those who drafted for him, came vigorous denunciations of those who had defied the royal will with insurrection and rebellion in Lincolnshire in 1536–37, and those whose domestic treason was linked with threat of foreign invasion. There was a defensive tone to some of the writing and an explanation of certain governmental actions. In the second of these documents or letters it was stated that the Privy Council, which at Henry's accession "the most were lawyers and priests," was now composed of more nobles. This statement was probably a response to rebel criticism of the king's elevation of parvenues. But then the letter continues, underscoring how little stock was indeed taken of the practical knowledge and worldly wisdom of dukes and bishops:

> And for because it is more than necessary to have some of our Privy Council learned in our laws and acquanted with the policies and practices of the world, we, by the advice of our whole Council before named, did elect and choose into our Privy Council, and also into their rooms, Sir Thomas Audley, knight, our chancellor, and the Lord Cromwell, keeper of our privy seal.

A barrage of complaints against the low-born Wolsey and Cromwell were met by a battery of exhortations to those of high station to be better prepared for giving counsel and participating in public life. In 1559, William Cecil,

Lord Burghley and faithful minister to Queen Elizabeth I, added his weighty opinion that "the wanton bringing up and ignorance of the nobility forces the prince to advance new men that can serve."

Despite inroads of humanist theories of education and the urging of More, Ascham, Elyot, Richard Pace, and others, it was still considered essential to extend the benefit of clergy to peers unable to read. To this end a clause was drafted in a bill of 1547.[66]

TWO

The Direction of Change

Something of the direction of cultural and social change in the north of Europe can be suggested by reviewing particular references from the Flemish experience of the thirteenth through the late fifteenth centuries. E. Warlop, in his monumental history of the Flemish nobility from the ninth to the fourteenth century, concludes that even at the end of the Middle Ages most nobles were illiterate. This handicap worked against this order, making it increasingly difficult for them to fulfill their commanding role in the administrative aspects of government. Their illiteracy did, on occasion, place them at the mercy of their own bailiffs. In April of 1224, Lord Gavere was to transfer a feudal abbey to the estate of Ninove; he was unable to do so, however, until the document had been translated into *teutonia lingua*. In a growing money-based economy, the nobles found themselves seriously disadvantaged. The second example concerns Jean de Lannoy, born about 1410 of a family of *grands seigneurs,* whose uncles had been leading advisors of Duke Philip the Good of Burgundy. Jean took service in the ducal armies and was, for fourteen years, stadholder of Holland. He captained a large contingent of Dutch volunteers coming to the aid of the duke against the rebels of the city of Ghent. He also undertook diplomatic missions to France and England for the House of Burgundy. In 1451 he was rewarded for his energetic devotion, becoming the fourth member of his family to be inducted into the Order of the Golden Fleece. At the ripe old age of fifty-two, he was transferred from the post of stadholder of Holland to governor of his own Walloon Flanders. Old age was good to him, for only two years later his wife bestowed upon him a son and heir. Shortly after the birth of little Louis de Lannoy, the father confessed that he had been spending sleepless nights worrying that he could not hope to be alive to advise his boy "at the age when he will have much understanding":

> I realize that my son and I can never be of the same time, for he comes and I go. . . . Therefore I decided to write this letter to my son so that if I do not live to the day when he can understand me, at least he will know by letter what my lips could not say to him, as often it is with lovers, who when they are together for love they cannot speak.[1]

These touching comments introduce the letter written in the father's own hand and dated May 3, 1465. Jean makes the modest disclaimer that he has no intention of setting up an educational program: this he will leave to "wise men, clerics, historians, and rhetoricians." But the father does intend to give the son very personal reasons why the lad must acquire Latin, take part in school disputations, be attentive to the Bible, and read books on ethics, economics, and, in particular, politics:

> Those who have learned and retained much, and who have the greatest desire to learn and know, attain great good, honor, and riches. . . . This has often caused me deep displeasure not for envy of them but, because of my simplicity and slight knowledge and because I was never put to school. I therefore know and can know nothing. I realize that this chance is for me lost and gone, never to be recovered, for I do not see or expect any remedy as to Latin or other studies. No day passes that I do not regret this, and especially when I find myself in the council of the king or of the Duke of Burgundy, and I know not nor dare not to speak my opinion after the learned, eloquent legists and *ystoryens* who have spoken before me. For I do not know the order or manner of speaking and can say nothing, but "Master John or Master Peter has spoken well, and I am of his opinion." Whence I have often felt deep shame and humiliation in my heart.

With more fathers like Jean de Lannoy, and obedient sons like Louis, prospects for educating the nobles of Burgundy must have improved. Certainly the foundation of the University of Dôle in Franche-Comté, with official backing of Duke Philip the Good, aimed at encouraging the learning in knightly and aristocratic circles. Indeed, these were the orders whose cooperation the duke most needed. The astute Fleming Philippe de Commynes regretted that in his youth he had not mastered Latin like other of his countrymen who had gone to study the tongue of Cicero and Virgil at the schools of Louvain, Cologne, and Paris. The matriculation register for the first three decades after the founding of Louvain suggests that Philippe may have been quite correct: a "reasonable sprinkling" of students designated *nobilia* is recorded, but in numbers they are nothing like what Oxford had to boast of 150 years later. Commynes, the keen observer of society, then matched the French lords against those of Netherlands-Burgundy: the French were proud of their ignorance, did not know languages, were incapable of running their estates, and, worst of all, could not offer good "civil counsel."[2]

In both England and France we have an extensive, and sometimes troubled, discussion of what has been appropriately designated "this nameless class"—those who now administered and gave counsel to the crown in greater numbers. Charles Loyseau, in his *Traité des ordres et simples dignitez,* spoke of "honourable hommes" and "honestes personnes," and Sir Thomas Smith, in his *De republica Anglorum,* written in the 1560s, spoke of "the fourth sort or classe." These were the better educated and legally trained men gaining prestige and political influence at the expense of clergy and nobility. Moreover, discussion and debate concerning the giving of counsel and advice to the crown was itself taking a different tack. Cautionary memoranda, such as those written by Sir John Fortesque, did nothing to further the notion that the nobility were the king's natural counselors. In his tract, *The Governance of England,* he urged King Edward IV to receive counsel from "the wysest and best disposed men that can be ffounde in all parties off this lande." In addition, they were to be sworn in and required to take an oath—something magnates considered an affront to their dignity. Fortesque's prescriptions correspond closely with the realities of politics in the reign of Edward IV: the notion that nobles were indeed the king's natural counselors did suffer a reverse. This trend was to continue under the first Tudors.[3]

In the next century, in the Netherlands, the mild remedies of educational reform and the easy diagnosis of the derelictions of aristocrats such as Lannoy and Commynes were displaced by more rigorous analysis. Instead, a more bitter medicine was prescribed. The influence of Machiavelli's *Art of War* was at work in the writings and teachings of that polyhistorian and philosopher of the University of Leiden, the humanist Justus Lipsius. Ranking Machiavelli in the company of the ancient thinkers Plato and Aristotle, Lipsius emphasized the Florentine's conceptions of obedience and loyalty to the state, as well as the unalterable military obligation of society and of citizen. A reading of Roman history and an assessment of contemporary European military experience made it apparent that the aristocracy must be disciplined in the martial arts and be eager to transmit this virtue to their troops through drill and training. The ideal officer, loyal in politics, was not to be motivated by an appetite for glory, but rather by a code closer to the ethos of professionalism. Lipsius presented a copy of his *Politicorum libri six,* published in 1589, to his sometime student Maurice of Nassau. This work has been characterized as providing "the intellectual basis of the Dutch small reforms." The lesson extracted buttressed the notion of the officer as a professional serving the community. Maurice of Nassau was perhaps the single soldier most responsible for sparking the first flames of the much heralded "military revolution" to come in the next century. Max Weber's conclusions on this question are brief and to the point: "It was discipline and not gunpowder which initiated the transformation . . . gunpowder and all the war techniques associated with it became significant only with the existence of discipline."[4]

To give political advice to the crown was no easy matter, and the ambiguities of the speaker's position also eluded any simple set of classical educational tags. Furthermore, traditional recipe books instructing in matters political, especially the giving of counsel, looked somewhat old-fashioned to literati of the sixteenth century. The reading of ancient history and of the experiences of their own times, even by such gifted commentators as Christianne de Pisan, of the previous century, seemed platitudinous. Like earlier writers, the author of *Livres du corps de policie* drew heavily on that favorite fount of morality, Valerius Maximus's *Facta et dicta memorabilia,* to illustrate the proposition that successful rulers must rely upon "old wise men" for guidance in statecraft. English commentators added to the familiar biblical references to King Rehoboan the terrible instances of Edward II, Richard II, and Henry VI, in which mischief and grief came to kings and kingdoms when monarchs heeded the advice of upstarts and craven youths. In 1465, when Clarence, Warwick, and the Archbishop Neville rebelled against Edward IV, this was their version of recent English history. Indeed, it reveals as much about the mechanics of present politics as about past history:

> First, where the said kings estranged the great lords of their blood from their secret council, and were not advised by them, and taking about them others not of their blood, and inclining only to their counsel, rule and advice, which persons took no respect or consideration to the welfare of the said princes, nor to the commonwealth of this land, but only to their singular honour and enriching of themselves and their blood . . . by which the said princes were so impoverished that they had not sufficient livelihood or goods whereby they might keep and maintain their honourable estate and ordinary charges within this realm.[5]

In the reign of Henry VII, Edmund Dudley, in *The Tree of Commonwealth,* was to reiterate the same advice. The king must "take counsell of good and wise men, for thei y' drede not god syldome gyve good counsell, and syldome it profiteth a prince to gyve confydence to young counsell." On the one side we have lessons drawn from history of the political chaos certain to ensue if the ruler follows the advice of the reckless, whereas on the other we observe an optimism as to the efficacy of classical moral precepts. The less the political experience of the humanistically educated, the more likely they were to believe that *bonae litterae* would serve to promote the public good and enhance the political virtue of the ruler. No easy resolution of this dilemma was forthcoming, albeit the consequences for political discourse and civic rhetoric were real enough.

Cardinal Pole's reputed recollections of a conversation he had had many years before with that "messenger of Satan"—Thomas Cromwell—the accuracy of which is historically suspect, yet remains as a vivid illustration of the dilemma so often pointed up in the rhetorical literature concerning counsel and advice. At Cardinal Wolsey's house, in 1528 or 1529, just after Pole's first return from Italy, Cromwell raised the general question: What was the first duty of a prudent counselor to the prince? Pole responded that, above all things, the counselor must consider his master's honor. He then continued his discourse giving two different principles as to the nature of honor and that of expediency. Cromwell retorted that such theories were praised in schools and universities but were not applauded in the secret councils of princes. A truly prudent advisor must first study the leanings, inclinations, and prejudices of the prince. Cromwell ended his immoral reflections by recommending that Pole relinquish his old-fashioned scholarship and read instead a book by a modern writer whose practical view of politics and government stood in solid contrast to the illusory and dreamlike thought of a Plato.[6]

Present-day scholars do not accept Pole's recollections at face value, nor do they credit Cromwell's pointer toward Machiavelli's *The Prince*. This soon-to-be bible for hard counsel was as yet unpublished. Still, the conversation stands as vividly cautionary and exemplary. The exchange—real or reconstructed—exposed the persistent dilemma of those who negotiated the king's business in a milieu illuminated or darkened by the new rhetoric and the Tacitean-Machiavellian historical vision. One should first acknowledge that the dangers were indeed real for those transacting the king's business. The court of Henry VIII was a reminder to all of just such risks. In his early masterpiece, the *History of Richard III*, likely started around 1513, Thomas More appears to be presenting the terrible fate of that king as a caution against possible derelictions of the young reigning monarch. In this history, composed in Latin and English, More portrayed the popular and sensible response of people to Richard III's feigned refusal of the crown:

> they said that these matters bee kynges games, as it were stage playes, and for the more part plaied vpon scafoldes. In which pore men be but yᵉ lokers on. And thei yᵗ wise be, wil medle no farther. For they that sometyme step vp and playe wᵗ them, when they cannot play their partes, they disorder the play & do themself no good.[7]

In England, both rhetoric and idiom in which counsel was to be rendered were enriched, shaded, and varied through borrowings from Continental humanists. From the time of Erasmus and Vives in the early sixteenth century, Latin and vernacular writings were freighted with more complex models of discourse allowing for conveyance of information and opinion in an urbane style with particular literary attention devoted to cultivating the ability to see both sides of an argument. Scholastic syntax, the specialized vocabulary of lawyers, ecclesiastics, and other professionals, was considered, perhaps unfairly, too inflexible and therefore inadequate for the rhetoric of counsel. The More (the persona of the author) of the *Utopia* understood very well how tricky, if not treacherous, was the linguistic landscape between the philosophical and the courtly, between flattery and hard truth. A man of letters and humanist inclination who came to court counseling the need for broad social reform would, in the judgment of More, be rather like a character in a Plautian Latin comedy attired as a philosopher, choosing to speak at the very moment when "the household slaves are making jokes at one another." The fictitious Thomas More (Morus) of the dialogue did, however, approve of play acting in politics. He urged on Hythlodaeus in these ringing words: "whatever play is being performed, perform it as best you can, and do not upset it all simply because you think of another which has more interest."[8]

Germane to the daunting difficulties of the giving of advice is the so-called "Dialogue of Counsel" of the *Utopia,* in which Morus confronts the pressing arguments of the traveler Hythlodaeus on the questions of moral duty and public responsibility. Agreeing that "academic" philosophy was useless in the councils of the king, More opts for a "practical" philosophy—a rhetorical philosophy, if you will—"which knows its stage, adapts itself to the play in hand, and performs its role neatly and appropriately." Again More issues a summons to political action heavily freighted with humanistic appreciation for rhetorical device:

> If you cannot pluck up wrongheaded opinions by the root, if you cannot cure according to your heart's desire vices of long standing, yet you must not on that account desert the commonwealth. You must not abandon the ship in a storm because you cannot control the winds. On the other hand, you must not force upon people new and strange ideas which you realize will carry no weight with persons of opposite conviction. On the contrary, by the indirect approach you must seek and strive to the best of your power to handle matters tactfully. What you cannot turn to good you must make as little bad as you can.[9]

1

To speak of the political experience of the precocious city-states of north and central Italy during the fourteenth and fifteenth centuries, and then to argue persuasively for a tilt towards civility as well as for the genesis of a rhetoric sensitive to the exigencies of public life, does of course involve much more than the delineation of the theme of the domestication and pacification of rural and town nobles. Certainly the Italian urban experience was critical for shaping new educational ideals and programs deemed appropriate for a Northern European aristocracy in the sixteenth and seventeenth centuries. This can readily be appreciated by cataloguing the borrowings from classical and humanist sources by literati of England, France, and Spain. Often the best works containing protracted discussions of the relationship between "good letters" and "good arms" were like the equally impressive dialogues on the nature of true nobility, translations from the Latin or the Italian. The links between scholar and soldier, in the view of Montaigne—the wisest of all Frenchmen—could be curious:

> That man you can see over there, furiously beside himself, scrambling high up the ruins of that battlement, the target of so many volleys from harquebuses; and that other man, all covered with scars, wan, pale with hunger, determined to burst rather than to open the gate to him! Do you

think they are in it for themselves? It could well be for somebody they have never seen, someone plunged, meanwhile, in idleness and delights, who takes no interest in what they are doing.

And this man over here, rheumy, filthy, blear-eyed, whom you can see coming out of his workroom after midnight! Do you think he is looking in his books for ways to be better, happier, wiser? Not a bit. He will teach posterity how to scan the verse of Plautus and spell a Latin word, or else die in the attempt.[10]

Despite a penchant for ironies and even a tendency to perceive the bleak side of public service, we recognize the momentum lent to the humanistic literary endeavor by the force of state-building, the strengthening of bureaucracies, the regularization of particular forms of public administration, and the enforcement of public law. In France reforms of the army in the fifteenth century resulted in greater specialization and professionalism. Perhaps the critical moment came, at least for England, in the early sixteenth century, when civil servants were separated from the king's household. We then have the sustained importation of notions and values that might loosely be termed "civically humanistic," as well as key ideas more inclined to professionalization in government. A Platonic functionalism favorable to the formation of an administrative cadre of secretaries and intendants did, in theory at least, purport to render regimes more effective. Such a view was most fully developed in the Florentine republic in the last part of the Quattrocento; it was to resonate in the political writings of Thomas More and his generation.[11]

In the case of France, the locus of change might be the last four decades of the seventeenth century, when emphasis on the military definition of nobility as virtuous action was challenged by more complex classical perspectives. A traditional vocabulary had hardened over time under the pressure of contemporary politics. The nobility tended to be regarded almost exclusively in social and functional terms. Now the moral significance of *noblesse* was lent fuller meaning. It was only with the 1570s that Castiglione's *Courtier* (translated into French almost forty years earlier), along with a spate of other classical texts and humanist dialogues, added a moral and esthetic dimension to the vexing question of what constituted *de vera nobilitate*. Unlike an older feudality, this nobility was to be more remote from the demotic language and culture of a subaltern world. *Prise de conscience* and the search for an appropriate role for the nobility led to a heated debate concerning the education and style of life suitable for the *noblesse*. One literary work must stand for many: Eymar de Froydeville's *Dialogues de l'origine de la noblesse où est déclaré que c'est d'icelle et ses inventeurs* (Lyon, 1574) speaks for an academy for educating the nobility. The author advises the reader: "One of the main reasons thus for the ruin of the Nobility is that it lacks scholarship and learning and does not consider itself to lead a respectable private life." Often in the humanist dialogues the old nobility, addicted to carousing, hunting, and hawking, gave as good as they got, denigrating the new education as a sure road to poverty and oblivion. This, however, only tended to lend a realistic tone to the conversation.[12]

2

Our concern here is not with offering some all-purpose explanation for the metamorphosis of the nobility in particular or presenting any monocausal theory for explaining the generalities of social change. Instead, we shall explore features of the linguistic shift which seem fundamental to the formation of a civic ethos. This ethos was gradually to rival ancient codes of ethical solidarity and obligation. We might begin to examine this shift by reviewing the influence on the European scene of classical rhetoric and Italian literati such as Ariosto, Castiglione, Della Casa, and Tasso. Castiglione's *Book of the Courtier* revised radically the code of courtly responsibilities, emphasizing the art of urbane converse and lightly held knowledge. In very different ways, but to the same end, Ariosto and Della Casa, along with Pulci and Boiardo, trivialized the heroic, demystified *cavalleria,* and even parodied the exercise of power. Tasso released the virtuous and high-minded individual from the harsher and more brutal demands of honor. This approach, surely worthwhile, would, however, tend to restrict our search by not going beyond the text to the bedrock of language. Is it possible to expose some of the deeper levels of meaning latent in social experience by examining linguistic change?

As indicated earlier, the vocabularies of chivalry and spirituality (or religion) underwent significant mutations. We observe subtle modifications in the meanings of such crucial terms as *nobility, honor, merit, courtesy,* and *glory.* It is well to recall that humanist writings on grammar and rhetoric were prone to explore the public and communal aspects of language. The merits of classicism devolved on such issues as the collective linguistic authority of the citizens of Rome, and whether contemporaries had the rights and skills to participate therein. The use of the word *glory,* not surprisingly, lost some of its older association with vanity, as did the words *fame* and *reputation.* The term "gentilezza" was more often linked with *urbanità,* and not so dependent on spiritual qualities. *Courtesy* was released from an elaborate world of etiquette and rituals to be increasingly associated with civility *(vivere civile).* Ideas of grace and beauty were losing something of their purchase on moral and spiritual qualities. Insights into love's suffering formed the tie between courtly *amour* on the one hand, and Neoplatonic and mystical love on the other. The region between the two domains was colonized by a refined and overelaborated psychology. The art of being pleasing to others was freighted with mistrust and suspicion of opportunism. Discourse on female beauty became oversubtle and strained. The erudite Bernardo Tomitano (1517–76) opined that "beauty without gracefulness is like a fish lure without bait."[13]

To follow the debate as to this turn of meanings, from Commynes to Montaigne in France or from Henry Medwell and Sir Thomas Elyot to Ben

Jonson and John Donne in England, is to appreciate contemporary awareness of the inability of language to register the ambiguous and problematic when featuring ethical questions of comportment and politics. A deep interest in visual signs was itself indicative of the problem of language; perhaps they expressed intention more adequately than did the word. Humanist pedagogy opted for rhetorical strategies favoring arguments on both sides of a moral dilemma, thereby recording with greater shading subjective values and psychological states. The stylistic advantages of *copia* as a rhetorical tactic were widely advertised as allowing for the more ample (copious) representation of variety *(varietas)* in nature and human affairs. The rhetorical figure of Ironia (irony) was gradually and anxiously being naturalized, allowing for a more patient exploration of the vast continents between the actualities of behavior and politics and the normative realm of what ought to be. As we have observed in matters spiritual, such diverse terms as *conversation, charity, atonement,* and *penance* underwent subtle modifications. Nowhere was the shift more marked than in the emotionally charged areas of reparation, revenge, love, and evil. Indeed, one might suggest that an archaic vocabulary which had once worked to bond the physical, social, and spiritual had lost certain of its creative forcefulness. Complex and sophisticated versions of syntax were neglected. Humanist grammar featured the study of autonomous human practice.[14]

3

Of course no single set of causes can be unveiled to highlight the change. Still, certain parallels between language change and social change suggest that displacement of an archaic matrix in the area of language had its analogue in the realm of political and social experience. Just as with language and instruction in grammar and theory, so too in politics we discover that the intellectual thrust was toward a critical and novel self-consciousness. Turning back to More's *Utopia,* one realizes that giving good counsel while exercising rhetorical tact may not lead to any easy resolution of political issues. Throughout More's dialogue the claims of "good lordship," "honor," "chivalry," "magnificence," and "display" have been mocked, if not subverted, with consummate irony. But in the penultimate sentence, More's persona voices his abiding skepticism concerning

> . . . that feature which is the principal foundation of their whole structure. I mean the common life and subsistence without any exchange of money. This latter alone utterly overthrows all the nobility, magnificence, splendor, and majesty which are in the estimation of the common people the true glories and ornaments of the commonwealth.

Nobilitas, magnificentia, splendor, and *maiestas* were, in the public perception, essential for bonding society together. At the end of this searching inquiry, what the people revere—received ideas—have political value not to be dismissed lightly. Certainly these archaic values were suspect, and worse, but one cannot deny their functional utility. The same responsible ambivalences were entertained by Sidney in the *Old Arcadia*. On the one side, kings would turn political life into theater, replacing reasoned political debate with pageant and spectacle, but, on the other, the work cannot be altogether dismissive of the popular need for such rituals. In the end this piece of imaginative literature (and it was here in the sixteenth century that political theory was generated) disclosed just how vital ceremony was for sustaining the social order.[15]

Erasmian humanism in general, and Thomas Elyot and Richard Pace in particular, concerned with pedagogy for the sons of nobility and instruction for princes, did not reckon the social consequences of their scathing critique of the style of life of magnates and rulers. Thomas More did, however, albeit his critique of chivalry, exaltation of riches, and extravagance of honorific ideals was proclaimed in Latin. He balanced this condemnation with a skeptical disclaimer as to social consequences of reforming these practices of conspicuous consumption out of existence. Without riches, magnificence, and display the bonds of society might not hold. Classical Latin, with its austere and rational word order, could be most hospitable to an objective view of a society in which the common folk required ritual and splendor of noble lifestyle to inspire awe and reverence for the ruling orders. In the next generation, however, with Ralph Robinson's vernacular translation of the *Utopia,* More's penultimate sentence and its complex syntax lost ironic shading. The sarcasm of the original became an outright expression of anxiety. In Robinson's English version a conventional vocabulary was employed freely to convey the author's appreciation of the abiding social and political values of "gorgeous" gestures, trappings, and ceremonies. He transformed the *Utopia* from a republic to a monarchy: Utopus was now a king, and the magistrate elected by the citizens was a prince. Here we have a measure of More's daring—albeit in a language reserved for the few conoscenti. In the following generation, with Sidney and his circle, schooling in Machiavelli, Guicciardini, and Gasparo Contarini had expanded the lexicon of political discourse. The observation "that most princes (seduced by flattery to build upon false grounds of government) make themselves, as it were, another thing from the people" offers an example—only one of many—of Sidney's anticipation of a republican political idiom of the next century.[16]

But for Sidney, Greville, and their English circle there were sharp and troubled moments. No easy recommendations were forthcoming, and in fact Sidney cautioned his brother Robert that while Venice was deserving of admiration and study, the laws and customs of England made for a very different type of governance. Warnings were issued against the "discoursing sort of men" who would alter state and society. Oscillation between the currents of intellectual innovation and rhetoric as an instrument of demystification of political ritual and social custom, on the one side, and the harsh fact that received ideas and rites have value, on the other, were indeed in fruitful competition. Something of the same sensibility is discovered in Rabelais, Spenser, Shakespeare, and Cervantes. Attractive features of their literary work derived from an engagement with radical elements in the oral culture, as well as from a serious preoccupation with innovative currents. Archaic diction, the riches of folklore, and vivid expressions of popular culture are self-consciously appropriated to literary ends. Often the mark of sophistication in the literature stems exactly from this self-awareness. So, too, does literature gain cachet by skeptical recourse to analogical argument. This response was nurtured by the several norms of neoplatonic and hermetic texts. Likewise, rival semantic programs challenged the notion of natural correspondence or linkage between words and things. The dream allegory and, indeed, sustained allegory, the versified sermon, the didactic lament, flyting, aureate diction, encyclopedism, personification, and a raft of other literary forms and tactics for bonding were becoming most unfashionable. When the best writers resorted to them, it was often with a conscious and playful sense of literary archaism.[17]

The iconoclasm of Protestant reformers, beginning with Carlstadt, the recovery of Sextus Empiricus and the widespread influence of this psychologically disturbing classical text, skepticism from Agrippa to Charon, Montaigne's siding with Heracleitus and Cratylus on the certainty of flux and change over and against the uncertainty of knowledge, the critique of resorting to etymologies and proper names as sources for the revelation of truth, arguments rendering dubious the prospect of acquiring knowledge from Aristotelian or scholastic definitions and quiddities—all of this did little to enhance the secure status of the linguistic sign and fix the correspondence between signifier and signified. Ficino, in his commentary on Plato's *Cratylus,* had contended that the doctrine of permanence held only for the supercelestial world of Ideas or Forms, not this our sublunary world. Both Aristotle and the humanists in their very different ways, and for very different reasons, came to the conclusion that language was a matter of convention. The more empirically minded, such as Francis Bacon, distrusted language, desiring that it be more tightly disciplined—more a function of facts. The scholastic language of speculation and rhetorical eloquence were suspect. Was it possible to jettison the variety of ordinary languages and establish a philosophical language whose morphology would more accurately reflect the content of nature?[18]

Doubts were raised that the sign was artificial and, therefore, a construct; prospects for any repair were problematic and sometimes bleak. If the sign was conventional and arbitrary, then grounds for semantic optimism remained uncertain, if not treacherous. Semiotic animism or faith in the sign and its capacity to be animated by its referent became the stuff of high drama and literary analysis. Segregation of folk or popular culture (the little tradition) from high culture (the great tradition) induced heightened self-consciousness concerning the felicitous outcome of any easy correspondence between man and nature or ready parallelism between the natural world and scientific belief. Allowing for the reading of the human mind in terms of the living and breathing physical universe was matched by a candid acknowledgment that no sure epistemological basis obtained for having confidence in the successful outcome of any such effort. Drama was often constructed from the deluded endeavors of characters to make epistemological theory conform to human requirements. In such intellectual comedies as Shakespeare's *Love's Labour's Lost*, the game of dispensing with rhetorical tropes, thereby making contact with reality, proves in the end to be a protracted illustration of just another rhetorical trope. Expressions of hope in the possibility that universal laws of the natural world would prevail in the microcosm of man were often subverted by mordant wit, skepticism, and epistemological despair.[19]

4

Recently, the historian of religion John Bossy has explored the transformation of the language of sacramental discourse, suggesting that such mutations can be located in this most sensitive of areas. He has not, however, offered any substantial explanation for this phenomenon; in fact, he goes out of his way to dismiss any theories connected with society and the economic market. Keith Thomas, in his new book *Man and the Natural World,* has sensitively analyzed the growing chasm between the archaic, folkloristic, and popular ways of looking at the natural world, on the one side, and the more learned and impartial views, on the other. Thomas allows that this deep sea change in the archaeology of the mind occurring in the period here under consideration may have been a particular aspect or consequence of a general trend. Michel Foucault, in his highly influential work *The Order of Things: An Archaeology of Human Sciences,* argues that the sixteenth and seventeenth centuries witnessed the shift from mental procedure operating by resemblances and correspondences, by sympathy and antipathy, to one manipulating a system of identities and measurable differences. How this shift to what Foucault calls "the classical frame of mind" was caused remains mysterious.[20]

What Foucault perceived as dominant features of high thought and science were themselves the consequences of change already in process from at least the late Dugento and early Trecento. Their beginnings surface in the town experience and culture of north and central Italy. Humanistic pedagogy drastically simplified the traditional, logical content of instruction, adapting the study of language to oratorical ends. Currency and effectiveness of language were considered essential for "good letters" and "good speech." The false strategy of reification was attacked on grounds that it distanced discourse from the human context. Great distinctions were permitted between thought and reality in the interest of rhetorical decorum. The domain of human activity required the lexical strategy of commodiousness in order to avoid reductionist representation of passions and interests.

The relationship between *res* (things) and *verba* (words) became increasingly metaphoric. The Italian vernacular, so admirably suited for its narrative context with its directness of style, its loosely joined and insubordinated sentence, now achieved a new flexibility allowing it to explore broader philosophical concerns and problematic issues. It gained the range and vocabulary essential for establishing a variety of literary genres. Allegory was used more self-consciously when linkages were set in place between the mundane and otherworldly. Greater toleration for error and "fictive deviance" permitted such genres as the pastoral, the epic romance, the mock epic, and satire to flourish. A literary commonplace was the portrayal of the metaphor of life as a play: Lucian's *Menippus* was a fruitful source for this topos. The poetry of vituperation was tamed with steady recourse to Horatian urbanity and wit. Errancy and distraction in discourse were less certain to be attributable to sin and a fall from grace, and more likely to be reckoned the products of human limitation. Anxious self-love was often fondly treated and regarded as killing the capacity for pleasure.[21]

Distinctions between subject and object, appearance and reality, and *res* and *verba* were not sure to be remedied by recourse to speculative thought or grammar. Of course ambitions for closure persisted and hopes of reconciling departures between the domains of private and public continued bright, if not shining. We observe new and old notions residing side by side, sometimes jostling, sometimes mingling in colloidal solution. The relative value of the study of law versus medicine, the active versus contemplative life, celibacy or marriage, the dignity of the laic condition over and against those in orders, or knight and cleric—these were durable themes. The persistence of the varied and contradictory formulations of the concept of nobility remained a hardy perennial. Was its quintessence derived from birth, function, deed, or form? These were major preoccupations. Humanist rhetoric enabled authors to take an apparently neutral position in these contests by utilizing the dialogue form to convert ideas into drama.

So, too, we discover that old and new definitions of *state, society,* and *law* enjoyed a widening literary circulation. These debates, along with such topics as friendship and family, had their origins in the Italian republican city-states where quotidian experience, Aristotelian philosophy, and the classical revival worked to create a heady mix. Strong definitions of good and evil, with the one being the antithesis of the other, were less likely to achieve an absolute literary victory. This was increasingly true as more attention was paid to the history of other civilizations, each with its own moral system. For the purpose of literary effectiveness, consideration was accorded to arguments stemming from ethical relativism. Even those received ideas bringing spiritual solace and psychological comfort were sharply contested. In Florence at mid-Quattrocento, public lectures and debates engaged in by humanists and literati featured definitions of vernacular literature and poetry, that is, the nature and legitimacy of contemporary culture. General questions concerning texts and historical and legal sources prompted disputes as to their authenticity. Contests between philological passion and pedagogical vocation led to further dispute as to the problematics of scholarly investigation. The very definition of literature and poetry was at risk: Was it an instrument for ethical and moral formation or for *ascesa contemplativa?* Self-consciousness about stylistics led to discussion of whether Dante's poetry had more *res* (content) than *verba* (form). Does Petrarch's poetry have more *verba* than *res?* What is the relationship between form and content? Can eloquence overcome the possible disjunction? What is the role of rhetoric? What are its limitations? How substantial is the need for a technical and philosophical vocabulary for resolving the separation of appearance and reality?[22]

The revolution in conceptualization first manifested itself in the scholasticism of the late thirteenth and early fourteenth centuries. Here we observe the pressures at work on language influenced by what C. S. Lewis delineated as the "subjectivism of an objective age." The debate concerning modes of signifying *(modi significandi moderni),* modes of being, and modes of understanding produced a spate of treatises intended to analyze and describe parts of speech and syntax according to possible relationships between these *modi.* This rush of activity was, however, for the most part contained within the framework of the sacramental system. Advances were made in the science of speculative grammar by *modistae* (grammarians) of the thirteenth and fourteenth centuries, but the study of language as a phenomenon of convention standing in opposition to the notion of the natural presence of meaning did not make dramatic headway. It did not displace an archaic natural matrix.

In hermeneutic theory, as well as in modes of reading the Holy Scripture, a heroic effort was made to reconcile disquieting facts concerning the origins of linguistic signs with the desire to preserve or retrieve the natural representation of meaning. Despite attention to the dislocation of language from its source (the Tower of Babel) or object of meaning, both hermeneutics and grammar remained steadfast in their ambition to stabilize signification. Saint Anselm's researches into language in the eleventh century had culminated in the thirteenth with a quest for a universal grammar believed to be the rock on which the different grammars of all languages could be secured. The prospect that the nature of linguistic signs was arbitrary, while disturbing, only tended to fuel intellectual ambitions to create a science of grammar. Masters in the arts faculties of the universities teaching *grammatica speculativa* were generally paid two times as much as teachers of literary grammar. The grammarians' appreciation of the separation of language from meaning did not induce them to relinquish age-old attachments to the ancient linguistic paradigms of Priscian and Donatus. Parts of speech were defined in terms of their semantic function. Incorporation of this semantic component can be traced back through the domain of analogical grammar to the precincts of Aristotelian definition of classes of terms and logical strategies.[23]

5

To the south, in Italy, humanist grammatical manuals did not share the concern of the best scholastics for the logical and metaphysical foundations of language. Lorenzo Valla (1407–57), in his encomium on Saint Thomas Aquinas, took contemporary theologians to task for their awe and reverence for "what they called metaphysics and *modus significandi* (modes of meaning) and other things of that kind." They harbor almost as much respect for these notions as they do for newly discovered spheres or planetary epicycles. In north and central Italy debates which in other parts of Europe were likely to be contained within the framework of the sacramental system were vernacularized, finding a laic and literary domicile. The metalanguage generated by the grammarians of the later Middle Ages *(modistae)* reflected its own autonomy and sufficiency rather than undertaking analysis of the dictions of usage. *Modistae* projected the semantic classification from language onto thought and reality; linkages were developed through schemes of *modi* bonding grammar, logic, and ontology. Therefore, it comes as no surprise to observe that linguistic phenomena tended to be perceived as rooted in conceptions of mind and the structure of reality.[24]

In the instruction of the early Florentine humanist Coluccio Salutati, emphasis on good Latin was itself an expression of laicism, since it automatically repudiated the technical vocabulary of the Schools. Rhetoric and humanistic education encouraged argument on both sides of a question without heavy reliance on syllogistic logic. Clarity of discourse between educated laymen sharing the cultural heritage of the classics was coming to be highly valued. Salutati's censure against the famous and influential Dominican preacher Fra Giovanni Dominici of Florence bears repeating:

> I would like all churchmen to have been and to be proficient enough in grammar so that we would hear them using *no* barbarous words, *no* syntactic errors, *no* words coined at variance with analogy, *no* words in inappropriate meanings, *no* words placed where they do not belong.

The lessons of classical rhetoric were understood as foreclosing the prospect of certainty in favor of mere probabilism in the interest of promoting urbane exchange and civility. Arguments in dialogues were frequently consonant with the professional commitment and outlook of the speaker, even reflecting his idiosyncrasies and obsessions. Imitating Cicero's expository, Plato's philosophical, and Lucian's dramatic dialogue, conversation was marked by the casual and informal. Literary talent was spent on lending verisimilitude to the setting. The reader was called upon to exercise discrimination, thereby enhancing the range of his practical reason. The essential requirement for the reader was this heightening of practical reason or prudential judgment necessary for the active civil life. From Coluccio Salutati's *De nobilitate legem et medicine* (1399) to Pontano's *De prudentia* and *De fortuna* (last decade of fifteenth century and first decade of sixteenth), we observe the multiplication of rhetorical strategies for combining structured argumentation with authorial skepticism. Challenges to received political opinion could be so forcefully advanced that the reader would be compelled to fall back on simple civic virtues. Skepticism in the first instance was neither an epistemological tool nor an expression of spiritual despair, but, rather, a rhetorical device for strengthening the strategies of argumentation on both sides of a question *(in utramque partem),* so that the reader might develop his abilities for deliberation in a world in which possibilities were so abundant. Again, received opinion cast down by over-clever reason could demonstrate the clear need for simple faith and abiding trust. Literary talent operated to sustain the decorum of the dialogue, distancing it from the harsh encounter of the medieval debate with its proclivity for the didactic. Rhetoric worked to create dialogue and fictional forms in which a more open ethical syntax obtained. This worked along with an appreciation of Ciceronian definitions of eloquence and prudence as moral, not intellectual, virtues to prompt the active pursuit of the good rather than the contemplative life.[25]

An archaic vocabulary operating to link *res* and *verba* was itself subject to serious and sustained investigation, as well as open to parody and literary fun. The central tradition of humanistic research into language tended to marginalize the prospect of "acceding to a natural, rather than a conventional language." Counter examples such as hieroglyphs and cabalism tended to be only passingly influential. Cratylism—the natural bond between word and thing—was retained as a hypothetical possibility that *ex contrario* clarified the condition of discourse which itself was exiled from the nature it was supposed to imitate. The locus of this natural bond was not to be found in the real world but, instead, in some utopian community. As has been noted, the art of rhetoric itself was valorized as an instrument of demystification demonstrating that traditional social and political rituals were no more than tropes. Grammar was no longer to be regarded as the ground on which the split between words and things, characteristic of the language of the fallen world, was to be healed. Nor was the whole of human history to be represented as in Dante's *De vulgari eloquentia,* as the history of language, with the edenic idiom of Adam being lost through human sinfulness and the proud Tower of Babel.[26]

Discourse in the real world, according to humanist investigations, bore only the most distant and imperfect relationship to that Eden or Utopia where sacred ties and bonds prevailed. The new intellectual impulse moved away from such felicitous identities and similitudes characteristic of an archaic community toward an idiom in which the ideals of language and associative life were not to be manifested in terms of linguistic correspondence or an ethos of solidarity. Grammar became less polarized, allowing language to become more personal—less ideological and political. Humanization of discourse permitted the dramatization of a process whereby the immediate world of social obligation lost something of its physicality and moral magnetism. Strong definitions of good and evil, with one being the antithesis of the other, were less likely to win an easy victory. Increased attention was invested in the history of different civilizations, each with its own moral system, and this encouraged a certain moral relativism. Humanist rhetoric worked toward a doctrine of responsibility and freedom, losing something of the nostalgia for a primordial and edenic innocence. The figure of speech of Irony was naturalized to mask the painful recognition that the tragic antithesis between good and evil did not always obtain. Concern for a middling range of behavior located in that ambiguous zone between the ascetic and heroic promoted a graded register of emotion so that such words as *envy, anger, fear,* and *melancholy* became polyvalent. These and like words tended to be demoted from the pantheon of vices as meanings were shaded to work against the imposition of any philosophical dualism.[27]

The Italian vernacular experienced change through the appropriation of neologisms; but the idiom was also porous and everyday language transmogrified by the pressures and opportunities of everyday existence. If society's presuppositions are embedded in language, and if we can best understand the minds of the people of the past through the symbols they use, then the widening register of key words should offer us occasional clues as to the direction of social change. To return to the subject of social obligation and the loss of something of its physicality and moral magnetism—a critical topic for the purpose of the present investigation—we observe how the term *obbligato* both extended and relaxed its significance. In early Tuscan texts the sense of obligation was virtually absolute. *Pietà* could be synonymous with obligation. The idea of filial and kinship responsibility was strict and boundless. One was obligated to the poor of the world; one was obligated not to enjoy the world or its delights. Ties of love and friendship were palpable and strengthened by a solemn and ceremonial vocabulary of *cortesia.* Over the centuries the vocabulary of obligation tended to lose its ritual character, becoming more abstract and less mired in the soil of fealty and allegiance.[28]

6

With Petrarch vernacular poetry and the Latin epistle moved toward a fuller presentation of what might be termed the "drama of evasion." Responsibility and obligation for the spiritual well-being and salvation of others was too lofty a task for progressive literati. Enough that they should concern themselves with their own voyage toward the far shores of blessedness. Human frailty was less the signpost for the collective miseries and derelictions of humanity, that is, Everyman; instead it was the mark of the "cross-grained nature of man." Out of this recognition of individual frailty emerged the comic drama of mobility of mind, with consciousness incapable of being bounded by tragic closure. Invocation of the contradictory and fleeting nature of thought diminished the stern claims of social accountability. The public field of renunciation and ascetic actions was miniaturized. Petrarch's poetic loyalty was to the experience of the world and not to some rational order. The fragmentary character of the sequence of his lyrics, with oscillation between love and sin, allowed for no heroic amalgam. Advanced literature sanctioned the refusal to extend the realm of the heroic to the bounds of the theological. Petrarch separated rhetoric and a theology of faith from philosophy.[29]

In the next century ordinary natural usage of language was privileged by Lorenzo Valla over logical formalism. Aristotelians were criticized for their proclivity for converting empty forms into moral imperatives, for example, the mean into the ethical quality of moderation. For the logical purposes of purifying or regulating the terms of an argument, Aristotelians transformed relational constructs into entities. Also, they could not resist the temptation to attribute substance to such terms as *bonum,* which is an *actio.* Proper definitions of virtue stem from action and linguistic usage rather than from deduction of place in a philosophical system of formal relations. The canons of rhetorical decorum, so concerned with context, were utilized to confute Aristotelian reifications.[30]

In the regional literature of Tuscany, words were losing something of their strong meaning, as well as their sense of imminence. *Carità* was less likely over the centuries to achieve literary representation as involving exchange of greetings, kisses, meals, and a hundred other tokens. Nor was one so likely to be received in an audience *caritativamente* by a superior with a *cartatevoli animi.* Abstract usage would in time realize itself in the vernacular: when one loves charitably, one loves in a disinterested fashion. *Pace,* too, was at first defined in its strong sense, owing much to the theological idea of "unity of peace." The conception of ideal concord of Saint Augustine carried the premise of the withering away of—at least in the modern sense— state and society. Peace involved numerous concrete acts of pardon and reconciliation. The kiss of peace, the formal conditions of peacemaking between feuding families, the entry of peace agreements in the account books of merchants when claims had been satisfied, and the appointment of *Defensori della Pace,* these were all manifestations of the impulse to realize, in concrete form, the spiritual and material benefits of that joy which, in Dante's words, "passeth understanding." Both *carità* and *pace* were *doni del Dio* (gifts of God) intended to cure the *superbia* (pride) of sinning mankind.[31]

By the end of the fifteenth century, neither charity nor peace were to be relied upon for weaving sacred bonds: the social benefits of humility were not

so certain. Institutions of Christianity were not regarded as saving mechanisms of this world, nor was the peace of Christ perceived as being of this
world. Sociability was less likely to be expressed in ritualized greetings and
ceremonial salutations. By the same token, insults and curses were not *de
rigueur* upon termination of social ties. The traditional obligation of aversion
was dissipated, and courtesy as a mechanism for generating mutuality and
obligation was no longer seen as reliable. The heroic message of joyous
death, so favored in the warrior culture of an earlier time, lost its stirring
appeal. Pride was no longer a social phenomenon consisting of placing rank
above sociability; it could now be dramatized in metaphysical and promethean terms. The esthetics of behavior was elevated programmatically at the
expense of the exchange of gifts and favors. Honor was sufficiently objective
to outlast an individual's assertion of it. In the novella and political handbook, the play of advantage and self-interest appeared in the foreground, thus
reducing notions of the effectiveness of obligation and fidelity. Humanist
literature, at its most optimistic, celebrated the prudential as the subjective
virtue capable of transcending self-interest. The converse was of course that
pessimistic reading of human nature as being irreducibly selfish and not for a
moment deflected from obsessive pursuit of self-interest by sentiments of
social solidarity. At its boldest, this literature glamorized the running of risks
when contesting the contingent and unforeseen.[32]

In the *Decameron,* Boccaccio gave literary acknowledgment to citizen
comedy with his treatment of the very fluid and hitherto little explored social
space between court and aristocracy on the one side, and the lowly world of
artisans, vagabonds, and rogues on the other. This was a realm in which
courtship and romance were not overplayed; often lovers were motivated by a
fascination with intrigue and deception and blessed with talent for negotiat-
ing in a world of hard bargaining. These patterns of social maneuvering
received literary nourishment from the recovery of the New Comedy of
antiquity in late fifteenth-century Italy. The world of Plautus and Terence was
freighted with domestic motifs and peopled with jealous husbands and impatient Griseldas. Young men plotted against the old to gain money or a pretty
girl, or both. Religion as a force for informing social ties was conspicuous for
its absence, as were other impulses leading to grand allegiances and extravagant loyalties. In this fiction trickery and deceit were metaphors for a society
where opportunity for mobility, wealth, and sexual favor were the coin of
imagination. This debased currency replaced an archaic treasure in the
reader's fantasy.[33]

7

Art lost certain of its preoccupation with sumptuousness: the preciousness
of materials grew less important than the skill of the artist. Florentine
contracts between artist and patron reveal a greater proportion of payment
for work done than for gold, ultramarine, and lapis lazuli. Moving away from

flattering the eye and surface attraction, the avant-garde Florentine sculptor and painter demonstrated how distanced he was from the applied art of the craftsman. Donatello had less need for polished and marvelously chased surfaces. Shunned too was the firm line that was the hallmark of the artist's mastery of his craft. Likewise, the careful finish practiced by the artisan who was required to meet the standards of the guild was no longer prized by progressive painters. Artistic creation was becoming an activity separated from practical use. Art collecting would, by the sixteenth century, be less concerned with the original purpose for which an object had been made. Creative energies and theories about them focused upon an imitation of nature rather than concentrating on its magical transformation. Imitation of nature, rather than imitation of other craftsmen, signified loss of ritual purpose in production of art as well as decline of talismanic meaning.[34]

Religious art, like devotional manuals and saints' lives, had portrayed holy men and women as protectors and intercessors. Instruments of divine grace, they were to be honored. These holy men and women out of primitive Christianity and the Church were to be venerated, not imitated. Indeed, God's omnipresence stood behind them, and their merits were hardly accessible to viewer, listener, or reader. The devotional manual, the lives, and the paintings offered proof and example of sanctity. Like preaching itself, the aim was to bear witness and testify, rather than to edify and call for emulation. Humanist art and literary criticism liberated the sermon, the saints' lives, and painting from a ritualistic context and offered theoretical and systematic justification for changes already in evidence in literature and the arts in Tuscany since the late thirteenth century. Narrative and biographical strategies were bringing the sacred and the lives of holy men and women closer to the experience of the faithful. Leon Battista Alberti, writing in the first part of the Quattrocento, generalizing from Tuscan accomplishment and, drawing upon classical rhetoric, argued that, in the case of painting, the aim of historical representation was not to verify or document an event but to move the viewer to virtuous deeds. The definition of history *(istoria)* was altered to encompass a heroism less distanced, more civic, more edifying, and more readily emulated.[35]

Just as art lost secure ties with the ceremonial and liturgical, so too in Tuscany and Emilia rhetorical manuals indicate that language was relaxing its hold on ritual eloquence. Rhetoricians in thirteenth-century urban centers such as Florence and Bologna were public officials serving in chancellories or active professional teachers of their art, or both. Instruction in letter writing (a principal area of competence) was transformed over the century. With Guido Faba in the 1220s and 1230s, the epistle assumed a syllogistic form, with the parts logically linked and concluding with a logically congruent proposition. A century later, instruction in this discipline was more open and less certain to be indentured to rigidly hierarchical conceptions of society. The need to gain the benevolence of the reader had required a mellifluous combination of words. Oral effects were produced by obeying the rhythms of the *cursus*. Adherence to a few basic rules gave the document a ritual-like quality. Style was keyed to the social level of the recipient, for it was necessary "to stroke all the strings of a hierarchical instrument." The document or letter was constructed so that the internal elaboration of dignity and status corresponded exactly to the public occasion.

By the early fourteenth century, however, instruction in these rhetorical arts in Tuscany and Emilia was moving away from the more formal strategies of persuasion with its reliance upon proverbs and *sententia*. The narrative account was now considerably expanded. Avoidance of extravagant metaphors and a more limited idea of elegance were advertised by teachers of the rhetorical arts as being essential if speakers and writers were to establish and hold the trust of audience and readers. This injunction was especially pertinent for those actively engaged in the art of public speaking. The orator must be moderate in his speech, since excessive elegance breeds mistrust. Already from the time of Giotto there were painters who abandoned the boundless horizons of the chivalric romance for a more limited moral continent. A more severe ideal than that of sumptuousness, color, captivating detail, and courtly elegance made a lasting impression on the Tuscan artistic imagination. Masaccio did not seek ecstatic visions but insisted upon the priority of visual truth over interior fantasy. His painting accepted limits centering on the foreground in which the human drama was being enacted. To be tautological: man is more socialized because society counts for more. Sociability is not expressed through rites and ritual acts but through a common idiom of word and gesture. Austerity and sobriety were the benchmarks of civic life and nature was treated with easy freedom. Worthy of recollection is the fact that the ethic of civic humanism extolled public monuments and buildings rich in splendor over and against the modest and sober architecture of private life.[36]

The sense of limits in advanced Tuscan art of the early Quattrocento stood in sharp contrast to the Flemish strivings for infinity. Flemish realism was inspired by a symbolic vision. In the North, painting was more than painting: a painting was a real object in itself and precious—nothing short of a form of magical persuasion. Made of expensive materials, it was a tangible piece of luminous matter—literally an *objet d'art*. The observation that Florentine Renaissance artists were less satisfied with portraying a world sustained by magic and enchantment than were their Northern European counterparts is essential for following Erwin Panofsky's mapping of the European arts in the fourteenth and fifteenth centuries. According to the testimony of the Portuguese artist and chronicler of the opinions of his times, Francesco de Holanda, Michelangelo commented at length on the nature of the differences:

> Flemish painting pleases all the devout better than Italian. The latter evokes
> no tears, the former makes them weep copiously. This is not the result of

the merits of this art; the only cause is the extreme sensibility of the devout
spectators. The Flemish pictures please women, especially the old and very
young ones, and also monks and nuns, and lastly men of the world who are
not capable of understanding true harmony. In Flanders they paint, before
all things, to render exactly and deceptively the outward appearance of
things. The painters choose, by preference, subjects provoking transports of
piety, like the figures of saints or of prophets. But most of the time they
paint what are called landscapes with plenty of figures. Though the eye is
agreeably impressed, these pictures have neither art nor reason; neither
symmetry nor proportion; neither choice of values nor grandeur. In short,
this art is without power and without distinction; it aims at rendering
minutely many things at the same time, of which a single one would have
sufficed to call forth a man's whole application.[37]

With Giotto we observe an accommodation between the idealism and
rigorism of a clerical tradition and the compelling desire of lay persons to live
a life in this world as Christians pleasing in the sight of God. Balancing the
exigencies of sacred and profane allowed for fuller attention to the biographical and narrative. New structures of narrative relevance were achieved in the
generation of Donatello, Brunelleschi, Masaccio, and Ghiberti. This revolu-
tionary development occurred even before Leon Battista Alberti's inspired
effort to bring rhetorical techniques from classical authors to bear on the
artistic production of his day. The priority of the works of that generation
over the coinage of a formal vocabulary of art criticism (the first since
antiquity) does suggest that practice came before theory. The accomplishment of new narrative techniques and the achievement of three-point perspective permitted a more detached view of man and society. Built into the
theory of perspective was a recognition of the transitoriness of the social and
natural worlds. Neglect of abundance of detail and repudiation of the poly-
phonic narrative enabled the historical imagination to take pleasure in the
geometric, the symmetrical, and all that was open to mathematical calculation. Three-point perspective allowed for the expression of a consciousness
aware of the boundaries between art and life.[38]

The poet gradually lost the mantle of prophet and role of inspired
dreamer; poetry was released from courtly entertainment and celebration of
occasion. Petrarch, with disciplined artifice, distanced himself from the poet
of daily consumption, court recitation, the marketplace, the maker of songs,
and riddling games of love and forfeit. It can be argued that the idea of drama
and theater was spawned during these centuries, as plays were released from
their commitment to the liturgical calendar and imperatives of community. In
an earlier time in Italy, and indeed in the north of Europe in the fourteenth
and fifteenth centuries, no play could hope to find an audience without a
public festival to release actors and audience from routine occupations and
obligations to their lords and masters. In Italy the separation between private
performance and public occasion served to enhance the theatricality of

performance while reducing the charge of the didactic. Would it be stretching a point to suggest that the very conception of painting, literature, music, and drama, which to some extent we share today, depended upon the subtraction of culture from its traditional function? In time works of art would be treated visually, away from the guide book's attention to miracle and relic. How telling was the appearance of the picture frame! So too was the release of the portrait from the devotional image. Leonardo da Vinci created his oeuvre not to satisfy clients and patrons but to please the most gifted artists: "Those who do not will fail to give their picture the foreshortening, relief and movement which are the glory of painting." Drawing, formerly not considered an art, but rather a functional technique appropriate to a certain professional competence, was assessed very differently by Leon Battista Alberti: "It is not unusual . . . to see a good circumscription—that is a good drawing—which is most pleasant in itself."[39]

8

If one follows the bitter controversy chronicled so expertly by Lucy Gent in her recent book, *Picture and Poetry 1560–1620,* one comes to appreciate the difficulties in the paths of even the best educated Northern European men and women in endeavoring to accept the notion that art and poetry were fiction-making requiring illusionistic devices and deceitful artifice. The trompe-l'oeil verisimilitude of art to life was a radical and disturbing fiction. To deceive the eye was to engage in an immoral act, and this was most troubling to the good conscience of a thoughtful and spiritually minded Tudor public in far off England. To create an imaginary world different from actuality was to do nothing less than counterfeit or posit untruths. The Tudor rhetorician and literary critic George Puttenham argued, heatedly, against transgressing "the ordinary limits of common utterance." He favored "plainesse and simplicitie" in speech and writing over and against a "certaine doublenesse" achieved with guile. His opposition to the figure of Irony, which deceived plain folk, was resolute, with only poets exempted, but, even for them, strictures remained against "doublenesse." One remembers Shakespeare's ironic disavowal of the "Sweet smoke of rhetoric," in *Love's Labour's Lost* (III,i,58), as well as the invocation of "a Muse of fire, that would ascend / The brightest heaven of invention," in *Henry V* (I,prologue, 1–2).[40]

To affirm, as Sir Philip Sidney had done in his *Defense of Poetry,* that humans live in two worlds, that of culture and that of nature, required the appropriation of ideas and idioms from the writings of Continental humanists and critics (in particular, the Italian, Lodovico Castelvetro). The technical vocabulary for explaining the creation of an imaginary world (a world of art, civilization, and culture) different from the world of actuality (the first world) called for importation of a language of criticism from Italy. It was very difficult to move beyond a language of contemplative wonder. Esthetic sensation induced by contemplation of art was dissipated in pious emotion and vague sentiments of astonishment. The very notion of *creation* and *create* traditionally carried a heavy freight of spiritual disapproval. These were pejoratives more often than words of acclaim. One has but to read Shakespeare in order to perceive the extent to which these terms continued to convey negative rather than positive connotations. From *Macbeth,* we have: "Or art thou but / a dagger of the mind, a false creation / proceeding from the heat-oppressed brain." From *Hamlet* we have: "This is the very coinage of your brain / this bodiless creation extasie / is very cunning in." From *Comedy of Errors* we have: "Are you a God? Would you create me new?" How can the creature who has been created create himself? How can man rival God, who is the only creator? Further, to make truth depend too much on individual experience (the authorial voice) and not on collective wisdom was to run serious intellectual risk. The importation of such bothering and alien ideas as perspective theory, placed the expression of consciousness on the borderland of separating art and life.[41]

New fashions worked to advance the notion that prestige was to be demonstrated by learned taste rather than conspicuous display. Art that yielded its meaning too easily to the vulgar was to be scorned. The firm line—signature of the guild artist and witness to the mastery of his craft—was spurned. Techniques for projecting the illusion of spontaneity multiplied, allowing for presentation of experience never to be repeated. Learning was characterized by its informal and amateur quality, with casual urbanity, instead of through a display of technical proficiency and structured debate. In manuals of social conduct, self-fashioning and civility were now prominently featured where once heroic virtues had obtained. Self-mastery, when confronted with the power of reality, was not so likely to be achieved through following traditional precepts of pedagogy or models from the *chansons de geste* or taking counsel from *mirrors for princes.* Flexibility and continual adjustment to changing circumstance, each feeding the other, were the hallmarks of manuals of conduct and rhetorical handbooks. In discussions of appropriate models for political conduct the disjunction between reality and appearance was sharpened, allowing for recognition that good customs and a just ethic were not always sufficient for fostering the victory of public virtue.

Leonardo Bruni Aretino appreciated the coercive character of law and the certainty of its mutability: "Things are legitimate in Florence which are condemned in Ferrara." Poggio Bracciolini, at his most rhetorical and radical, constructed a dialogue on that old chestnut: Which is superior, law or medicine? His *Historia tripartita,* consisting of three after-dinner conversations *(Disceptiones conviviales tres),* set in his villa at Terranuova, halfway between Arezzo and Florence, in the summer of 1449, recounts the opinions of three speakers, each of whom had taught at the Florentine university in the 1430s and 1440s. The palm for originality and scoring on the opposition goes to the doctor Niccolò da Foligno, who characterized the law in these deprecating words:

> Only the mob and the common people are bound by your laws. The ties of legality exist only for them. Serious, intelligent and modest men need no laws. Their lives have their own laws, for their education and the formation of their character leads them automatically to the exercise of virtue and to good manners. . . . Strong men transgress and reject the laws that seem suitable enough for the weak, for cowards, for pedlars and the miserable rabble, for the lazy and the poor. . . . It is a fact that all great deeds worthy of being remembered have their origin in injustice and violence, in short, in the breaking of the law.[42]

This brilliant display of rhetorical virtuosity was extended to include the experiences of Rome and Athens: without disregard for laws, the Roman Empire would never have been constructed; the Athenians would never have been able to further the arts, and no advances of civilization would have been possible. Further, the legislators in antiquity well understood that useful and needed laws required divine sanction if they were to be imposed on a recalcitrant population. Not surprisingly, these rhetorical fireworks have been compared to the stirring analysis of a Machiavelli whose challenge to traditional notions of behavior was so effective. The crimes of infidelity and betrayal were psychologized and hypocrisy highlighted as essential for successful social maneuvering. The idea of open conflict and conception of perennial discord as ineradicable elements in society found privileged expression in Florentine historiography. Was it possible in the domain of politics to construct bridges over that chasm between the blindness of natural impulse and the claims of civic prudence? Literary space was opened between folly and crime so that degrees of culpability could be registered with precision. The influential *canzoniere* of Petrarch, now so often imitated, disclosed the many ways of love with an appetite for ambiguity far beyond the poetics of a Catullus or an Ovid. The play of mind and soul was featured with an intensity and measure beyond the reckoning of classical Roman poets.

> I find no peace, and all my war is done,
> I fear and hope, I burn and freeze like ice;
> I fly above the wind, yet can I not arise . . .

Meanwhile, the precincts of literature were more open to manifestations of affection through the expression of filial piety, domestic virtue, and the joys of family life. Less literary attention was devoted to the representation of affective ties through rhetorical extravagances highlighted by apostrophes to the gods and goddesses and profligate use of lugubrious adjectives. More subdued expressions of grief, appropriate for private mourning, found poetic voice. One recollects Wyatt's lament for Cromwell and Surrey's for Wyatt as being suitable for the private moment rather than the public occasion. On his return from a diplomatic mission to Italy in 1527, Wyatt introduced the absorbing theme of love into English poetry, to be treated neither allegorically nor with customary earthy frankness. The elegy, too, came into popularity with its diminished moral rigor and lessening of anxiety concerning the expression of emotion. The pastoral eclogue of Theocritus and Virgil, with its companionable shepherds and prize songs, sanctioned the contemplative life as a legitimate adjunct to the active. In this way the deadly sin of sloth was converted into the dignified ideal of classical *otium* (leisure). In England in the sixteenth century, Continental influences, particularly Italian, worked to modify the medieval aureate manner, with its lofty tone, as well as to nudge traditional literary tastes away from preference for ballads about death in battle and the ancient poetry of satire and complaint.[43]

Influential manner books demonstrated how inappropriate heroic virtues, stoic self-control, and asceticism were for so complex a civil society. Of course vulgarized stoicism with its demand for equanimity in the face of misfortune was not displaced from the kingdom of proverbial wisdom. But in advanced literature, self-pity and psychological collapse were better resisted by mockery and ironic self-awareness. The stylized way to respond to rejection and loss of dignity was through the force and play of wit. For the disconsolate, conceits and witticisms were a first resort. The lyric sensibility was privileged, and Petrarch chose this form to present a model of sentimental biography with flaws and all. His *Triumphs,* often printed together with his *Canzoniere,* had formerly been admired as a treasure house of encyclopedic learning. Now they were valued as poetry and interpreted as the allegory of the spiritual progress of the human soul. Public entertainments, frescoes, tapestries, medals, emblems, and pageants testify to the popularity and ready adaptation of the *Triumphs.*

The vocabulary of inner tension and distress (manifestations of human frailty) was enriched with special attention to human inconstancy. Lovely landscapes and troubled seas, with the ready use of antitheses, oxymoron, and hyperbole, allowed readers to participate in the unheroic mobility of human consciousness. Christian awareness of pagan myth produced bittersweet echoes of better times in distant lands. The burden of the soul's uneasy balance and the call for darkened rhetoric was soon to be lightened by easier devotional and meditative impulses. Florentine neoplatonism offered a less demanding, less aristocratic brand of mysticism. Marsilio Ficino adumbrated an essentially laic version of theology: the mind freed of those illusions induced by the senses and by deceptions of imagination will be liberated for conversion toward God. Against the naturalistic and technical philosophy of the peripatetics (Averroists and Aristotelians alike), as well as against the esthetic reductionism of the poets with their passion for images, Ficino would erect his own *docta religio* that was certain to secure the ties between Pallas and Themis.[44]

9

The revival of Senecan tragedy gave space to individual moral responsibility, notwithstanding the bitter and arbitrary play of fate. In matters spiritual and social, the highest valor and the "sublime virtues" were not often put to the test. As we have observed, sociability no longer signified extravagant gestures, nor were man's political impulses inflated to encompass an infinite capacity for being companionable. Gradually, similes and metaphors for portraying political conduct were no longer drawn from the discourse on friendship. Among leading commentators on political life, a more depersonalized language evolved. Civil conduct, good and bad, was not being gauged by the human talent to sustain fellowship or the proclivity to undermine associative bonds. Extravagant entertainments and gestures of boundless hospitality designed to achieve a reputation for largess were denigrated in favor of more modest "civil" expenditures. The Venetian humanist Francesco Barbaro visited Florence in the summer of 1415 with his teacher Guarino. While there, he was guest in the home of Lorenzo and Cosimo de' Medici, sons of Giovanni di Bicci. He established friendships with literati of the city, as well as with the young Lorenzo. For Lorenzo he wrote *On Wifely Duties (De re uxoria)*, in honor of the forthcoming nuptials of Lorenzo and Gianevra Cavalcanti. What made the work so popular in its time (fifty manuscripts survive, almost all from the fifteenth century) was the lively and informed commentary on contemporary and ancient mores and customs. In the proem to book 2, the author reviews, tastefully, the question of the wedding gift, justifying his present not from his store of wealth but from his pen. In so doing, Barbaro gracefully indicates his assessment of changing customs:

> Our ancestors, my dear Lorenzo, were accustomed to making gifts on the occasion of the marriages of their friends or relatives as a token of the obligations that they felt or the love they bore toward the couple. Now this custom (as has happened to many others instituted by our ancestors) is no longer observed among us. For it happens that many people, for a variety of reasons, often borrowed money so that they could give the finest presents to those who were usually very rich. And in sowing these gifts (if I may speak in this way), they seem to me to be imitating those Babylonian peasants for whom (as the father of history, Herodotus, writes) fertile fields were expected to return two-hundredfold, and often even three-hundred-fold. I would call these fields anything but fertile and fruitful; but even though they were very poor, these people sent presents to the very rich while they themselves lacked everything and the wealthy had plenty. For this reason, driven on by hope for gain or for money, they lent their property at high interest. But I think they deserve to be deluded in their hoped-for riches because they were trying to gain reward by means of a deceitful liberality and were striving for many and great advantages.[45]

In celebrating the couple, Barbaro was not merely instructing the young wife in domestic virtues, but he was also monumentalizing the family as the rock on which civic life and Venetian Florentine polity was founded. Civility was less certain to be anchored in a world of courtesy, chivalric protocol, and etiquette. The speech of Carlo Marsuppini in Poggio Bracciolini's dialogue *An seni sit uxor ducenda* of 1439 (dedicated to Cosimo de' Medici) is telling. When discussing the institution of marriage and the taking of a wife, Marsuppini concludes: "And so I consider it most proper to want to live a sociable life and accommodate myself to civil existence." Even the priest Ficino, with his commitment to a Platonic dualism of flesh and spirit, celebrated matrimony:

> Man, almost like a god, maintains his species through having descendants. Gratefully he restores to nature what she has given him. . . . Like a happy and true sculptor he sculpts his living image in his children. . . . Moreover he is in possession of a domestic republic in miniature in which he exercises the force of his whole intelligence and virtue. . . . And finally there is this to be considered: either wife and family are a sweet solace and take many a burden from us, or they are a thorough schooling in moral philosophy.[46]

To condemn marriage was to be without humanity. Is not humanity realized through engaging in life in society?

> For this reason, if you wish to be men and genuine sons of the gods, you must legitimately multiply by generating, nourishing and educating children. Because in this way you are similar to God and imitate Him. And remember that you, in guiding your family with the utmost care, are educating yourselves to be experienced and honoured members of the earthly city, worthy of the heavenly city.

Classical ideas of the self-sufficient citizen, soldier, and patriot—not militarily or politically dependent on others—were the centerpiece of civic humanism. At the same time, the canons of rhetoric permitted a certain flexibility of moral imperatives. Classical ethics, so venerated, were in particular instances mistaken: this was true when hard definitions of *caritas, fortitudo,* and *iustitia* were given a too sure structure and force. The register of meaning of key public virtues lost much of its univocality. In discussing politics humanist historians tended to locate the cause of events in the free decisions of men: choices made by men were capable of being understood by men. Citizen independence was secured against despotism by property rights and the willingness of the individual to accept a condition of approximate equality with others. The ideal of an unspecialized style of life, wherein the citizen successfully discharged varied public duties at different moments, was quintessential. In this classical view men were not sociable out of a sense of mutual deference. In matters religious, humanists were less willing to accent obligatory sets of ritual observances. Indeed, the very notions of repayment, restitution, atonement, and penance as forms of satisfaction were, as we have noted, characterized as barbarous and uncivil. Florentine neo-platonism was a meditation on life laced with consoling recitations of ancient myths. Genial and encouraging in spiritual outlook, it rendered the soul the lynchpin between the worlds of matter and Mind. While belonging with the material world, still, men and women had immortal souls which partook of the divine. No longer doomed by Original Sin, and not entirely dependent on God's grace, the soul held within its power the capacity to rise by dint of reason and love (an ineradicable longing for its heavenly abode) to its true celestial home. The soul was the principle of movement in the world of matter and was itself in motion toward contemplation of eternal truths in the realm of Mind.[47]

Valla, in his *Annotationes in Novum Testamentum* (1444), boldly admit-ted that "none of the words of Christ have come down to us, for Christ spoke in Hebrew and never wrote anything down." To Saint Jerome's statement that each and every biblical codex was corrupt, Valla added the following caution: ". . . if only after four hundred years the river had become too murky, need we be surprised that after a thousand years—for we are sepa-rated from St. Jerome by that many years—that river never having been purged carries both mud and refuse." The study of classical Latin and philology encouraged the humanist to feel free to retreat from the more severe translations of crucial biblical passages toward a more subjective and psychological rendition. For example, Romans 5:3, "We will not repent of our faith," could be stated less harshly with classical overtones as, "We will not be ashamed of our faith." As we have noted, from Valla through to Erasmus, interpretation of Romans 5:12 (the text cited for the doctrine of Original Sin) was a matter of substantial concern. Valla would not exempt God from responsibility for hardening the heart of the sinner. Erasmus, on occasion, was willing to suggest that the progeny of Adam sinned by imita-tion of their forebear, not by virtue of grim inheritance. The solemn exalta-tion of chastity and virginity was an easy target for invective and satire. Sacrifices of the *sanctimoniales, virgines et continentes,* the detachment of holy men and women from earthly goods, and the celebration of voluntary poverty were no longer providing ready coin for the minting of a new spiritual vocabulary. Perhaps the most revealing instance of this seismic shift can be observed in the changing Tuscan iconography of the Saviour. In the ad-vanced fine arts the road to redemption was no longer so likely to be portrayed as being secured by the victimization and torments of Christ. The scapegoats whose sufferings and sacrifices were exchanged for the redemp-tion of humankind lost their near-monopoly on the artistic imagination. This at a moment when the torments of Christ were achieving new heights of dramatic intensity in the north of Europe.[48]

Quattrocento Florentine literary critics also registered an awareness of the decline of primitive and archaic forms of discourse and exchange. The raw and rude *(rozzo* and *rudis)* stylistics of Dante were singled out to characterize that first age when the poet and his language were one with the world he described. As in social and religious life, so, too, in the vernacular poetics, language was not segregated from the universal things with which it participated. When Pico della Mirandola commented upon the poetry of Lorenzo de' Medici, he contended that his friend and contemporary had benefited from the best of Dante and Petrarch. Dante's style was "horrdus aspe et stregosus rudis impolitus" when compared with the ornate and "dulcis" lyricality of Petrarch. Pico, like other critics, was evenhanded in his commentary, acknowledging that the sense of Dante's epic was "grandior et sublimior," whereas Petrarch's oeuvre was more polished. The Magnificent Lorenzo had successfully combined the distinct virtues of each poet, navigating between the raw but sublime style of Dante and the lyrical, amorous philosophy of Petrarch. Imitation of the best qualities of the two poets did indeed serve as an inspiration to Michelangelo, with his awareness of the singular values of each. Politian, the finest Latin poet of the century, incorporated the literary values of the "furious" and the "ornamental" styles in his poetic ideal of "docta varietas." In the next century, the Florentine canon and poet Francesco Berni (1497?–1535) continued to find the vocabulary of pretty *parole* and profound *cose* effective when charging the followers of Petrarch of Berni's day with merely uttering *words,* whereas a Michelangelo uttered *things.* This abbreviated account of stylistics, though venerable, may, in a general way, prove fair.[49]

10

Literary historians, from Giambattista Vico in the seventeenth century to Erich Auerbach, Harold Bloom, John Freccero, and Thomas Greene in the twentieth, have praised Dante for being at one with his own severe poem: "In the rhetorical figures of the schools, he saw vestiges of the original concrete and sensuous thinking of men who believed that in employing words and concepts they were seizing hold of things themselves." Influential modern literary interpreters, such as Charles Singleton, have been critically attentive to Dante's method of writing, characterizing it as an imitation of God's way of writing in the Holy Scriptures. A textual conception of truth, whereby texts were everywhere interposed between experience and reality, worked along that undifferentiated boundary between things, thoughts, and language. How different was that literary subjectivity which, as we have noted, recognized more clearly its distance from the things itself, relying upon words apart from things. Indeed, the emergence of the first Italian literary prose in the *volgare* in the thirteenth century, with its elemental and *rozza* syntax, has been portrayed as impoverished both in its power to establish abstract relationships and its ability to achieve nuanced evaluations. This literary assessment of the quality of early Italian vernacular does, at the same time, acknowledge its arresting power and penchant for the factual and unelaborated. We are at a moment of extreme intellectual economy, when thought still adhered to things, fixing a rude interdependence.[50]

Similar observations have been offered by literary critics when considering the transformation of prose stylistics of the English vernacular in the early sixteenth century. The English prose of the previous century was admirably suited to its narrative context, achieving remarkable effects by using monosyllabic words in a series of loosely joined and unsubordinated sentences. The prose of Sir Thomas Malory's *Morte Darthur* (1470) is stunning in this regard:

> Therefore, Sir Launcelot, go to thy realm, and there take thee a wife, and live with her with joy and bliss, and I pray thee heartily pray for me to our Lord, that I may amend my mis-living. Now, sweet madam, said Sir Launcelot, would ye that I should return again unto my country, and there wed a lady? Nay, madam, wit you well that shall I never do; for I shall never be so false to you of that I have promised.[51]

The older syntax, with its accurate account of the factual and everyday, was, in the next century, to serve as ballast so that the ship of language, while pridefully sailing the seas of abstract and philosophical discourse, might yet be steadied by concrete illustration and factual analogy. One thinks on the prose of Francis Bacon and his essays which evolve from simple declarative sentences into the open classicism of broad philosophical vistas. One does not have to go to the end of the century, however, to appreciate this new tactic in the vernacular. Sir Thomas Elyot, humanistically trained and eager to assert the claims of the public world over a recalcitrant nobility and gentry, brought to bear the recently imported classical techniques, with their abundance of abstract nouns and complex sentence structure, to further philosophical discourse. This appreciation of the wealth of the classical tradition was played out in a language also responsive to the time-honored and more elemental forms:

> Augmentation of honour and substance . . . not only impresseth a reverence, whereof proceedeth due obedience among subjects but also inflameth men naturally inclined to idleness or sensual appetite to covet like fortune, and for that cause to dispose them to study or occupation. Now to conclude my first assertion or argument, where all thing is commune, there lacketh order; and where order lacketh, there all thing is odious and uncomely. And that have we in daily experience; for the pans and pots garnisheth well the kitchen, and yet should they be to the chamber non ornament. Also the beds, testers, and pillows beseemeth not the hall, no more than the carpets and cushions becometh the stable.[52]

If we were to venture into serious fifteenth-century prose literature, we would discover a world both highly elaborated and ceremonial. Prose stylistics in the vernacular favored a heavily pompous language little preoccupied with the relative subordination of words and clauses. This would be true even in weighty discourse where it was disadvantageous to have words and expressions fall outside the syntactical order. The solemn and circumstantial rhetoric, with its formulas and repetitious conventional gestures and invocations, made social ties concrete. Processions of prepositional clauses, pageants of apostrophes, and parades of adverbial phrases, accompanied by acclimations of pleonestic and quasi-pleonestic expressions, recall to mind the overblown and ponderous style of legal and diplomatic documents. In these public writings language itself became an amalgam—a kind of cement—for strengthening the bonds of obligation and responsibility. Through a form of literary profligacy language became a warrant for delivery of promises and pledges of fidelity. The numerous invocations during this time of God, the Virgin, and the Saints have a strong affinity with the rhetoric of legal and diplomatic agreement. Reminiscent also of the public document are the repetitive formulas aiming to strengthen the will of the believer to meditate on things spiritual; the hammering language operates to channel energies that, if left free, might wander aimlessly.[53]

Again, how different was that literary subjectivity which, as we have noted several times, recognized more clearly its distance from things themselves, relying upon *parole* apart from *cose?* To what extent do changes in literary language and artistic symbolism and iconography provide evidence of the onset of a more problematic relationship between linguistic sign and referent? To what extent do changes in vernacular expression replicate consciousness of these problematics? To what extent do these transformations parallel structural change in social, political, and economic life? To what extent were these mutations refracted in word and image? Deliberate restriction of vocabulary and evocation of strongly expressive words has been singled out by modern literary critics of the Italian vernacular as the mark of the emerging extension of the poetic register of experience. In England too, in a later day (the early sixteenth century), prose writing has been similarly assessed by critics. Erasmus had commented that More "exerted himself to acquire a flexible prose style, making experiments of every kind." Of course these trials were carried on in Latin. From his earliest forays into English prose (the *Life of Pico della Mirandola*), however, the English is most vivid when it retains its Latin word order: "Great libraries, it is incredible to considre, with how mervelouse celeritee he readde them over." His *History of Richard III* is a highly polished and stunning example of historical narrative. The extraordinary stylistic control may well have been a result of the probability that More composed his Latin and English versions at the same time. A brief sample from this work suggests something of its distance from Mallory, while at the same time presaging literary prospects for Shakespeare and the Elizabethan theater:

> Where he went abroad, his eyes whirled about, his body privily fenced, his hand ever on his dagger, his countenance and manner like one alway ready to strike again; he took ill rest at nights, lay long waking and musing, sore wearied with care and watch, rather slumbered than slept, troubled with fearful dreams, suddenly sometime start up, leap out of his bed, and run about the chamber, so was his restless heart continually tossed and tumbled with the tedious impression and stormy remembrance of his abominable deed.54

In both Italian prose and poetry attention has been called to a sensibility characterized by the limits of experience. Confident notions that it was possible to penetrate the historical or fictional surfaces of poetic texts voiced by a Dante (*Inferno* IX: "ponder the doctrine that is hidden below the veil of strange verses") or a Boccaccio ("the essence of poetry is to conceal truth under a veil of fitting fables") were rivaled by a humanist hermeneutic. The frustrating experience of mapping a classical text was ensured by its remoteness. Resistant to penetration, the text might require an "archaeological subreading." In the Latin dialogue we observe that any ready moral prescription can run counter to the demands and claims of civic life. So too we notice a sense of restraint in the quest for spiritual remedies: to make this search artistically and literarily effective, it might well be necessary to acknowledge pulls on the human will working in an opposite direction. A feature of the most advanced art of a Donatello or Michelangelo was the ineradicable conflict between Christian humility and pride in artistic achievement. Such tensions nourished the deeper impulses of these artists instead of stunting their talent. The search for the truths of experience and of the tangible world did not lessen the compelling authority of divine revelation. Figures of celestial beauty, such as the *Madonna of the Rocks* of Leonardo da Vinci, were located in grottos of true geological formation replete with botanically accurate renditions of shrubs and plants. Michelangelo's *Pietà* presented an image of idealized and sublime beauty which yet remained astonishingly human.55

The pursuit of spiritual quiet and solitude could not still the appetite and love of glory. Moral struggle and spiritual torment were freed from ontological claims. The history of the world and of the self lacked ontological grounding. Claims of cultural expression were being understood more modestly and were not so likely to be asserted as an authoritative reflection of external reality. The grand model was scaled down in favor of more limited and fragmented insights expressed in lyrical subjectivity, the poetics of discontinuity, the immediacy of the essay, the miniaturizing of the epyllion, the familiarity of the letter, the isolation of the *pensée,* and the openness and probabilism of the dialogue. Of course perspective theory in the arts and autonomy of Renaissance painting provide a telling symbol of the repudiation of the idea of mental procedures as operating by resemblances. The need for illusionism became an imperative, with the artist self-consciously feigning and counterfeiting a reality. We have a significant instance of the unsettling impact of perspective and the demands of verisimilitude on a religious object. In Umbria in the last part of the Quattrocento, the procession standards, with their representation of the Mother of Mercy, were in conformity with the new standards of Renaissance realism. The effect was to convert a sacred image into a religious object. This transformation proved emotionally costly, as an image was "perverted by the charms and fascination of culture."[56]

1 1

In the social world, as well as in the domain of language and culture, an archaic and ceremonial idiom was rivaled by a vocabulary more flexible. The essence of things, the true, the absolute, and the need to validate through textuality were less beguiling, even less seductive. The criteria utilized were much more ductile as the grammar of social relations tilted away from its traditional matrix. Political and military events, and their interpretation, did not so readily turn on the ethos of a single order or its ability to live up to its oaths, pledges, and agreements. Perhaps we can glimpse something of the complex character of this displacement, and even gain an appreciation of its psychic cost, by recounting the observations of the Florentine chronicler, Matteo Villani on the career of Niccolò Acciaiuoli. Writing in the early 1360s, Villani describes the elegance and liberality of this great statesman and Florentine citizen who served as principal advisor to the queen of Naples. The chronicler cannot fault this paragon of chivalric virtue "con animo più cavalleresco che mercantile" who chose royal service over the citizen business life. Yet, because of his virtues of magnanimity and generosity of spirit, he must suffer exile. His very grandeur posed a threat to the liberty of the city, and, therefore, he accepted voluntary banishment. His style of life from the great *loggia* where feasting and hospitality were the order of the day and night to his retention of bands of followers, revealed his noble nature. But like the good Scipio Africanus, this citizen, "onesto e di bella maniera," pursued a life more *signorile* than republican. This was the same Niccolò much beloved by Boccaccio, of whom the author of the *Decameron* was to make sport: this grand seneschal of Naples believed in the historical facticity of the Arthurian legend and would create a contemporary chivalric order replicating exactly the noble ways of old. How to generate a vernacular in which traditional customs and behavior were surveyed with both detachment and sympathy! By the early fifteenth century in Tuscany the classical dialogue form of the humanists comes to the fore, and we observe the forensic debate on the nature of true nobility. This genre contributed to the extension of a vocabulary and formation of more open categories for reviewing the complex questions pertaining to the true nature of nobility. Buonaccorso da Montemagno, the Tuscan civic humanist, recapitulated the variety of arguments on this much disputed topic in his *De nobiltate,* and it was this text which Caxton published in an English translation done by John Tiptoft in 1481. Buonaccorso's work became the basis for Henry Medwell's innovative interlude *Fulgens and Lucres* (1497). Medwell was chaplain to Cardinal Morton, Thomas More's benefactor, and well equipped to appropriate the rhetorical strategy of maintaining the fiction of ethical neutrality. The drama was located in a sphere of "good faith were one can debate without intimidation."[57]

In the Italian vernacular, words such as *onore, utile, naturale, interesse, nobile, regionevole, rischio, merito, dono, discipline, grazia, conversazione, fama, gloria, virtù, maniera,* and a host of others became polyvalent, allowing for a wider register of meaning. Rhetoric itself was designed for verisimilitude, not the representation of reality. The structure of thought was revealed in speech. Allegory came to be perceived as a continuous metaphor with mythology the first allegory. In Latin we observe a softening of such key words as *otium* and *negotium. Otium* did not preclude fulfillment of civic duties nor did *negotium* negate the prospect of cultivated leisure. The requirement of good letters and good arms could be brought into harmony. Passions such as *invidia* and *ira,* as well as self-love, gained range of meaning, moving, like the idea of nobility, from anchorage in a rigid philosophical dualism toward the open sea of comprehensive multiplicity.[58]

Eloquentia was distanced from *sapientia,* with any strict connection rendered ambiguous. Words lost their hold on the world. An illustration of this can be discerned in the changing meaning of the word *conversazione.* In the *Convivio,* Dante spoke of having had from earliest days *benevolenza* and *conversazione* with another. The equation between talk and incurring good will was apt. The word *conversazione* signified "living or behaving in an environment of other persons—in heaven, or even with women—or in intimacy with things." One achieved good will from it and also one could achieve yet another form of satisfaction by having carnal conversation. There was also "sacred conversation" because, when two people spoke, God was present. What was novel was the coining of the term *la civile conversazione.* Not synonymous with gaining benevolence or achieving satisfaction or being intimate with heaven, the world, or a woman, it became a self-conscious activity whereby comportment in society was taught. A model for the humanists, it became one of the keys to education through which instruction in grammar and language might be conveyed by conversation rather than rule and precept. How different was the art of civil conversation from that of contemplation with its truths and rules. Finally, conversation was much more than speech: it was the very foundation of conjugal society. In a later day, the classically trained and humanistically minded John Milton summed the matter up with delicacy: conversation with one's friend and wife provided for "the solace and satisfaction of the mind."[59]

Angelo Decembrio, the Italian humanist of the Quattrocento, in his *Politia literaria,* when introducing the reader to the pedagogy of Guarino Guarini, identified *politia,* not with the Greek city or republic but with the Latin idea of culture. The same meaning is expressed by Crinito, in his idea of "honesta disciplina," and by Valla in his conception of "eligentia," with human culture defined as resting essentially on urbane converse. Standards of discourse were much indebted to the exigencies of civil conversation, with its preoccupation for verisimilitude and interest in the probable rather than the certain. Advanced literature moved away from rhetoric and dialectic as proof became increasingly involved with strategies for evoking the illusion of spontaneity and informality. An appreciation for the casual and seemingly random worked to certify the authenticity of exchange of views and opinions. Textuality calling attention to literature as literature gave way to oratory and its devices, which projected the illusion of uninterrupted discourse. Archaic foreclosure was in process of being evaded. No longer was the trademark of courtesy to be detected in verbal effusions of magnificence and public display. Honor was being detached from its material manifestations. The ancient meaning of *compagnevole,* as giving aid to another person, was becoming obsolete. *Gentilezza* was being associated with the acquisition of *civiltà* and command of the resources of high culture (a knowledge of arts and letters). *Gloria* was less certain to be reduced to sheer vanity and *fama* less likely to be dismissed as worthless in the face of the ravages of time. The Florentine humanist Matteo Palmieri, who sought to transform *caritas* into a civic virtue, was glowing about the benefits of fame to individuals and community:

> It is not possible to say whence a man comes; but it is certain that there is in our hearts a longing for future centuries which compels us to seek eternal fame, a happy condition for our country and enduring health for those who are about to descend from us.[60]

Patience was being translated from an otherworldly virtue of resignation in the face of life's vicissitudes to a restless preoccupation with perfection. Soft definitions of *good* and *evil,* once intoned by a Machiavelli or a Guicciardini, altered the lexicon of political ethics beyond easy moral repair. In *Discorsi,* II, Machiavelli wrote:

> When I come to reflect upon the course of events, I reach the conclusion that the world is the same. There has always been good and bad; but the good and bad have differed from country to country.

The idea of original sin was perceived under the influence of the Greek Church Fathers by both humanist and theologian, not as something to be paid for or for which satisfaction must be given or for which atonement must be made. Sin was characterized as a condition of illness, not of guilt, and salvation was viewed as a restoration to health rather than a process of atonement. Even the definition of *obligation* was undergoing revision; more abstract conceptions were rivaling concrete notions. An idiom more relaxed tended to loosen its hold upon the physical and social world. To make peace with one's enemies or secure the good will of one's friends had required some objective compensation or satisfaction. But in Tuscany by the fourteenth century words of tribal and Germanic origin, such as *guidrigildo* (blood price), *guiderdono* (countergift), *guiderdonatore* (countergift giver), and their ilk, had become exceedingly rare. In the thirteenth century the *guiderdono* had been a regular synonym for the act of paying interest. In fact, the persistence of the conception of interest and gift suggests that the vocabulary of an archaic world was displaced only gradually, and sometimes incompletely. The word *interest (interesso)* was used by the Florentine chronicler Giovanni Villani during the first part of the fourteenth century as a synonym for damage or harm done to the commune. This usage goes back to a much earlier time, both in French and Italian, to equate *dammaggio* with *interesso*. Not surprisingly, one also finds records of the payment of interest in which *interessi* and *spesi* are coupled with *danni* (losses).[61] Slowly, and sometimes under circumstances of acute tension, did the idea that individuals might establish meaningful relationships based upon a frank recognition of ties of self-interest achieve literary currency. Again, in the early fourteenth century, a redaction of the *Statuti dei mercanti di Calimala* required the consuls of the guild, along with *frati,* to see that fellow members pardon each other for interest taken during the course of business in the previous year. "Guiderdoni overo interesse per l'anno" was to be forgiven "per amore" of one guildsman for another. Words such as *interest, grace, courtesy, benevolence, sympathy* were slowly released from indenture to a domain of mutualities and obligation. The archaic meaning of *benevolenza* was voluntary payment of tribute. In the thirteenth century, loans were recorded by Sienese merchants in their correspondence as having been made "a sua cortesia"; this of course indicated that the loan was made without interest. To perform a charitable act was to reduce one's debt to God, who was, in Dante's words, "sire de la cortesia." It was this sublimely courteous Lord of all Lords who turned his soul so that it might perceive the glory of the blessed Beatrice. The author of *La vita nuova* was following the blessed Saint Francis and the blasphemous Iacopone da Todi in celebrating the courtesy of God toward man. When interest was returned to the commune on the public debt by bond holders, its restoration was recorded in the Monte of 1345 with the words "pro amore communis." One was obligated through the exchange of favors, and one was obligated through sin. Conversation in its archaic meaning was acquired through experiencing the customs and habits of life lived in common. By the sixteenth century it was being defined by Castiglione and others as a colloquium carried on with discretion, elegance, and amity among friends. In an early time, *grazia* often signified favors and benefits, as well as the thanks accorded for them. The first poets writing in the vernacular in the thirteenth century regarded gratitude as a right of the favor-giver that merited great respect from the beneficiary. This too was to be transformed into an esthetics of elegance and refinement of style, both literary and personal.[62]

1 2

In the vocabulary of politics we also observe something of the same seismic shift. In the Trecento chronicles of Giovanni and Matteo Villani, the synonym for alliances and treaties was "solemne obbligagione." Ceremonies of peace and rituals of reconciliation were structurally necessary to the civic life of the thirteenth-century north and central Italian communes. While these rites persisted over the centuries, they tended to become increasingly marginal and ceremonial. The highwater mark was clearly in the thirteenth and early fourteenth centuries, and this was a time when numerous magistrates and officials were specifically created and charged with defending the peace—a peace almost synonymous with the good order of the city. As the structures of the territorial state were put in place, the need for the exchange of tokens, pledges, olive branches, and the kiss of peace became the stuff of pageant rather than of *Realpolitik*. Ideas of unity had been closely bonded to the idea of peace. The conception of *concordia* of Saint Augustine heralded the withering away of the state. The weaker the state and the more pacific the times, the greater the likelihood of a citizenry made one by the triumph of love and charity. Gradually, however, this theological-political rhetoric receded before new modes of discourse less devoted to the ideal of concord and harmony among the social orders and estates. The political community was conceptualized as being less dependent on the actions of "boni cives," who were "amantes iustitiae et tranquillitatem," susceptible to the imperatives of *caritas* and *misericordia*. Instead, views which had formerly been marginal and anonymous were now advanced with a heightened self-awareness. Accompanying the call for union and peace among magnates, *popolani,* and artisans was the resolute and specific admonition to maintain "the full faith and credit of the commune." The need for tranquillity was now matched by the requirement of providing "de securitate status." A new style of political leadership emerged with a handful of politicians and statesmen advising the government. These select figures were not spokesmen for guild corporations or any one of a myriad of corporate bodies but, rather, very much in the mold of civic personalities. From the conventional and somewhat old-fashioned point of view, these civic personages could indeed be branded as guilty of the horrendous sin of *superbia*. This was one of the major differences between such chroniclers as Giovanni and Matteo Villani on the one hand, and the new humanist history of Leonardo Bruni Aretino, who frankly recognized the need for self-assertive and dynamic, rather than corporate, leadership on the other. In the Florentine Quattrocento, humanist historiography and rhetoric assigned to the leader and statesman a noble role, giving him a classical political stage on which to act. Florentine sculptors created the first civic space staffed with civic monuments of exemplary leaders unrivaled since the days of Greece and Rome.[63]

Simultaneous with the civic art of the generation of Donatello, Brunelleschi, and Alberti, we observe the beginnings of a systematic segregation of private and public sentiments. The demanding and costly tradition of spontaneity, gregariousness, extended courtesy, and widespread sociability was now in competition with a conception of civility marked by new dining customs, new table utensils, new household furnishings, new organization of interior domestic space—all of these working to restrict ancient commensality and open ways of living. As the *vita civile* achieved status as an ideal, it operated to sanction the scaling down of archaic obligation, which may seem ironic. But civil society did reduce the need for the fortified palazzo as well as requirement for making public display of munificence and power. Indeed, public exhibitionism was challenged as an ideal in this civil society, so that conspicuous consumption became an indoor activity sheltered behind imposing palace facades.[64]

Whatever the idealization of the civic virtues, their play in public life was problematic and limited. There was, of course, Machiavelli's penetrating question voiced in his *Discorsi* I, 18, as to "whether in a corrupt state it is possible to maintain a free government." Strict were the margins of objective possibilities. In the kingdom of historical necessity, room for moral intervention and the will of the individual was not ample. Those who would modify reality could not modify its laws. In reflecting on politics it was becoming more difficult to place in the foreground the might of traditional solidarities, the power of obligation, or the successful workings of conciliation and reconciliation. We have already noted that the flowering and proliferation of magistracies and political corporations formed to the ends of pacification were an achievement of the communal age (the Dugento). By the late fifteenth and early sixteenth centuries advanced Florentine political thinkers were likely to highlight the play of advantage and self-interest when representing contemporary historical drama.[65]

Humanist thought in general was surely not creative in spawning grand ideologies or even a substantial body of systematic political philosophy. This had been a sterling accomplishment of an earlier day. The study of history no longer was certain to confirm the commonplace of the vanity of human wishes, but rather to sanction the wisdom of the proposition of the vanity of wishing for too much. Social struggles were perceived as having certain positive value. Ambition in politics was recognized as a virtue, provided it was not inordinate. History was less likely to be a record of the tragedy of social disorder and civil wars. Had not the Roman plebes in their bitter contest against the *optimates* acquired a robust commitment to the *patria?* The civil and military character of pagan religion was not only acknowledged but also recognized as lending structure to society and meaning to individual acts. Cohesion and authority existed in classical times, and the question was, upon what was it grounded? More likely on citizen military service than *caritas.* To what extent was citizen unrest and discontent the result of defects in political institutions or human frailty? Surely, benevolence and sympathy among the citizen body were not reliable cornerstones for state-building. What was the nucleus of common conviction that gave extralegal cohesion to a people? What lent authority to ordinances and inspired faith in power? These and a battery of other queries were posed energetically and called for response. The search for answers tested the resources of archaic social and political thought over the next centuries, first in Italy and then, later, in the north of Europe.[66]

Transformation of a traditional political vocabulary with attendant moral precepts and the coinage of a new civic idiom has been documented for Florence. In the minutes of the *Consulte e Pratiche* are the records of the opinions of influential and, sometimes, informed citizens summoned by the *signory* to advise on a variety of public issues. In the digests of their speeches we have evidence as to the ways in which the need to improve statecraft and diplomacy operated to promote formulation of such concepts as *ragione dello stato, interesse, virtù, fortuna, necessità,* and so forth. Here, in these public debates, we discover the soil that nurtured the political lexicon of a Machiavelli or a Guicciardini. Distant from traditional moralizing precepts, this language was itself bred on calculation. Its aim was to steady the tiller of a ship passing through the turbulent waters between the Scylla of exaggerated fears and the Charybdis of illusory hopes. Exposed to arbitrary currents and tides of uncontrollable power, the need for *ragione* was compelling, albeit the lamp of reason had but few candle power. A reading of the minutes of these sessions in the late fifteenth and early sixteenth centuries suggests that the minting of this new coin occurred against the backdrop of untrammeled confidence in an older currency. Yet a tilt was evident: advice to princes and republics could not be given with sublime assurance without some reckoning of this new idiom.[67]

1 3

Michel Foucault's exclusive focus on the later centuries (principally the seventeenth) calls attention to acts which he believes represented an ultimate transformation in culture and consciousness. Featuring these crucial developments, he ignores the centuries of change during which grounding for this transformation was in process. Moreover, the shift in awareness, so central to his argument, was far from decisive and complete. In addition, by highlighting the last stages of these mutations in language and mental habits, Foucault does not have any strategy for generating hypotheses as to possible causes for this cultural revolution. Perhaps by examining particular aspects of Tuscan social and cultural development from the thirteenth through the sixteenth centuries, with side trips to other regions of north and central Italy, as well as the north of Europe, it may be possible to suggest some of the forces working toward change. Comparison with Northern Europe may permit us to indicate features of the political and economic landscape inhibiting or favoring these changes. Crucial for my argument is the notation that mounting recognition of the limits and constraints exercised by an overdetermined world of archaic obligation, feudal solidarity, and communal restriction was first put at risk in the south in the late thirteenth and early fourteenth centuries, and in the north of Europe some two centuries later.[68]

One aspect of this change, and perhaps not a trivial one, was the displacement of an overdetermined, linguistic protocol in favor of discourse more relaxed and capable to copiousness (amplification). New literary forms—less imperialistic—acknowledged more fully their distance from the reality they sought to characterize. This decline in the totalitarian claims of culture was already apparent in scholastic thought but was not to find sustained expression in the literature of north Europe until the sixteenth century. In Italy, the first generalized evidence of this cultural modesty had appeared some three centuries before in the humanist and vernacular idioms, as well as in the arts with their new strategies for integral representation of forms in space. The religious image became an instrument of spiritual persuasion rather than mnemonic device. No longer defined in terms of its relationship to a spiritual prototype, the figure was valorized for its capacity to generate "jeu d'illusion" of lived life. As a consequence of accepting certain conventions (often drawn from antique rhetoric), *imagines viventes* replaced *imagines agentes,* so essential for the mnemonic tradition.

By comparing developments in the north and south of Europe, albeit impressionistically, it may be possible to offer a hypothesis that the onset of a civil society sanctioned by different notions of exchange was essential to the formation of a new cultural vocabulary. The difficulties in generating such a vocabulary should not be underestimated; nor should the contribution of this language be disvalued when considering the extent to which it enhanced prospects for change. That the transformation was so gradual, and movement so crablike, calls for considerable intellectual patience. One thinks of the obstacles confronting the Tudor translator of Castiglione's *Courtier.* When Thomas Hoby would render into English the Italian words *stile* or *maniera,* he wrote, "the trade and manner of the courtier." In the same vein, he will speak of the "kind of trade" of a Leonardo or Raphael. He renders Castiglione's "statue antiche di marmo" in the ducal palace into the stuff of a warehouse. In English, the statues become "ancient images of marble and metall."[69]

THREE

The Colloidal Solution

In the interest of generating hypotheses concerning differences in cultural forms and vocabulary between Northern and Southern Europe from the fourteenth through the sixteenth century, two geographic areas have been selected: north and central Italy and far-off England. To begin with a very obvious difference is to feature the question of the bonds and relationships of associative life. If one surveys the ties of obligation at the apex of English society, one is struck by the extent to which they diverge from the Tuscan model. At the upper-reaches of English society relationships reveal certain elements which can legitimately be classified as archaic. To my mind it is not sufficient to describe England of the fourteenth and fifteenth centuries merely as feudal, but, rather, it is essential to examine in some detail those practices and strategies cementing aristocratic relationships bringing stability to that society. A system of relationships resting upon complex forms of land tenure was the product of a fluid society where land was exchanged for personal allegiance—this at a time when land was both less available and easier to part with. This system has sometimes been described as "bastard feudalism," providing, as it did, the fundamental bond between the lesser and greater aristocracy, that is, gentry and nobles. This intricate matrix of ties formed the structure of power within society, lending coherence and style to the behavior of an elite. The castles and households of great noblemen were the chief centers of social influence and strength; from them originated those concentric, often overlapping, circles constituting the lord's "affinity." Loyalty was secured by life annuities, so that men were bound by life indentures and in this way lords could be sure of retaining a man's service. Only the insignificant were without their lord. The Warwick affinity was a series of concentric circles with the earl at the center reaching out to councilors, estate servants, stewards, household officials, and Warwickshire gentry holding their own lands and their own residences. The boundaries of affinity included annuants holding no office, ranging from the lawyer retained for professional services to lesser gentlemen and yeomen who were well-wishers of the lord. A system grounded in rewards of honors, high office, enfeoffment with land, gifts, pensions, and strategic marriages was in place. On festive occasions peasants found the lord's domicile the center of beneficence. Rich

gifts symbolized both power and humility. The line between chivalric largess
and Christian charity was indeterminate. Most aristocratic charity assumed
the form of casual gifts with the Church serving as intermediary. Rich men
were entrusted by God with stewardship of wealth. *Dives and Pauper* speaks
of the rich and lordly as "Goddis revys and Goddis baylys," and this of
course was a commonplace in the didactic and admonitory literature of late
medieval England.[1]

Influence emanating from castles and households of great nobles radi-
ated over the countryside; service in such a household enhanced reputation.
The remarks of Giacomo Soranzo, the Venetian ambassador under Edward
VI and Queen Mary, are worth quoting:

> The nobility, save such as are employed at Court, do not habitually reside in
> cities, but in their own county mansions, where they keep up very grand
> establishments, both with regard to the great abundance of eatables con-
> sumed by them as also by reason of their numerous attendants in which
> they exceed all other nations, so that the Earl of Pembroke has upward of a
> thousand clad in his own livery.

The humble and well-born were assembled to take their place in the
retinue of a great lord as he progressed from one castle or manorhouse to
another in peripatetic fashion. Retainers enhanced a lord's "worship" or
influence, enabling him to further his own interests and that of his dependents. Patronage, good lordship, protection, and pageantry formed the binding cement of late medieval society. The relations between medieval magnates
were as important in the everyday world as they were in the accounts of
chroniclers. In the mid-fifteenth century the greater part of the battle-ready
military was composed of retinues of magnates. In addition to the tenants of
magnates, there were lesser lords who had bound themselves to the potentates of the realm and from whom they frequently received a type of uniform
(livery) and badge which they wore as a sign of their clientage. This was their
due along with contributions toward their maintenance. Private retinues
owing loyalty to territorial magnates were at the center of the order and
disorder of fifteenth-century England. The secret of rule rested in the king's
using the elite rather than bypassing it. Legal innovation magnified by juristic
accident often worked to make the feudal world operate according to its own
morality and assumptions. It is very doubtful that the king conceived of any
other solution than that of attracting or compelling a turbulent feudality to
participate with its wealth and local prestige in the work of an embryonic
state. As soldiers, judges, councilors, and representatives, these nobles
contributed willingly or unwillingly to the formation of networks of command and obligation. War service was of course most essential. In Henry
VIII's early campaign (1513), just over one-half the army of 25,000 men were
retainers of peers.[2]

When Englishmen of the fifteenth century wrote about their society, it was generally in time-honored and conventional language. The modern-day historian E. F. Jacob has described it clearly:

> English speculation about government and society in the 15th century was less political than moral and dogmatic. The study of man and his duties in the community, his moral nature and his rights was, with a few exceptions, left to homilists or to regents or to the universities, where a handful of teachers in the faculties of arts and theology considered questions about the moral excellence of a citizen mainly as a branch of theology or in relation to the obligations of the classes or grades in society.[3]

Fifteenth-century English monarchs were expected to maintain order, do justice, defend their subjects and the realm from rebellion or invasion, and, when required, captain their armies in war. The effect of the ideal ruler on his kingdom was often conveyed in the imagery of meteorology, as movement from the turbulence of tempestuous passions to the calm of tempered reason. Indeed, the political science of the fifteenth and sixteenth centuries was no political science at all, depending as it did on the language of correspondence and metaphors of nature. The vocabulary of politics was close to the language of the cosmos; that of the social world approximated the language of the natural world; and that of the economic world the language of bodily functions. It was as if any upset to the natural order made men, in the words of Macbeth, "float upon a wild and violent sea." When economics was written about in the fifteenth century, it was as a means toward power rather than as an end in itself. It was conventional to frame public policy in the name of some general pinciple such as "the common profit," or "the profit of the realm," or "the nurturing of love." Parenthetically, it should be noted that a low status was accorded to the writing of history. The great age of historical enterprise of the monastic houses had been impressive. After the Norman Conquest and the attendant social disruption, feelings of resentment and pain for a lost heritage stimulated efforts for a historical reconstruction. Links between community and the past were achieved by rendering its physical being. History solemnized the memory of "a great army of benefactors, craftsmen, saints and enemies." The aim was total recall of the past in order to give the community its identity in the present. This historical reconstruction was inspired by a quest for continuity.[4]

No self-perpetuating, self-important tradition of historical composition existed in fifteenth-century London; nor was there a successor to Froissart in fifteenth-century England. History was not important as propaganda for the monarchy of the fifteenth century. In the fourteenth century an exception to the proposition that historical imagination was the last requirement for an intellectual had been the Londoner Andrew Horn. Much influenced by the Florentine civic rhetorician Brunetto Latini—a literary figure celebrated but slighted by Dante—Horn took many cues from this instructor in the science of politics. There were significant differences, however: when discussing the discord and struggles besetting Italian towns, Latini expressed casual regret about the spirit of faction and use of coercion in elections. Horn followed Latini but placed the blame for disorder in London on wealth, intrigue, and the retinues of the great. In so doing, he may well have been responding to the particular conditions prevalent in the politics of his city.[5]

In England, where the roots of urban culture were shallow, extreme conditions of social conflict were rare, and, therefore, historical sensibilities were limited. As yet there was no well-secured city interest to balance the authority of the landed. Urban institutions were often designed to be inimical to the play of market forces. Towns were economically weakened in the fifteenth century as industry evaded the surveillance of guilds for the freer atmosphere of the rural village. Only in towns with developed industries, which were dependent on distant markets for their supplies and outlets, were social tensions more than sporadic. The habit of thinking of men in high places as being supported by some supernatural sanction was pervasive. The central psychological prop of inequality, both political and economic, was the respect the indivdual had for authority. Merchants controlled their staff of apprentices and servants in a style resonating with the vocabulary of paternalism and gestures of lordship. People thought in terms of a series of ranks from which they were more likely to fall than to ascend. Politicians spoke in a language redolent with the imagery of courtesy, friendship, service, and love. The shame of losing a lawsuit may have been as important to a litigant as the value of the land in dispute. Law depended to a disturbing degree on the cunning of a pleader, a judge, or counsel. The outcome was often determined by the uncertain recall of a statute in a yearbook case or the willingness to debate and contest, rather than resolve. Procedure in court instilled a habit of absolute verbal precision, since a case might be invalidated by an inaccurate *contre*. Vagueness of the law led to the dominance of accident rather than remedy. The narrative art was no novelty to the pleader of the fourteenth century, whose role has been compared to that of romance author and singer of tales. Fiction and stage performance bearing restraint and stability were essential if law was to benefit community.[6]

1

Status was inexorably bound to public ceremony, ritual, and display. Although the medieval affinity was no longer military, this did not lessen the attractions of the chivalric code. Indeed, in the later Middle Ages ardor for chivalric spectacle and extravagance intensified. Wardrobe accounts for the early 1360s describe the entire English royal household assembled at Christmastime, with each member's status defined by the quality, quantity, and color of garments. Clothing was an art form and so, too, was fine tailoring.

Similarly, the intricacies of cooking were celebrated. Honor was to be gained at the banquet table, or at the court of Richard II of England, with the preparation of a cookbook. What Lawrence Stone, the English historian, has termed "the old country ways" entailed giant kitchens and hordes of servants, thus enabling the nobility to keep "open house" to all comers. Of course rank prevailed: to eat "humble pie" was to eat meat at the lower end of the table. In the late fourteenth and early fifteenth century, as many as seven hundred household servants were required at the English court; the great lords might make do with only two or three hundred. This was a world in which the traffic in archaic forms and rituals was brisk: pageantry, pomp, hospitality, pensions, and gifts were structural features of this society, and they were necessary for inspiring loyalty and good will. Even menial service was not considered dishonorable, and gregariousness was highly prized. In religious houses too the aristocratic style of hospitality and gaudy display, with armies of servants and retainers, was in vogue.[7]

The churchman Robert of Grosseteste's rules for the management of his own household were translated into French by him for the use of the countess of Lincoln (ca. 1240). The author provided an ethical base for the noble style of life and customs in the Hall. The ideal behavior was to set forth great quantities of food displaying generous hospitality: leftovers were to be so abundant that enough could be distributed for alms. To eat before all the people was an act of courtesy, and to recycle food was to pay tribute to the exigencies of the moral economy of medieval society. Surviving manuscripts indicate that Grosseteste's rules were widely circulated during the next two generations. The image of Chaucer's Franklin, who, unless ill or fatigued, made a particular effort to eat in the dininghall because it was certain he would gain much benefit and honor by this public appearance, follows the line already etched by Grosseteste. Dinners and suppers outside the Hall, in secret places and chambers, brought no honor to lord or lady. In a later day, when these customs were not so securely championed, those who divided the organization of space in their great houses, separating the public from the private, were designated as "keeping secret house." The poet and moralist William Langland (Piers Plowman) regarded the abandonment of the Hall in favor of the pursuit of private luxury as a sure sign of the decline of society— largess was neighbor to caritas. The public character of society was ratified by a plethora of rules encouraging rollicking good fellowship, communal feasting, and the exchange of pledges and gifts. This style of life, so antithetical to private selfishness, spoke against waste and concealment in favor of a redistributive economy.[8]

The durability, and even systematization, of numerous archaic rituals are confirmed in the massive letter collections of the fifteenth and early sixteenth centuries. Chronicles were replete with exhaustive descriptions of festivals and tournaments. The writings themselves were richly illuminated with artis-

tic representation enclosed within the forms of social life. When Froissart
brought his chronicle to Richard II,

> the king asked to see the book which I had brought and I took it to his
> chamber, for I had it ready with me, and laid it on his bed. He opened it and
> looked inside and it pleased him greatly. Well it might, for it was illumi-
> nated, nicely written and illustrated with a cover of crimson and velvet and
> with ten studs of silvergilt and golden roses in the middle and two large
> gilded clasps richly worked at their centers with rose-trees.

The priest Froissart went from princely court to princely court aiming to
please noble patrons with the elegant social tone of his prose and poetry. The
poet, as minstrel and professional entertainer, committed his art to an external moral purpose. His work was ritually stylized, and for it he might receive
a pension or an ecclesiastical sinecure. This was the happy fate of the poet
and renowned composer Guillaume Machaut.[9]

The late development of prose and high evaluation of poetry, as well as
the petitionary form of much of the verse, have been considered by literary
scholars as essential features of an archaic culture. Archaic values, as expressed in that literature and art, have also been judged as demanding and
narrow. Even such an advanced poet as Chaucer was to leave numerous
poems unfinished, giving them a mocking and jocular ending. If we include
the *Retraction,* the case becomes stronger. So ruthless and conventional are
their piety that they "serve to make Chaucer's peace with the world rather
than his poem." Morality was systematized into a critique of the estates or
orders of medieval society. Moral judgments were stern; rank and responsibility could never be divorced. Ethical difficulties pressed upon those
writers exploring a middling ground between perfect courtesy and churlish
manners. Ideals were too strict for a man of the world, yet Middle English
literature offered few alternatives. Pride, pomp, and self-display were part of
the repertoire of aristocratic status, and the power essential for maintaining
that network of structures undergirding everyday life. Chivalric education
nurtured lofty expectations concerning the privileges of rank and power.[10]

The finest writers in the north of Europe were aware of the conflicting
grounds on which moral evaluations were made. Against *surquedrie*—that
high pride so often inveighed against these writers—was recommended the
spiritual tonic of humility and self-abasement. This conflict reached beyond
the realm of literature into the lives of the English aristocracy of the fourteenth and fifteenth centuries. Other conflicts abounded in this literature, as
we find presentations of a pragmatic, unheroic version of life a counter to the
decline of chivalric idealism. At this time, also, poets of the caliber of
Chaucer, Gower, and Langland were consciously cultivating a more ambiguous view. The best of the literature demonstrated that a nobleman was "a
man for all of that," and the need for charity and compassion was a social

imperative of the highest order. Reason and appetite must not be left in stark confrontation. The sentiments of honor and chivalry must provide the mean uniting them, thereby integrating the civilized man. Yet modern-day critics of fifteenth-century English literature have observed that subscribing to the chivalric virtue of courtesy, in the sense of treating kindly those who are weak and defenseless (an idea prominent in earlier romance works), underwent decline. These same critics suggest that, beginning in the latter part of the fourteenth century, English literature (particularly that of the alliterative tradition) was characterized by a radical disenchantment with "virtually every institution invented by man." In light of the French tradition, two impulses were informing English literature: one toward a functional use of the courtly convention and the other toward a realism that suggests comic disenchantment.[11]

In England we have a vital tradition of political and social satire. To be taken in by the glamor of society was, in the opinion of leading English writers, to suffer that devastating affliction, perhaps best described as an acute form of spiritual myopia. Certainly, readers of the *Canterbury Tales* were made aware that just such an affliction had been visited upon the fictional "I" of the poet, who was taken in by the high status, sophistication, and elegant manners of his betters. In the *Tales,* Chaucer presents a vision of a social world imposed on a moral universe: the Pilgrim cannot perceive what indeed the dazzling, attractive externals of life represent. English literature of the period was intent upon inducing readers to reject the proud and arrogant style of life of an archaic society. One thinks of Long Will in *Piers Plowman* explicitly seeking after the Good but entirely unable to evaluate correctly what it is he sees. Mankind, the protagonist of the *Pearl*, whose heart is fixed on a transient good that has been lost but who, for the most natural of reasons, confuses earthly with spiritual values. One thinks of Gower's *Confessio Amantis* and the old man searching for an impossible earthly love, which seems to him the only good.[12]

One also observes the painting of Northern Europe and the International Style celebrating an aristocratic civilization lent coherence by enchantment, display, and the bounteous reservoirs of emotional credit. Even one of the great pioneers of naturalism in the North, the Master of the Hours of the Maréchal of Boucicaut, could not be a naturalist in principle. The reality of nature and of quotidian life was, in his way of thinking, but one aspect of a world, the other sphere of which was dominated by the esthetic and social habits of an aristocracy requiring—even demanding—the utmost in artificial stylization. In literature the moralist defined most austerely what ought to be, yet his fictional representation served to ratify the pride, largess, and magic of archaic ceremonies and rituals serving to order society. Gower, Chaucer, Langland, the political moralists, and the anonymous author of the alliterative *Morte Arthure,* believed that the chaos man sees all about him was in fact created by man himself. Modern historians of late medieval England portray a society given structure through lineage, patronage, affinities, liveries, maintenance, retinues, castle armories, private armies, and clientage. Only very gradually did the balance turn in the late sixteenth century against this retaining system, and only then do we find something approximating a civil society coming into being. Before that, archaic culture was both the ground for durable social relations and a field for harsh criticism. This should alert us to certain differences between Tuscany and the north of Europe. Also, it should make us more sensitive to those conditions favorable to the reception of the ideas of the Continental Renaissance. Circumstances for the reception of ideas from classicial rhetoric, humanistic education, civil conduct, domestic architecture, political theory, and the new literary and art criticism were rendered increasingly propitious as a result of the gradual displacement of an archaic social structure by a civil society. Ideals of heroic virtue were scaled down and those of chivalry were metamorphosed into paradigms of courtliness and decorum. The proper finalities of the *vita civile* worked to domesticate a warrior caste.[13]

2

Clearly, the term *archaic* must be amended and its meaning deepened if we are to appreciate the transformation to a civil society and to recognize the grounds for borrowing from Italy. We have already noted how delight in the splendor of the world was countered by a pious impulse to repudiate it. The strength of asceticism and its disclaimers about the vanity of all temporal things was itself enhanced by the magnetic force of an extravagance and display structurally essential for ordering society. Historians of late medieval, Northern European cultural vocabularies—from political theory to tomb sculpture, novels, and poetry—have called attention to the radical disjunction between temporal claims of honor, authority, and the insignia of office on the one hand, and the radical insufficiency of the individual in the sight of God on the other. When polarities were overcome, conceptions of eternal bliss could be coupled with unabashed praise of voluptuousness. Freedom between intimacy and the world was often the privilege of mystics.

Let me suggest that what was quintessential for the emergence of a civil society was a quality best described by the word *patience*. A borderland between the pleasure principle and its antithesis, the reality principle, had to be colonized before nature and nurture, youth and old age, passion and a sense of measure, pleasure and pain, conviviality and solitude, avarice and charity, and love and death would not be placed in stark confrontation. This vocabulary was coined under great stress over three centuries in the south of Europe as archaic forms receded ever so gradually. Awe at the spectacle of power or fame or beauty—each doomed to destruction—was more likely now to lead to a comment on greatness rather than on death. The literary consequence was a fascination with the strength that was frail, the fame that was fleeting, and the beauty that was dust. A sense of temporality inspired men to be aware of their true nature, with the brevity of human life occasioning lament rather than a condemnation of it. A reluctance to rush to judgment, with the ability to endure opposition between elementary instincts and canonical moral imperatives, was the mark of advanced literature. Ethical problems were not certain to be conceived in terms of the grander conflicts of individuals with fortune or fate. The autobiographical impulse was less beholden to the penitential and confessional for stimulus. The new sentiment at work found more spiritual balance in introspection. The record of selfhood was more candid, admitting that the quest for success was to be valued. Through apprenticeship and years of professionalization, one could legitimate the self and even consecrate success. Portraits came to include the appurtenances of professionalism, with the man of affairs, the banker, the goldsmith surrounded by the tools of his trade. Even the humanist was depicted in the privacy of his study fortified with his books and manuscripts. Family pride, with its tableau of intimacy, was recorded in the new painting conveying the clear message of the success of the Tuscan household.[14]

3

Giovanni di Bologna served on the staff of the Archbishop Pechams from 1279 as notary and was to write:

> Italians, like cautious men, want to have a public instrument for practically every contract they enter into, but the English are just the opposite and an instrument is rarely asked for unless it is essential.

One is not obliged to take Giovanni's statement as an exhaustive description of thirteenth-century English record-keeping to be impressed by his forthright reaction as to differences between England and Italy in this regard. The word *fet* in Anglo-Norman or *factum* in Latin came to mean title-deed or charter only in the late thirteenth century. It was only at this late date that a deed was no longer considered as the physical act of conveyance symbolized by a piece of earth from the land and "livery of seisin." The sealed document made by the donor obtained public faith and credit more than a century after it had carried the day in the courts of Italy. Even then, anyone possessing a seal was considered competent by the English court to authenticate his own written act. In twelfth-century Italy, notarial authentication was the accepted form in communal courts. The dignity of the notary and the *publica fides* accorded his writings made him a public person indispensable for transactions in business and commercial life. In England the new and essentially literate procedures still seemed rather suspicious and alien. Elements of preliterate legal practice were retained to a much greater extent than in Tuscany. An English legal treatise, dating from the first half of the thirteenth century, contained this admonition:

a gift is not valid unless livery follows; for the thing given is transferred neither by homage, nor by the drawing up of charters and instruments, even though they be recited in public. . . . If livery is to be made of a house by itself, or of a messuage for an estate, it ought to be made by the door and its hasp or ring, by which it is understood that the donee possesses the whole of its boundaries.[15]

Giovanni di Bologna's assessment of the difference in status of the notarized document in communal Italy as contrasted with thirteenth-century England is not inconsistent with the results of modern-day research into literacy, record-keeping, and contractual relations in these two regions of Europe. One could, with considerable justification, argue that relations tended to be contractual in the South, whereas in the North they were more likely to be predicated on hierarchy. The requirement of written titles to land established in *quo warranto* cases was suppressed in the 1290s. Virtually every magnate holder of property did so according to custom and insofar as "the memory of the eldest inhabitant runneth not to the contrary." The king's government was compelled to recognize as legitimate tenure that which was held "time out of mind." When making comparisons, however, many cautionary words must be voiced: the differences between the regions were often the result of subtle shifts stemming from slight variations in the mix of the society and economy. Anyone who has studied the English land market in the thirteenth century or the London merchant in the fourteenth will appreciate how complex this mix was across the Channel. Yet one must bear in mind that the influence and power of leading London merchants seldom ran outside the walls of the town. Only a single family of merchant origin, the de la Poles of Hull, gained entry into the aristocracy. Furthermore, those English merchants succeeding in trade soon left the town to join the country gentry. Of course England was predominantly rural (perhaps 90 percent), whereas Tuscany was the most highly urbanized area in all of Europe. In 1500, London was the only town in all of England to have a population equal to that of a major Italian city—60,000 or so. The second city in the kingdom had only 12,000 inhabitants and would not have rated as an important urban center in north or central Italy. Furthermore, it would be simplistic to make comparisons based on class or even upon rural/urban dichotomies. Certainly, such contrasts have a general validity, but they obscure the contradictions and complexities of society in the North and South. By following the more obvious path, we would obscure rather than illuminate the more subtle cultural distinctions. If we examine closely the culture of Tuscany—that most precocious of all regions in fourteenth- and fifteenth-century Europe— we find it differing in degree but not in kind from that of England. Moreover, change was gradual and contradiction persisted. Perhaps this point can be clarified if we look more closely at the evidence for Tuscany. In comparing Northern and Southern Europe, we recognize that differences in value were relative, not absolute. Change can only be appreciated if we are aware of the persistence, force, and durability of tradition.[16]

4

Unique as a source for the Tuscan experience are the many family diaries, memorials and *ricordanze* surviving from the late thirteenth century. Perhaps better than any other written record, these *ricordi* illuminate the ambiguities and tensions of the Tuscan cultural mix. By examining the contraditions and shading of attitudes and values, we can make certain distinctions between the cultural idiom and grammar of Italy and that of the north of Europe. Comparable evidence for England does not appear until the late sixteenth and early seventeenth centuries, and the timing is of significance. Only then, in Elizabethan London, do we have a robust literature projecting similar sets of conflicts as those set forth in the personal memoranda and vernacular books of advice composed by the Florentines. Already, among the earliest of these Italian *ricordanze,* we observe two contrasting impulses at work: at the one pole the espousal of the values of caution (even mistrust), self-control, moderation, and the husbanding of wealth and emotion, while at the other we note the persistence of the attraction toward the blood-feud and vendetta, the force of wider clan loyalties, the lure of conspicuous consumption, and appeal of conviviality. At one boundary we have the advocacy of that line of conduct predicated upon reserve and suspicion, leading in its most radical form to a sense of alienation; at the other, the espousal of the archaic code which, in its most extreme form, led to hospitality, generosity, casual friendliness, and violence. The former favored privatization with a lower level of emotional interaction with one's fellows, whereas the latter called for the formation of expensive networks based on emotional display and material extravagance. No clear victory was achieved by either value system, and, in fact, it was a result of tensions between the two that change came about. But change there was, and its course led to a modification of archaic values with a tilt toward civil society.[17]

Indeed, the drama of Florentine vernacular writings, from the novella to diary, drew inspiration from the contest between moral and social norms grounded in privacy and reserve over and against an etiquette more generous, if not profligate. The anthropologist Pierre Bourdieu has analyzed the ethic of liberality characteristic of an archaic society in which affection, obligation, and fear were generated by the liberal exchange of goods—both material and psychological. The exchange of gifts, challenges, words, and affection resulted in the never ending transformation of energy into honorific ritual and symbol. Bourdieu characterizes this exacting round of activity as "an endless reconversion of economic capital into symbolic capital." The world of sentiment was joined to the world of goods, with service and courtesy constituting the symbolic capital. Against a semipublic lifestyle of an archaic world stood norms less liberal and more reserved: in the end these were to exert their influence; a line of conduct more patient and distrustful would be idealized. Likewise, a range of emotions more sublimated and privatized would be legitimated. At the same time the values of courtesy, generosity, and honor were not to be displaced but transvalued. Demands on wealth and generosity were sanctioned by older social values, but often they made the fulfillment of new social ambitions impossible. Hard bought by rough experience, and not atypical, was the counsel of Giovanni di Pagolo Morelli, of about 1400, to his progeny, entered in his *Ricordi:*

> Do not ever trust anyone; be clear in things and still more with a relative or friend than with outsiders, but [deal this way] with all, use notarial forms, with free obligations to a guild, do not trust what is written in books, except by third parties.[18]

If one reviews the Tuscan diaries and family books from the late thirteenth century to the Quattrocento *Della Famiglia* of Leon Battista Alberti, one can observe the persistence of the lure of an archaic world of courtesy preoccupied with those modes of behavior justly termed *onorevole.* This world created a network of social and psychic obligations conferring upon its denizens the reward of high prestige and social credit. Against this were voiced the equally persistent anxieties and reservations subverting this demanding code. The single most common fear was that the patrimony of the family would be consumed in an extravagant lifestyle with its numerous social obligations. The Florentine merchant Giovanni da Uzzano spoke for many when condemning the prodigal son: "And in effect he consumed a greater part of his patrimony that his father left to him in *cortesia.*" In the *Cronica domestica* of the lawyer and eminent political figure of the mid-decades of the Trecento, Donato Velluti, we observe the stigmatization of a cousin who wore himself out playing the "nobleman," of a wastrel brother, and of another kinsman who was a good troubadour, sonneteer, as well as excellent player on the lute. Another relative was a good horseman, an equerry, expert in everything save business affairs. Finally, Velluti's comments on his brother, Filippo, were entirely disapproving: the prodigal son, on his return from Sicily, wore "grand dress" and rode a horse with extravagant caparison. This flaunting of chivalric style may have been suitable in another realm, but not in the Florentine republic.[19]

Florentine *ricordanze* were insistent in their call for moderation and the withdrawal of emotion, energy, and wealth from archaic commitments to a broader community. Such a shift did not disvalue the claims of honor, but suspicion and caution were intensified against those rituals of courtesy, as well as emotional and material extravagance. In the domain of actions discussed in these family memorials and handbooks the call was for greater discrimination. If one follows the unfolding of the literary impulse from the Trecento's Paolo di Messer Pace da Certaldo to Leon Battista Alberti in the

Quattrocento, one observes a leaning toward new modes of civility away from archaic forms and codes. The claims of kinship and hospitality were narrowed and the demands of ancient solidarities lessened. At first the *ricordi* present in bald and unequivocal form archaic rules for politics and the governance of family life. Attribution to women of the role of peacemaker recalls the Germanic epic with the figure of the female as "peace weaver" mitigating hostilities between warring clans. Early domestic chronicles evoke shades of the ancient tribal epic. Relations between fathers and sons could be exceedingly harsh, and limited sentiments were invested in daughters or wives. Paolo di Messer Pace da Certaldo, in his *Libro di buoni costumi,* advised his progeny thusly:

> The wife is a vacuous thing and easily influenced; she confronts great risks when she is separated from her husband. Therefore, keep women at home, keep them as near to yourself as possible, and return home frequently to keep an eye on your affairs and hold them in fear and trembling. Make certain that they always have work to attend to in the house and never permit them to be idle.[20]

Daughters were not to be taught to read, unless they were to become nuns, and wives were often perceived as untrustworthy partners who, upon the husband's death, would be certain to take their wealth back to their natal household. Between fathers and sons one could be sure of obedience only as long as the former controlled the patrimony: once it was turned over to the son, the friend became an enemy wishing his father dead. Most striking is the absence of guilt for the pursuit of feuds and vendettas in the early *ricordanze.* In books of private memorials the word "quietanza" was entered to indicate the payment of a debt in coin or blood. Similarly, the operation of penal solidarity and collective liability for debts and crimes were recorded in a matter-of-fact way in the memoirs. By the time of Alberti, this commitment to archaic forms and codes had softened and would become the stuff of elegy and nostalgia. Emotion and affection were less often represented as finding expression in wider loyalties and more likely to be seen in terms of their domestic and private aspects. Noteworthy is the fact that it was precisely at this time that family members most prone to engage in extravagant forms of behavior, once calculated to bring honor to the clan, were now regarded as a threat to the social standing and patrimony of the lineage.[21]

The passing of this liberal style of life, with its prizing of largess and courtesy, was to become the subject of literary drama. The tale of Federigo degli Alberighi is one of the wittiest and most tender in Boccaccio's *Decameron.* This gallant knight, obeying the precepts of aristocratic and courtly behavior, follows the gaudy path of splendid excess bringing himself to ruin. His romantic career terminates upon the making of a most fortunate marriage. With sympathetic irony, Boccaccio concludes the novella by affirming that at least Federigo had become a "good household manager." Such was the hard-won wisdom of the knight, who relinquished grandiose dreams to accept the humble role of *buon massio* and law-abiding rate-payer. This was a literary moment in which the narrative art made a lasting conquest. Urbanity and civility brought authorial tact. The road to the art of Ariosto and La Fontaine was paved with literary poise, and the question of whether the author was mocking or sympathetic to his chivalric protagonist should not even be asked.[22]

Beyond the boundaries of the more familiar admonitions to avoid ostentation and the routine warnings to shun knightly excess, costly obligation, and extended courtesies were new territories with new versions of urbane comportment. A civility less devoted to publicity and self-advertisement favored elegance and refinement more privatized and less communal. Tastes were reflected in more domestic forms so that the minor arts decorated the interior space of the palaces of the well-to-do. Models of new lifestyles were celebrated which had little in common with traditional household rituals of sociability and commensality. The portrait of the fastidious Florentine humanist Niccolò Niccoli, drawn by the fifteenth-century bookseller Vespasiano da Bisticci, is classic:

> He had a housekeeper to provide for his wants, and was one of the most particular of men in his diet as in all else, and was accustomed to have his meals served to him in beautiful old dishes; his table would be covered with vases of porcelain, and he drank from a cup of crystal or of some other fine stone. It was a pleasure to see him at table, old as he was. All the linen that he used was of the whitest. Some may be astonished to hear that he possessed a vast number of vessels, and to these may be answered that, in his day, things of this sort were not so highly prized as now; but Nicolao, being known all over the world, those who wished to please him would send him either marble statues, or antique vases, or sculpture, or marble inscriptions, or pictures by distinguished masters, or tables in mosaic. He had a fine map of the world on which all places were given, and also illustrations of Italy and Spain. There was no house in Florence better decorated than his or better furnished with beautiful things.

With patrician investment in private space and embellishment, advanced tastes were less public. The tax law of 1427 (the *catasto*) exempted the dwelling place and furnishings, thereby favoring domestic cultural and sumptuary expenditure.[23]

The loyalty of well-to-do Tuscans became increasingly focused inward on the conjugal core and outward on the territorial state, rather than on the bloodline and marriage. State intervention in the life of the family intensified when the republic guaranteed the payment of dowries (*Monte delle Doti*, 1434) to purchasers of this form of state assurance. Well-to-do investors stood in a new relationship to public authority. Intervention in the form of political remedies was well in evidence in the legislative enactments of the Florentine communal councils. Throughout the fourteenth century, petitions were regularly received and approved permitting individuals to be released from responsibility for the actions of kinsmen deemed in these times too violent but, which in an earlier age would have been judged entirely honorable. The signory acted in turn both to confer a type of supermagnate status on the most obstreperous of the nobles, thereby disfranchising them, and to bestow full citizenship with political rights (*popolano* status) on the more law-abiding lineages. The Ordinances of Justice (1293–95), the basic Florentine law, enforced principles of collective liability with exceptional vigor, so that the disadvantages of ancient solidarities competed with the benefits of mutuality. Magnate status, defined by shared resources and systematized organization of family life as a tight lineage, was in decline. The Tuscan experience, with fraternal solidarity, was generally short-lived: brothers remaining under a common roof for any long period of time was the exception, not the rule. Traditional private alliances and peace pacts were not so strategically significant in a republic where legal arrangements were more likely to hold. Family solidarity exacted a price, and this, along with demographic pressures, frequently operated to advantage partable inheritance over maintenance of joint property. Finally, the force of advanced ethical thinking was very much against the conception of joint or blood liability. The humanist Coluccio Salutati regarded these archaic codes as entirely reprehensible.[24]

5

When the art historian Erwin Panofsky defined the Renaissance as having a sense of disjunction or separation from the past, he was, in my opinion, focusing too exclusively upon a narrow historical consciousness. That Petrarch and certain of his contemporaries regarded the Middle Ages as being without luster, if not light, and that they saw themselves as distanced from classical and Christian antiquity is not at dispute here. What, in my view, should be featured is a broader sense of criticism and rejection commencing roughly with the generation of Giotto, Petrarch, and Boccaccio. The critique, even displacement of elements of an archaic culture, was in evidence at that time, and, although it did not advance consistently on all fronts, it was initiated, however unsteadily. Over the next century and a half the challenge mounted and awareness intensified as writers and artists distanced themselves from the attraction of ancient rituals, customs, and images. The humanist and architect Leon Battista Alberti was fascinated by the variety of customs and religious beliefs of the ancient peoples. Burial practices were transformed over time, as were the rituals. Deep were his reservations concerning particular rites and prayers of antiquity, which he regarded as "polluting the skies." Especially scornful was he of the extravagant funereal customs. The social utility of the tomb and the restrained comportment of the living were, in his view, the true marks of decorum and civility. You will remember that two generations before this Petrarch had denounced the extravagant ceremonies of burial and mourning with their lamentation and keening. These barbaric customs were entirely contrary to civility and the good order of the city. Petrarch exhorted the ruler to act decisively to curtail funereal excess. Buttressing this conception of the requirements for civil life was a definition of lay piety divorced from a world of archaic rites and social obligations.[25]

Indeed, it would be possible to cite examples of descriptions of mourning and burial practices over subsequent centuries demonstrating a growing sense of distancing from ancient and archaic rituals. One calls to mind the fifteenth-century account by the Florentine traveler Cristoforo Buondelmonte and the informative descriptions of a series of his humanistically minded contemporaries. In most instances it is clear that writers dealing with archaic rituals were well aware that even in their day such practices persisted in remote rural regions. Giglio Gregorio Giraldi wrote: "It was truly the custom among women of the ancient world to ululate and to tear their hair and cheeks and, which, at the very moment I write, still persists in Sabina and throughout all of Latium." The distancing from mourning practices, as well as the rituals of chivalry and tournaments, already evident in the literature of Petrarch's generation, was, as I have suggested, part of an objectification or, if you will, historicization of emotional and ritual practices once at the structural base of an archaic society. This disjunction was the conscious registering of the tilt in Italian society toward the displacement of archaic and communal forms. It is essential to recognize that this displacement was in no sense radical, involving as it did a gradual and, in certain instances, incomplete modification of a mix between those values and practices essential to an archaic culture over and against forms more pertinent to a civil society. In fact, if a single rubric obtained for describing this transformation, it might be from archaism to civility.[26]

We have already noted Francesco Barbaro's proem to his *On Wifely Duties,* in which he recapitulated ancient customs—long out of date—pertaining to wedding gifts. Barbaro's generation and that of his Florentine host to which the work had been dedicated (Lorenzo de' Medici, 1415) had forgotten rituals of gift exchange practiced only a few generations back. In those days wedding gifts were rendered as tokens of obligation in the hope that, by sowing these gifts, one would fertilize the field of benevolence so that, like the cultivators of old described by the father of history, Herodotus, in return they would reap a harvest two or three-hundredfold. By the early sixteenth century, humanists were reflecting systematically on rituals of alliance and social solidarity. Around 1500 the Roman humanist Marco Antonio Altieri composed a dialogue entitled *Li nuptiali.* His intent was to instruct the Roman aristocracy on ancient marriage customs. With this in mind, he reviewed the Roman and Lombard heritage, thus laying the foundation for an "anthropology of alliance." His interest was both historical and practical, for he saw great value in ancient wedding customs and sought to persuade his contemporaries to abandon their moneygrubbing in favor of old-fashioned forms of social exchange. Altieri perceived the virtues of popular rites and festivities, especially those connected with nuptials. To reconcile civil order and religious order, he endeavored to decipher the ritual heritage. Using the standard of classical antiquity, he worked toward the creation of an ethnology of marriage. With the early sixteenth century, the historical perspective of literati toward custom and ritual surrounding birth, marriage, and death had moved well beyond the antiquarian. In the case of Altieri, knowledge gained from a study of past customs was of civic and political utility for the reformation of the dissolute Roman patriciate of his day. The rites of society were recognized as essential for securing social ties and, as such, were reckoned as critical marks of past civilizations. The civic religion of pagan times was understood as contributing mightily to the health and longevity of that most splendid of all governments—ancient Rome. Archaic customs and ceremonies were no longer regarded as quintessential threats to the effectiveness of civil government and society. Instead they were perceived as reinforcing ties between the individual and the state. Religion might enhance the power of the ruler, and the question as to whether religion emanated from a natural human need or was the cold-blooded projection of authority was vigorously debated. This scandalous doctrine, derived from the *De rerum natura* of the Roman philosophical poet Lucretius, was a significant sign of the extent to which humanistic views on politics and religion were infiltrated by ethnographic preoccupation.[27]

Petrarch's letters reveal him in the act of discovering and publicizing the startling fact that antiquity was different from his own world, and his propaganda influenced profoundly his literary contemporaries. He took the step that an archaic society must make in order to reach a self-consciousness about itself—maturity. Not only did he conduct a concerted critique of archaic ideals of culture, calling them into question, but he vividly and forcefully recognized the possibility of a cultural alternative. With abundant confidence he was to pose the following rhetorical question: "In what book do we read that Cicero and Scipio were skilled at the joust?" We can observe how ubiquitous the notion of style became from this sentence, which Poggio Bracciolini wrote in a letter to Guarino in 1416: "What is there that could be more delightful, more pleasant and more agreeable to youth and to the rest of the learned world than the knowledge of those things whose acquisition makes us seem learned and what seems more important, stylistically polished?" To achieve such refinement and polish one must be aware of the distance between urbanity and a rude, archaic world. The humor of Poggio's *Facezie* was often grounded in just such distinctions: in one of his literary anecdotes, he describes a visit made by a group of peasants to an artist of Arezzo from whom they intended to order a crucifix for their church. When the artist saw these "zotici ed ignoranti" men, he had to suppress laughter and, when hearing that they wanted a crucifix, he asked if the Christ should be living or dead? They conferred among themselves for a long time, deciding, finally, that they preferred a living Christ: "If He didn't please their fellow countrymen, they would have it killed immediately." The sharpening of social boundaries between city dwellers and peasants, between an urban literary elite and the unlettered, occurred at a moment when awareness that religion as a force for social cohesion was magnified. Festivals and folk spectacles lost much of their popular and derisory character. The spontaneous and disruptive impulse of the carnival was domesticated. Harsh opposition between the "true religion" of Christianity and pagan worship was muted. An interest in classical precedent led to learned quotation and allegory. The display of technology and scientific skill in mounting public entertainments enhanced the viewer's confidence that control could be exercised over the social and natural worlds. Technical mastery rendered critical commentary of folkways and festivals ever more marginal. The problem of magic and witchcraft was confronted historically for the first time in the early sixteenth century by Gian Francesco Pico and others. Soon folkways and customs were to receive the benefit of codification as they were trivialized and elevated into literature.[28]

Petrarch, in his dialogue *Physic against Fortune,* has Ratio (Reason) condemn the effect on us of works of art in these ringing words: "It is the preciousness, as I suppose, and not the art that pleases you." Indeed, the grounds for movement away from an archaic culture were being advanced by successive generations of commentators on the arts, from Petrarch through Alberti. The International Style was enormously popular in Florence; yet contracts with painters were less eloquent about the use of gold and ultramarine. By the fifteenth century the dichotomy between the quality of materials and quality of artistic skill was a persistent motif in Florentine dialogues on painting and sculpture. This theme held its literary ground, whether discussions centered on ascetic denigration or public enjoyment in the texts. The need to flatter the eye with marvelously chaste surfaces and costly gilding, which would glorify the materiality of the object, was no longer so commanding and absolute an esthetic imperative. Distanced from archaic conventions, the disjunction between naturalistic tendencies and ritualized presentation became a new domain to be investigated programmatically. In this time of transition it was possible for literati and artists to present the claims of the new and the old with patience and equanimity. Giotto portrayed the miraculous as dramatic and tension-filled, yet situated it in a natural context, as if the viewer were a spectator.

One thinks, for example, of Simone Martini who projected a vision of grace and waning chivalry set in a shifting borderland between the secular and spiritual worlds. Frequently there lurked beneath the surface of the new art compositional and iconographic relationships to time-honored motifs: one thinks of Donatello's *Judith and Holofernes* and its debt to the psycho-machia tradition. Brunetto Latini, Dante's dishonored mentor, had a deep literary appreciation for the fate of a society suspended between elegant courtly ideals and a burgher ethic of morality. This sensibility was of course much enhanced in the *Decameron* as Boccaccio achieved a tactful diction when recording the magnanimity and generosity of a nobility over and against the prudential values of the citizen world. Moreover, the author registered an ironic distance from the archaic world of folk culture when tolerantly chronicling ancient rural ways. Not surprisingly, then, Boccaccio's ideas of culture and poetic inspiration carried both traditional and novel connotation. At the very center of his literary consciousness was the belief that the poet owed as much to the direct inspiration of God as to human talents. Petrarch was perhaps even more attentive to the gift of divine grace. Further, both he and Coluccio Salutati, while willing to make a specific determination and legitimation of the work of an artifact as an artistic creation, were still ambiguous concerning the moral and spiritual appropri-ateness (the vanity) of taking pleasure in art.[29]

6

Petrarch acknowledged, albeit reluctantly, the power of chivalric literature to shape the imagination of his contemporaries. He noted in the *Trionfi d'Amore,* with some pathos: "Here are those who fill the pages with dreams." Like several of his literary contemporaries, Petrarch denounced tournaments as "dangerous folly," understanding well that such charac-terizations would gain the assent of the very few. Historians of fourteenth-and fifteenth-century Italy have ignored the persistence and durability of ancient social customs and economic practices in the quest for the fools gold of modernity and protocapitalism. But even in such an advanced urban center as Florence, we recognize that key terms like *mundium* and *launechild* were to disappear from notarial formularies only after several centuries, and practices of *ordalia* and *faida* lost their hold only gradually. In fact, Germanic ways, though in decline, still retained much of their symbolic character: one thinks immediately of the bridesgift, the legitimacy of vendetta, the payment of composition by nobles for crimes, and certain leading rituals associated with knighthood. Only after repeated state intervention were blood-feuds limited to the principals in a quarrel—this only in the early fifteenth century. Trial by combat, mentioned in communal statutes of the thirteenth century, disappeared only with glacial speed. Homicide was regarded as a personal crime for which, upon occasion, restitution might be made. Lombard mar-riage rituals were still followed by nobles in the distant reaches of the Florentine territory at the end of the thirteenth century. Only after constant communal objection and legislation was the right to bear offensive weapons circumscribed. Comparable legislative campaigns were launched against costly betrothal gifts and excessive displays of wealth or hospitality. The sumptuary laws were only moderately successful as the many forms of conspicuous consumption, so essential for legitimating archaic styles of life and ratifying social obligations, proved robust and resistant to communal law. Finally, it should be noted that standard accounts of Florentine economic history emphasizing the spirit of capitalism and the absolute centrality of big banking, are as misleading as they are unilluminating.[30]

Florentine tax law did not encourage capital investment, but, rather, the construction of sumptuous residences stocked with works of art, libraries, furniture, gaudy utensils, and the many products of the goldsmith's art. A reading of Florentine *ricordi* that suggests that riches evolved from thrift, not investment, is unexceptional. The ideal of economic self-sufficiency (autarchy) was fundamental for estate planners as well as villa builders. The Florentine *ricordi* continue to carry a cargo of proverbial wisdom directed against public expenditures and the "sudden gains" of private speculators. Never do these authors lose sight of the commanding figure of Dante the moralist—that resolute opponent of "legge nuova," "gente nuova," and "subiti guadagni."[31]

As a source of power, riches had to compete with knowledge, honor, nobility, reputation, friends, and even natural beauty. Poverty could indeed come from misfortune, but it was more likely to be caused by luxury, sloth, or folly. The emphasis on the modernity of Florentine banking and credit operations by such scholars as Raymond de Roover and Federigo Melis called attention to advanced Tuscan business techniques—particularly the vocabulary of accounting. But this technical progress failed to lead to a fully developed banking system. Individuals have been identified as bankers who were in fact speculators in money changing. Furthermore, the persistence of prohibitions against usury does not entirely explain the absence of evidence in the merchant account books for the exaction of interest. The very language of credit continued to bear the imprint of a system of exchange appropriately described as pertaining to a gift culture. One strategy for concealing interest on particular types of deposits involved the making of a gift by lender to borrower for the use of the latter's money. It was not always simple to distinguish between gifts and loans. The word for savings was gradually divested of its traditional connotation of hoarding, and ever so slowly came to mean active investment. Meanwhile, in the account books of city dwellers owning land in the countryside *(contado)*, relations betweeen the landlord *(oste)* and sharecroppers *(mezzadri)* as revealed in the Catasto of 1427 were a complex weave of obligations with debts tailing into gifts and favors.[32]

Only against the backdrop of archaic social practices, rituals, and exchange operations can we understand the character of a new and often fragile culture. Here is a sage observation of Adovardo in Alberti's *Della Famiglia:*

Our country will not tolerate from one of its citizens an overgreat success in the career of arms. This is wise, for it would endanger our ancient liberty if one in our republic, instead of gaining his will by winning the approval and love of the citizens, could by threat and force of arms go wherever his spirit carried him, wherever fortune seconded him, and wherever times and conditions allowed and beckoned him.[33]

The strength and appeal of Ambrogio Lorenzetti's panoramic fresco "Good and Bad Government," in the Town Hall of Siena, stems from the juxtaposition of a society pacified and in concord over and against the horrors of one in which pride runs roughshod and fear looms over all. It is not possible to explain the lure and attraction of new cultural views without devoting equal attention to the pull and force of countervailing sensibilities. Even the rather scientific and neutral topic of town planning received dramatic treatment. Leon Battista Alberti's *De re aedificatoria,* completed in 1450 and published in 1485, featured sharp differences of opinion among his contemporaries—principally Florentines—with an archaic conception of urban social organization pitted against newer notions:

There may perhaps be some who would prefer to have the habitations of the gentry separate by themselves, quite clear and free from all mixture with the meaner sort of people. Others are for having every district of the city laid out, that each part might be supplied at hand with everything it could have occasion for, and for this reason they are not against having the meanest trades in the neighborhood of the most honorable citizens.[34]

Any number of humanist treatises and dialogues would support the observation that arguments on both sides of a question were marshalled without giving any easy victory to the new over the old. This would obtain whether the issue involved definitions of nobility, the legitimacy of wealth, or the value of civic participation. Full intellectual measure was accorded the psychology of the speakers championing these divergent views. Alberti's *Della Famiglia* is a ready example, and in it we observe how effectively and artfully the author dramatizes conflicting values of speakers as they discourse on the pain and pleasures of the emotional life of the family man. All the anxieties a father suffers for his young offspring, so prone to disease and death, are catalogued against a listing of the joys. At the very center of the debate is a residue of thought and feeling not to be overcome by cold rationalism or well-informed pessimism or threadbare optimism. When Adovardo is confronted with the observation that it is folly to fear over the health of children, for whose sickness there is no remedy, his rejoinder is worth quoting:

Anyway, I do not want to argue with you or quarrel over fine points. I am satisfied that you consider unwise whoever continues to fear what he cannot cure. You should hardly judge me mad, however, for all that I frequently cannot help worrying about my children. If you do, you must consider all fathers utterly foolish, for you cannot find one who does not struggle mightily and is not filled with fear at the threat of losing those who are dearest to him. If you blame them for this, you condemn fatherhood itself.[35]

Archaic society breeds antithetical responses and values. Abnegation, withdrawal, and asceticism stand as stark counters against the extravagant investment of emotion and capital in the world of honor and reputation. To retain one's poise in the face of these conflicting claims is the mark of advanced literature and art. All the time, however, we must recognize how fragile was this construct. In Alberti we have nostalgia for the clan and the advantages of family solidarity balanced against his keen awareness of the indifference and cruelty of near-kinsmen. Trust in relatives and confidence in friendship were balanced against the terrible risks of standing surety or making loans. Indeed, Alberti provides the reader with a catalogue of excuses for refusing just such favors. Endorsing the public life, yet recognizing that it was full of pretense, vanity, and lies is a mark of humanistic rhetoric. Valuing profit and advantage does not foreclose the bald conclusion that "the minimum of enslavement, then, is to work for love and not for payment." Among advanced Florentine political thinkers such as Francesco Guicciardini, we are struck by the care and attention he lavished upon a world of intimate obligation. Not disdainful of communal wisdom, his *Ricordi,* like so many other Tuscan books of reflection, was mindful of material rewards, as well as of that currency of civil society: offices, good will, trust, and good counsel. Networks of benefits created social bonds, and these were sustained through family support and friends. From this world of personal initiative and interests came the proverbial wisdom of small-scale society with its common stock of assumptions. But having understood this, what course did Guicciardini offer his reader? The need for intellectual and emotional distancing was primary. Discretion, recognition that each situation is different; these insights never deteriorated into an easy didacticism, smug casuistry, nor did they lead to the stratagems of a blithe truism.[36]

7

Clearly, other terms must be added, and it would be simplistic to believe that a term such as *archaic* could be used to map the jagged landscape of a complex civilization. We have already noted the intellectual authority and moral force of asceticism, abnegation, and withdrawal. To retain one's literary poise while occupying ground between those polarities required enormous patience, as well as a recognition (often pained) of the limits of human understanding. Yet, with Italian literati, from Petrarch through to Alberti, we do have stunning examples of a literature able to retain a balance while colonizing that territory between those polarities. Similarly, we have the first fictional forays into that zone between the largess of a noble order and the parsimony of the burgher. The novella was an exercise in the patient exploration of the bravery and generosity of a warrior caste done without denigrating the dignity of law-abiding merchants. The humanist dialogue was also the beneficiary of a strong measure of patience; literati from Petrarch to Alberti granted ample recognition to the limits of human understanding, without falling victim to epistemological despair. The abiding question posing the sturdiest of intellectual dilemmas was also the source for creativity: Could secular culture be so positioned in relation to religious faith that it could retain authenticity without surrendering to otherworldliness or capitulating to a crude materialism?[37]

Radical conceptions of divine transcendence and God's inaccessibility worked to deny the possibility of any sure knowledge of God and His intention in creating the world or even of the world itself. Late medieval scholastic philosophy, particularly that practiced by the English Franciscan William of Ockham, placed great conceptual pressure on language. The idea of divine omnipotence was carried to its bitter end through routines of logical disputation, so that there were no reasons knowable to man that might explain why God actualized this universe rather than another. Ockham carried the radical dissociation between theology and metaphysics, and between divine and human knowledge, to their very limits. In Italy, instead, the foremost literati exploited the domain of dialogue and fiction, where the incompatible might be left unreconciled, unresolved, and even fruitful. Classical influences operated in the long run toward proportion, order, and harmonious unity in literature and the fine arts. By adhering to its canons, the true and the false would, as far as possible, achieve the delicate balance of a fictitious probabilism.[38]

We can realize something of the difference between the literary and artistic poise and patience of Northern and Southern Europe if we consider the reception of the works of Boccaccio and Petrarch. Surely it was not the Boccaccio of the novella or the classically minded defender of poetry who influenced the Northerner: rather, it was Boccaccio the moralist standing in the tradition of Boethius and Seneca. He was memorialized as the "doctor of patience in adversity." It was *De casibus virorum illustrium* and *De claris mulieribus,* with their obsession with the inconstancy of human fate, that galvanized intellectual interest—not the *Decameron.* "Messire Jehn Bocace" had a reputation as a type of *impresario* of the fickleness and malevolence of fortune among the writers of the North. The poet Georges Chastellain composed *Le Temple de Bocace,* fixing that name to the work of consolation for Queen Margaret after her escape from the terrible wars in England. What would be more consoling than a detailed review of the tragic destinies of men and women of those days?[39]

Judging from the number of Boccaccio manuscripts surviving from the fifteenth century (eighty-three for the Latin and over one hundred for Laurent de Premierfait's French translation), it was the Latin works, especially *De casibus,* that had an exceedingly large circulation in the North. The English poet John Lydgate, at the express command of Humphrey, duke of Gloucester, the most important bibliophile of fifteenth-century England, did a translation of *De casibus* based on a French amplification made by Laurent for the Duc de Berry. The French text converted Boccaccio's scorn of those *viris illustribus* who through avarice, idleness, and corruption caused virtue to decline and led the people astray. Boccaccio's contempt for the overmighty was replaced by servile admiration for the princes of this world. Laurent, who was a professional writer and translator at the court of Charles V, produced two versions of *De casibus* at the request of the Duc de Berry (1400 and 1409). Laurent converted Boccaccio's reflections on the intricate relationship between history and human passion into a handbook for nobles intent on learning historical lessons from the fall of princes. The second version was much expanded, the literary tactic of amplification almost completely obscuring Boccaccio's artistic devices. The Florentine's perspective on his characters was lost under that inflated literary impulse common to much of Northern European writing, which aimed for the encyclopedic. Finally, the Northern penchant for reducing complex moralizing into easy didacticism was here in full view. In *Troilus and Criseyde,* Chaucer transformed Boccaccio's flaming romance into a hard indictment of courtly love: a radiant beauty was debased and a valiant knight died, and all was for naught. Human frailty was such, and chance and change ruled over all, so that all one could do was forgive and forget. It was on these grounds that the poet refused at the last to condemn Criseyde.[40]

John Lydgate, in his turn, compressed the unwieldy French version of *De casibus,* removing passages offensive to the English and adding a long section in praise of his native country. It was the courtly side of Boccaccio that interested the best of the English poets such as Chaucer. It is likely that the first reference to Petrarch that Chaucer knew was in a letter from Philippe de Mézières to Richard II of England in which the French author referred to the tale of patient Griselda, later to be translated by Chaucer. Philippe regarded himself as Petrarch's "special ami" and described the tale as "escripte par le solempnel docteir et souverain poete, maistre Francois Petrac," based on "la cronique autentique." He had no knowledge of its derivation from the stories of the last day in Boccaccio's *Decameron.* (The French translation of the *Decameron* did not come to England until the sixteenth century. In any case, the French version was never able to replicate the generous moral atmosphere of the original, in which no string of adjectives could exhaust the ethical or esthetic meaning. It was not possible for the French translator to capture such a "mediate and indirect form of discourse," which worked to convey multiple systems of possible moral criteria.)[41]

The standard view of Petrarch taken by the Northerner was voiced by Jean de Montreuil, when he referred to the author of *De remediis* as a "most devout Catholic and very moral philosopher." Petrarch was, then, not the poet of the *canzoniere* or *Trionfi,* but a moral philosopher and a very Christian Cicero. The mystic Denis the Carthusian borrowed from Petrarch his poetic lamentation for the loss of the Holy Sepulchre. Literary efforts to follow the rhetorical tactics of the epistolary style of the Florentine chancellor Coluccio Salutati in official correspondence bore little fruit. Endeavors to introduce classical rhetoric into public documents, and even a zeal for classical refinement, were to a large extent a response to Petrarch's taunt that there were no poets and orators worthy of note outside Italy. A French movement of literary renewal of about 1400 had only trivial impact.[42]

It was the courtly Boccaccio upon whom poetic and scholarly interest was focused: it was the ascetic and moralistic Petrarch, rather than the humanist scholar, who was to engage the interest of fifteenth-century Northerners. *De remediis* and *Historia Greseldis* were the only two works of Petrarch to be translated into the vernacular in the later Middle Ages. The latter was of course a Latin rendition of the most didactic of Boccaccio's *Decameron* tales. From Petrarch's translation came Chaucer's *Clerk's Tale* of patient and saintly Griselda. *De remediis* was rendered as a collection of *sententiae* of stunning banality. Judging from surviving manuscripts, these two works, and the penitential psalms and *De vita solitaria,* enjoyed great popularity. (These were of course Petrarch's most ascetic writings.) No single piece of manuscript evidence exists to support the contention that Petrarch's Italian lyrics were circulated in the north of Europe before the last quarter of the fifteenth century. We have only Chaucer's lone translation of the Petrarcan sonnet "L'amor non è" inserted into his *Troilus and Criseyde.* Translations of the *Trionfi* began to appear in France in the 1470s. In England in the fifteenth century, poetry for the most part was intended as didactic rather than entertainment. The penchant of writers for social and religious commentary suited the intellectual mood of the times. The verse of John Lydgate, full of information and sage advice, was quite representative of the writing of the period. Lydgate's fifteenth-century readers knew and delighted in the "low Canterbury Tales." But within the prevailing canons of literary taste there was no concept whereby these tales could be treated as serious literature. Thus, because of their "low style," they went largely unmentioned. The prejudice for "high style"—the "golden aureate" language—prevailed. The poet Thomas Usk spoke of Chaucer as Love's Servant, "the noble philosophical poete in English." Lydgate regarded Chaucer, above all, as the poet of the sententious utterance and as "that noble Rethor that alle did excelle."[43]

8

A recent biography of Thomas More argues very effectively that his early writings are fundamental for understanding his personality. More is portrayed as oscillating between extremes: his English poems projected a near Manichean view of life, whereas his translations of classical texts (Lucian) gave him cues for responding to the world without despair. His earliest Latin epigrams show how tenuous and unstable was his world view and how quickly the pendulum could swing from hope to despair. His *Nine Pageants* was an imitation of Petrarch's *Trionfi,* and the discomforting ironies were invoked by More with a fierce originality. The visual images capture the violence without conveying any of Petrarch's sense of "beneficent purpose." Mutability denied men any chance of temporal happiness. More's translation of Giovanni Francesco's life of his uncle Pico della Mirandola *(Vita Pici)* demonstrated little interest in the intricacies of Pico's genealogy, the historical facts of his life, or the exact details of his erudition. More's involvement was with that conflicted figure torn between worldliness and spirituality. The juxtaposition of *eruditio* and *pietas* as irreconcilable was cautionary in charting the moral dangers besetting one aiming for success in the world of secular learning. One can certainly argue that More suffered inordinately from the deadly contest between the consolations of the spirit and pulls of the flesh. When King Henry VIII attacked the sacrament of marriage, More opposed him for the first time. Only this sacrament made "the flesh acceptable in the sight of God."[44]

If one pursues the theme of Petrarchan adaptation by English poets, one observes that contrasts and contradictions continued to be exaggerated. The first English poet to know and use Petrarch's verse was of course Thomas Wyatt, and he was unable to capture the emotional shading of the original. Tension between experience and the poetic convention absorbing it was acute. To compare Petrarch's sonnet "Io non fu' mai d'amar" with Wyatt's "Was I never yet of your love greved" is to contrast Petrarch's nuanced imagery and metaphysical spirituality with the Englishman's brutal and urgent literalness. Here are the two texts:

PETRARCA

Io non fu' mai d'amar voi lassato
   unqu'anco
Madonna, ne sarò mentre ch'io viva
Ma d'odiar me medesimo giunto a riva,
E del continuo lagricar so stanco;

E voglio anzi un sepolcro bello e bianco
Che il vostro nome a mio danno si scriva
In alcun marmo, ove di spirto priva
Sia la mia carne che pò star seco anco.
Però, s'un cor pien d'amorosa fede
Puo contentarvi senza farne strazio.
Piacciavi omai di questo aver mercede.
Se 'n altro cerca d'esser sazio
Vostro adegno erra; e non fia quel che
   crede,

WYATT

Was I never yet of your love greved
Nor never shall while that my liff doeth
   last;
But of hating myself that date is past

And teeres continuell sore have me
   weried.
I will not yet in my grave be buried
Nor on my tombe your name yfixed fast.
As cruell cause that did the sperit son
   hast
Ffrom th' unhappy bonys, by great
   sighes sterred.
Then, if an hert of amourous faith and
   will

Di che amor e me stesso assai ringrazio.

> May content you, withoute doyng greiff
> Please it you so this to doo releiff
> Yf othre wise ye seke for to fulfill
> Your disdain, ye erre, and shall not as ye
>   wene;
> And ye yourself the cause thereof hath
>   bene.45

Chaucer, Petrarch's younger contemporary, celebrated him in Clerk's Prologue (l.31–34) as a "lauriat poete," but his only verified use of Petrarch's vernacular poetry is his translation of one sonnet. "S'amor non è" (*Rime* 32) forms the song of Troilus (Canticus Troili) in book I of *Troilus and Criseyde* (l.400–10). Petrarch's sonnet is an account of his feelings, and no easy rule or moral can be drawn: this is how things are. Chaucer misunderstood the text "S'amor non è che dunque è quello ch'io sento," taking it to imply the human propensity for error and man's lack of wisdom. His variant of Petrarch's seafarer's image conveys a vague sense of helplessness: "Alas! what is this wondre maladie?" Petrarch, on the other hand, directs his poetic inquiry toward the question of whether this incomprehensible feeling is love or not. Chaucer would have Troilus ask a metaphysical question whose reply the Italian poet had taken for granted: "Does love exist or not?" Troilus would know "what then is love?" while Petrarch concentrates on the self and on the singularity of the experience. Words such as "bona" and "ria," used by Petrarch to particularize the character of his love, become counters for generalization in the poetry of Chaucer. The Englishman is more theoretical and remote, whereas Petrarch conveys the illusion of subjectivity, first by placing in the foreground his own thoughts and feelings, and then by presenting contrasting but intellectually balanced perspectives on experience. His imagery is deployed to further an analysis of interiority. The suffering lover, his storm-tossed boat with no ballast of wisdom, bears a cargo of error. (This twelfth line Chaucer omits and the seafaring metaphor becomes slight.) Bereft of reason the bark must flounder, driven by the tides of passion. We have Petrarch, not the penitent but the poet, caught up in the alternation between vain hopes and vain sorrows. The poet's anguish is fed by a desire which he is unable to consummate or conquer, and this state of mind finds expression in paradox or oxymoron:

> If I might I would be more sane
> But new violence drags me unwillingly away. I desire one thing;
> To another my mind urges me on. I see what is better and approve it;
> I follow the worst.

Focusing on the conflicting demands of personality and not merely those engendered by sexual conflict, Petrarch highlighted longings to realize the poet's mission, the dangers of both pride and despair in his craft, the struggles of literary composition, and the passion for literary mortality: "Mortal grace, gestures, words have been the chief / Interest of my soul."[46]

These Petrarchan conflicts bespeak a conception of literature as literature, not as symptom of a typical social activity. Chaucer is poised between oral and literary culture. (Indeed, an argument can be made that much of what we term "medieval English literature" is just that.) Out of the Italian experience stemmed a ratification of the idea of what it is to be a poet and achieve mastery over emotion. Further, an appreciation for the ample prospects of the vernacular was voiced confidently. But even with English authors most sensitive to the intellectual achievements of the Italian vernacular, it would be necessary to freight their writings with legitimating philosophical passages. Chaucer of course harbored philosophical ambitions and found Boccaccio's *Il Filostrato* deficient in "doctryne." He added philosophical passages from Boethius's *De consolatione philosophiae* (book 2) to his appropriation of the Boccaccian narrative, whether they contributed to the dramatic purpose or not.

One of the first English translators from the Italian, Henry Parker, Lord Baron Morley (a member of Wyatt's circle), considered it necessary to defend his version (ca. 1550) of Petrarch's *Trionfi* by referring to the "theological secret declared therein." Northern European literati found it difficult to distance reason from appetite without the intervention of doctrine ostentatiously clerkly or resorting to an idealism conspicuously courtly. The translations from Italian (Boccaccio to Matteo Bandello) were prefaced by extensive moralistic and didactic disclaimers. The complexity of experience was brilliantly suggested by English poets, but harmony between reason and passion was only possible momentarily, and then through stylistic artifice. Slowly, however, the balance was restored between a sympathetic re-creation of earthly life and a harsh moralistic perspective. So too was the contrast between a gentle lyricism extolling youth and beauty and the grim fact of the futility of human desires being mitigated. Distancing from the claims of an archaic society was finding more ample expression in the drama and poetry of Tudor England. Chester, Coventry, and York mystery plays were becoming recognizably old-fashioned and archaic. Christianity, having the power to present belief in pictorial form, had heavy competition from more literary ideas. A more balanced presentation of the life of Christ and His teachings was encouraged by Continental humanism. In the fourteenth and fifteenth centuries the theme of the Passion and the Nativity were favored; by the Tudor period we observe a growing appreciation for a fuller biblical stage play. The new dramatic style weakened the hold of the Corpus Christi theme.[47]

Chaucer's middle style had been visual and iconographic. Now the literary impulse was toward abandoning description of any processes of experience directly. The central core of the numerous Tudor handbooks of rhetoric was devoted to linguistic strategies allowing for variety of discourse.

"Copia" was to be achieved by amplification of an idea through profusion of figures of speech. The rhetorical quest was for a formal beauty distanced from the natural use of language. The high style of spectacle and archaic language, with its epic use of titles, was being replaced by an eloquence both more dignified and more measured. Spenser, in his *Letter to Raleigh,* disclosed his intent in composing *The Faerie Queene,* taking up the theme of variety and arguing that the difficulties were only apparent and would be recognized as a source of pleasure:

> To some, I know, this Methode will seeme displeasaunt, which had rather have good discipline delivered plainly in way of precepts, or sermoned at large. . . . But such, me seeme, should be satisfide with the use of these dayes, seeing all things accounted by their showes, and nothing esteemed of, that is not delightful and pleasing to commune sence.[48]

9

Playwrights such as Ben Jonson were acutely conscious of archaic dramatic forms, perceiving that the allegorical personifications of past times no longer satisfied sophisticated taste. Indeed, dramas of the late sixteenth and early seventeenth centuries were less likely to be embodied sermons of theatrical happenings easily reduced to theological argument. The ability to tolerate disjunction and endure the claims of emotion and the secular world, with all its life-enhancing follies and triviality, became the mark of advanced writings: witness the measured reflection on a great variety of themes from honor to revenge and suicide. In order to be rhetorically effective, it was essential that writers review in ever more explicit detail the catalogue of options, explicating them copiously. To exercise patience was an emblem of the new civility and urbanity. To ratify the pleasure principle with the same imaginative force with which one endorsed the reality principle was to qualify for the appelation of *sage*. These are the words of Sir Thomas Browne, whose eloquence was replete with "magnificent variations on the double theme":

> But man is a Noble Animal, splendid in ashes, and pompous in the grave, solemnizing Nativities and Deaths with equall lustre, nor omitting Ceremonies of bravery in the infamy of his nature.[49]

Listen to the tactful commentary of Sir Philip Sidney on intellectual opportunity and the fallen state of man:

> This purifying wit—this enrichening of memory, enabling of judgement, and enlarging of conceit—which commonly we call learning under what name soever it come forth, or to what immediate and soever it be directed, the final end is to lead us and draw us to as high a perfection as our degenerate souls made worse by their clayey lodgings can be capable of.[50]

Of course, Hamlet's lines are almost too familiar to quote:

What a piece of work is a man, how noble in reason, how infinite in faculties, in form and moving, how express and admirable in action, how like an angel in apprehension, how like a god: the beauty of the world; the paragon of animals; and yet to me, what is this quintessance of dust?

Book I of the *Utopia* dramatizes the costly choice confronting Thomas More: Will he join the court of Henry VIII taking up public service or not? As we have already observed, in the debate between Morus and Hythlodaeus the harsh conclusion was inescapable: the overmighty listen not to wise and experienced counselors: " 'Deaf indeed, without doubt', I agreed, 'and, by heaven, I am not surprised. Neither, to tell the truth, do I think that such ideas should be thrust on people, or such advice given, as you are positive will never be listened to.' " But then Morus, expanding upon Menippus's skeptical judgment in Lucian's *Necromantia,* avers that there is "alia philosophia ciuilior," which enjoins one to play one's part in the drama at hand, so that the piece will not end in a tragicomedy. This *alia* philosophy, "more civil," allows one to endure the separation between public and private, which is, after all, the mark of a civil society. This practical philosophy does not seek for the kind of dominion or certainty characteristic of an archaic culture; nor does it retreat into abnegation or despair. Toleration of the storms one cannot control and not abandoning ship on the roughest seas, while recognizing the ineradicable nature of evil, constitutes the essence of literary poise: "For it is impossible that all should be well unless all men were good, a situation which I do not expect for a great many years to come."[51]

There is in More a recognition of the radical insufficiency of any pragmatic philosophy. To accept fully this gulf between private and public is to repudiate virtually all the teaching of Christ, for did He not forbid such dissembling to the extent that "what He had whispered in the ears of His disciples He commanded to be preached openly from the housetops." The anguish which was to follow More for the next sixteen years was the burdensome one of the awareness of the disjunction between courtier and philosopher, active and contemplative life, being and seeming, and the opposition between the claim of the soul and the exigencies of civil society. Wrestling with his own human nature, he seldom triumphed. Yet he must not appear as the driven and sinful man he well knew he was. But withal, there was the literacy character, the More of the *Utopia,* able to endure that problematic zone between private and public. In the eyes of modern literary critics this was no small achievement:

We may also wonder whether the price which Hythlodaeus asks us to pay is too high—not so much the cost involved in losing all that has been bequeathed to us, but rather the loss in terms of human personality itself.

Given Hythlodaeus's isolation from the rest of humanity, can we really trust him to lead us into the promised land?[52]

The injunction to "play one's part" and the imagery of the world as a stage gained a rhetorical hold on Tudor literature unprecedented in the history of English letters. From More's bleak observation, previously noted, on royal politics in his *Richard III*—"These matters be king's games, as it were stage plays, and for the most part played upon scaffolds"—to Queen Elizabeth's more objective comment—"We princes . . . are set on stages, in the sight and view of all the world duly observed"—we see the force of role-playing and the public world. Self-fashioning and the construed identity of *The Courtier* were lent warrant by the very influential treatise of Castiglione. Thomas Hoby's dedicatory epistle reveals an appreciation for the rhetorical tradition from which *Il cortigiano* had originated:

> Cicero, an excellent Oratour, in three bookes of an Oratour unto his brother, fashioneth such a one as never was, nor yet is like to be; Castilio an excellent courtier, in three bookes of a Courtier unto his dear friend, fashioneth such a one as is hard to find, and perhaps unpossible. Cicero bringeth into dispute of an Oratour, Crassus, Scevola, Antonius, Cotta, Sulpitius, Catallus, and Caesar his brother, the noblest and chiefest Oratours in those daies. Castilio, to reason of a Courtier, the Lord Octavian Fregoso, Sir Frideric his brother, the Lord Julian de Medicis, the Lord Cezar Zonzaga, the L. Frances comaria Della Rovere, Count Lewis of Canossa, the Lord Gasper Pallavisin, Bembo, Bibiena, and other most excellent Courtiers, and of the noblest families in those daies in Italie.[53]

If we were to trace in some detail Italian influence in the new courtesy books, we could follow the trajectory from Castiglione's *Il cortigiano* to Stefano Guazzo's *Civile Conversation*, discovering that the fashioning of polite gentlemen was extended to acting in society at large rather than in the court. To see this ideal democratized (or at least gentrified) and given political specificity, we can turn to the writings of that influential scholar and pedagogue, Richard Mulcaster (1530–1611). Headmaster of Merchant Taylors School in London from 1561, for some twenty-five years, and then headmaster at St. Paul's, he stood firm for civic idealism:

> For the good bring vp of yong gentlemen, he that taketh no care is more than a foole considering their place and service in our countrie.[54]

The humanist conviction that Latin classical texts (not surprisingly, Cicero and Horace) shaped the private man for furthering the public good, seldom found a less stinting endorsement:

> For those who serve in publik function do turn their learning to publik use, which is the natural use of all learning: so such as live to themselves either for pleasure in their studye, or to avoid foren truble do turn their learning to

a private ease, which is the privat abuse of a publik good. For the common weall is the measure of everie mans being, which if anie one respect not, he is not to live in it.[55]

Mulcaster's textured appreciation of English history was coupled with a reverence for tradition and a sensitive consciousness of changing custom. His was an English linguistic patriotism enriched by classical humanism and responsiveness to the new Continental literature: "I love Rome, but London better; I favor Italie, but England more; I honor Latin, but worship the English." All of this and more he communicated to his long-time student Edmund Spenser, whose *Faerie Queene* was rich recompense to an educator whose devotion to the public good received epic sanctification. Civilized order was the centerpiece of a metaphysical celebration, just as savagery and disordered license were the dark side of a bestial universe.[56]

1 0

To suggest that the reception of key Italian and classical texts depended upon social transformation from an archaic, communal culture to a civil society is to underscore the fact that distinctions between nature and culture, government and society, and public and private were accorded full, sometimes troubled, but often playful, recognition. Indeed, the representation of the exigencies of the public world and the vocabulary of civility were both enhanced and enlarged during Tudor times. From fourteenth-century texts we have terms such as *civil law* and *civil* [Roman] *lawyer*. But only in the sixteenth and early seventeenth centuries did the term *civil* take on that broader meaning of "to civilize." In *As You Like It* (II,vii,96), Shakespeare speaks of "smooth civility." Bacon, in his *Essays on Counsels Civil and Moral,* will note that vagabonds are to be considered "of no civil society or corporation" (ca. 1590). In a later edition (1616) he contends that "a Citizen is a profession of civility." In an anonymous dialogue of 1579 on *Civil and Uncivil Life,* the author will exhort gentlemen to leave the boorish environment of the countryside for the city. The notion of civility bore a heavy cargo of the stuff of urbanity as handbooks for gentlemen revealed a marked disdain for the pastimes of country life. In the cities—the arena of civil life—communal ritual was being transformed into performances, often professionally organized. Indeed, government distrusted the spontaneity of archaic festival and celebration. In larger towns such as Coventry, Hull, Leicester, Northampton, and others, magistrates imposed discipline. Protestant attacks brought down the maypole, Morris dancing, the many forms of *charivari,* and the "topsyturvidum" of Hocktide and Shrovetide. In these and other major festivals, social norms had been inverted through burlesque and parody. Now, town governments, animated by a sense of civic pride and ambition for social control, foreclosed the innocent and not so innocent ribaldry and riot of the world of ancient festivals. These folkloristic rituals did more than let off steam or inspire social cohesion; their mockery was a defense—if not an assault—against the pride of the overmighty.[57]

The character of the Fool, so popular in the festive life of former days, came now to typify the idle and boisterous countryman. On the Elizabethan stage the Vice and Virtue figures and other allegorical personfications of the morality play withered in the glare of change. The remnants of these archaic personages were transformed into individualized characters as the "morall" was increasingly preoccupied with the improvement of manners and civil conduct. Ben Jonson believed the times were too sophisticated and that the "Vice figure of the morality play" was not "attir'd like men and women o' the time"; no longer was he clad in a "juglers jerkin, with false skirts, like the knave of Clubs" or brandishing his "wodden dagger." In his preface to *The Alchemist* he took exception to the dramatic romances of the day, arguing both on esthetic and ethical grounds that they "runne away from Nature." To run away from nature was, in Jonson's view, to abdicate the poet's proper function of holding up a mirror to society. For advancing this opinion he was judged "a mere empiric"—an author who relied on his observation, making only "nature privy to what he indites [writes]"[58]

Jonson is at his critical best when ridiculing the fairy queens and magical monster figures of olden times. Marvels, anachronisms, and fanciful freedom of time and place were shunned in favor of those progenitors of the reality principle—verisimilitude and poetic justice. In the last decades of the seventeenth century we have in London an illusionist theater of scenes and properties. Theoretical arguments concerning the Aristotelian unities of time and place were debated. Indeed, the whole question of restraint and self-control was dramatically modified. In an earlier time, drama was preoccupied with the comedy of the loss of physical control. The humor of many of the religious plays, as well as such newer works as *Gammer Gurton's Needle* (1552) and George Gascoigne's *Supposes,* contained excremental humor and anxiety concerning incontinence which, when considered along with Ulpian Fulwell's *Like Will to Like* (1568) and other dramas, suggests that anal humor and anxiety were a metaphor for the loss of moral control. The new dramaturgy was one of sexual innuendo and double entendre. Emphasis upon the subtleties of human transactions is itself an evidence of the civilizing process.[59]

At a moment when the idiom of the courtly lover was translated into public entertainment, and chivalric behavior was perceived as reckless rather than prideful, we notice that Tudor translations of Italian manner books apprehend the unheroic message with stunning banality. The grand virtues of fortitude, magnanimity, and liberality were in the run of daily affairs not often to be put to the test. The importation of educational programs, rhetorical studies, and handbooks from Italy to the north of Europe bore the imprint of that civic purpose framed to temper the extravagant, sometimes violent, and often heroic behavior of an obstreperous nobility. As was previously mentioned, Queen Elizabeth's principal minister, William Cecil (Lord Burleigh), observed in 1559 that "the wanton bringing up and ignorance of the nobility forces the Prince to advance new men that can serve." Sir Thomas Elyot, in the first English book to be written on education (*The Boke Named the Governour* [1531]), offered the reader the ripe wisdom of the classics of Latin literature, as well as ample gleanings of sage counsel from Erasmus, Castiglione, and Petrarch. All of this was intended to serve as preparation for an order of landed magistrates dutifully officiating in the name of the crown. It was necessary for Elyot to state scornfully the following: "Some . . . without shame dare affirm that to a gentleman it is a notable reproach to be well learned and to be called a great clerk. . . ." The title of one of his chapters is, "The education or form of bringing up of the child of a gentleman, which is to have authority in a public weal." Especially useful toward this end was the study of history through which

> a yonge gentilman shal be taught to note and marke nat only the ordre and elegancie in declaration of the historie, but also the occasion of the warres, the counsailes and preparations of either part . . . the fortune and successe of the holle affaires.

Elyot had borrowed extensively from Francesco Patrizi's *De regno et regio institutione,* among other sources, to advocate instruction for gentlemen in carving, painting, singing, and the dance. In particular, the dance engaged the author's attention, taking up four chapters in his book. In addition to being a pleasure in and of itself, it served as a metaphor of universal concord. Further, the dance furnished the most appropriate symbolism for conveying figuratively an active engagement with society. One accepted one's designated role, never breaking time and measure, contributing to the harmonious integration of one's own steps with one's fellows. The activity of dancing embodied the conception of the right ordering of society, and from the dance came compelling images expressive of the social benefits of personal restraint. Along the same line was the elevation of the art of horsemanship, which also served as an emblem of the human ability to tame the passions and dominate brute nature. But Elyot was writing in the first part of the sixteenth century and had to be reassuring to his gentleman reader. There was something vulgar and menial about certain of the arts. His audience was more suspicious and less cultivated than that of Castiglione; therefore, he advised gentlemen that practicing the arts during one's leisure hours was not as demeaning as it would be in the case of a craftsman doing it for hire:

> I intend not . . . to make a prince or nobleman's son a common painter or carver, which shall present himself openly stained or imbrued with sundry colours.

Although such assurances were unnecessary for arts like riding, Elyot still felt compelled to write that "a gentleman playing or singing in a common audience impaireth his estimation."[60]

11

At court a domesticated nobility was ideally to learn a style of life predicated upon self-cultivation and tact. Over the century social imperatives and social graces were resolutely linked to those accomplishments designed to demonstrate new paradigms of civility. Indeed, the language of chivalry was being divested of certain of its ties to an archaic culture whose structural base rested upon the exchange of favors, gifts, and services. The idiom for expressing these traditional forms of social negotiation was acquiring flexibility and new dimension. In verse, beginning with Wyatt, the dramatic moment highlighted rejection of courtly idealism as inappropriate to the poet's immediate circumstance. Among later-day poets, chivalric culture was marked by a burdened self-consciousness that such an ethos was heroic but reckless. The notion of service lost something of its romantic quality, assuming the aspect of a negotiated settlement between lord and lady. A key word like *trouth* was no longer securely grounded in metaphysical or religious speculation. One can trace the temporal odyssey of such words as *grace* and perceive how the archaic meaning of material favor was transvalued until it achieved an esthetic quality. As we have noted, the English word *isolate,* which was appropriated from the French of the sixteenth century, who in turn had borrowed it from the Italian, referred to an individual who was without retinue or following. Indeed, the culture of Queen Elizabeth's court would keep competition in display within bounds by imposing a code of manners upon the courtier. The word *elegance* appears to have made its entry into English at this time. Etiquette required one to distance oneself from the bait of power and wealth, whereas elegance signified the accomplishment of a cultivated nonchalance. The need for distancing, as well as for *urbanitas,* worked to expand the register of meaning of such concepts as courtesy and honor, taking them far beyond the realms of fidelity and exaction of social credit.[61]

The word *elegance* may have been introduced into English through Lorenzo Valla's humanistic philological text *Elegantiarum libri* (on the elegance of the Latin tongue). The *Oxford English Dictionary* gives as a first instance: "Elegant oratours with their oracions garnished with elegancy" (1502). This usage suggests something of the extension of the civil and public dimension of language. Meanwhile, advocacy of the new learning went beyond the bounds of criticism of an old-fashioned magnate lifestyle. This was not the complaint literature or estate satire of an earlier time. Furthermore, the thrust of these criticisms could not be parried by almsgiving and largess. A sampling of opinion as evidenced in contemporary literature indicates that the boundaries of disapproval breached new territories. The poet John Skelton's disdain for the style of life of the old nobility is well known:

> . . . noble men borne
> To lerne they have scorne,
> But hunt and blowe an horne,
> Lepe over lakes and dykes
> Set nothyng by polytykes,

Not so often cited are the lines from his *Colin Clout:*

> But noble men borne to learne they have scorne . . .
> Set nothing by polytykes.

Of course politics refers to the science of politics, and this probably signifies Aristotle. Thomas Wilson, in his influential work on logic, wrote: "The polliticall lawe doeth cause an outward discipline to bee observed even of the wicked." In a thesaurus of 1565 (Cooper), we note that under the entry *civilis* we have "scientia civilis, morall philosophie, the politic." The early impulse toward educational reform in sixteenth-century Tudor England garnered much of its strength from the desire to transform the nobility into a governing order able to fulfill its civic responsibilities. Handbooks on statecraft became books of approved civic comportment. Criticism of the semi-public ostentatious way of life, characteristic of an older aristocracy, became increasingly strident. But more than criticism was involved.[62]

The last private castle in England, Thornbury in Gloucestershire, had been built as far back as the early years of Henry VIII. This has been explained as a consequence of the emergence of a new civil culture at the top of English society. Subsequently, this castle and eleven others reverted to the crown on the attainder of Buckingham. Indeed, the crown seems to have pursued a deliberate tactic of collecting castles. Furthermore, the Tudors refused to create new great families through gifts of land and titles. We must not, however, infer from this that the Tudor government harbored any fixed hostility toward bastard feudalism or conclude that the nobility was unmindful of the advantages of being secure in their holdings. Nobles might profit from political disorder but had no natural interest in doing so. In 1592, Lord Buckhurst explained to Gilbert, earl of Shrewsbury: "Your lordship must remember that in the policy of this Common Wealth, we are not over ready to encrease of power and countenance to such great personages as you are." Elizabeth and Burghley exercised great caution when confronted with aristocratic intransigence. Reliance was placed on the slow shift of habit and custom over a considerable period of time, rather than on any ruthless intervention by government to achieve the "good order" of society.[63]

Awareness of change is disclosed in the numerous writings of perspicacious commentators on the late Tudor and Stuart social and political scene. Different from the stinging polemics directed against old-fashioned nobles and gentry who preferred to educate their sons in hunting and hawking rather than letters, these new assessments proved more historical and measured than rhetorical and strident. Furthermore, the later-day evaluations were less likely to proffer idealistic schemes for social improvement, tending to be contented with reporting transformations in habits and customs. John Selden (1584–1654), jurist, antiquary, and scholar, was direct and pithy in his statements in his *Table Talk* when gauging the nature of historical change:

> When men did let the lands under foot [that is, for less than their value], the tenants would fight for their landlords, so that they had their retribution; but now they will do nothing for them, nay, help the first, if but a constable bid them, that shall lay the landlord by the heels, and therefore 'tis vanity and folly not to take the full value.

> Knight's Service in earnest means nothing, for the lords are bound to wait upon the King when he goes to war with a foreign enemy, with, it may be, one man and one horse, and he that does not is to be rated so much as shall seem good to the next parliament. And what will that be? So 'tis for a private man that holds of a gentleman.[64]

Historical interest was engendered by reflections on the war between York and Lancaster of the past century. Fought by magnates and overmighty subjects, this War of the Roses stimulated Francis Bacon to ruminate on the social circumstances of that troubled interval before the reign of Henry VII. Bacon believed the consequences of this civil war were significant for the lifestyle of nobility and for the yeomanry emancipated from dependence on them:

> First, concerning the nobility . . . Touching the command, which is not indeed so great as it hath been, I take it rather to be a commendation of the time, than otherwise: for men were wont factiously to depend upon noblemen, whereof ensued many partialities and divisions, besides much interruption of justice, while the great ones did seek to bear out those that did depend upon them. So as the kings of this realm, finding long since that kind of commandment in noblemen unsafe unto their crown, and inconvenient unto their people, thought meet to restrain the same by provision of laws; whereupon grew the statute of retainers; so as men now depend upon the prince and the laws, and upon no other; a matter which hath also a congruity with the nature of the time, as may be seen in other countries; namely, in Spain, where their grandees are nothing so potent and so absolute as they have been in times past.

The *Prerogatives of Parliaments,* attributed to Sir Walter Raleigh, offered a more radical evaluation of the decay of private military power and its subsequent replacement by public authority:

Counsellor of State. "Was it not so ever?"

J.P. "No, my good lord, for the noblemen had in their armories to furnish some of them a thousand, some two thousand, some three thousand men, whereas now there are not many that can arm fifty."

C. of S. "I hold it not safe to maintain so great an armory or stable; it might cause me or any other nobleman to be suspected, as the preparing of some innovation. . . . Such a jealousy hath been held ever since the time of the civil wars over the military greatness of our nobles, as made them have little wills to bend their studies that way. . . ."

J.P. "The power of the nobility being now withered, and the power of the people in the flower, the care to content them would not be neglected, the way to win them often practiced, or at least to defend them from oppression."

One could multiply instances of apprehension of decline, not only in the number of armed retainers, but also in outlays for idle servants, extravagant hospitality, open entertainment, and the thousand rituals and gestures quintessential to good lordship. One could single out the progressive breakdown of the page system of education in great houses, whereby the young had in an earlier time gained entry into military careers. A very different tuition was in place with an almost exponential increase in gentry and aristocratic attendance at universities and Inns of Court. Gentry and nobles were turned away from gaining honor and influence through heroic gestures of liberality and magnificence. The old ideal of the *domus* as open was challenged as were the casual ways of the countryside. Rural duties and homespun lavishness were rivaled by new notions of refinement and delicacy. Detachment from an archaic civilization was often troubled, and the adoption of courtier literature from Southern Europe was bitterly criticized for advocating the cultivation of artifice and subterfuge. Had the rough country ways been truly superseded? Had largess and ideas of casual charity become peripheral of social experience? Was largess indeed the queen of virtues? Were alms best provided at castle gate and manor? Did not these donations and bequests recycle the wealth of the community? Was not the increased distance between respectability and roughness a vital social issue? Did the new lifestyle with its imported architecture disassociate the governing order from the real problems of country life? Was not the decline of hospitality linked closely with the reluctance to employ many of the "tall fellows" whose service had once been an obligatory part of every great estate? Did not open hospitality provide relief for the poor and strengthen communal bonds? Was this not also true of ancient festivities and holidays?—those living reminders of traditional solidarities. Did retreat of the lord and his peers from open dining not undermine "good neighborhood"? To many Tudor commentators on the conventions of moral responsibility, the social consequences of renouncing older obligations were truly dire.[65]

1 2

Much of the new literature being translated from the French and Italian, judged to be an "underground library" for Cambridge men, worked toward a very different end. Perception that an ancient network of reciprocal obligation was in competition with a different model of social order was deeply troubling. The lines recited by Ben Jonson's character Carlo Buffone in *Every Man Out of His Humor* (I,ii,37–39) dripped with irony: "To be an accomplished gentleman, that is, a gentleman of the time, you must give o'er housekeeping in the country and live altogether in the city amongst gallants." Shakespeare's Roman plays were to be the occasion for a protracted examination of the failure of time-honored aristocratic virtues, such as bravery, bellicosity, preoccupation with martial honor and attention to public fame, magnificence, and generosity. These jewels in the crown of a noble ethic were, however, to be found flawed and imperfect by a younger generation more pragmatic, materialistic—less romantic and less imaginative. The lesson of Castiglione was not lost: "Many times men of courage are sooner knowne in small matters than in great," this in Hoby's translation. It was the small virtues rather than the heroic and spectacular ones that proved durable and essential for social success. One recalls Peterson's translation of the Florentine Giovanni della Casa's *Galateo,* freighted with that civic wisdom partial to the small virtues of daily commerce which oblige one person to another. These polite habits and correct manners of speech are required much more often than the grander and more extravagant virtues of moral courage, generosity, and fortitude.

Francis Bacon, in his "Of Ceremonies and Respects," sanctioned and extended this social insight:

> He that is only real had need have exceeding great parts of virtue; as the stone had need to be rich that is set without foil. But if a man mark it well, it is in praise and commendation of men as it is in gettings and gains: for the proverb is true, *That light gains make heavy purses;* for light gains come thick, whereas great come but now and then. So it is true that small matters win great commendation, because they are continually in use and in note: whereas the occasion of any great virtue cometh but on festivals. Therefore it doth much add to a man's reputation, and is (as Queen Isabella said) like *perpetual letters commendatory,* to have good forms.

Tudor literature cultivated an ambiguous relationship with a more solemn world of obligation, vows, and heroic duty. Manuals of conduct such as *Il cortigiano* called for cultivating those skills required to camouflage the Herculean efforts needed to satisfy the strenuous code of chivalric conduct.

A wide and bitter debate ensued as to the legitimacy of following conventions of noble behavior governed by immoral feigning and *beau semblant*. The debate about "imaginative artifice" was for the modern-day premier critic C. S. Lewis at the very center of Tudor literary and visual culture: "What is in question is not man's right to sing but his right to feign, to 'make things up'." The call for graceful negligence and that art which conceals art, posed linguistic and moral difficulties for the English translator of Castiglione's *Courtier.* Hoby's rendition of *sprezzatura* or *grazia,* as simplicity or recklessness, suggests how easily the conception of cultivated nonchalance could shade into dissimulation and insincerity.[66]

The poet's part as moral guardian must not be too prominent and his moral judgment should recede in a type of infinite regress until it approaches esthetic perception. Withal, it will be essential that the imperatives of secular life, no matter what their ethical roots, not lose authenticity by capitulating to rigorous moralism or otherworldliness. Movement in Spenser's *The Faerie Queene* was unpredictable and fluid, conveying the illusion of human experience. Acute consciousness of artifice and the fictive was a necessary condition for a heightened awareness of the recreative aspects of culture. This view allowed for distancing from a more heroic code. Francis Bacon was to write: "The mind of man is more cheered and refreshed by profiting in small things than by standing at a stay in great." Whether play was to be judged valid, albeit gratuitous, or whether serious claims were to be made, the rules of stylistics required that didactic goals be disguised. An aversion for bare moral discourse animated the arts and the spate of rhetorical manuals now achieving currency. Rhetoric was averred to be "right pleasant" as a persuasive art discovering probabilities rather than truth. Paradigms for social life emphasized that decorum and its absence were truly as variable as "the sundrie circumstances that mens affaires are." Style and eloquence were equated with civilization, and the expression of civility, as Ben Jonson was to maintain, no longer was lodged in "bare form" or "meere ceremony." George Puttenham was to write in his influential book *The Art of English Poesy* (1589) that it was poets and orators "that by good and pleasant persuasiveness first reduced the wild and beastly people into publicke societies and civilities of life, insinuating into them under fiction with sweets and colourie speeches, many wholesome lessons and doctrines."[67]

Literary terms were identified in the new rhetoric (the debt to Castiglione was clear) with notions of proper conduct. Correlations were commonplace between poetry and civility. Sir John Harrington (Elizabeth's godson), in his "Brief Apology for Poetry," which was prefaced to his translation of Ariosto's *Orlando Furioso* (1591), maintained that poetry should be employed and read "as was intended by the first writers and devisers thereof which is to soften and polish hard and rough dispositions of men and make them capable of vertue and good discipline." (*Orlando Furioso* was to go through twenty editions in less than a century.) Dancing, fencing, riding, and the cult of bodily grace called for the importation of Italian masters. This extension of the range of social accomplishments was often attributed by contemporaries to the Continental influence. Roger Ascham, humanist pedagogue and tutor to Edward VI and Elizabeth, who would marry colloquial energy with elegance—"the pure fine talk of Rome" (echoing in the comedies of Terence)—was the target. He perceived the incidence of disciplined beauty in quotidian social comportment: in social behavior as well as in art, one must be instructed in *beau semblant*. It was Castiglione who provided a rationale for fakery in art, and it was his countrymen who stocked the arsenal of art criticism. Art and literature were replete with deception and deceits—the very figures of language offer "meere illusions to the minde." Regrettable it may be that they are false, but it is precisely those "meere illusions" which engage the mind. If one recollects Erasmus's forthright but playful acknowledgment of the benefits of civility and society, more was engaged than the mind of man: Things which men laugh at are things which are ridiculous, but it is they and they alone that "make society pleasant and, as it were glue it together." Gabriel Harvey praised his friend Edmund Spenser calling him "an Inglishe Petrarck" who, following his model, "gratiously confined Love within the limits of Honour; Witt within the boundes of Discretion; Eloquence within the Termes of Civility." Peter Haylyn recommended Sir Philip Sidney's *Arcadia* to the reader as a "book which besides its excellent language, rare contrivances and delectable studies, hath in it all of the strains of Poesy, comprehendeth the universal art of speaking and to them that can discerne and will observe, notable rules for demeanour both public and private."[68]

1 3

Honor and reputation were to be gained through grace and elegance. Cultivated nonchalance was to mask rivalry in politics and competition for sexual favors. The movement of literary styles was toward a new politeness and urbanity, making the conventions and customs of an older world seem less fashionable. The Venetian ambassador to England remarked acerbically: "The magnates are mostly hated for their vain ostentation, better suited to their ancient position than their present condition." Particular codes of the orders, professions, and trades were being rivaled by a conception of society distanced from archaic notions. Deploring the irresponsibility of an aristocracy, the provinciality of a gentry, and the technicalities and narrow horizons of the professions, the humanists of the first part of the sixteenth century proposed educational remedies. In former times the treatment of the various estates of society in prose and poetry tended toward exhortation to heroic virtue or satirization of rampant vice. For example, extortionate lawyers were repeatedly reminded of their Christian duty to rectify wrongs and injustice regardless of personal sacrifice. The lawyer must not sell his services or put his skills out for hire, since they were gifts from God. Thomas Starkey (ca. 1499?–1538), humanist and student of law at Padua, wrote most of his *Dialogue* between Reginald Pole and Thomas Lupset in that north Italian city. He was, as we have noted, seriously engaged with training the scions of gentry and aristocracy in "the discipline of the common weal." In the first conversation between Pole and Lupset, the latter berates the former for pursuing an otiose life of scholarship:

> You know right well, Master Pole, that to this all men are born and of nature brought forth: to commune such gifts as be to them given, each one to the profit of other, in perfect civility, and not to live to their own pleasure and profit, without regard of the weal of their country, forgetting all justice and equity.[69]

The value of the lawyer to society was self-evident to Starkey, who proposed that the problem of selling knowledge should be resolved not through any appeal to altruism or heroic Christian virtue, but through limiting the practice of law to men who were educated in virtue, had the requisite legal training and sufficient income to live independent of fees. The wealth of the aristocracy was not at issue, nor was their failure to live up to an exalted code at stake. They were to be publicly educated in knowledge and virtue so they would be responsive to the wider claims of state and society. Young men were to be delivered from careless private tuition and brought together to be educated in the civil arts as well as in feats of arms. Thus the age group would be placed above family loyalty or devotion to clannishness. Such schools for achieving these ends might be located in the "over many" monasteries and abbeys where the children could be raised together in the discipline of the commonweal. Plans for institutional military education worked, albeit very hesitantly, against the notion that the right to command was ensured by noble birth and familiarity with the sword. The study of ancient history, literature, and rhetoric was judged as having a practical as well as moral value for all who might be summoned to positions of command. For the lawyers and justices too, a broader education was also certified.

Sir Thomas Elyot's *The Boke Named the Governour* was more legalistic and patriotic than the Italian sources from which he borrowed so heavily. As we have mentioned, the work would go through eight editions in less than half a century and was most influential in representing Continental ideas to gentry and aristocrat. Scions of these two orders having their own "revenues certain" were to constitute the magistrate class. Having inherited political and social authority, they must be educated to participate in public life. Elyot agreed that a legal education was useful to that end but should not be too narrow or begun at too early an age. The student should first read philosophy, master the skills of eloquence and oratory, and acquire the numerous social graces recommended by Continental manuals on polite behavior before specializing. Knowledge "for use" was the end of "all doctrine and study"; in the conclusion of *The Governour,* Elyot fixed this desideraturm "in good counsel, wherein virtue may be found (as it were) his proper mansion and palace."[70]

A conception of society being purveyed called for less technical preparation, with emphasis on the social and civil arts rather than on mastery of role and heroic virtues. Mastery of role was sometimes disadvantaged as handbooks of good counsel were converted into manuals of statecraft. Advancement of notions of flexibility in the conduct of public affairs was a mark of sophisticated writing. Meanwhile, the eloquence of an earlier age was being converted into high drama and entertainment. The cultural hero advanced by the new education was, more often than not, the cunning and flexible rhetorician Odysseus, rather than the fighting man Achilles. One thinks of the lines of Golding's influential translation of Ovid:

> The Lords were moued with his woordes, & then appeered playne
> The force that is in eloquence. The lerned man did gayne
> The armour of the valeant[71]

Literary evidence suggests that writers such as Sir Philip Sidney, John Lyly, and others most open to new ideas were reluctant to endorse narrow judgments or authenticate strict codes. Dramatic attention was placed upon observation of the mind at work, rather than enumeration of moral doctrine. Lyly portrayed characters struggling to reason their way to appropriate behavior. Lucilla speaks with pathos in *Euphues:* "If Nature canne no waye resist the furye of affection, how shoulde it be stayed by wisedome?" In his *Defense of Poesie* or *Apology for Poetry* (as the two quartos of 1595 name it), Sidney made a defense not of poetry against history, but of fiction against fact. Images in the arts had the power to bring a man "to a judicial comprehension" of matters. In a complex fiction such as the *Arcadia,* all sides of questions were vividly dramatized. In his *Life of Sir Philip Sidney,* Fulke Greville offered a telling description of the work:

> In all these creatures of his making, his intent and scope was, to turn the barren Philosophy precepts into pregnant Images of life; and in them, first on the Monarch's part, lively to represent the growth, state, and declination of Princes, change of government, and Lawes: vicissitudes of sedition, faction, succession, confederacies, plantations, with all other errors, or alternations in publique affairs. Then again in the subject's case, the state of favor, disfavor, prosperitie, hospitality, travail, and all other moodes of private fortunes or misfortunes. In which traverses (I know) his purpose was to limn out such exact pictures, of every posture in the minde, that any man being forced, in the straines of his life, to pass through any straights, or latitudes of good, or ill fortune might (as in a glass) see how to set a good countenance upon all the discountenances of adversitie, and a stay upon the exorbitant smilings of chance.[72]

Instead of harsh assessments about the frailty of a wormish humanity or exaltation of altruism and self-sacrifice, humans must learn to live with their imperfections, recognizing their own weaknesses in others. Of course one thinks of Shakespeare's plays, from *King Lear* to *Measure for Measure*. Hamlet bears eloquent but tragic witness to the failure of deep penetrating wit to transcend the limits of its own condition. Sidney was concerned with the world of culture (that of "nice art") over and against "brazen reality" (that of natural necessity). About these matters he did not confront the reader with overmuch solemnity while making his serious point:

> This purifying wit—this enrichening of memory, enabling of judgment, and enlargening of conceit—which commonly we call learning under what name soever it come forth, or to what immediate end soever it be directed, the final end is to lead us and draw us to as high a perfection as our degenerate souls made worse by their clayey lodgings can be capable of.

While man bears full degradation and the mark of the Fall, it is the office of the poet to present the world as it ought to be. The poet brings home to man the degradation of his immediate condition, while at the same time giving him instruction and delight by offering him an ideal vision. This Sidney has learned from the Continental literary scene—that poetry may serve as a companion and guide in times of uncertainty and rough conflict.[73]

Christopher Marlowe believed that his sophisticated "tragic glass" would displace the scorned ancient drama of "the jiggling veins of rhyming mother wits." From Ben Jonson to John Selden to Thomas Hobbes and Samuel Butler, we observe a deepening appreciation of the disjunction between an archaic past and the present. Hobbes, in *Leviathan*, compared the Roman Saturnalis to English "Carnevalls and Shrove-tuesdays liberty of Servants." Samuel Butler introduced a detailed account of the ancient custom of ridiculing a cuckold for mock heroic effect in his *Hudibras*. There the man was permitted to be beaten by his wife; Butler was sufficiently distanced from folk practices to recognize their solid good sense.[74]

Rhetoricians perceived an association between Graeco-Roman comedy and contemporary religious harvest rituals. Puttenham, the literary historian, wrote on the topic of revenge with a neutrality owing much to his long view of culture. When defining a certain "auncient forme of poesie by which men did use to reproach their enemies," he wrote:

> There be wise men, and of them the great learned man *Plutarch* that tooke upon them to perswade the benefite that men receive by their enemies, which though it may be true in manner of *Paradoxe*, yet I finde mans frailtie to be naturally such, and alwayes hath beene, that he cannot conceive it in his owne case, nor shew that patience and moderation in such greifs, as becommeth the man perfite and accomplisht in all vertue: but either in deed or by word, he will seeke revenge. . . . This made the auncient Poetes to

invent a meane to rid the gall of all such Vindicative men; so as they might be a wrecked of their wrong. . . . And this was done by a maner of imprecation, or as we call it by cursing and banning of the parties, and wishing all evill to a light upon them, and though it never the sooner happened, yet was it a great easment to the boiling stomacke.[75]

Antiquarianism, which for the most part had been an isolated interest—almost conspicuous for its absence—became a serious intellectual preoccupation in Tudor times. In an earlier age an interest in the past had been nurtured by a careful, almost obsessive, search for precedents. Such a quest was seldom inspired by a firm recognition of historical discontinuity between past and present. When the Italian humanist historiographer Polydore Vergil was invited to England by Henry VII, he created something of a scandal by rejecting the fabulous and legendary accounts of the reign and exploits of King Arthur. The new perspective on the past provoked bitter controversy, but it also stimulated Tudor antiquarians and typographers such as John Bale and John Stow to study the past in a radically new spirit. An edition of Chaucer, a survey of London, the preservation of old manuscripts, and a keen appetite for philological learning led educated men to conceive of English literature in a new way. It would be difficult to find a parallel in an earlier time for Puttenham's discussion of the most commendable English authors. In his *Art of English Poesie* (1589), one finds a sense of excitement emanating from his belief that this is a new and better cultural age. He sees in the past "a certain martial barbarousness" and a "rude and homely manner of vulgar poesy":

In the latter end of the same King's reign (Henry VIII) sprang up a new company of courtly makers of whom Sir Thomas Wyatt the elder and Henry Earl of Surrey were two chieftans who having travelled into Italy, and there tasted the sweet and stately measures and style of the Italian poesy, as novices newly crept out of the schools of Dante, Ariosto and Petrarch, they greatly polished our rude and homely manner of vulgar poesy from that it had been before, and for that cause may justly be said the first reformers of our English metre and style.[76]

1 4

Creation and borrowing of imaginative structures for distancing dramaturgy from ancient custom and folk culture was the task of Tudor playwrights. The rituals from old plays became cryptic and arbitrary actions—fossil remnants. Entertainments by amateurs on holidays were transformed from social forms into esthetic experiences. The comic mode was no longer so securely wedded to the seasons and social occasions of Candlemas, Shrove Tuesday, Hocktide, May Day, Whitsuntide, Midsummer Eve, Harvest-home, Halloween, and the twelve days of Christmas with the finale on the Twelfth Night. Here is Shakespeare's Induction to *The Taming of the Shrew:*

Messenger. Your honour's players, hearing your amendment, Are come to
play a pleasant comedy; . . .
Sly. . . . Is not a comonty a Christmas gambold or a tumbling trick?
Bartholomew. No, my good lord; it is more pleasing stuff.
Sly. What, household stuff?
Bartholomew. It is a kind of history.
Sly. Well, we'll see it. Come, madam wife, sit by my side and let the world
slip. We shall ne'er be younger.

The distancing from a holiday world, where the boundaries between play
and audience were drawn in sand, was becoming increasingly the mark of an
advanced literature. On the wane was the impulse to foster the many illusions
designed to redress or strengthen traditional solidarities. Likewise, the parody and reversal of communal ties through representation of Lords of Misrule, which allowed for privileged moments of license, now were placed in
very different literary settings. Humanists had been critical of the traditional
pursuits of the lower orders. In the *Utopia,* Thomas More would discipline
and regulate the lives of the lowly. Edmund Spenser, despite his sympathy
and antiquarian interest in Irish legends and customs, would come down
hard on the popular and living traditions of the simple folk of that bedeviled
land. Literati were on the whole concerned with promoting civility, and this
ordering of society was defined in substantial measure by its distance from
popular culture with its high evaluation of spontaneity and conviviality.
Shakespeare in *Henry VI,* has the Duke of York, who was scheming to
provoke Jack Cade to make insurrection, describe Cade's prowess in the wars
in Ireland thusly:

> his thighs with darts
> Were almost like a sharp quill'd porpentine;
> And in the end being rescued, I have seen
> Him caper upright like a wild Morisco,
> Shaking the bloody darts as he his bells.

Cade was the perfect lord of a rebellion which was represented as a type
of Saturnalia. The antiquarian John Selden was to see the festival in its
historical relationship to the ritual of the ancient Romans: "Christmas suc-
ceeds the Saturnalia, the same time, the same number of holidays; then the
master waited upon the servant, like the Lord of Misrule." The rude juxtaposition of ritual license over and against the harsh realities of country life
was being artistically transformed. In place of ritual release we have the
literary creation of the pastoral myth with all its romantic conventions. In *As
You Like It,* Touchstone comically puts down Rosalind's effusive sentimen-
tality for the lovesick shepherd Silvius. His realistic appraisal of harsh
country life is not entered against a folk and archaic mythology, but over and
against the literary legend of the pastoral, which has deluded Rosalind and so

many of the other courtiers taking refuge in Arden forest. (II,iv,46ff.) How different is the Puck of *A Midsummer Night's Dream* from the Robin Good-fellow of folk custom and Christmas games. The traditional vice figure survives only in Shakespeare's songs, ironic asides, and the epilogue. How distant is the Ariel of *The Tempest* from the mythic Kobold, the servant sprite who answered his master's call. In *The Tempest* he has become "a spirit too delicate / to act . . . earthy and abhorred commands. (I,ii,273–75)[77]

Thomas Nashe, writing in 1592, perceived the figures of popular leg-end—"the Robbin Goodfellowes, Elfes, Fairies, Hobgoblins of our later age"—as being identical with that "which . . . fantastical world of Greece ycleped Fawnes, Satyres, Dryades and Hamadryades." The humanistically oriented Gabriel Harvey was particularly scornful of contemporary popular writers who pandered to degraded public tastes by adopting folk themes and archaic forms. He castigated the author Robert Greene's "Greeness" as well as the general addiction to "piperly extemporizing and Tarltonizing." (Dick Tarlton was the court jester for Henry VIII.) Harvey also reproached Nashe, who responded to criticism by posing a serious query: "Is my stile like Greenes, or my ieasts like Tarltons?" Indeed, if one reads a major work of Nashe's, such as *Summer's Last Will and Testament,* one observes not only the author's engagement with popular and folkloristic forms, but also his impulse to stand clear and sophisticated—apart from that archaic world. "Traveling the skies" is qualified by the certainty that such a trip will make a fearful racket; the beauty in "gold breathing" is undercut by the fact that the gold is only breath and "meals" are paired against miracles. We are well on the way to Ben Jonson's comic mix of zest and revulsion for cunning, license, and glamorous luxury. But we have also arrived at a moment when Jonson, collaborating with Inigo Jones, architect and scene designer, will compose the yearly masque for the court of the Stuart kings. Realistic illusionism converted the masque into the spectacle celebrating the miraculous moral and civil authority necessary to check the energies of destruction and chaos. Set design, stage machinery, moveable scenery and perspective staging, which Jones had learned from the Italian theater, contributed the sense of the power of art to impose order on the world. Learned tastes had outrun the appetite for misrule, bear-baiting, and carnival. Viewed from the perspective of the popular theater, however, these spectacles were little more than infant's playthings:

> *What* petty things they are, wee wonder at? like children, that esteeme every trifle; and preferre a *Fairing* before their Fathers: what difference is betweene us, and them? but that we are dearer Fooles, Cockscombes, at a higher rate? They are pleas'd with Cockleshels, Whistles, Hobby-horses, and such like: we with Statues, marble Pillars, Pictures, guilded Roofes, where under-neath is Lath, and Lyme; perhaps Lome. Yet, we take plea-sure in the lye, and are glad, wee can cousen our selves.[78]

1 5

Perhaps the single most important mark of advanced literature and thought was the sense that the society of earlier times—idealized, of course—was passing. Ben Jonson, in plays such as *The Alchemist* and *Bartholomew Fair,* however paradoxically, privileged certain behavior coinciding with individual and contractual rights. Self-consciousness concerning the tenuousness of human solidarity was elevated to an operational principle. But overall, Jonson's own stance was characterized by ambiguity: in his later years, after his successful career as playwright was over, he demonstrated an increasing affinity for archaic subjects and rural folklore. His fond poetic hopes for the return to the golden world and oral culture of Old England found expression in Robin Hood's speech in the unfinished work *The Sad Shepherd:*

> I should think it might be
> As 'twas, a happy age, when on the plains
> The woodmen met the damsels and the swains,
> The neatherds, plowmen, and the pipers loud,
> And each did dance, some to the kit or crowd
> Some to the bag pipe, some to the tabret moved
> And all did either love, or were beloved.[79]

No features of declining sociability were more certain to be offered as testimony than those of hospitality, good lordship, and good housekeeping. Literary witness was abundant on the score of the social price paid for the dissipation of mutuality and decline of "charitable time." In his poem to Penshurst, Jonson celebrated the residence of the Sidney family at Penshurst, not as a place of repose for repairing the damage of city life, but as an estate serving the community, not a retreat but an emblem of public virtue. All who came within its sheltering walls partook of the spirit of self-sacrificing generosity. Beyond this, Penshurst was praised as a part of nature executed by honest masons unconfined by canons of style. Here we observe the ambiguity of Jonson's position: on the one hand he attacked art and architecture because they fostered illusion, and, like the masque, they were but "toys"; on the other, he described poetry as an art disposing men "to all civil Offices of Society . . . the absolute Mistress of manners . . . which leads on and guides us by the hand to action with a ravishing delight and incredible Sweetness."[80]

Jonson, like so many of his literary contemporaries, was capable of dramatizing new versions of culture and society with the same wit and authority as he could cast them into doubt. Still, the question persisted as to whether art and architecture, rhetoric and poetry, with all their "make believe," were able to reclaim man from beastly life and facilitate his entry into the social order. An earlier literature had celebrated society in terms of companionship, obligation, gratitude, and duty. Cohesion was lent through pomp, emotional display, enchantment, and the exchange of courtesies. The darker subtext of society linked sinner to sinner, and the prospect of emotional detachment was inversely proportional to the depth of insight into the human condition. The living were inextricably linked with the dead and expected to work for their salvation—sometimes their vindication. The guilty at law were linked, at least in theory, with those who, but for the grace of God, would join them in climbing the gallow steps. Each individual had a claim on the other. Perhaps Shakespeare's King Lear, that regal representative of the old order, says it best when appealing to daughter Regan:

> 'Tis not in thee
> To grudge my pleasures, to cut off my train,
> To bandy hasty words, to scant my sizes,
> And, in conclusion, to oppose the bolt
> Against my coming in: thou better know'st
> The offices of nature, bond of childhood,
> Effects of courtesy, dues of gratitude.

The speech of Edmund in *King Lear* is indicative of the frightening dimension of the void directly abutting that of the King's archaic domain:

> Thou, Nature, art my goddess; to thy law
> My services are bound. Wherefore should I
> Stand in the plague of custom, and permit
> The curiosity of nations to deprive me,
> For that I am some twelve or fourteen moonshines
> Lag of a brother? Why bastard? wherefore base?
> When my dimensions are as well compact,
> My mind as generous, and my shape as true,
> As honest madman's issue? Why brand they us
> With base? with baseness? bastardy? base, base?
> Who in the lusty stealth of nature take
> More composition and fierce quality
> Than doth, within a dull, stale, tired bed,
> Go to the creating a whole tribe of fops,
> Got 'tween asleep and wake? Well then,
> Legitimate Edgar, I must have your land:
> Our father's love is to the bastard Edmund
> As to the legitimate. Fine word, 'legitimate'!

Edmund, Goneril, Regan, and Cornwall see things in "a continuous present," so that past obligations are utterly disvalued and a shallow rationalism trivializes antique moral codes. Having no memory of responsibility and free from the "plague of custom," they would create a society bound together by force and appetite—the converse of Lear's old order sustained by communal tradition infused with memory. Certainly, this new society, presented with such imaginative intellect by Edmund and a host of

Elizabethan stage villains from the time of Christopher Marlowe to Marston and Tourneur, had high dramatic credentials. The joys and horrors of being released from battlefield obligation, amorous service, filial piety, and political duty were as heady as they were appalling. Characters were unprepared to pay debts of gratitude or exchange courtesies. As types the Elizabethans themselves increasingly came to define them as Machiavellian: men and women obeying only the twin realities of interest and force.[81]

The very popular Elizabethan theater produced a drama in which the ancient order of society based on obligation and communal tradition was juxtaposed against a new order in which networks of political and emotional attachment no longer held. Nor could a race of "Senecal Men," no matter how heroical, repair this perversion of relationship. Even those characters drawing strength, as did George Chapman's heroes from some prelapsarian green world with its "native noblesse," were in the end to be baffled. They brought not ethical virtue to a perverse world but only a fierce and excessive energy. For all their vitality they were certain only of finding their own destruction. How wise and yet how unrealistic were the words of Clermont d'Ambois: "To live with little and to keep within a man's own strength still." But he cannot escape, and the ancient claims of the world were forced on him by the ghost of his dead brother Bussy summoning him to his sacred obligation of revenge. From this time-honored duty murders most foul and Clermont's suicide were to follow as the night the day (*The Revenge of Bussy d'Ambois* (1610?).[82]

T. S. Eliot's anachronistic literary judgment that Prince Hamlet exhibited emotional responses "in excess of the facts as they appear" serves only to disvalue widely held and deeply felt Elizabethan sensibilities concerning the propriety of aborting mourning practices. Equally disturbing were the hasty remarriage and indecent festivities. A brave ruler's untimely death, incest, the adulteration of family blood, affront to honor, and tyrannicide were at stake. The prince's fear of ghosts and hell was certainly real and widely shared by the audience. Dr. Samuel Johnson was closer to Hamlet and his times than was T. S. Eliot. He understood that while the prince and the play charms and fascinates, "it does horridly shake our dispositions." Nearer to Hamlet, he knew and dreaded that "hunger of the imagination which preys upon life." Hamlet's chief energy is what Claudius speaks of as "his brain still beating." This brain cannot dismiss the primitive duty of revenge nor banish the haunting voice of his father, the old king, from a heroic age crying for vindication of his high honor. Yet, withal, this archaic ideal cannot inspire him, for it does stand in clear opposition to the very moral terms of human existence. Man is a mixed creature whose nature, at least in some measure, demands that he sympathize and cherish rather than murder and kill. Still, there is no easy escape from the dilemma: Hamlet cannot follow the advice of mother and surrogate fathers (Gertrude, Claudius, Laertes, and Polonius) urging restraint, the exercise of caution, and acceptance of what cannot be changed. Old Hamlet's words, "adieu! Remember me," are stronger than the sensible and balanced exhortation of Claudius to confront life's occasions "With mirth in funeral and with dirge in marriage."[83]

But the claims of an archaic society and the weight of communal responsibility could not be discredited by any shallow rationalism or easy skepticism. On the other side, however, no ready, dramatic defense of the rightness of ancient codes was intellectually satisfying. If Claudius's rationalism is stunted, hear how naive and callow are Malcomb's revelations of his true character to Macduff:

> I am yet
> Unknown to woman, never was forsworn,
> Scarcely have coveted what was mine own,
> At no time broke my faith, would not betray
> The devil to his fellow, and delight
> No less in truth than life. (IV,iii,125–30)

Hotspur's idealism is as menacing to any civil order as is Falstaff's sensuality. Drama permitted a fuller exploration of the so numerous and diverse claims governing any society. Techniques borrowed from Continental humanist rhetoric allowed writers to argue with dexterity on either side of a question. Dramatic devices were expanded to give verisimilitude to abrupt and disconcerting shifts in points of view. Archaic notions of family and patriarchy were pitted against the rights of young lovers. The ideals of chivalry and honor were posed against the need for civil order. The duties of vassalage and hospitality were juxtaposed against private ambition. The active life was set against one of contemplation. Opposing definitions of kingship and regential authority were favored topics for debate.[84]

1 6

We observe a pedagogy being imported which had been established in Tuscany in the early fifteenth century. There rhetoric was regarded as an art of persuasion as well as of inquiry. Its study was set apart from a world of habitual expectation to be located in a sphere of "good faith" where ethical neutrality prevailed. Philosophically, its announced concern was with probabilities rather than truth. Borrowings from this rhetoric, further enhanced by Erasmus, Agricola, and others, stocked the Tudor grammar school and up. Speeches in praise and in blame, arguments in *utramque partem, sententiae* confirming an argument and mimesis of persons in highly emotional states, these were the hardy staples of Tudor pedagogy. Multiplication and variety in interpretation of motive and cause were coupled with short, witty opinions and a proliferation of meanings of terms to enhance human understanding. Questions of ideology and politics were converted into psychological dilemmas by posing a series of stock questions: What does it feel like to suffer exile from one's homeland or lose one's children? How can one rise to nobility in the face of the buffets of misfortune? How can human imagination deal with the different demands of reality?[85]

Values and obligations were naturalized, even domesticated, by being lent full psychological play and a more ample social context. Honor was no longer gained exclusively through humility, allegiance to a feudal lord, duty to God, or service to a lady. The thirst for fame and immortality were rendered with stunning rhetorical force in Elizabethan drama. So commanding and eloquent was the language that it could baffle the conventional moral expectations of the London theatergoer. Listen to Cleopatra as she prepares for death:

> Give me my robe, put on my crown, I have
> Immortal longings in me. Now no more
> The juice of Egypt's grape shall moist this lip.
> Yare, yare, good Iras; quick: methinks I hear
> Antony call, I see him rouse himself
> To praise my noble act. I hear him mock
> The luck of Caesar, which the gods give men
> To excuse their after wrath. Husband, I come:
> Now to that name, my courage prove my title! (V,ii,279–87)

Drama, prose, and poetry owed much to humanist rhetoric and the revival of fashionable classical studies. Encouragement was forthcoming for writers of tragical histories to explore the workings of that proud imagination, impatient with limits, preying on life, and tempting men to self-assertion. This lure to imperial power was undeniable, making men believe they were more than mortal. The end of the tragical drama, however, was that man was tempted to play roles he was unable to sustain. Comedy, again much indebted to its classical antecedents, demonstrated that the desire for the limitless and unbounded only made men ridiculous. The potential for laughter increased as the opposition between imagination and reality was magnified. Exhilaration with freedom from social restraint was evidenced by the Promethean ambitions of language. The pleasure principle was indeed better adapted for survival in the world than idealism. But very soon an amoral sense of life took over as the pleasure principle was played out. The very literary embodiment of spontaneity and pleasure—the jolly Falstaff—was finally reduced to intoning the ugly rule of life, big fish eat little fish: "If the young dace be a bait for the old pike, I see no reason in the law of nature but I may snap at (Justice Shallow)." Even in the lyrical world of Illyria (*As You Like It*), when love and reconciliation seem to obtain, Festa, the clown, offers the grim reminder to the audience, in the last song, that "the rain it raineth every day."[86]

Violations against sacral kingship, sacred honor, the rituals of hospitality, responsibility for revenge, and kinship loyalty were chronicled relentlessly. Yet a rebellious subjectivity remained intact. Private visions and passions were charted with particularity, and concern for nuance of motive was explored patiently so that inner heresies were rendered as dramatically compelling as public orthodoxies. Spenser contested the reigning public fictions while embracing them at the same time. Shakespeare expended boundless literary energy seeking to account for Hamlet's madness, Lear's folly, Troilus's love, Shylock's greed, and Macbeth's betrayals, but yet the mystery of character was not dispelled. The formidable Shakespeare critic Samuel Coleridge's characterization of Iago as "the motive-hunting of motiveless malignity" is apt. His is an instinctive antipathy that found reasons as an afterthought. In the end, we do not have an answer to Horatio's query of Hamlet: "Good my Lord, what is the cause of your distemper?" Not only do grand distractions and mighty wrongs work to subvert a character's claims to serenity and wisdom, but also petty passions and eccentricities are likely to undo him. Indeed, pettiness often accompanies political greatness. Oddities of temperament were more prone to be catalogued than heroic indifference in the face of the vicissitudes of fortune. Certainties lose their shape under the implosion of private passions. Furthermore, efforts to offer facile explanations of private mystery can be resisted. Hamlet will not permit Guildenstern to extract from him the reasons for his distemper and melancholy. Instead, he shoves a recorder into the unwilling hands of Guildenstern, admonishing the false courtier and gullible members of the audience in these words:

> HAMLET: Will you play upon this pipe?
> GUILD: My lord, I cannot.
> HAMLET: I pray you.
> GUILD: Believe me, I cannot.
> HAMLET: I do beseech you.
> GUILD: I know no touch of it, my lord.
> HAMLET: Why, look you now, how unworthy a thing you make of me! You would play upon me; you would seem to know my stops; you would pluck out the heart of my mystery; you would sound me from my lowest note to the top of my compass; and there is much music, excellent voice, in this little organ; yet cannot you make it speak. 'Sblood, do you think I am easier to be played on than a pipe? Call me what instrument you will, though you can fret me, you cannot play upon me. (III,ii)

The new linguistic habits grounded in Continental rhetorical strategies and nurtured by classical influences permitted a fuller dramatization of conflicting demands. The rhetoric of paradox used by poets and philosophers since ancient times now became something of an epidemic, for it seemed so promising as a tactic for doing justice to human ambiguity and life's complexity. The marriage of the techniques of classical comedy to philosophical dialogue had been learned by humanists such as Alberti and Erasmus from their reading of Lucian and other classical authors. Erasmus's *Praise of Folly* demonstrated a control of thought and expression most commanding when coupled with the urbane appearance of easy achievement. Erasmus's *Colloquies* was but one of the many literary texts popular in Tudor England from which students could learn rhetorical techniques for colonizing the middle ground between man's pride and his mortality, between human achievement and wormish circumstance, and the life of pleasure over and against the claims of duty and honor. Classical influences from Roman poetry (for example, the Horatian odes and epistles) were assimilated to produce an equilibrium and fluidity of ethical precept. The classical tragedies of Seneca proved enormously popular, and in their Elizabethan resurrection they did not offer instruction as was the wont in the genre concerning the vanity of human desires. The new tragedy was instead exemplary and openly political. Insistence on mortality highlighted rather than detracted from the yeastiness and zest of life; insistence on mutability did not efface the zeal for engagement. If verisimilitude of character portrayal was to be achieved, then Plutarch's advice stood high:

> The imitation that does not show an utter disregard of truth brings out, along with the actions, indications of both vice and virtue commingled; as is the case with that of Homer, which emphatically says goodbye to that of the Stoics, who will have it that nothing base can attach to virtue, and nothing good to vice, but that the ignorant man is quite wrong in all things, while, on the other hand, the man of culture is right in everything. These are the doctrines that we hear in the schools; but in the actions and in the life of most men, according to Euripides, 'The good and bad cannot be kept apart But there is some commingling.'

In 1579, Thomas North's translation of Plutarch's *The Lives of the Noble Grecians and Romans* was published based on the French version of Jacques Amyot. Like the French work, North's English translation offered to contemporary readers, in a prose both virile and sonorous, the texture of historical experience as lived by a pantheon of flawed heroes. North believed the reader would benefit since "it is better to see learning in noble men's lives than to read it in philosophical writings."[87]

In Elizabethan England poetry was identified with what we moderns might call drama or fiction. T. S. Eliot defined the wit of the poet in that age so: "It involved a recognition, implicit in the expression of every experience, of other kinds of experience which are possible." The human predicament was beyond precise calculation. Wit permitted and civility required that poetry portray high endeavor and sensuous ease with equal literary force. Verse could sustain a conversational and relaxed tone even when explicating the terrors of the onset of ugly old age and bodily decay. In earlier centuries (the fourteenth and fifteenth) the English lyric operated within strict conventions organizing experience around the binary poles of winter/summer, sickness/health, hot/cold, youth/old age, and pleasure/pain. Now we observe a modulation of feelings and judgments. A sustained poetic effort was initiated to project a vision of society and culture in which even the most heroic figures were marked by a dissonance between private desire and public purpose. No hero in Spenser's *Faerie Queene* goes unmarked by the exaction of the price for this costly choice. The English epic, from Sidney and Spenser to Chapman and Milton, gave full measure to this disjunction. If it could not be overcome in life, can it be overcome in art? In his youthful poem on the Passion, Milton evoked the dilemma of Hercules when describing Christ:

> Most perfect Hero, tried in heaviest plight
> Of labours huge and hard, too hard for human wight.[88]

1 7

Any slighting of the inner attraction of eros, of ease and contemplation, must diminish the heroism of choice between *otium* and the *vita attiva*. (New Italian critics—particularly Tasso—observed that the genius of Homer was that he was never more consistent than nature.) The fuller and more explicit the treatment of the passions and their psychology, the more real the lure of the world, and the more dramatic character and plot. Indeed, this was as true for the pastoral form as for the epic. In the former, worldly aspiration was renounced because the game was not worth the candle. But neither the world nor the game could be denigrated, for that would drain the choice of meaning. Society and its attraction and imperatives must be lent more ample literary recognition no matter what the ultimate moral intention of the author happened to be. Comedy called for a knowledge of mankind's pretentions and foibles. By holding the proverbial mirror to society, comedy worked to inform the spectator's judgments concerning the manners and humors governing human relations.[89]

Esthetic theory, first imported from Italy and then from France, distanced comedy from the mongrel form of mingling clowns and kings. Rhetoricians gained a historical perspective on archaic culture, discerning an association between Graeco-Roman comedy and religious harvest rites. The Italian critic and poet Guarini gave new status to the comedic and pastoral forms, separating them from old-fashioned notions of celebrating popular spontaneity and rural innocence. His commentaries and pastoral poetry were inspirational to the English writer. The once heated debates between those offering instruction in the learned principles of the mimetic role of the arts over and against those "purists" who regarded such teachings as licensing, lying, and counterfeiting were becoming a thing of the past. Perspective theory in the fine arts was gradually gaining converts to its geometric strategies for creating the illusion of three-dimensional space. The English tradition of drawing viewed as a functional technique was challenged by foreign critical theory, which regarded it as an art. Indeed, the English had been without a critical vocabulary for the arts and literature that could treat such new developments as perspective and chiaroscuro.[90]

Humanist criticism and paraphrases from classical texts lowered the barriers between tragedy and comedy. Boundaries between the familiar and remote, between high drama and farce were readily negotiated by Jacobean playwrights. The ideals of love and chivalric adventure were presented by advanced writers in the knowledge that their authority rested simultaneously in their "apparent reality and actual ideality." A critical perspective on the romance was initiated in which the artificial world of the writer was distinguished from the real world. In the latter realm pain was real and the romantic pose only a pallid gesture. The mock epic would soon dramatize the commingling of the extraordinary and the trivial: heroic style housed banal content. In tragedy we witness a distancing between human and ultimate causality. The heroics of Marlowe's Faust and Tamburlaine are displaced by the ironies and surrealistic horrors of John Webster's *The Duchess of Malfi* and *The White Devil*. All that remains for Webster's larger-than-life figures is rhetorical gesture and descent into madness. Political tragedy is informed by a Tacitean, almost Machiavellian, perspective on public life, in which confidence in the ability of traditional virtues to alter the course of history fades under the harsh glare of experience. Tragedy in general becomes more romantic and narrowly theatrical. Finally, comedy dramatizes the power of civil society to tame the extravagant norms of an archaic world. Values become synonymous with appearance so that honor is identical with reputation and truth with sharpwittedness. The distinction between affectation and habit grows dimmer over the seventeenth century.

The power of society is no longer so likely to be dramatized by the force of shared responsibilities, loyalties, and allegiances. In fact the opposite is true: dramatic interest is focused upon those conventions, customs, and manners which protect characters from despair and save institutions from anarchy. The theater separates the gulls and dupes who are swept away from the true wits who learn to swim in the treacherous tides of the oceans of the world. Romantic comedy which freed individuals from the accidents of time and place was in decline: characters must adjust their manner to suit the ways of the world. Just below the intricate surface of manners and humors lurked the naked face of self-interest. Discourses on morality were increasingly required to debate for or against humanist views that ethical principles were grounded in intersubjective customs and practices. Since they were not objective in the natural law sense, they were therefore culturally and historically relative.[91]

A series of sharp disagreements centering upon the role of noble virtues in the life of society were to contribute significantly to the development of English social and political thought. Here we observe disputation as to whether gratitude, generosity, and fortitude could serve as more than ideals for the select few. Did gifts, benevolences, exchange of courtesy, and those many benefits flowing from reciprocity act to create a durable sense of social solidarity? Hobbes, like Machiavelli, was to dissent wickedly on these matters, maintaining that rivalry was commonplace between the obliged and the obliger. The heroic drama of the period is tinged with the sadness prompted by unattainable ideals. Hobbes himself will write for those who would prosper, but he understood very well those human beings more properly preoccupied with concerns of honor rather than of mere survival and prosperity. Yet these grander ethical ideals cannot be reckoned as essential parts of the workings of a political structure. There certainly was a context in which principles of generosity were not an aberration. Hobbes's political philosophy was, however, a deliberate departure from this context. He wrote for "tame men" and was not alone in asserting that in a civil state "fortitude is a royal virtue and though it be necessary in such private men as shall be soldiers, yet for other men the less they dare the better it is for the commonwealth and themselves." Between Hobbes and such intelligent opponents as Clarendon stood the disagreement concerning the place of generosity in the *Leviathan*. For Hobbes it was too rare to be presumed upon—an ideal "only a select minority can aspire." John Locke will soon speak loftily about the "generous Temper and Courage of the English Nation." But to read Locke is to discover that generosity is a virtue not to be expected or presumed upon outside the limits of the family.[92]

18

The hypothesis that three times in the history of Western culture (sixth–fifth century B.C. Athens, fourteenth- and fifteenth-century Florence, and sixteenth–seventeenth-century Northern Europe) the tilt was away from an archaic society can be suggested. This tilt was crucial to the formation of a new critical vocabulary in the fine arts, literature, political philosophy, and ethics. In each instance an archaic culture lost pride of place: artists, literati, and the philosophically minded responded by relaxing grammatical, poetic, and epistemological links between words and things, appearance and reality, and images and the world. Literacy and philosophical debate was initiated and sustained as to the legitimacy of employing self-conciously rhetorical devices and fictional strategies to overcome this dissociation. Illusionism in the arts was regarded by moralists as counterfeiting, or worse. Resolute defenses of poetry were proclaimed against detractors who distrusted new techniques for creating the appearance of verisimilitude. Critics in each of the periods argued manfully that attempts to deceive the senses through mimetic representation or the use of perspective in the arts was ethically reprehensible and certain to bring dubious benefit to society. This disjunction was predicated upon a heightened awareness of the gap between nature and convention (meaning as attached as a natural part of a thing over and against meaning as arbitrarily imposed by man). Appreciation of possible incompatibilities between private and public morality was therefore heightened. The debate was conducted against the backdrop of a sharpened awareness of historical discontinuities. One can peruse Plato's *Cratylus* recapitulating competing theories as to the origins of language or read the *Republic* with its many-layered definitions of justice and discover the dramatic contest between views appropriate to a Homeric aristocracy over and against those of the new aristocracy of the city-state. These same arguments were pregnant with meaning for the humanists of Florence in the fourteenth and fifteenth centuries and for their confreres in France and England in the sixteenth and seventeenth.[93]

Patience was required to locate the subterranean passages between the subjectivity of human choice and objective social circumstance. The pursuit of truth was grounded in eloquence with more sophisticated accounts of the operation of human discourse. Rhetoric taught probabilities rather than truth. The toleration for disequilibrium between narrative and gloss was on the rise. It is noteworthy that in Greece and Italy the ability to endure and explore this disjunction resulted in the beginnings of a perceptual revolution. The creation of new perspectives were essential for projecting the illusion of reality as shared, measurable public space. This was a realm in which the archaic imagination was domesticated and the extravagant quest for ritual, ceremony, and enchantment as principal sources of security and pleasure lost certain energies. It was to be the Florentine Alberti, with his intense appreciation for civility and urbanity, who counseled his countrymen to renounce the search for the "marvelous."[94]

In the North the artistic imagination could not readily tolerate the separation between private and public, the disjunction between narrative and gloss. Only in the late medieval scholastic philosophy do we observe the conceptual pressure on language and its operation; even then the debate was contained within the sacramental system. Northern vernacular literature camouflaged or ignored such problems. The same cannot be said for their Italian contemporaries (from Dante and Petrarch on), whether writing in Latin or in the vernacular. Here distinctions were made between history and romance. In the North the materiality of objects received splendid artistic embellishment, whereas in Tuscany an artistic vocabulary was being coined to affirm the priority of visual truth over interior fantasy. No world of private yearnings could achieve an easy triumph over brute fact; nor was the frustration of private hopes and dreams to achieve the esthetic pathos characteristic of the Northern artistic imagination. One has but to look at Northern European tomb monuments to appreciate the talent invested in the harsh juxtaposition of the lugubrious and the triumphal. But the diffusion of the Italian practice of replacing the figure of the decomposed cadaver with the *nudité heroique* was emblematic of changes to come. Perhaps we may be going a bit too far in mentioning that Catherine de' Medici, horrified and filled with loathing upon viewing a macabre, naturalistic tomb effigy of her own self, immediately commissioned a second figure more to her taste—a representation of a reclining Venus. This would certainly stand as an example, albeit extreme, of the pleasure principle distancing itself from the reality principle. Estheticism challenged didacticism; private delight was coming to rival public display; learned content challenged ceremonial function; and artistic skill was championed over the preciousness of materials.[95]

Epilogue

The Fragile Construct

In the late Roman Empire and early Middle Ages, words which had had two sets of meanings, the one abstract and the other concrete, were relatively sure to lose the former. Bruno Migliorini, the scholar of medieval Latin and Italian vernacular, gives numerous examples indicating the early medieval preference for the concrete and tendency to welcome the vivid and highly colored. He cites, among numerous other words, the term *exemplum*: it survived in *scempio,* which originally signified "a slaughter capable of serving as an example." To this list belongs *gradus,* surviving as "a step," and not as "degree"; *putare,* which in Latin had meant either to cut or think or believe, survived only in *potare* (to prune); *stirps* survived as *sterpo,* meaning stub or offshoot. Predominant attention was lavished on material and vulgar fact. The list can be greatly augmented and reflects part of a semantic shift whereby events were rendered graphic and palpable by a vocabulary clinging to the word it would describe. This transition also involved a movement in the vulgar Latin away from indirect discourse, so that we have a world free of rhetorical editing. The use of direct discourse served to make deeds and events visible and concrete, presented in all their materiality and sensuousness.[1]

My purpose here is not to explore changes in the Latin syntax, grammar, or stylistics of the early Middle Ages, but rather to suggest that in important respects the literature, recorded discourse, and even quotidian documents were the mirror image or the reverse of those rhetorical and lexical habits of the later age we have been considering under the rubric of "tilt toward civility." The crux of the difference may well rest in the fact that in the earlier time we observe the contraction of a civil society, whereas in the later age we perceive its extension.

In my previous book, *Medieval Italy: Constraints and Creativity* (Bloomington, Ind., 1981), I attempted to explore possible relationships between linguistic change and the transformation of associative life in north and central Italy during the eleventh and twelfth centuries. The force of literal ties and the authority of concrete logic were attenuated as confidence in the durability of social and economic arrangements was enhanced. Abstract economic bonds and modes of exchange permitted new forms of associative life to flourish. In an earlier time a necessary material rapport existed between person and object. The need to make concrete the relationship between men and their possessions *(gewere)* had its analogue in such practices as *mundium,* in which wardship over women and minors held by the father or guardian was transferred to the husband only after payment of the bridesgift. This was a world in which women, gifts, pledges, and oaths were exchanged in a manner well understood by the anthropologist studying primitive and archaic societies. Guarantees were required for fulfilling daily obligations, with agreements sealed by the exchange of sacred tokens or pledges. Frequently, the pledge or *wadia* was equal in value to the debt incurred: the oath was sacred and a personal guarantee was required for those going surety.

The number of instances in which ties of obligation were lent concrete form could readily be multiplied. Creditors acknowledged their debts *per lignum et chartam,* and it is difficult to distinguish a pawn or pledge from a document as a source of obligation. The notion that writing in itself could be a cause of obligation was tenuous at best. This, then, was a world of narrow loyalties, demanding kinship ties, and exacting primary allegiances. The individual was enclosed in a literal world where the materiality of bonds was immediate and certain. Movement toward release from an archaic world structured upon networks of primary obligation was first clearly reflected in the slackening of blood ties. This loosening of bonds was dramatized by the holy man who solemnly and publicly disavowed the once-sacred duty of pursuing the blood feud. Kinsmen had inherited the duty of revenge. The two most influential religious figures in Tuscany in the eleventh century, Romualdo and Gualberto, both vociferously renounced this time-honored tradition, refusing to settle family scores in the bloody, tribal way. Religious reformers and spiritual leaders, from Damiani to Saint Francis, challenged that bedrock of aristocratic insensitivity, the payment of composition for settling violent crimes. Holy men were the most relentless critics of these archaic practices and were to propose very different networks of relationships based on empathy, compassion, and love. Their trust was increasingly invested in the power of abstract ties. In the eleventh and twelfth centuries the holy man was at the cutting edge of social change, advancing new possibilities for the relationship between the human and the divine. Of course these prospects had their analogue in the changing character of quotidian social and economic arrangements. In Tuscany we observe the beginnings of a harsh critique of the world of gift culture at mid-eleventh century. A bitter campaign launched by Giovanni Gualberto and other Florentine reformers was mounted against ecclesiastical institutions accepting gifts in return for spiritual benefits. These Florentine monks and clerics attacked this nefarious practice, rejecting the widely held and time-honored idea that wealth was a sign of divine favor and a proper means of gaining salvation.

It can be argued that the impetus for the transformation of certain archaic values originated principally from the clergy, their lay confreres, and supporters of church reform. Dissatisfaction and social criticism found sustained expression in religious and reforming thought. With the initiation of the Tuscan *volgare* as a literary medium in the thirteenth century, we observe the beginnings of a long-term investment in a vernacular accommodated for commerical negotiation and political transaction. The rise of the territorial state was a vital force in shaping this metamorphosis. Terms such as *commune,* designating a political institution, *popolo* as a synonym for a particular type of regime, as well as *podestà* for chief foreign magistrate or governor of the city are but a sampling of a lengthy catalogue. The term *contado,* designating the countryside subject to the commune, was appropriated from the word *contado,* as land subject to a royal count; *contadino* was a worker on the land. The circulation of money produced a rich vocabulary: *ragione* came to mean account or bookkeeping, and from it stemmed *ragioniere* or accountant. The language of accounting and exchange, as well as that of public finance and private credit, increased exponentially.

The word *ragione* was a particular favorite in the deliberative sessions of the Florentine signory. Through the exercise of "reason" it might be possible to discern durable landmarks for mapping policy behind the clouds of chaos generated by arbitrary actions of rulers and states. But even so, there was no world of rational order in the domain of politics. Devotion to reason was especially intense because the citizenry felt itself vulnerable to capricious and untamed forces. *Fortuna* and *necessità* made a mockery of many a rational calculation.[2]

Multiplication of points on the linguistic compass allowing for extension of meaning of key words has been one of our major interests. Of course language steeped in anterior images, while wrestling new images from a traditional idiom, did not break its ties with the past. A key word, such as *virtù* in Italian, or *vertu* in French, or *virtue* in English, had a talismanic power signifying potency, and this ran well back into past times. The semantic change was in part the result of the revival of classical meaning. The key word *virtù, vertu,* or *virtue* was used not just in the Christian sense of virtue or in the archaic sense of potency but came to signify valor and heroism à la the classical. In addition to this series of meanings, human accomplishment itself came to be designated as man's *virtù;* from this emerged the term *virtuoso,* one usage being to designate an individual as having a taste for the fine arts and an appetite for collecting antiquities. We observe in this instance how the register of meaning covered points on the linguistic spectrum running from the preternatural to a particular definition highly indentured to the civil and social.

A revealing instance of linguistic transformation is to be found in the declining archaic usage of the word *merito.* A commonplace in the Tuscan *volgare* of the thirteenth century, it had served as a metaphor for representing the attractive notion of payment as reward for good deeds and labors. It was recompense for services and even religious offerings, and, like *dono* (gift), it was employed as a substitute for payment of interest. A battery of such words continued to retain currency through the thirteenth century, even persisting beyond: their usage, however, was becoming increasingly formulaic, and this is a vital piece of linguistic evidence. The need for such vocabulary was clearly to portray a heroic conception of exchange, and only gradually was this perspective on everyday transactions to be deflated. To represent payment or reward, not as consequence of some heroic or generous effort, but rather as the result of a self-interested and mundane negotiation was both esthetically and morally unappealing. Yet the fabric of commercial and civil life was replete with just such modest, unheroic, and occasionally disreputable deeds. The scaling down of the meaning of the word *merito,* with its ultimate formulaic usage, is but one instance of the deflation of the currency of an epic vocabulary. The word *omaggio,* in addition to its traditional definitions, came to include a mere sign of respect. *Grazia* came to signify, in addition to its archaic sense of favor or benefit, physical elegance; *honor* was now born from human encounter and, like courtesy, was miniaturized and privatized, implying only slight obligation: more telling was its definition as "respect for prevailing social convention." To the spectrum of meanings of such words as *piacere,* the classical revival added the sense of pleasure as a condition and mainspring of existence to the traditional definition of the word that had featured the sinful, the dark, and the guilty. The passions also were lent higher ethical credit: grief, anger, and ambition, among others, received meanings that provided social, if not psychological, validation. The noble and ignominious were no longer so likely to stand as deadly opposites in a linguistic world where philosophical dualisms did not exercise their customary monopoly. Several of the seven deadly sins (avarice, sloth, luxury, and so on) were perceived as contributing—however indirectly—to certain social benefits. In contemporary texts of the Quattrocento and Cinquecento, *utile* was balanced against *onore.*

Virtue in an archaic society tended to be public, serving to create obligation. Over the centuries key words such as *dishonor* assumed, in addition to their strong meanings, weaker ones such as loss of dignity. The archaic usage of this word carried the explicit charge of concrete damage; now, with the prevalence of an emergent civil society, we observe key terms becoming polyvalent. We have spoken before about the conception of *virtus;* in archaic times its synonym was *Heil. Virtus* or *Heil* included a belief in divine power operating through royal and saintly figures. The king, by exercising his *Heil,* gave protection to pilgrims and merchants. The onset of catastrophe or strokes of misfortune was seen as an indication that once-powerful figures had forfeited divine favor. The surest signs of *virtus* were to be found at shrines of the popular miracle-working saints. *Virtù* in the hands of a Machiavelli or Guicciardini had a genealogy reaching back into a murky primordial past. Like so many other key words, this term did not lose its roots in the preternatural. Further, its archaic forebears were never at rest and could be evoked to benefit a poet or embarrass a polite writer. In the fine arts it would be another century before Bernini severed subjective experience from pretersubjective ritual. The novelist Henry James struck a grim balance on this divorce: "Modern Tombs are a skeptical affair . . . the ancient sculptors have left us nothing to say in regard to the great, final contrast."[3]

If we examine usages of the word *ceremony,* we may be able to appreciate something of the direction and complexity of change. Negative usages of this key word appear over the centuries, with Erasmus virtually dismissing *ceremielae* as "trivial little ritual nonsense." *Ceremoniale* was the Italian for a book listing rule of etiquette, and over the centuries *ceremony* came to mean *ceremonial.* To the archaic usage of ceremony as pomp or solemnity or as a pure act of courtesy, one must add a series of highly self-conscious transformations. Ceremony as a communal, performative sign was on the one hand deflated. Religious rituals and observances were regarded by humanistically minded reformers such as Erasmus as being formal, external, and empty. Scholars of manners such as Giovanni della Casa contended that there was precious little difference between ceremonies, falsehoods, and dreams: they were all equally insubstantial and a tribute to nothing but human vanity. While some were appalled at the excessive use of ceremony in the Roman Church, there was of course the other view. Opposing the foregoing were writers on politics and civil society who perceived the value of ritual. Machiavelli would contend that republics wishing to maintain themselves free of corruption and decay must also retain, uncorrupted, the ceremonies of their religion. Of course republican Rome was the model, and if Machiavelli and Guicciardini differed from Erasmus and the Christian humanists, it was because they believed that ritual and ceremony were essential for the proper functioning of a civic society. Agreement as to the negative usage of the word, wherein ceremonies were regarded as formal and external, did not preclude the fact that they had utility.

When one traces the extension of the register of meanings of the word *ceremony,* one becomes aware that its value in religious life became problematic and that self-awareness concerning its role in a civil society heightened. Criticism of the rituals of Christianity for subverting civic virtues served as a backdrop for asserting the value of pagan, state ceremonies. Estranged from its archaic roots, ceremony was nonetheless seen as valuable for inculcating political devotion and social bonds. In matters pertaining to social comportment, ritual and artifice were appreciated because they did not disrupt social cohesion. Prudence and decorum were situational and were also rhetorical imperatives intended to generate flexibility of character.

An appreciation that myth lent shading to sensibility enabled writers to create a superindividual reality, yet this reality was acknowledged as humanly constructed and humanly comprehensible. The discordant attractions of earthly values on the one side and Christian ideals on the other were dramatized rather than resolved. Easy to say that the thought of death must always be before one's eyes. But when Petrarch raises the difficulty of the mobility of the human soul always tossed by new passions and preoccupations, then Saint Augustine's admonition loses its urgency. The tendency to interpret traditional wisdom in psychological terms and to examine political counsel in esthetic terms favored the rhetorical strategy of amplification or *copia*. This rhetorical tactic worked as a generative principle dedicated to reproducing the variety of nature and the multiplicity of moral options. Preference was marked for dialogue and debate over any one-sided literary formulation. Humanist pedagogy was preoccupied with invention or the finding of arguments. Indeed, the more closely one looks at crucial texts, the more one is likely to perceive the conscious resistance against systematizing discourse. Humanist thought operated in a general way to contain the epistemological threat by the practice of social consensus. Both sides of a question must be argued with the intent that the individual could arrive at a socially useful pragmatic truth.

A quotation from Erich Auerbach's *Mimesis* evaluating Rabelais' rhetorical art conveys something of the social imperative of the new literature:

> Almost all the elements which are united in Rabelais' style are known from the later Middle Ages. . . . The way in which these elements are exaggerated and intertwined produces an entirely new picture. . . . Late medieval works are confined within a definite frame, socially, geographically, cosmologically, religiously, and ethically; . . . But Rabelais' entire effort is directed toward playing with things and with the multiplicity of their possible aspects; upon tempting the reader out of his customary and definite way of regarding things, by showing him phenomena in utter confusion; upon tempting him out into the great ocean of the world, in which he can swim freely, though it be at his own peril.[4]

Auerbach's comments on Montaigne illustrating the essayist's contention that it was necessary to come to terms with a world not sustained by a heroic ethos or resolute philosophical conviction are also worth citing:

> And—still more significant—among all his contemporaries he had the clearest conception of the problem of man's self-orientation; that is, the task of making oneself at home in existence without fixed points of support. His irony, his dislike of big words, his calm way of being at ease with himself prevent him from pushing beyond the limits of the probable and into the realm of the tragic. But the tragic appears as the highly personal tragedy of the individual, and moreover, compared with antiquity, as far less restricted by traditional ideas of the limits of fate, the cosmos, natural forces, political forms, and man's inner being.[5]

Favoring the pragmatic art of communication, the problematics of inquiry, debate pro and contra, and amplification of argument encouraged proliferation of lexical aids, guidebooks, and maps intended not to promulgate, in Descartes' words, "la vrai method," but to persuade "per l'exemple et par la coustume." What weighed on language was the multiplication of meaning as the register was extended from the strong toward the weak. Words such as *dignity,* which once carried a heavy spiritual cargo and unequivocal commitment to heroic endeavor, were now perceived more modestly as the consequence of a concern for the betterment of humanity and the attendant receipt of human admiration. The notion of glory was desanctified and the ideal pretentions of pride naturalized. *Discipline,* once synonymous with norms and rules to which one submitted, now also signified something one learned. *Satisfaction* never lost its literal meaning of doing penance or rendering compensation for an insult. In early Tuscan vernacular texts and statutes, satisfaction was essentially a promise made that would secure performance of a particular agreement. As we have noted, one could give satisfaction (or security) for the good behavior of a third party. Over the next centuries this range of archaic activities, including reparation for sin and satisfaction for vendetta, was augmented as the idea crossed into new frontiers of meaning more psychological and abstract—closer to pleasure and fulfillment. *Dishonor* moved from the strong definition of concrete damage to the weaker one of loss of dignity, and *eloquence* from harsh persuasion to subtle and subliminal influence. The word *stato,* as has previously been observed, continued to pertain to one's grade or condition or patrimony or good fortune or power. In fact, *la potenza* was regularly conjoined with *lo stato.* Over the centuries these archaic definitions were jostled aside by the less literal, less concrete, more abstract conceptions of *state.*[6]

I have rehearsed this catalogue of words at the close of this book in order to underscore the following impressions: First, the movement of language and symbol was mixed and gradual; the new did not replace the old but enhanced the fluidity of semantic usage. Second, this transition was replicated in several fields of creative endeavor, particularly in the fine arts and literature. If one considers a single intellectual enterprise, such as the defense of poetry to which so many literati contributed, one is bound to observe how cautious and crablike its movement from the thirteenth through to the late fifteenth century. Here, as in many other intellectual enterprises, the difficulties should not be underestimated, nor should the fact that many of these changes transpired in Italy over more than three centuries. The Italian Renaissance was the locale for the coining of a new vocabulary in fields such as art history and literary criticism, and here we observe change which can be calculated logarithmically rather than geometrically. In England and Northern Europe time was telescoped, and this mattered a great deal. If one reads Erwin Panofsky or Thomas Greene, one should bear in mind that the sense of anachronism which they believe to be quintessential, was never fully realized—at least until the seventh century. The very term, as we have noticed, does not surface until the sixteenth century, making, perhaps, an early appearance in Florence. This suggests something of the struggle involved in achieving a sense of historical distance from the past. Neither Greene nor Panofsky offers any social explanation for the emergence of the generation of this new historical perspective. If there is merit in my argument, then we should appreciate the struggle to find a vocabulary and a literary and artistic style for expressing disjunction from an archaic past. No easy task, this.

The observations of Paul Oskar Kristeller on the intellectual history of the Renaissance have influenced two generations of scholars. After many years of dedicated research devoted to seminal thinkers and leading ideas, Kristeller has voiced a certain disappointment. In his *Renaissance Thought, the Classic Scholastic and Humanist Strains* (New York, 1961), pp. 17–18, he characterized humanism as a movement that cannot properly be considered either philosophical or theoretical. His grim conclusion states that humanist works,

> often seem to lack not only originality, but also coherence, method, and substance, and if we try to sum up these arguments and conclusions, leaving aside citations, examples, and commonplaces, literary ornaments and digressions, we are frequently left with nearly empty hands. Thus I have not been convinced by the attempts to interpret these humanistic treatises as contributions to speculative thought.

Kristeller has explored the intellectual terrain from the fourteenth through the sixteenth centuries. Bernard Williams, another eminent historian of ideas, has examined philosophical texts of the seventeenth century, writing principally on Descartes. Looking back on the Renaissance, he, too, discerns a confusion of possible answers to philosophical and theoretical questions stemming from an inability on the part of leading thinkers to generate prototypes for this knowledge. Further, these thinkers are without any settled belief about how to acquire such an understanding.

> In the Renaissance, a confusion of possible answers was generated to this question of what capacities could lead to knowledge. Many Renaissance thinkers, particularly in Italy, understood this task to be not just the establishment of knowledge about the classical past, but also the revival of the attitude to knowledge which existed in that past. But this understanding was itself surrounded by great uncertainty about what the powers of the ancients consisted in. . . . This incapacity to tell the difference between the power of words and the force of argument (prevalent, then as now, in Paris) contributed to the sceptical disorientation which existed in Descartes's time. Having discarded the rundown traditional logic which then was current (for which Descartes sustained a life-long contempt), and the answers to sceptical argument provided by the Aristotelian tradition, adventurous thinkers were uncertain what dialectical weapons could counter scepticism.[7]

Neither Kristeller nor Williams have an abiding interest in answers to those questions involving civic comportment, good arms, good letters, and giving of counsel, both spiritual and political, which so engaged the humanists. Parenthetically, it should be noted that in fifteenth-century Tuscan vernacular usage, *filosofia* could signify "counsels of mundane wisdom," sometimes different from and sometimes compatible with "Christian counsel." Whether the humanists intended to resolve philosophical problems or not is of singular consequence to the historian of ideas. Williams, however, believes a priori in the retrograde character of this movement with its confusion "of the force of reason with the power of the spoken word. . . ." Contributing little to speculative thought, Williams quotes, with approval, Descartes' wonderfully dismissive comment concerning the humanist's preoccupation with history:

> . . . nor shall we come out as philosophers, if we read all the arguments of Plato and Aristotle, but can form no sound judgement on the matters in question: we shall have learned, not the sciences, but history.[8]

But it was precisely the concern of literati and humanists with history and the force of the written and spoken word that permitted language and vicarious experience to colonize imaginatively an ever-widening zone between reason and necessity, instinct and lucidity, love and duty, prudence and liberality; between anguish and loathing on the one side and unpretentious wisdom on the other; between careful scrutiny of the defects of human nature and the serene acceptance of the most unflattering portrayals of man. Instinct could not be crushed or nature silenced. The idea of nobility was reconciled with that of humanity. Descartes himself in his *Traité des Passions* conferred prestige on the noble passions. His purpose was not to crush desire by an act of will, but to seek for a condition of concord between the impulses. The high status of love was harmonized with the demands of society. Feelings of guilt linked to the satisfaction of desire were attenuated by favoring soft definitions of sin and evil. This owed less to traditions of religious thought and more to the new literature with its valorization of self-esteem and dismantling of archaic pridefulness. Stoic ethics were those occupied almost exclusively with human grandeur. The notion of ease *(facilité)* was not so readily associated with cowardice. Facility or facileness, like skill or art or cunning, was valued, as interest in the means of achievement challenged a traditional preoccupation with end or outcome. Prejudice against gaining advantage through discipline and training was somewhat dissipated. The idea of glory became more humane and benevolent, and, therefore, the need for self-assertiveness was less compelling. The prestige of love was reconciled with the claims of society. The idea of social discipline, while regulating this passion, did not divest it of its archaic grandeur.[9]

Notes

In my notes I have offered suggestions for further reading in lieu of a bibliography. These suggestions are not intended to be comprehensive; rather, they feature the more recent writings which, I feel, present new interpretations and suggest possibilities for new investigation.

INTRODUCTION

1. For a contemporary assessment of the political role of Giano della Bella, who is credited with working strenuously to implement the Ordinances of Justice (the basic Florentine constitution), see Giovanni Villani, *Chronicle,* trans. R. Selfe and P. Wicksteed (London, 1906), pp. 309–15. Cf. also, D. Compagni, *The Chronicle,* trans. E. Benecke and F. Howell (London, 1906), pp. 29–31, 49–51. A new translation of Compagni's chronicle, entitled *Chronicle of Florence* (Philadelphia, 1980), has been rendered by Daniel Bornstein. See esp. pp. 14–22. On Sylvestro de' Medici, who in the opinion of contemporaries saved the city from ruin at the hands of the lower orders and their allies in 1378, see M. Becker, *Florence in Transition: Studies in the Rise of the Territorial State,* 2 vols. (Baltimore, 1968), 2: 78–79, 146–47, 177–78. The poet, Franco Sacchetti, made a play on Salvestro's name calling him "Salvation of the World" (Salvator Mundi). Cf. also, G. Brucker, *Florentine Politics and Society, 1343–1378* (Princeton, 1962), pp. 358–89.

2. G. Villani, *Chronicle,* p. 449.

3. Ibid., pp. 212–13. For a life of Latini, See T. Sundby, *Della vita e delle opere di Brunetto Latini* (Florence, 1884), including commentary by R. Renier, I. Del Lungo and A. Mussafia. For a recent study, see C. T. Davis, *Dante's Italy and Other Essays* (Philadelphia, 1984), pp. 171 ff.

4. For a Latin transcription and Italian translation of this key work of Bruni's, see E. Garin, *Prosatori latini del Quattrocento* (Naples-Milan, 1952), pp. 44–99.

5. For Filippo Villani's biography of Francesco da Barberino, see *Croniche storiche di Giovanni, Matteo and Filippo Villani,* ed. I. Dragomanni (Milan, 1848), 7: 38–41. On the "new citizens," see M. Becker, "The 'Novi Cives' in Florentine Politics," *Mediaeval Studies* 24 (1962), 35–82.

6. G. Holmes, in his recent work *Florence, Rome and the Origins of the Renaissance* (Oxford, 1986), pp. 78–88, considers the influence of Aristotle's *Ethics* and *Politics* on Dante and his literary contemporaries.

7. The appetite for practical knowledge and useful information on topics ranging from child rearing to meat carving, from how to learn to live to how to learn to die has been judged to be among the most prominent intellectual features of the English literary landscape in the fifteenth and early sixteenth centuries. See H. Bennett, *English Books and Readers, 1475–1557,* 2nd ed. (Cambridge, 1969), pp. 65–152, and his "Science and Information in English Writings of the 15th Century," *Modern Language Review* 39 (1944), 1–8. Compare English interests with the literary concerns of Tuscan merchants and patricians, as disclosed by their inventories of books. Commonplace in the Florentine holdings are Dante's *Divine Comedy,* Boccaccio's *Decameron,* and Petrarch's *I Trionfi.* Also, civil education is revealed by holdings—particularly the works of Cicero. See C. Bec, *Les marchands écrivains: Affaires et humanisme à Florence* (Paris, 1967), pp. 301–30.

8. B. Latini, *La rettorica,* ed. F. Maggini (Florence, 1915), p. 23; *Li livres dou Tresor,* III, 1.2, ed. F. Carmody (Berkeley, 1958). Cf. also, H. Wieruszowski, " *'Ars*

dictaminis' in the Time of Dante," in *Politics and Culture in Medieval Spain and Italy* (Rome, 1974), 359–77.

9. I am completing a manuscript on Florentine wills and pious benefactions from 1000 to 1500, and will discuss this transformation in some detail.

10. Noteworthy for its treatment of the revival of classical oratory in late Trecento and early Quattrocento northern Italy, is J. McManamon, "Innovation in Early Humanist Rhetoric: The Oratory of Pier Paolo Vergerio the Elder," *Rinascimento* 22 (1982), 3–32. Cf. also, J. Banker, "Giovanni di Bonandrea and Civic Values in the Context of the Italian Rhetorical Tradition," *Manuscripta* 18 (1974), 3–20.

11. The word *conversation,* often referred to in the present book, was in medieval parlance, frequently used to designate the practice of religious life after a deliberate renunciation of the world in favor of God. See S. Bertelli, F. Cardini, and E. Zorzi, *Italian Renaissance Courts,* trans. M. Fitton and G. Culverwell (London, 1986), p. 182.

12. For a discussion of the Medici *ricordanza* and its reflections on family history in the late Trecento, see G. Brucker, "The Medici in the fourteenth Century," *Speculum* 32 (1957), 1–26. For the comments of the member of the Alberti family and his retrospective on the early history of the clan, see *Biblioteca Nazionale Firenze, Fondo Magliabechiano,* II–IV, 378, c. 32.

13. J. Banker, in his " 'Ars Dictaminis' and Rhetorical Tradition at the Bolognese University in the fourteenth Century," *Medievalia et Humanistica,* n.s., 5 (1974), 153–63, examines the relationship between rhetorical strategies and social transformations in the late thirteenth and early fourteenth centuries in Tuscany.

14. For the comments of K. B. McFarlane, see his "The Wars of the Roses," *Proceedings of the British Academy* 34 (1964), 97–119, esp. 117. For the quotation from Fortescue, see his *De laudibus legum Anglie,* ed. S. Chrimes (Cambridge, 1942), p. 119.

15. The quotation from the Boke of St. Albans is discussed by D. Morgan in his "The Individual Style of the English Gentleman," in *Gentry and Lesser Nobility in Late Medieval England* (New York, 1986), p. 30.

16. The citation and translation of Tasso is to be found in C. Brand, *Torquato Tasso: A Study of the Poet and His Contribution to English Literature* (Cambridge, 1963), p. 47.

17. F. Nietzsche, *Beyond Good and Evil* (New York, 1954), no. 258, p. 576.

1. THE TILT TOWARD CIVILITY AND THE WINDS OF CHANGE

1. R. Williams, *Keywords: A Vocabulary of Culture and Society,* expanded ed. (London, 1985), pp. 291–93. Cf. also, L. Febvre, *A New Kind of History,* ed. P. Burke (New York, 1973), pp. 219–57; J. Bossy, "Some Elementary Forms of Durkheim," *Past & Present* 95 (1982), 3–18, and his "Blood and Baptism: Kinship, Community and Christianity in Western Europe from the Fourteenth to the Seventeenth Century," *Sanctity and Society: The Church and the World,* ed. D.Baker (Oxford, 1973), 129–46. Very useful is T. Finkenstaedt, E. Leisi, and D. Wolff, *A Chronological English Dictionary* (Heidelberg, 1970). New words from the *Oxford English Dictionary* [hereafter, *OED*] are listed alphabetically, year by year.

2. R. Williams, *Keywords,* p. 293. On mutations in the language of trade and commerce, see J. Pocock, "Early Modern Capitalism: The Augustan Perception," in *Feudalism, Capitalism and Beyond,* ed. R. Neale (Canberra, Australia, 1975), 62–85, and J. Appleby, *Economic Thought and Ideology in Seventeenth-Century England* (Princeton, 1976), chap. 2. Q. Skinner, "Language and Social Change," in *The State of Language,* eds. L. Michaels and C. Ricks (Berkeley, 1980), 562–78, treats the changing meaning of key words, and especially useful for the present inquiry is his discussion of shifts in the usage of the word *commodity.* H. Lefebvre, *Le langage et la*

société (Paris, 1966) offers a general theoretical discussion of problems implicit in relating language to social and economic practice.

3. For an informed and sensitive discussion of this controversy and many other issues and disputes central to my argument concerning the tilt toward civility, see J. Bossy, *Christianity in the West 1400–1700* (Oxford, 1985). Cf. also, N. Elias, *The Civilizing Process: The Development of Manners,* trans. E. Jephcott (New York, 1971). For further bibliography on the themes of manners and conviviality, see F. Heal, "The Idea of Hospitality in Early Modern England," *Past & Present* 102 (1984), 66–84. For a more detailed treatment of Veronese's encounter with the Inquisition and the changing of the title of his painting from *Last Supper* to *Feast at the House of Levi,* see T. Pignatti, *Veronese* (Venice, 1976), pp. 55–58. Useful for background on art criticism and the Catholic Reformation, is A. Quint, *Cardinal Federico Borromeo as a Patron and a Critic of the Arts* (New York, 1986). Cf. also C. Paleotti, *Discorsi intorno alle imagini sacre e profani* in P. Barocchi's *Trattati d'arte del Cinquecento* (Bari, 1961), 2: 16–503.

4. H. Holborn, *Ulrich Von Hutten and the German Reformation,* trans. R.H. Bainton (New Haven, 1937), pp. 18–19. Cf. also the classic account of obligation and cultural responsibility of nobles (perhaps a bit idealized) by Otto Brunner, *Adeliges Landleben and europäischer Geist* (Salzburg, 1949). On intergroup pledging and village cohesion, see the model study of E. DeWindt, *Land and People in Holywell-cum-Needingworth* (Toronto, 1972), pp. 243 ff. For a recent study of family and the ethos of solidarity, see B. Hanawalt, *The Ties That Bound: Peasant Families in Medieval England* (Oxford, 1986). Mervyn James's *Society, Politics and Culture: Studies in Early Modern England* (Cambridge, 1986) is a magisterial work treating the ties emanating from concepts of honor among English magnates and gentry in the late fifteenth and sixteenth centuries. Cf. also his earlier study, *English Politics and the Concept of Honour 1485–1642, Past & Present,* Supplement 3 (1978). Estate accounts of the earl of Northumberland and the notes and remarks of their steward, George Clarkson, provide a snapshot of an estate community in sixteenth-century northern England. Here we have a "common wealth" defined by the benefits, duties, and rights arising from social bonds. The lord was to be "fully answered of his accustomed servyce and suncyent rent." To exact more would, in the language of stewardship, be to violate order and go against "conscience." See M. James, *Society, Politics and Culture,* p. 277. One does not desire to present a glossy picture of sixteenth-century nobles, but at the same time the moral context of their lives need not be diminished. A single document might stand for many to illustrate the extent to which an ethic of responsibility could be internalized. The duke of Anjou made his last will and testament in June of 1584. First he asked forgiveness from the king from whom he held a large *apanage,* and whose liberality he had enjoyed. The duke knew all too well that he had irritated his majesty: "You have augmented my means by your kindness, and what is more, you have allowed me to assist myself from the revenues of my domain, and to secure a portion of it with my creditors. I have been gratuitously assisted, however, by many lords and gentlemen, your subjects, most of whom have inconvenienced, impoverished, and nearly ruined themselves in my service. My servants have served me faithfully, each in his own charge, and I have not had the means to repay them as I would like and as reason dictates. Even the majority of them have not been paid. I owe around 300,000 *écus* to many different subjects of your kingdom, and I carry to the grave their earnings, their tears, and their wailing, without having the means to discharge myself to God and men . . . I beg you to continue my revenues for four more years and to employ them to this effect, that is to say, to acquit my debts and to pay my servants' wages, whom I ask you to employ for two further years. . . . Finally, the Netherlands have bestowed upon me most dearly the titles of duke and count, which they still owe me. And if I have any power in their behalf, I

pray them to transfer everything to you, to whom (and equally to your successors) I leave and give all rights and pretensions that I have been able to acquire in this respect, by virtue of the official treaties that I have made with them. Moreover, Cambrai can serve as a bulwark, acquired and won by the means you have given me. I remain obliged to defend its citizens, who with such affection and devotion threw themselves into my arms. I beg you in God's name, my Lord, to accept what I possess by right and authority in this place, and to put an end to the oppression and desolation of such good people." Cf. M. P. Holt, *The Duke of Anjou and the Politique Struggle during the Wars of Religion* (Cambridge, 1986), pp. 210–11.

5. J. Bossy, *Christianity in the West,* pp. 155–56. For a general discussion of new research on possible relationships between changing religious beliefs and altered patterns of social behavior, see Keith Thomas, "An Anthropology of Religion and Magic," *Journal of Interdisciplinary History* 6 (1975), 91–105. For a sensitive appraisal of Borromeo and Catholic-Reformation sentiments, see H. O. Evennett, *The Spirit of the Counter-Reformation* (Cambridge, 1968). Cf. also, C. Borromeo, *Instructiones fabricae et supellectilis ecclesiasticae* in P. Barocchi, *Trattati d'arte del Cinquecento,* 3: 3–113. On neighborly obligation and the exacting requirements of spontaneous charity as sources of personal anxiety, the bibliography is extensive, but see especially, M. MacDonald, *Mystical Bedlam: Madness, Anxiety and Healing in Seventeenth-Century England* (Cambridge, 1981), pp. 104–8. A MacFarlane's *Witchcraft in Tudor and Stuart England* (New York, 1970), chaps. 12, 15, 16, and Keith Thomas's *Religion and the Decline of Magic* (New York, 1970), chap. 17 present ample evidence for psychological tensions generated by conflicting claims of individual advantage and well-being over and against the requirements of fidelity, openhandedness, and almsgiving.

6. For Italian language usage and changes in meaning over time, see *Grand dizionario della lingua italiana,* ed. S. Battaglia (Turin, 1962–); *Vocabolario degli Accademici della Crusca* (Venice, 1612; reprinted, Florence, 1974); B. Migliorini, *Storia della lingua italiana* (Florence, 1963), 3d ed. For French usage, see E. Littré, *Dictionnaire de la langue francaise,* 7 vols. (Paris, 1963). For English usage, see *Middle English Dictionary,* ed. H. Kurath and S. Kuhn (Ann Arbor, Mich., 1952–). I wish to thank my student Jay Smith for providing me with materials from the French experience in his unpublished paper, "From the Noble Point of View: *Crédit, Gage* and the Values of the Early Modern French Nobility." For additional information on English usage, see *The New English Dictionary on Historical Principles,* ed. J. A. H. Murray et al., 13 vols. (Oxford, 1888–1933). Cf. also, M. Tilley, *A Dictionary of the Proverbs in England in the Sixteenth and Seventeenth Centuries* (Ann Arbor, Mich., 1950). For Latin, see *Thesaurus linguae latinae,* 9 vols. (Leipzig, 1900–); A. Souter, *A Glossary of Later Latin to 600 A.D.* (Oxford, 1949); H. Walther, *Proverbia sententiaeque latinitatis mediiaevi,* 6 vols. (Gottingen, 1963–69); C. DuCange, *Glossarum mediae et infimes latinitatis,* 7 vols. (Paris, 1840–50).

7. Georges Duby, "L'émergence de l'individu: Situation de la solitude XI–XIII siècle," *Histoire de la vie privée,* ed. P. Ariès and G. Duby (Paris, 1985), 2: 502–8. Cf. Brian Stock's review of this volume in the *Times Literary Supplement* (5 September 1986), 983–84. The significance of the constriction of essential sociability as the individual experienced contrasts and ruptures within the many concentric circles of social life, is discussed by P. Braunstein, "Approches de l'intimité XIVᵉ–XVᵉ siècle," in *Histoire de la vie privée,* 2: 526–619. The corollary of the recession of sociability is the tendency to experience self through these contrasts and ruptures. Cf. M. Becker, "An Essay on the Quest for Identity in the Early Italian Renaissance," in *Essays Presented to Wallace K. Ferguson,* ed. J. Rowe and W. Stockdale (Toronto, 1971), 295–311.

8. P. Chaunu, "Mourir à Paris (XVᵉ–XVIIᵉ siècles)," *Annales E.S.C.* 31 (1976), 45,

for statistics on restitution of usury is perhaps a bit overprecise but still revealing. See J. Bossy's comments, *op. cit.*, p. 40. On mortality rates for British ducal families, see T. Hollingsworth, "A Demographic Study of the British Ducal Families," *Population in History*, eds. D. Glasser and D. Eversley (London, 1965), 354–78. On the taming of the ancient English nobility, see K. McFarlane, *England in the Fifteenth Century: Collected Essays* (London, 1981). He sees the emergence of a "chastened, indeed craven mood" among nobility with the coming of the Tudors. They were now "more self-effacing, less sure of their mission to coerce high-handed rulers, congenitally wary, convinced of the benefits of passive obedience" (p. 117). They had probably learned this somewhat dispiriting lesson of obedience as far back as the mid-fifteenth century. Cf. p. 260.

9. See P. Fleming, "Charity, Faith and the Gentry of Kent, 1422–1529," *Property and Politics: Essays in Later Medieval English History*, ed. T. Pollard (New York, 1984), 36–58, esp. p. 37, where the piece of doggerel is cited. On the vital moral and spiritual issue of the stewardship over property by the rich and their duty to the poor, see Isiah, 58:7; Ezekiel, 18:5–9; Matthew, 25:35–36. Moral theologians allowed that in case of extreme need, all things were once again to be considered as held in common, and therefore a man could, either by stealth or openly, take possession of the goods of another. Baptista Trovamala's *Rosella casuum* is noted several times by Thomas More in his "Debellation." If the need was not extreme, the individual was required to provide in other ways, even if this meant begging. Saint Antoninus, *Summa* 2. 1. 14.) See *The Complete Works of St. Thomas More*, Yale ed., eds. S. Surtz and J. Hexter (New Haven, 1965), 4: 332–33. Theft as a permissible alternative to starvation had the support of civil lawyers and, in 1279, was lent papal sanction. See W. Ullmann, *The Medieval Idea as Represented by Lucca de Penna* (London, 1946), p. 154. The common law of medieval England considered theft in time of necessity, if below the value of twelve pence, as unpunishable. *The Mirror of Justices*, ed. W. Whittaker (Selden Society, 1895), p. 141. This and other references are discussed in Keith Thomas's "The Social Origins of Hobbes Political Thought," in *Hobbes Studies* (Oxford, 1965), 221–25.

10. P. Wicksteed, *The Latin Works of Dante Alighieri* (London, 1904), p. 153. For a thoughtful appraisal, see A. P. d'Entrèves, *Dante as a Political Thinker* (Oxford, 1952). For treatment of the Latin and vernacular version of the *Ethics* of Aristotle, which was so influential, see C. Marchesi, *L'etica nicomachea nella tradizione latina medievale* (Messina, 1904). E. Moore, in his *Studies in Dante* (Oxford, 1896), 1: 339–42, gives over one hundred fifty quotations from the *Ethics* in Dante's poetry and prose. On Boethius and Chaucer, see T. Stroud's, "Boethius' Influence and Chaucer's Troilus," *Chaucer Criticism*, ed. R. Schoeck (South Bend, 1961), 2: 122–35.

11. The quotation is cited by L. C. Knights, "Shakespeare's Politics: With Some Reflections on the Nature of Tradition," *Interpretations of Shakespeare*, ed. K. Muir (Oxford, 1985), p. 96. Knights's article offers a cogent discussion of the changing political language of literary discourse, pp. 85–104. For an informed consideration of the ideas of John of Salisbury on the ordering of the Christian life, see R. W. Southern, *The Making of the Middle Ages* (New Haven, 1968). Also useful for an analysis of John of Salisbury's *Policraticus*, is S. Painter's *French Chivalry: Chivalric Ideas and Practices in Medieval France* (Baltimore, 1940), pp. 68 ff. Cf. John of Salisbury, *Policraticus* 5. 2; 6. 21–22; 6. 24–25, trans. J. Dickinson, *The Statesman's Book of John of Salisbury* (New York, 1927), pp. 64–66, 245–48, 256–65. In the *Policraticus* (bk. IV,4), provisions of the *Corpus Juris* were fused with biblical teachings from the Book of Deuteronomy in an elaborate effort to create a theory of statecraft.

12. For a full discussion of the movement of charity and mutual aid to professional civic welfare organizations, see Brian Pullan's *Rich and Poor in Renaissance Venice* (Oxford, 1971). On the topic of charity, religion, and the poor, K. Wrightson and D.

Levine, *Poverty and Piety in an English Village: Terling 1525–1700* (London, 1979) offers valuable insights. H. Baron, "Franciscan Poverty and Civic Wealth as Factors in the Rise of Humanist Thought," *Speculum* 37 (1938), 1–37 provides an indispensable analysis of changing values and opinions on the subject of poverty and wealth. Cf. also the comments of M. Becker, "Aspects of Lay Piety in Early Renaissance Florence," in *The Pursuit of Holiness in Late Medieval and Renaissance Religion,* eds. C. Trinkaus and H. Oberman (Leiden, 1974), 170–86. For Northern Europe, John Pound's *Poverty and Vagrancy in Tudor England* (London, 1971) contains a useful bibliography and a selection of representative documents.

A balanced treatment of the relatively ineffectual structure of poor relief in the later Middle Ages is provided by B. Tierney in his *Medieval Poor Law* (Berkeley, 1959), pp. 108–32. Cf. also W. Jordan, *The Charities of London, 1480–1660* (London, 1960), pp. 280 ff. For a critique of the monasteries and the extent to which they succeeded in fulfilling their charitable office, see D. Knowles, *The Religious Orders in England* (Cambridge, 1959), 3: 264–68. G. Elton's article on a discarded draft of a poor law, more comprehensive than the one passed in 1536, should be noted: "An Early Tudor Poor Law," *Economic History Review* 6 (1953), 55–67.

13. A. Ferguson, *The Articulate Citizen and the English Renaissance* (Chapel Hill, N.C., 1965), pp. 256 ff. treats Thomas Starkey's definition of *state*. The *OED.,* 2: 447, credits Thomas Starkey with being the first to use the word *civility* to signify good polity and an orderly state of the country as opposed to anarchy. F. Gilbert, in his *Machiavelli and Guicciardini: Politics and History in Sixteenth-Century Florence* (Princeton, 1965), pp. 177–78, 328–30, examines Machiavelli's influence in promoting a wider use of the word *state* in its more abstract, modern sense. With the dissemination of Machiavelli's novel ideas of a political society as a collective body having its own laws, the meaning of the word *stato* could be extended to fill this need without difficulty. E. Benveniste, *Le vocabulaire des institutions Indo-Éuropeenes* (Paris, 1969), 2: 9, provides a comparative analysis of the political vocabulary of the West and its institutions with that of other cultures. Cf. also M. Sahlins, *Islands of History* (Chicago, 1986), pp. 44–47 for a discussion of Benveniste's insights. A. O. Hirschman, *The Passions and the Interests: Political Arguments for Capitalism before Its Triumph* (Princeton, 1977) offers an urbane treatment of the nuances of linguistic changes and the possible correlation with social mutations. Keith Thomas, in his "The Social Origins of Hobbes Political Thought," 185–236, proffers salubrious counsel on problems connected with the transformation of political and social language.

14. Alison Brown offers a useful survey of recent scholarly writings on humanist political thought covering not only Florence but also Continental Europe. See her "Platonism in Fifteenth-Century Florence and Its Contribution to Early Modern Political Thought," *Journal of Modern History* 56 (1986), 393–413. Of course classical political writing was influential not only because of it content, but also for its stylistic virtues: these included *urbanitas, subtilitas, incredibili dicendi copia,* and *divinae sententiae.* For typical humanistic comments appreciative of the need for elegance, see Leonardo Bruni, *Epistolarum libri VIII,* ed. L. Mehus (Florence, 1741), I: 16–17. Cf. also F. Geldner, *Die Staatsauffassung und Fürstenlehre des Erasmus von Rotterdam* (Berlin, 1930), pp. 85–90. For G. R. Elton's compact and incisive comments, see "England and the Continent in the Sixteenth Century," *Reform and Reformation: England and the Continent c. 1500–c. 1750,* ed. D. Baker (Oxford, 1979), 3–10. For France, see Donald Kelley, "Guillaume Budé and the First Historical School of Law," *American Historical Review* 72 (1967), 807–34.

15. Petrarch's quote, "How a Ruler Ought to Govern His State," in *The Earthly Republic,* ed. B. Kohl and R. Witt (Philadelphia, 1978), p. 73. For the text of the letter, see F. Petrarch, *Rerum senilium liber XIII ad magnificum Franciscum de Carraria*

Paduae dominum: Epistola I qualis esse debeat qui rem publicam regit, ed. V. Ussani
(Padua, 1922). For further evidence of the influence of Plato's *Republic* on the thought
of humanists considering that which was termed "civilem societatem," see Francesco Patrizi's *De institutione reipublicae* (Paris, 1534), I.3–4, fols. 6r–7r. Cf. also A.
Renaudet, *Erasme et l'Italie* (Geneva, 1954), pp. 9–12.

16. D. Norbrook, *Poetry and Politics in the English Renaissance* (London, 1984),
pp. 49 ff. mounts a sensitive treatment of the relationship between literature and
politics in seventeenth-century England, with emphasis upon receptivity to continental ideas. B. Guenée, *States and Rulers in Late Medieval Europe,* trans. J. Vale
(London, 1983), pp. 124–30, discusses the political vocabulary of administration (the
term *secretarius*). On the changing character of feudalism in England, see J. Bean,
The Decline of English Feudalism 1215–1540 (Manchester, 1968). On political theory,
C. Morris, *Political Thought in England: Tyndale to Hooker* (London, 1953). On the
topic of education in England, see Lawrence Stone, "The Educational Revolution in
England, 1560–1640," *Past & Present* 28, 41–80; Joan Simon, *Education and Society
in Tudor England* (Cambridge, 1966), pp. 291 ff.; M. H. Curtis, *Oxford and Cambridge
in Transition, 1558–1642* (Oxford, 1959), pp. 54 ff. The classic account of Continental
intellectual and religious influence on England is F. Seebohm, *The Oxford Reformers*
(London, 1928). More recent assessments are those of L. Miles, *John Colet and the
Platonic Tradition* (London, 1962) and J. K. McConica, *English Humanism and
Reformation Politics under Henry VIII and Edward VI* (Oxford, 1965). G. Brizzi, in
his "Strategie educative e istituzioni scolastiche della Controriforma," in *Letteratura
italiana,* ed. A. Rosa (Turin, 1982), 1: 899–904, offers evidence as to the social
composition of students in Florentine schools in the late fifteenth and early sixteenth
centuries. A substantial number were drawn from the artisan and *minori* families of
the city. For France, see F. Furet and J. Ozouf, *Lire et écrire: L'alphabétisation des
Français de Calvin á Jules Ferry* (Paris, 1977), 1: 199–228.

17. E. Garin's numerous writings serve as a systematic exposition of the leading
ideas of Florentine civic humanists. See esp. his *L'educazione in Europe, 1400–1600:
problemi e programmi* (Bari, 1957) and *L'umanesimo italiano: filosofia e vita civile
nel Rinascimento* (Bari, 1952). For an account of the relationship between Florentine
republicanism and the rise of civic humanism, see H. Baron, *The Crisis of the Early
Italian Renaissance,* 2 vols. (Princeton, 1955). The present account, as well as my
Florence in Transition, are admiring of Hans Baron's contribution to our understanding of civic humanism, but do not share his focus on foreign policy and the war with
Milan as primary causes for its onset in Florence. Instead, my focus centers on
economic and social developments responsible for the decline of guild corporatism,
the ethos of service, blood and lineage allegiance, magnate power, honorific codes and
a host of penal and fiscal liabilities intended to extend networks of private obligation.
Concomitant with these changes was the rise of the territorial state serving as a
magnet to attract fiscal and emotional citizen investment. Republicanism, while a
vital ingredient, was only part of a mix as the vocabulary of politics and society
underwent gradual revision away from an archaic lexicon. For a discussion of the
impact of classical rhetoric on preaching and the transformation in the church setting
toward a type of deliberative assembly, see J. O'Malley, *Praise and Blame in Renaissance Rome: Rhetoric, Doctrine and Reform in the Sacred Orators of the Papal
Court, ca. 1450–1521* (Durham, N.C., 1979).

18. H. Baron, "Franciscan Poverty and Civic Wealth," p. 22. In 1420, on a site
where the ancient statue of Abundantia was believed to have stood, a column figure
by Donatello bearing the cornucopia and other emblems of prosperity was erected.
Though since lost, a representation of this figure, along with three other statues
placed on tall freestanding columns, *all'antica,* can be seen in the Walters Art Gallery
in Baltimore. C. Seymour, Jr., *Sculpture in Italy 1400–1500* (Baltimore, 1960), pp. 6–7.

19. P. Bracciolini, "De avaricia," in *Prosatori latini del Quattrocento,* 218–30, esp. 276. Aristotle's views were congenial to the more open and less didactic dialogue form. Although the Greek philosopher agreed that virtue was most vital for happiness, he did not believe that it was possible to deny the role played by wealth, high birth, power, and honor. These so-called "external goods" did constitute "good fortune" and were under no circumstances to be easily dismissed. When considering the critique of the hypocrisy of clerics and friars on the subject of the acquisitive instinct and legitimacy of wealth, it should be recalled that the chancellors of the Republic of Florence (Salutati, Bruni, and Poggio Bracciolini) wrote numerous *litterae commendatitae,* in addition to political *missive.* Many of these letters were addressed to the pope and cardinals, as well as other high churchmen, charging certain ecclesiastics with *avaritia.* Especially deplorable in the judgment of Poggio was the conceding of benefices to foreign prelates. These benefices were often ecclesiastical holdings under Florentine jurisdiction, and the result could be that these foreigners neglected their duties, and churches and convents fell into disrepair. Instead of serving "ad Dei laudem et honorem," these church holdings came only to benefit private individuals. In a letter to Pope Nicholus V, typical of many others, Poggio complained, "just as a wife has need of the presence of a husband, so monasteries require a spouse that will govern them with care and solicitude." See D. De Rosa, "Poggio Bracciolini cancelliere della Repubblica Fiorentina," in *Studi e Ricerche* 2 (1983), 217–50, esp. 233. Cf. also *Archivio di Stato,* Firenze, *Missive,* 40, c. 18r.

20. Carol Lansing, "Nobility in a Medieval Commune: The Florentine Magnates, 1260–1300," (Ph.D. dissertation, University of Michigan, 1984), considers in detail and with substantial documentary evidence, the tendency of magnates to rely upon public tribunals and other civic institutions for enforcement of agreements and resolution of conflicts. An assessment of the significance of the decline of magnate violence in Fourteenth-century Florence is presented in M. Becker, "Changing Patterns of Violence and Justice in Fourteenth- and Fifteenth-century Florence," *Comparative Studies in Society and History* 18 (July, 1976), 281–96; cf. also the general study of crime in fourteenth-century Florence by U. Dorini, *Il diritto penale e la delinquenza in Firenze nel secolo XIV* (Lucca, 1916), pp. 38–64, in which he offers statistical evidence based on samplings of the judicial records indicating the decline of a variety of violent crimes. M. Becker, in his "A Study in Political Failure: The Florentine Magnates (1280–1343)," *Mediaeval Studies* 27 (1965), 272 ff., correlates the decline of magnate political power with their inability to expand their stock of social and economic ideas. When confronted with the crises of the 1340s, they resorted to tired and outmoded measures. Cf. also, M. Becker, "Florentine Popular Government (1343–48)," *Proceedings of the American Philosophical Society* 106 (1962), 360–82. On Donato Velluti and his expressions of satisfaction at having settled a feud with a rival house, see his *Cronica domestica,* ed. I. del Lungo and G. Volpe (Florence, 1914), pp. 66–70. Velluti tells us that he feared being implicated in the vendetta, although he was not a principal to the quarrel; one of his forebears, murdered in the early fourteenth century, had left a sizable legacy of 500 florins to anyone avenging his death. One of the difficulties stemming from these quarrels was that they could be extended into foreign territories and interfere with business and banking. Cf. *Cronica domestica,* pp. 29–30.

21. For a recent analysis of Salutati's views on perpetual leasing, reprisals, and extension of liability to include malpractice among dentists and responsibility among contemporary Jews for the Crucifixion, see R. Witt, *Hercules at the Crossroads: The Life, Works and Thought of Coluccio Salutati* (Durham, N.C., 1983). Also germane to an understanding of this humanist's views on such themes as bloodguilt and liability for the crimes of kinsmen, see D. De Rosa, *Coluccio Salutati: il chancelliere e il*

pensatore politico (Florence, 1980). G. Brucker and M. Becker, "The *Arti Minori* in Florentine Politics, 1342–1378," *Mediaeval Studies* 18 (1956), 93–104, discuss the impact of the participation of the "new citizens" in public life. For an analysis of the role played by *novi cives* in sponsoring legislation against overmighty magnates, see M. Becker, *Florence in Transition* 1: 223–28. It was precisely in the early fifteenth century that a form of limited liability investment and the time deposit were instituted. Legislation was enacted in 1408 allowing businesses to accept capital *in accomandita* without committing the investor to the unlimited liability of the partners. Cf. R. Goldthwaite, "The Medici Bank and the World of Florentine Capitalism," *Past & Present* 114 (1987), 14. The Court Merchant (Mercanzia) registered limited liability companies, or *accomandite,* thus providing legal protection to investors. In the case of business failure, these investors were liable only for that amount of capital recorded in the registers of the Mercanzia. R. Litchfield, "Les investissements en commerce des patriciens florentins au XVIIIᵉ siècle," *Annales E. C. S.* 24 (1969), 685–721. Cf. also, M. Carmona, "Aspects du capitalisme toscan au XVIᵉ et au XVIIᵉ siècles: Les sociétés en comandite à Florence et à Lucques," *Revue d'Histoire Moderne et Contemporaine* 11 (1964), 81–108.

22. On the doctrine of Atonement in the Reformation, see J. Rivière, "Redemption," *Dictionnaire de théologie catholique,* Vol. 13 (Paris, 1937) and G. Aulén, *Christus Victor* (London, 1970). Cf. also J. Rivière's *Le dogme de redemption au début du moyen âge* (Paris, 1934). The idiom of the older notion of man's disobedience to God was very like the vocabulary of feudalism with its focus on the feudal custom of *diffidatio.* For a discussion of this vocabulary, as well as an assessment of Saint Anselm's contribution, see R. Southern, *Making of the Middle Ages,* pp. 234–38. T. Tentler's *Sin and Confession on the Eve of the Reformation* (Princeton, 1977) analyzes very effectively the changing content of the confessors' manuals. On the doctrine of purgatory, two recent studies illuminate changes during the later Middle Ages: J. Rosenthal, *The Purchase of Paradise* (London, 1972), and M. and G. Vovelle, *Vision de la mort et de l'au delà en Provence, Cahiers des Annales,* vol. 29 (Paris, 1970).

23. *Epistolario di Coluccio Salutati,* ed. F. Novati (Rome, 1891–1911), 2: 303–4. See also, E. Garin, *Italian Humanism: Philosophy and Civic Life in the Renaissance,* trans. P. Munz (Oxford, 1965), p. 28; Witt, *Hercules at the Crossroads,* pp. 350–53; *Earthly Republic,* pp. 93–114.

24. See C. Trinkaus, *In Our Image and Likeness: Humanity and Divinity in Italian Humanist Thought* (Chicago, 1970), 2: 517–613, the chapter entitled "Italian Humanism and the Scripture." Cf. also, "The Religious Thought of the Italian Humanists and the Reformers: Anticipation or Autonomy?" in *The Pursuit of Holiness in Late Medieval and Renaissance Religion,* 339–70. J. Bossy, "Holiness and Society," *Past & Present* 75 (1977), 119–37 is a sparkling essay bristling with ideas about world and spirit.

25. Recent work on "bastard feudalism" and its variants are legion. For a useful summary and careful analysis, see C. Armstrong, *England, France and Burgundy in the Fifteenth Century* (London, 1983), pp. 212–18. The fundamental account is that of K. McFarlane, *The Nobility of Later Medieval England* (Oxford, 1975), and his *England in the Fifteenth Century: Collected Essays,* with an incisive introduction by G. Harriss (London, 1981). For Lord Hastings, see W. H. Dunham, *Lord Hastings' Indentured Retainers,* in *Transactions of Connecticut Academy of Arts and Sciences,* vol. 39 (New Haven, 1955), pp. 1–175. Cf. also, I. Rowney's revisionist study, "Resources and Retaining in Yorkist England: William Lord Hastings and the Honour of Tutbury," in *Property and Politics in Late Medieval English History,* ed. T. Pollard (New York, 1984), 139–58. It is also essential to reckon that bastard feudalism provided a network of patronage well attuned to the ambitions and interests of

English gentry, as well as of the nobility. The crown and nobility used the bastard feudal affinity to retain the loyalty and service of an increasingly variegated armigerous class within the ancient tradition of good lordship and chivalry. Bastard feudal society merits the study of gentry as well as nobility—the below as well as above. Cf. M. Jones's introduction to the recent collection of papers published under the title of *Gentry and Lesser Nobility in Late Medieval Europe* (New York, 1986), pp. 7–11. Cf. also, C. Richmond, "After McFarlane," *History* 58 (1983), 46–60.

26. For a review of military history, see F. Gilbert, "Machiavelli: The Renaissance and the Art of War," in *Makers of Modern Strategy from Machiavelli to the Nuclear Age,* ed. P. Paret (Princeton, 1986), 11–31, esp. 12–14. For a general discussion of war and its effects on society in the late Middle Ages, see P. Contamine, *Guerre, état et société à la fin du moyen âge: Études sur les armées des rois de France 1337–1494* (Paris, 1972). The author suggests that the demilitarization of France in the later Middle Ages was accompanied by a heightened valuation of soldiering as a noble vocation. Cf. also, J. Henneman, "The Military Class in the French Monarchy," *American Historical Review* 83 (1978), 946–65. J. Wormald in *Lords and Men in Scotland: Bonds of Manrent* (Edinburgh, 1985), considers in detail the nature of Scottish ties of obligation in the fifteenth and sixteenth centuries. For a study of the crown and the use of retaining knights with esquires to staff local offices and anchor provincial loyalties, see J. McKenne, "The Myth of Parliamentary Sovereignty in Later Medieval England," *English Historical Review* 94 (1977), 481–500. On the important subject of comradeship-in-arms and its decline after the reign of Edward IV, see A. Tuck, *Crown and Nobility 1272–1461* (Oxford, 1985), pp. 326–28. For a recent study of good lordship and the crown, see C. Given-Wilson, *The Royal Household and the King's Affinity* (Yale, 1985).

27. For a recent survey of evidence and interpretation on the relationship between the crown and nobles, see D. Carpenter, "King, Magnates and Society: The Personal Rule of King Henry III," *Speculum* 60 (1985), 39–71. For Scotland, see J. Wormald, *Lords and Men in Scotland.* H. Miller treats relations in the Tudor period; cf *Henry VIII and the English Nobility* (Oxford, 1986), esp. her conclusions, pp. 254–57. J. Lander's many articles are crucial for an interpretation of the relationship between king and nobles in the fifteenth century: see esp. "Bonds, Coercion and Fear: Henry VII and the Peerage," in *Florilegium Historiale: Essays Presented to Wallace K. Ferguson,* ed. J. G. Rowe and W. H. Stockdale (Toronto, 1971), 327–67. Gary Stuart De Krey, in his *A Fractured Society: The Politics of London in the First Age of Party* (Oxford, 1985), argues persuasively that the merchants of London seem in their commitment to be more often royalist or Tory than Parliamentary or Whig during the English Civil War. It was not until the late seventeenth century that merchant loyalties shifted and the term *bourgeoisie* can be invoked with confidence to designate this order and its political triumph.

28. On Burgundy and the chivalric revival, see W. Prevenier and W. Bloomans, *The Burgundian Netherlands* (Cambridge, 1986), pp. 282–372. E. Zorni presents a useful summary of the rituals of good lordship in "Cerimoniale e spettacolarità: Il tovagliolo sulla tavola del Principe," in *Rituali, cerimoniale, etichetta,* ed. S. Bertelli and G. Orifò (Milan, 1985), 67–84. G. Duby, in his *History of Medieval Art, 980–1440* (Geneva, 1986), pt. 3, pp. 13–14, gives a succinct discussion of the art of Northern Europe in the fourteenth and fifteenth centuries and its energetic effort to escape reality and realize a world of dreams. In so doing, the artist would render them visible and thereby capture them.

29. Guenée, *States and Rulers,* pp. 162–63. For a consideration of the continued prestige of the idea of chivalry, see A. Ferguson, *The Indian Summer of English Chivalry* (Durham, N.C., 1960), pp. 34–46. Recently, questions have been raised as to J. Huizinga's classical study of cultural decline in the later Middle Ages with its jaded

aristocracy and decadent chivalry. The work in question is, of course, *The Waning of the Middle Ages: A Study of the Forms of Life, Thought and Art in France and the Netherlands in the Fourteenth and Fifteenth Centuries* (London, 1924). See esp. M. Keen, "Huizinga, Kilgour and the Decline of Chivalry," *Medievalia et Humanistica* 8 (1977), 1–20. On balance it can be argued that Huizinga has a much more nuanced view of medieval chivalry and its role in politics and culture than do many of his critics. Cf. his "La valeur politique et militaire des idées de la chevalerie à fin du Moyen Âge," *Revue d'Histoire Diplomatique* 35 (1921), 126–38.

30. For a host of citations of books of comportment, see D. Régnier-Bohler, "Fictions," in *Histoire de la vie privée*, ed. P. Ariès and G. Duby 2: 316–75. References to the style of education prevalent in the noble household are of course legion. Of particular interest are the following: *Education in Early England*, ed. F. J. Furnivali, *Early English Text Society*, vol. 32 (1868), pp. 6–30; *A Collection of Ordinances and Regulations for the Government of the Royal Household* (London, *Society of Antiquaries*, 1790), pp. 42–48. In the metrical romance, *Ipomydon*, named after the youthful hero, the king gives the following instructions for the youth's upbringing in the royal household:

> Tholomew a clerk he toke
> That taught the chyld uppon the boke,
> Both to synge and to rede;
> And after he taught him other ded:
> Aftirward to serve in hall,
> Bothe to grete and to smalle;
> Before the kyng mete to kerve,
> Hye and lowe feyre to serve;
> Bothe of houndis and haukis game
> After he taught hym, all and same,
> In se, in field, and eke in ryvuere,
> In wodde to chase the wild dere,
> And in the feld to ryde a stede,
> That all men had joy of his dede.

Cited in James, *Society, Politics and Culture*, pp. 271–72.

31. For recent studies on English villages, their solidarities and antagonisms, see Hanawalt, *The Ties That Bound*, pp. 130 ff.; E. Clark, "Some Aspects of Social Security in Medieval England," *Journal of Family History* 7 (1982), 307–20; "Debt Litigation in a Late Medieval English Will," in *Pathways to Medieval Peasants*, ed. J. Raftis (Toronto, 1980), 261–67. Alan Macfarlane's revisionist essay, *The Origins of English Individualism: The Family, Property and Social Transition* (London, 1978) offers the thesis that the collective solidarity of the English village community was no longer the guiding force in rural life after the thirteenth century. His arguments have generally been criticized as seriously flawed and his thesis rejected. See D. Levine, *Journal of Interdisciplinary History* 11 (1981), 669–76; P. Hyams, *English Historical Review* 96 (1981), 605–7; J. Hatcher, *Historical Journal* 22 (1979), 765–68; C. Dyer, *Economic History Review*, sec. ser. 32 (1979), 600–1; S. Waugh, *Journal of Economic History* 39 (1979), 770–72; R. Hilton, *New Left Review* 120 (1980), 109–11. For a sensitive appraisal of the relationship between history and the Arthurian legend in the fifteenth century, see E. T. Pochoda, *Arthurian Propaganda: Le Morte Darthur as an Historical Ideal of Life* (Chapel Hill, N.C., 1971). For a review of fifteenth-century Flemish art and its bearing on the themes of reconciliation with one's enemies and the exchange of the kiss of peace, see C. Harbison, "Visions and Meditations in Early Flemish Painting," *Simolus* 15 (1985), 81–118, and also his review of B. Lane's *The Altar and the Altarpiece*, in the above journal, pp. 221–24. Bossy's "Blood and

Baptism," 138–62, treats the role of the Church in conflict, resolution, and peacemaking, with emphasis on the mass and the consecration of the host as a symbol of peace.

32. D. Nicholas, *The Domestic Life of a Medieval City: Women, Children and the Family in Fourteenth-Century Ghent* (Lincoln, Neb., 1985), pp. 47–61, 198–208. See also his "Town and Countryside: Social and Economic Tensions in Fourteenth-Century Flanders," *Comparative Studies in Society and History* 10 (1968), 458–85 and "Economic Reorientation and Social Change in Fourteenth-Century Flanders," *Past & Present* 70 (1976), 3–29. For the implementation of rituals of peacemaking and the use of the consecrated host to stop a city riot in Spain, see H. Kamen, *Spain in the Later Seventeenth Century* (London, 1980), pp. 180–81. For London in the fifteenth century, see *Six Town Chronicles,* ed. R. Flenley (Oxford, 1919), p. 146.

33. The ideal of psychic and moral self-sufficiency is perceived by C. Trinkaus as Petrarch's most important discovery in the domain of classical philosophy. Cf. *The Poet as Philosopher* (Yale, 1979), pp. 25–26. For Petrarch, solitude was a strategy of detachment and a variation on the monastic impulse. Withdrawal was not privileged as an exercise of heroic virtue and test of holiness; contemplation resulted in an appreciation of human frailty in its myriad and ever-intrusive forms. Scaling down of his essential sociability enabled him to confront his own singularity. This was no mere conventional portrayal of the contest between *otium* and *negotium.* Petrarch defined himself by a process of constriction that broke with the social ideals of hospitality, epic heroism, love service, and even the public rituals associated with "social death." For him dying well involved not excessive lamentation and the horrors of the death bed but instead signified living well. See A. Tenenti, *Il senso della morte e l'amore della vita nel Rinascimento* (Turin, 1957), pp. 108–30, 185–228; M. Vovelle, *La mort et l'Occident de 1300 à nos jours* (Paris, 1983), pp. 198–201.

34. On the difficulty of perceiving exchange as advantaging both parties, see Louis Dumont, *From Mandeville to Marx: The Genesis and Triumph of Economic Ideology* (Chicago, 1977), pp. 35–39; also, Hirschman, *Passions and the Interests,* pp. 25–42. The intellectual obstacles confronting thinkers who would eliminate the human "natural" social impetus to barter and exchange were daunting. Over time, and piecemeal, all economic relations would be required to be reduced to human, historical conditions. To trace this transition it would be necessary to survey writings from Hobbes to Vico to Marx. See A. Funkenstein, *Theology and the Scientific Imagination from the Middle Ages to the Seventeenth Century* (Princeton, 1986), pp. 17–18. For a discussion of Erasmus and the interpretation of crucial passages from the New Testament, see J. Tracy's review of Vol. 42 of *Erasmus's Collected Works,* ed. R. Sider et al., *New Testament Scholarship: Paraphrases on Romans and Galateans* (Toronto, 1984) in *Renaissance Quarterly* 39 (1986), 293–95. Cf. also, R. Coogan, "The Pharisee against the Hellenist: Edward Lee versus Erasmus," *Renaissance Quarterly* 39 (1986), 476–500.

35. For a general discussion of the archaic impulse toward wholeness of observer and object, see D. Brewer, *English Gothic Literature* (New York, 1983). For an assessment of language theory in the late Middle Ages and the consequences of not effecting a displacement from an "archaic natural matrix," see J. Gellrich, *The Idea of the Book in the Middle Ages: Language Theory, Mythology, and Fiction* (Ithaca, 1985), pp. 105–8; R. Howard Bloch, *Etymologies and Genealogies: A Literary Anthropology of the French Middle Ages* (Chicago, 1983), pp. 151–56. A. Spearing, *Introduction to Chaucer's the Franklin's Tale* (Cambridge, 1966), pp. 1–56, contains a useful review of the literary tendency to conflate the material aspect of what is seen with the moral and spiritual appreciation of the observer. On the question of the moral difficulties of accepting illusionism in the form of perspective theory, see L. Gent's excellent account in her *Picture and Poetry 1560–1620* (Leamington Spa, 1981). For references to Chaucer's use of the word *gentilesse,* see *Works,* ed. F.

Robinson, 2d ed. (Cambridge, Mass., 1957), pp. 87, 183, 536. For Thomas Malory, see *Works,* ed. E. Vinaver (Oxford, 1954), p. 280. The earliest English-Latin dictionary (ca. 1440), the *Promporium Parvulorum* starts by rendering "gentyl/genylmann/gentry" by the Latin "generosus-generositas," before going on to offer other meanings, the nuances of which, in the words of a recent commentator, serve to "mirror the discriminations of society." See D. Morgan, "The Individual Style of the English Gentleman," in *Gentry and Lesser Nobility in Late Medieval Europe,* ed. M. Jones (New York, 1986), 17–35, esp. p. 20. The dictionary offers separate vocabulary for "gentry (or gentilnes) of awncetrye (= ingenuitas), and gentry (or gentilnes) of norture and maners (= comitas)." Cf. D. Morgan, "Individual Style," p. 32.

36. Often the monastic ideal was transferred to the work-a-day world. The key word for writers such as Gower and Langland was *caritas.* M. Bloomfield, *The Seven Deadly Sins: An Introduction to the History of a Religious Concept, with Special Reference to Medieval English Literature* (East Lansing, Mich., 1952), pp. 69–80, 105–21, describes the eight deadly sins of John Cassian and the seven deadly sins of Gregory the Great. The latter's ordering was to become standard: pride, wrath, envy, avarice, sloth, gluttony, and lechery. This arrangement came to dominate and was replicated by leading theologians and popular writers alike. For the author of *Piers Plowman,* the spiritual enemy was sloth, and spiritual and social justice were no duality, bound as they were by *caritas.* Cf. John Bowers, *The Crisis of Will in Piers Plowman* (Washington, D.C., 1986), esp. chap. 4, "Sloth Personified and Transformed," 79–96. In *Gawain and the Green Knight,* the protagonist or persona of the poet is a flawed hero and penitential figure. His chivalric quest concludes with the knight's profound appreciation for the deep nature of human frailty. Cf. J. Bennett, *Medieval English Literature,* compiled by B. Gray (Oxford, 1986), pp. 430–52.

37. Cf. the comments of J. H. Hexter in the introduction to the Yale edition of St. Thomas More's *Utopia,* ed E. Surtz and J. H. Hexter, *The Complete Works of St. Thomas More* 4: i–ixxxi, and also E. Surtz's discussion, pp. civi ff. For Erasmus's appreciation of the variety of ways in which More gave full expression to ideas in his brilliant fiction, see J. McConica, *English Humanists,* pp. 40–43.

38. For a discussion of this quotation, see R. DuRocher, *Milton and Ovid* (Ithaca, N.Y., 1985), p. 25. Cf. *The Works of Ben Jonson,* ed. C. Herford and P. Simpson (Oxford, 1947), 8: 335, 338. Petrarch's letter to his brother Gerardo, of December, 1349, in which he draws on Aristotle's *Metaphysics* to elevate the status of poetry and role of the poet, is worth citing. Poetry is not to be subsumed under *artes liberales,* which were founded on the ideals of just measure and practicality. Poetry is "non vulgari forms sed artificiosa quadam et exquisita et nova." Cf. F. Petrarch, *Familiares,* ed. V. Rossi (Florence, 1935–44), 2: 301–2. In 1345, with the discovery of Cicero's *Pro Archia,* Petrarch had substantial ammunition for elevating the role of poet. Cf. G. Billanovich, *Petrarca letterato: lo scrittoio del Petrarca* (Rome, 1947), p. 4.

39. For a discussion of the value of fame and recognition to community and public world, see M. Stavig, *John Ford and the Traditional Order* (Chicago, 1964), pp. 218 ff. Fame as a factor in *regimen principum* evoked considerable ambivalence, but thinkers as varied as Bacon and Daniel shared Montaigne's view that while fame and opinion might be follies, they did have their uses in the governance of the earthly city. Cf. John Florio's translation of Montaigne's *Essays* (Everyman ed., London, 1910), 2: 355. Such a view of honor was markedly different from that of an earlier time, when it was maintained that it was lineage and blood that predisposed one to honorable behavior. Cf. James, *Society, Politics and Culture,* pp. 310–17.

40. On Erasmus's recollection of his early miseries with grammatical instruction, see B. Kimball, *Orators and Philosophers: A History of the Idea of Liberal Education* (New York, 1986), p. 76. For a full appreciation of the influence of Continental

rhetoric and biblical exegesis on the generation of John Colet, see J. McDiarmid, "Language: System to Act to Report; The Development of English Linguistic Thought in the Sixteenth Century," (Ph.D. dissertation, Harvard Univerity, 1980).

41. For the anecdote concerning the impatience of Henry VIII, see J. R. Hale, *Renaissance Europe: The Individual in Society 1480–1520* (New York, 1973), p. 256. On the more general subject of Henry VIII and patronage and education, see Simon, *Education and Society in Tudor England*, pp. 63 ff. For the quote from Coleridge, see E. Partridge, *The Broken Compass* (London, 1958), p. 218. The dying stage convention of homiletic allegory advantaged Elizabethan secular playwrights who could mix low and high moral seriousness. The Vice figure of the temptor of the moralities still trailed a Falstaff, thus giving him his double nature. The tilt from didactic to dramatic was both gradual and imaginatively fructifying. Cf. B. Spivack, *Shakespeare and the Allegory of Evil* (New York, 1979).

42. For an analysis of the significance of this quote, see S. Greenblatt, *Renaissance Self-Fashioning: From More to Shakespeare* (Chicago, 1980), pp. 2–5. Greenblatt quotes Sermon 190—"Hands off yourself. Try to build up yourself and you build a ruin"—as antithetical to the new Tudor humanistic ideals of self-fashioning. Cf. Peter Brown, *Religion and Society in the Age of Saint Augustine* (London, 1972), p. 3. For Gabriel Harvey's comments on the author of the *Faerie Queene,* see *Spenser: The Critical Heritage,* ed. R. Cummings (London, 1971), p. 57.

43. For a consideration of Sidney and his responsiveness to new intellectual currents and rhetorical strategies, see J. Altman, *The Tudor Play of Mind: Rhetorical Inquiry and the Development of Elizabethan Drama* (Berkeley, 1978), pp. 84–103. G. Zeevend, in his useful survey of sixteenth-century English writings on politics and society, *The Temper of Shakespeare's Thought* (New Haven, 1974), p. 16, treats Cranmer's views on ceremony.

44. D. Norbrook, *Poetry and Politics in the English Renaissance* (London, 1984), p. 104, discusses the quotation from Hoskins. On John Hoskins, see *Dictionary of National Biography,* 9: 1291–93, and J. Buxton, *Sir Philip Sidney and the English Renaissance* (New York, 1966), pp. 126–27.

45. On the not unrelated themes of architecture, poetry, country ways, and human waste, see W. McClung, *The Country House in English Poetry* (Berkeley, 1977), pp. 33–65. Cf. also, D. Javitch, *Poetry and Courtliness in Renaissance England* (Princeton, 1978). For France, see M. Fumaroli, "Rhetoric, Politics, and Society: From Italian Ciceronianism to French Classicism," *Renaissance Eloquence: Studies in the Theory and Practice of Renaissance Rhetoric,* ed. J. Murphy (Berkeley, 1983), 253–73. For a useful up-to-date bibliography on cultural exchange between England and Europe in the sixteenth century, see F. Whigham, *Ambition and Privilege: The Social Tropes of Elizabethan Courtesy Theory* (Berkeley, 1984), pp. 239–52. J. H. Hexter's "The Education of the Aristocracy in the Renaissance," republished in *Reappraisals in History* (New York, 1961), 45–70, stands as a model study. (The article originally appeared in *The Journal of Modern History* 22 (1950), 1–20.) On Ascham's notorious condemnation of *Le Morte Darthur,* see L. Ryan's edition of *The School Master* (Ithaca, 1961), pp. 68–70. *The Correspondence of Sir Philip Sidney and Hubert Languet,* ed. S. Pears (London, 1845), pp. 147–54, suggests something of the difficulty of tempering the extravagant requirements of honor and excessive appetite for glory. Languet writes the following to his friend Sidney: "You and your fellows, I mean men of noble birth, consider that nothing brings you more honor than wholesale slaughter." Languet seeks to establish the credentials of "wisdom." This is the hallmark of the governor, and his role necessitates a more expanded spectrum of qualities than the narrow compass of the heroic activism of those fired by honor and love of glory. "Ought not you," writes Languet, "adorned as you are by Providence with those

splendid gifts of mind to feel otherwise than men feel who are buried in the most profound shades of ignorance and think that all excellence consists in physical strength." See James, *Society, Politics and Culture,* p. 117.

46. T. Norton and T. Sackville, *Gorboduc* in *Medieval and Tudor Drama,* ed., J. Gassner (New York, 1963), p. 432. Contributing most to the onset of political chaos is the failure of the king to consent to the grave advice of honorable counselors, relying instead on the words of parasites. It is interesting to note that Thomas Sackville was a cousin of Queen Elizabeth who relinquished private literary work in favor of a career as a high-serving minister of state. See A. Ferguson, *Clio Unbound: Perception of the Social and Cultural Past in Renaissance England* (Durham, N.C., 1979), pp. 428–32, for a textured explication of the transition from the giving of counsel to the techniques of statecraft. Queen Elizabeth was appreciative of the legal research of William Lambardi for assisting her in understanding certain terms of ancient law when, as she put it, "force of arms did prevail," and before the "wit of the fox" was afoot. Cf. Donald Kelley, "History, English Law and the Renaissance," *Past & Present* 62 (1974), p. 32.

47. On the measured rhetoric of English poetry, see J. Miles, *The Continuity of Poetic Language: The Primary Language of Poetry* (New York, 1965), chap. 1. F. Tateo, in his *Umanesimo etico di Giovanni Pontano* (Lecce, 1972), provides a rich mine of insights into the linkage between language (rhetoric) and social comportment (moral philosophy).

48. See R. Pine-Coffin's introduction to the Penguin edition of Giovanni Della Casa's *Galateo* (Harondsworth, 1958). A. Di Benedetto provides a thoughtful discussion of the *Galateo* in the introduction to his *Prose di Giovanni Della Casa e di altri trattatisti cinquecenteschi del comportamento* (Turin, 1970). C. Mutini gives a succinct account of the career and writings of Castiglione, as well as extensive bibliography, in "Castiglione, Baldassarre," in *Dizionario biografico degli Italiani* (Rome, 1979), 22: 53–68. The passage from warrior to courtier to diplomat, and the requirements of education for making these transitions, is discussed by J. Guidi, "Le jeu de cour et sa codification dans les différentes rédactions du Courtisan," in *Le pouvoir et la plume. Actes du Colloque International, Université de la Sorbonne Nouvelle* (Paris, 1982), 97–117. Castiglione himself had fond memories of his mission to England in the time of Henry VII when he served as proxy for the duke of Urbino and was inducted into the Order of the Garter. Impressed with the royal family and its court, he praised the father and his excellently educated son, the present King Henry VIII. Cf. *Il libro del Cortigiano,* ed. G. Preti (Turin, 1960), pp. 395–96.

49. Giovanni della Casa, *Galateo,* trans. R. Peterson (Boston, 1914), pp. 11–17. See also the introduction to *Galateo* by R. Romano (Turin, 1975); A. Rochon, "Lo scrittore nella societa rinascimentale: sollecitazioni, pressioni, repressioni," *Problemi* 13 (1979), 177–211.

50. For treatment of the translations of Machiavelli's *Art of War,* see S. Bertelli and P. Innocenti, *Bibliografia Machiavelliana* (Verona, 1979). The *Arte della Guerra* was the only great work of Machiavelli's to be published in his lifetime. The *Discorsi* and *The Prince* were published in 1531 and 1532, respectively, three and four years after his death. L. Pieraccini, "Alcuni aspetti della fortuna di Machiavelli a Firenze nel secolo XVI," *Studi e Ricerche* 1 (1981), 221–72.

51. For a discussion of Taverner, an important figure in the dissemination of Continental humanist ideas into England and the context in which he operated, see Greenblatt, *Renaissance Self-Fashioning,* chap. 1. For further information on Taverner, see *Dictionary of National Biography,* 29: 395–96. On the value of history as an effective form of discourse, the comments of Thomas Blundeville are representative: "The way to come to that peace whereof I speake, is partly taught by the Philosophers in generall precepts and rules, but the Historiographers doe teache it much

more playnlye by perticular examples and experiences, and speciallye if they be written with that order, diligence, and judgement, that they ought to be." Cf. David Johnston, *The Rhetoric of 'Leviathan': Thomas Hobbes and the Politics of Cultural Transformation* (Princeton, 1986), p. 18.

52. For a sensitive appraisal of transformations in linguistic usage and the economy of chivalry and love service, see A. Spering, *Medieval to Renaissance in English Poetry* (Cambridge, 1985), pp. 283 ff. Cf. also, Greenblatt, *Renaissance Self-Fashioning,* chap. 7, for an analysis of the poetry of Wyatt. A public vocabulary purveying ambitious notions of sociability recedes and is sometimes matched by an enriched idiom of intimate and singular sensibilities. See T. Greene, *The Light in Troy: Imitation and Discovery in Renaissance Poetry* (New Haven, 1982), chap. 12: "Wyatt: Erosion and Stabilization," pp. 242–63.

53. C. L. Barber, *Shakespeare's Festive Comedy* (Princeton, 1959) is a masterful analysis of the dramatist's portrayal of the conflict between the mechanism of wealth and the generous social use of it. Barber is the first scholar of Elizabethan English literature to detail the tensions between archaic values and their opposition. Cf. also the fundamental study of L. Knights, *Drama and Society in the Age of Jonson* (London, 1962). For a recent work advantaged by new scholarship, see A. Marotti, *John Donne, Coterie Poet* (Madison, Wisc., 1986), esp. chap. 1, "Donne as an Inns-of-Court Author," 25–95.

54. The last duel of chivalry was fought in England in 1492 when Sir James Parker and Sir Hugh Vaughan met in mortal combat at a tournament in Richmond. See R. Bildich, *The Duel: A History of Dueling* (London, 1965), pp. 32–41; John Selden, *The Duello or Single Combat* (London, 1610). On the Continent the chivalric tourney was increasingly being regulated in ever-greater detail with rules covering everything from weapons to dress, and even the feasting and dancing afterwards. L. Stone, *The Crisis of the Aristocracy 1558–1641* (Oxford, 1965), pp. 242–50, provides a balanced account of change among English aristocrats and gentry as they took up the duel from the Italian school. The deadly rapier proved to be a great leveler, and protests against its use replicated those of Ariosto, Blaise de Montluc, and, of course, Don Quixote who had fulminated against cannon and gun powder as being entirely subversive of honorable battle. Cf. J. Hale, "War and Public Opinion in the Fifteenth and Sixteenth Centuries," *Past & Present* 22 (1962), p. 29. Montaigne, in his essay, "Cowardice Mother of Cruelty," (II, 27), expresses deep reservations about the art of fencing essential for the duel. He knows very well that this skill, learned from the Italians by the French, is "useful for its purpose." He denies, however, that it is "properly valor, since it draws its support from skill and has its basis in something other than itself." He speaks admiringly of the nobles who in his childhood would have done anything to avoid the reputation of good fencers, since the honor of combat "consists in the jealousy of courage, not of craft." For Germany, see W. Jackson, "The Tournament and Chivalry in German Tournament Books of the Sixteenth Century and in the Literary Works of Emperor Maximilian I," in *The Ideals and Practices of Medieval Knighthood,* eds, C. Harper-Bill and R. Harvey (Bury-St. Edmunds, Suffolk, 1986), 49–73.

55. On *mouvance* and the inclusiveness of vassalage, see J. Dubabin, *France in the Making 843–1180* (Oxford, 1985), pp. 239–45. The solemn exchange of sealed letters between great lords was replicated on a more modest level by pledges and agreements between esquires who, in the aureate language of chivalry, vowed to be "brothers-in-arms and live and die by one another." These allegiances involved the furnishing of ransom money and division of the spoils of war. Mutuality obtained in matters as diverse as business interests and affairs of honor. Cf. M. Keen, *The Laws of War in the Late Middle Ages* (London, 1965), pp. 48 ff.; G. Hindley, *England in the Age of Caxton* (New York, 1979), pp. 166–202. On the changing character of social ties and

the valorization of social distance, one can chart the amplification of the meaning of the vocabulary of privacy and isolation. R. Sayre, *Solitude in Society: A Sociological Study in French Literature* (Cambridge, Mass., 1978), provides a general treatment of these topics with extensive bibliography. Cf. also, B. Wind, *Les mots italiens introduits en francais au XVIe siècle* (Amsterdam, 1928), pp. 174 ff.

56. Julia Briggs' assessment of tension and ambivalence in courtly literature is cautionary, standing as a reminder to those who would treat this evidence as one-dimensional and mere propaganda. See her *This Stage-Play World: English Literature and Its Background 1580–1625* (Oxford, 1983), pp. 119–59. Cf. also, D. Javitch, "Rival Arts of Conduct in Elizabethan England," *Yearbook of Italian Studies*, 1 (1971), 178–98, and his "Poetry and Court Conduct," *Modern Language Notes*, 87 (1972), 865–82. For a recent characterization of Shakespeare's reading of Chaucer, see E. Talbot Donaldson, *The Swan at the Well* (New Haven, 1985). The theme of the evils of life at court has an ancient literary pedigree. For this period the celebrated letter of Eneas Silvius Piccolomini (later, Pius II) to Johannes von Eich (1444), was subsequently to be reprinted frequently under the title of "De curialium miseriis." Here we have an analysis of the psychology of the courtier with his appetite for the "honoribus seculi ac popularibus laudibus." See Silvius's *Der Briefwechsel* (Vienna, 1909), 1: 453–87.

57. On urbanitas and classical rhetoric (particularly Quintilian) and the social dimension of poetry, see R. Gill, "*Musa Iocosa Mea:* Thoughts on the *Elegies* in John Donne," in *John Donne: Essays in Celebration,* ed. A. Smith (London, 1972), 50–61. Cf. also the valuable comments of A. Gilbert, *A Literary Language from Chaucer to Jonson* (London, 1979). Works on Shakespeare's language are of course legion, but particularly helpful are M. Doran, *Shakespeare's Dramatic Language* (Madison, 1976), pp. 36–62; A. Hart, "Vocabularies of Shakespeare's Plays," *Review of English Studies* 19 (1943), 128–40; M. Joseph, *Shakespeare's Use of the Arts of Language* (New York, 1947).

58. The number of administrators required by the French crown increased approximately seven-fold from the early sixteenth century to the mid-seventeenth. In 1505 the figure was about 12,000 and by 1664 it was over 80,000; this total does not include armed forces. Roughly the same number administered the estates and law courts. See R. Knecht, *French Renaissance Monarchy: Francis I & Henry II* (London, 1984), pp. 14–16. Cf. also, J. Berenger, "Le problèm du ministeriat au XVIIe siècle," *Annales E.S.C.* 39 (1974), 166–92. R. Mousnier, in his *La vénalité des offices sous Henri IV et Louis XIII* (Rouen, 1945), pp. 105–14, calculates that the number of officials in Normandy was approximately 1,800 in 1573; by 1665 it had reached 4,100. It should be noted that the geographic extent of Normandy is approximate to that of Tuscany. On diplomacy and the role of the nobility, see P. Prodi, *Diplomazia del Cinquecento: istituzione e prassi* (Bologna, 1963); C. Vasoli, *La cultura delle corti* (Bologna, 1980), pp. 72–77.

59. On Edmund Harvel and his comments, see G. K. Hunter, *John Lyly: The Humanist as Courtier* (London, 1962), p. 28. P. Bénichou's work, *Morales du grand siècle* (Paris, 1948), pp. 168–72, discusses the subtle metamorphosis of heroic virtues among French aristocracy. For a recent treatment of French drama in the seventeenth century, see G. Braden, *Renaissance Tragedy and the Senecan Tradition* (New Haven, 1985), pp. 124–46. M. Roston, *Sixteenth-Century English Literature* (New York, 1982), pp. 25–28, provides an analysis of Ascham's rhetoric. G. Hibbard, in his *Thomas Nashe: A Critical Introduction* (Cambridge, Mass., 1962), furnishes a balanced treatment of the leading and often conflicted ideas of this literary innovator. Cf. also *Works of Thomas Nashe,* ed., R. McKerrow (Oxford, 1958), pp. 8, 14.

60. For the judgments of the well-traveled Fynes Moryson, see his *An Itinerary Containing His Ten Years Travel to 1617* (Glascow, 1907–8), 4: 174–6. One particular

insight is worth quoting: "The gentlemen [of England] disdain traffic thinking it to abase gentry, but in Italy, with graver counsel, the very princes disdain not to be merchants . . . [but] leave the retailing commodity to men of inferior sort. And by this course they preserve the dignity and patrimony of their progenitors, suffering not the sinew of the commonwealth upon any pretense to be wrested out of their hands. On the contrary, the English and French, perhaps thinking it unjust to leave the common sort no means to be enriched by their industry and judging it equal that gentlemen should live of their revenues. Citizens by traffic, and the common sort by the plough and manual arts, as divers members of one body, do in this course sell their patrimonies, and the buyers (excepting lawyers) are for the most part citizens and vulgar men. And the daily feeling [? feeding] of this mischief makes the error apparent, whether it be prodigality of the gentry (greater than in any other nation or age) or their too charitable regard to the inferior sort, or rashness, or slothfulness, which cause them to neglect and despise traffic, which in some commonwealths and namely in England passeth all other commodities, and is the very sinew of the kingdom." Cf. J. Wilson, *Life in Shakespeare's England* (London, 1954), pp. 27. On the collaboration between Jonson and Inigo Jones, see R. Strong, "Inigo Jones and the Revival of Chivalry," *Apollo* 86 (1967), 101–8; R. Strong and S. Orgel, *Inigo Jones: The Theater of the Stuart Court,* 2 vols. (London, 1973); J. Harris, R. Strong, and S. Orgel, *The King's Arcadia: Inigo Jones and the Stuart Court* (London, 1973); J. Webb, *Stonehenge Restored* (London, 1633).

61. A. Pini, in his *Città, comuni e corporazioni nel medioevo italiano* (Bologna, 1986), pp. 130–33, gives statistics on the number of notaries in the city of Bologna: there were 30 in 1250 and 280 by the end of the fourteenth century. For the same increment in Pistoia, see D. Herlihy, *Pistoia nel medioevo e nel Rinascimento, 1200–1430* (Florence, 1967), p. 264. For Florence, see D. Herlihy and C. Klapisch-Zuber, *Tuscans and Their Families: A Study of the Florentine Catasto of 1427* (New Haven, 1985), pp. 261–98. For the figures on France in the early sixteenth century, see R.J. Knecht, *French Renaissance Monarchy: Francis I and Henry II* (London, 1984), pp. 14–16. For additional documentation on Florentine lawyers and notaries, see R. Davidsohn, *Storia di Firenze* (Florence, 1965), 4: 221–51. Charles Davis's *Dante's Italy and Other Essays* (Philadelphia, 1984) contains valuable information on education and public life in Florence and other central and north Italian city-states.

62. For an analysis of a number of county elections disclosing that English voters were far from deferential and passive, see D. Hirst, *The Representatives of the People? Voters and Voting in England under the Early Stuarts* (Cambridge, 1975), pp. 44–47. On the changing education of the justices of peace, see J. Gleason, *The Justices of the Peace in England 1558–1640* (Oxford, 1969), pp. 82–85. For France, indications are that the figure of 12,000 for 1505, or thereabouts, rose to 80,000 by 1664; this total does not include armed forces. Approximately the same number administered the estates and law courts. See Knecht, *French Renaissance Monarchy,* pp. 14–16. Cf. also, J. Berenger, "Le problèm du ministeriat." C. Brooks, in his *Petty Foggers and Vipers of the Commonwealth: The 'Lower Branch' of the Legal Profession of Early Modern England* (Cambridge, 1986), takes a positive view of the role of attorneys. Their numbers increased (that is, attorneys in Common Pleas and in King's Bench) by almost 800 percent between the mid-sixteenth and mid-seventeenth centuries. Their fees were not so high as to prevent them from assisting numerous of the weak and exploited in defense of their property and rights against the overbearing and overmighty. The attorneys' contribution to the formation of a civil society is here argued vigorously and effectively. M. Kishlansky, in his *Parliamentary Selection: Social and Political Choice in Early Modern England* (Cambridge, 1986), pp. 2–21, 225 ff., opts for a view of the ritual nature of sixteenth-century parliamentary elections as being rarely contested, since to compete constituted an affront to the honor

of the candidate. He outlines an archaic system of political choice predicated on honorific values and suggests steps by which, over the next century, a ritualized process of social distinction, affirmation, and celebration was displaced by movement toward political calculation and competition for election.

63. For comments on William of Worcester and his judgments on historical changes, see M. H. Keen, *England in the Late Middle Ages: A Political History* (London, 1973), pp. 514–16. See also, William of Worcester, *The Boke of Noblesse*, ed. J. Nicholas (Roxburghe Club, 1860), pp. 77–78.

64. See R. O'Day, *Education and Society 1500–1800* (London, 1982), pp. 65–68 for a general view of what was novel in pedagogy. For particulars, see J. McDiarmid, "Sir John Cheke's Protestant Ciceronianism and Its Background," to be published. Sir Thomas Smith (1513–77), author of a seminal work on English politics, *De Republica Anglorum,* had studied at Paris and received his D.C. from the University of Padua; he was public orator at Cambridge and Henry VIII's first Regius Professor of Civil Law at that university. On the subject of the foreclosure of debate concerning noble participation in the King's Council resulting in the vindication of regular contribution of "new Men" (upstarts), see, John Guy, "The King's Council and Political Participation," in *Reassessing the Henrician Age: Humanism, Politics and Reform 1500–1550,* eds. A. Fox and J. Guy (Oxford, 1986), 121–47.

65. On Thomas Wilson and a variety of other matters pertaining to court talk, country speech, and rhetoric, see John King, *English Reformation Literature* (Princeton, 1982), pp. 49–53, 225 ff. L. Stone's "Educational Revolution in England," provides valuable statistical data. By the 1630s, perhaps one-half of the adult males could read and one-third of all adults were literate, after a fashion. This compares with figures collected for selected regions of north and south Italy for the fifteenth century. If Giovanni Villani's statistics are correct, the figure for England would roughly match that of Florence for the biennium 1336–38. Cf. *Cronica,* ed. F. Dragomanni (Milan, 1848), bk. XI,94, pp. 323–26; Davidsohn, *Storia di Firenze* (Florence, 1965), 4: part 3, 211–333, on education in Florence in the thirteenth and fourteenth centuries. Comparison of literacy figures for England and north and central Italy in the fourteenth and fifteenth centuries cannot be precise, but the difference appears marked: rates in England were perhaps one third to one half lower than those for the selected regions of Italy. See D. Cressy, *Literature and the Social Order: Reading and Writing in Tudor and Stuart England* (Cambridge, 1980). He confirms Stone's figures.

66. For a discussion of the quotation from William Cecil, see L. Salinger, "The Social Setting," *The Elizabethan Age* (New York, 1982), p. 46. It is worth noting that Cecil made provision in his household for a number of young aristocrats, several of whom were court wards. Cf. J. Briggs, *Stage-Play World,* p. 108. K. Levine, in his *The Social Context of Literacy* (London, 1986), pp. 74–76, discusses recent views on participation by nobles and gentry in the so-called Tudor educational revolution. See also, L. Stone, "Literacy and Education in England 1640–1900," *Past & Present* 42 (1969), 69–135. Ben Jonson killed a fellow actor in sword-fight and was charged at Old Bailey in 1598. He pleaded guilty and, in his own words to William Drummond, "called for the book" (Bible), got through the "neck verse," satisfying the court that he had "read like a clerk." Though he was branded at the base of his left thumb and his goods confiscated, Jonson had escaped the gibbet by pleading benefit of clergy. R. Miles, *Ben Jonson: His Life and Work* (London, 1986). Cf. also, *The Works of Ben Jonson,* ed. C. Herford and P. and E. Simpson, 1: p. 219.

2. THE DIRECTION OF CHANGE

1. See E. Warlop, *The Flemish Nobility before 1300,* 4 vols., 2 parts (Kortrijk, 1975–76), 1: 90–110; see N. Tolstoy's review of Warlop's detailed study in the *Times Literary Supplement* (22 February 1985), p. 22. Stone's *Crisis of the Aristocracy* p.

550, reports the comment of the Venetian ambassador: "The magnates are mostly hated for their vain ostentation, better suited to their ancient position than their present condition." Stone's chapter, "Conspicuous Expenditure," is the work of a master tapestry weaver of social history and is rich with detail and insights. In 1546 the Venetian ambassador to the French court reported that "offices are infinite in number and grow daily . . . half of which would suffice." Cf. Knecht, *French Renaissance Monarchy*, p. 15. On the foundation of academies for educating French nobles in "bonnes lettres," along with the martial arts and social graces, see R. Chartier and D. Julia, *L'éducation en France du XVIe au XVIIIe siècle* (Paris, 1976), pp. 170 ff. Cf. also, C. de Seysell, *The Monarchy of France of 1515,* trans. J. Hexter (New Haven, 1981), pp. 60–64. For a translation of Lannoy's letter to his infant son, see Hexter, *Reappraisals in History,* pp. 62–63.

2. On Commynes' political career (its ins and outs), see W. Prevenier and W. Blockmans, *Burgundian Netherlands,* pp. 196–200. For a sensitive appraisal of the literary style as an index to the character of Commynes, see Montaigne's reflections on the Fleming's writings: "Here you will find the language pleasant and agreeable, of a natural simplicity; the narrative pure, and the author's good faith showing through it clearly, free from vanity in speaking of himself, and of partiality or envy in speaking of others; his ideas and exhortations accompanied more by good zeal and truth than by any exquisite capacity; and, throughout, authority and gravity, representing the man of good background and brought up in great affairs." *The Complete Works of Montaigne,* trans. D. Frame (Stanford, 1948), pp. 305–6 (*Essays,* II, 10).

3. J. Guy, "King's Council and Political Participation," 121–26. Cf. also H. Miller, *Henry VIII and the English Nobility,* pp. 102–33; R. Storey, "Gentlemen-bureaucrats," in *Profession, Vocation and Culture in Later Medieval England: Essays Dedicated to the Memory of A. R. Myers,* ed. C. H. Clough (Liverpool, 1982), 90–129, considers the laicization of royal administration under the Lancastrians.

4. G. Rothenberg, "Maurice of Nassau, Gustavus Adolphus, Raimondo Montcuccoli and the Military Revolution of the Seventeenth Century," in *Makers of Modern Strategy,* 32–63. The quote from Max Weber's *Essays in Sociology,* trans. and eds. H. Gerth and C. Wright Mills (New York, 1946) is on page 34 of Rothenberg's article. Cf. also, M. Vale, "New Techniques and Old Ideals: The Impact of Artillery on War and Chivalry," in *War, Literature and Politics in the Late Middle Ages,* ed. C. Allmand (Liverpool, 1976), 60–67; P. Contamine, "Points de vue sur la chevalerie en France à la fin du Moyen Age," *Francia* 4 (1976), 255–85.

5. J. Guy, "King's Council and Political Participation," p. 125; *English Historical Documents 1327–1485,* ed. A. Meyers (London, 1969), 4: 300–1. From Plato on, the notion that political philosophy should be written for an elite was comfortably ensconced in literary tradition. Such sixteenth-century writings as Erasmus's *Education of a Christian Prince;* Guillaume Budé's *De l'Institution du Prince;* Sir Thomas Elyot's *The Boke Named Gouvernor;* and, of course, Machiavelli's *The Prince* (the *Discorsi* was dedicated to one who ought to be a ruler), offer lively testimony to the health of this tradition. The problem of rendering effective counsel to the ruler occupied More, Elyot, and Starkey, and they were practitioners of this venerable art. See Johnston, *Rhetoric of Leviathan,* pp. 72–73, 132–33.

6. On Thomas Cromwell, see the entry in *Dictionary of National Biography* (London, 1885–1900), 5: 198. Cf. also, W. Zeeveld, *Foundations of Tudor Policy* (Cambridge, Mass., 1948), pp. 105–8.

7. It might be useful to quote in full the translation from the Latin text of More's *Historia Richardi Tertii* in *The Complete Works of St. Thomas More,* Yale ed., ed. D. Kinney (New Haven, 1986), 15: 482–83. Buckingham, having offered Richard the crown, and the latter having pretended that this momentous business had not been

prearranged, the people departed for their homes. Some saw the pretense as shameless. By quoting More's account at length, it is possible to suggest something of his view of the cultivated moral ambiguity and theatrics of the politics: "But others appealed to tradition and the standard conventions of human behavior, according to which all great affairs must be executed with some sort of legitimate ceremony; indeed, some pretenses and the spectators did not pretend not to notice them. For when someone is ordained a bishop, he is twice asked if he would be willing, and twice he denies it devoutly, and the third time he is barely induced to say he would be willing in spite of himself, whereas even supposing he has not paid the prince any money, the bulls he has bought from the pope show how he has been angling for the title. And when someone plays an emperor in a tragedy, are the people unaware he might be a mere craftsman? But in such circumstances it shows such ignorance to know what you know that if anyone calls him what he really is, not what he is falsely supposed to be, he risks getting a good beating for a bad joke from that man's make-believe retainers, and quite rightly, since he went about to disrupt the whole drama with his untimely truth. In the same way, what they had just watched was a regal tragicomedy; the people had been summoned merely to watch, and a sensible person would do nothing else; certain people who had followed an impulse to get onstage and step in among the theatrical company had disrupted the drama through their inexperience and thus landed themselves in great danger." More's disenchanted version of the theatrics of politics did not dim the luster of his admiration for the prudent Cardinal Morton "who dyd farre exceed them all in wysdom and gravytie," thereby being able to survive the perfidy and treachery of the time of Richard III. Not only did he endure, but he was to become Henry VIII's chancellor and chief administrator. This artful, perceptive, and prudent civil servant, always ready to give counsel, served as an example to More at a critical moment, both in his personal and literary life: in 1516 he was writing the *Utopia* and had received a request from the crown to serve. See P. Kaufman, *The "Polytyque Churche": Religion and Early Tudor Political Culture, 1485–1516.* (Macon, Ga., 1986), pp. 133–34.

8. For a full discussion of the significance of More's ideas on rhetoric and the amplification of the discourse of counsel, see Ferguson, *Articulate Citizen.* For More's political service, see J. Guy, *The Public Career of Sir Thomas More* (Brighton, 1980). More's sensitivity to rhetoric and advice to princes is expressed in the *Utopia,* where he compares a counselor coming to court to urge the necessity of initiating some drastic reform with someone dressed as a philosopher who barges on stage during a moment in a comedy by Plautus when household slaves are making trivial jokes at one another. For a discussion of this and other insights into More's appreciation of the niceties of rhetoric, see Norbrook, *Poetry and Politics,* pp. 24–28. A. Michel, *Rhetorique et philosophie chez Ciceron: Essai sur les fondemente philosophique de l'art de persuader* (Paris, 1960) treats in detail the philosophical base for rhetoric. Cf. also, W. Howell, *Logic and Rhetoric in England, 1500–1700* (New York, 1961); W. Ong, *Ramus, Method, and the Decay of Dialogue* (Cambridge, Mass., 1958). After Machiavelli and the dissemination of his subversive ideas, the notion that the founders of ancient commonwealths—especially civil societies—used religion manipulatively to persuade their subjects that the laws which they had promulgated were divine in origin, became a feature of advanced political thought. For Hobbes and others, Moses and his successors, both Old Testament and classical, were perceived as instituting religious ceremonies to sustain the commonwealth and sovereign authority. Cf. Johnston, *Rhetoric of 'Leviathan'*; T. Hobbes, *Leviathan,* ed. C. Macpherson (Harmondsworth, Middlesex, 1968), pp. 172–78, 503–11.

9. *The Complete Works of St. Thomas More,* Yale ed., 4: 99. J. Hexter's *More's "Utopia": The Biography of an Idea* (Princeton, 1952) is unrivaled for its historical reconstruction of the stages of More's composition of the text of *Utopia.* The need for

a delicate appreciation for the strategies of rhetoric was sometimes at odds with the requirement that those counseling rulers and potential rulers must avoid speech that was idiosyncratic, esoteric, and exotic. Francis Bacon was to sum it up when he stated that the principles and reasoning of their science should be evident even to the "meanest intellect." This dictum was subscribed to by Erasmus, Sidney, Bacon, Hobbes, and a host of others writing on politics. The tension generated between their desire to be accessible to the mighty, yet not to be understood by fools, produced some of their best prose. See Johnston, *Rhetoric of 'Leviathan'*, p. 72.

10. Michel de Montaigne, *The Complete Works,* ed. and trans, D. Frame, pp. 177–78 (Essay, "Of solitude," I, 39).

11. Robert Estienne, in his *Grammaire françoise,* maintained that the royal court and tribunals of justice and finance qualified as temples of "good usage' for the vernacular: "I rely on those who during their entire lifetimes have frequented the courts of France, that of the king as well as of his Parliament in Paris and also his Chancellery and Chamber of Accounts in which places the language is written and pronounced in greater purity than in all others." Estienne Pasquier was more radical and would reserve for the learned men of the robe the privilege of establishing standards for vernacular prose: "Whoever would like to acquire judgment and intelligence in this language and take any degree, I would counsel him to frequent practicing law people for besides having exquisite speech, proper and familiar, making themselves accessible to the common populace (which is principal among them), the courtly or the most delightful speech of the King and the Court is well-known to them, sent back and forth by Letters or by Edicts of the ones or the others." For the translation of these passages and a description of their social context, see M. Fumaroli, "Rhetoric, Politics, and Society," 253–73, esp. 268–69. Note should be taken of the lowering of the temperature of polemical and fiery civic prose so prevalent in Quattrocento Italian humanist circles. By the next century education and discourse were rendered more appropriate for those serving as functionaries, diplomats, military men, or governors in secular or ecclesiastical states. See C. Dionisotti, *Gli umanisti e il volgare fra Quattro e Cinquecento* (Florence, 1968), pp. 32–72.

12. For a recent discussion of the debate concerning the upbringing of the French nobility, see E. Schalk, *From Valor to Pedigree: Ideas of Nobility in France in the 16th and 17th centuries* (Princeton, 1985). Cf. also, G. Huppert, *Les bourgeois gentilhommes: An Essay on the Definition of Elites in Renaissance France* (Chicago, 1977), pp. 8–13; J-M. Constant, *La vie quotidienne de la noblesse française aux XVIe et XVIIe siècles* (Paris, 1985). Comments and opinions by contemporaries on the vital issue of education of the nobility are beyond count, but Montaigne's observations, in his letter to Madame Diane de Foix, Comtesse de Gurson (*Essays* I, 28, trans. D. Frame), are worth quoting: "Madame, learning is a great ornament and a wonderfully serviceable tool, notably for people raised to such a degree of fortune as you are. In truth, it does not receive its proper use in mean and lowborn hands. It is much prouder to lend its resources to conducting a war, governing a people, or gaining the friendship of a prince or a foreign nation, than to constructing a dialectical argument, pleading an appeal, or prescribing a mass of pills. Thus, Madame, because I think you will not forget this element in the education of your children, you who have tested its sweetness and who are of a literary race (for we still have the writings of those ancient counts of Foix from whom his lordship the count your husband and yourself are descended; and Francois, Monsieur de Candale, your uncle, every day brings forth others, which will extend for many centuries the knowledge of this quality to your family)."

13. On Tomitono and the esthetics of opportunistic behavior, see Garin, *Italian Humanism,* pp. 153–60, 197 ff. Marc Fumaroli, in his *L'âge de l'eloquence: Rhétorique et res literaria en France de la Renaissance au seuil del'epoque classique*

(Geneva, 1980), analyzes the art of elegant conversation as governed by the stylistics of Pietro Bembo and his spirited advocacy of Ciceronian norms. Harmoniously proportioned, this Venetian, Ciceronian atticism achieved an equilibrium between *sprezzatura* and *neglegentia,* over and against the decorous. Jacques Amyot was to transpose and codify Bembo's literary strategies in French. For an earlier definition (first part of fourteenth century) of a *gentile uomo,* see that of the Carmelite, Guido da Pisa: "Questo gentile uomo, che m'e capitato a casa, m'è entrato si nel cuore, ch'io non so che vuole essere questo; la sua gentilezza, li suoi alti costumi, lo suo bello e ornato parlate, mi danno fede che sia nato dalla schiatta degl'Iddii." Compare this assessment of *gentiluomo* with later-day usage. Alberti, in the fifteenth century, will advocate that the gentleman abandon his "marvigiose gentilezza" in favor of the moremundane "uso civile." Machiavelli's definition of *gentiluomo* was even more prosaic: he was one who lived well on the income of his possessions (preferably lands) without exerting effort. See Battaglia, *Grande Dizionario della Lingua Italiana,* 6: 683.

14. On the first manual of grammar composed by a humanist, Guarino de Verona's the *Regulae grammaticales,* see W. Percival, "Textual Problems in the Latin Grammar of Guarino Veronese," *Res Publica Litterarum* 1 (1978), 241–54. Guarino's grammar is unoriginal, and its ingredients are to be found in the works of the grammarians of the preceding generation. His grammar is humanistic, not for its contents but for what it excludes. Unlike earlier grammars, it does not anchor this discipline in the logic and metaphysical constructs of scholasticism. See Percival's observations in his "Grammar and Rhetoric in the Renaissance," in *Renaissance Eloquence,* ed. J. Murphy (Berkeley, 1983), 303–30.

15. Perhaps it would be well to permit Erasmus' Dame Folly to have her say: "Nothing is so foolish, they say, as for a man to stand for office and woo the crowd to win its vote, buy its support with presents, court the applause of all those fools and feel self-satisfied when they cry their approval, and then in his hour of triumph to be carried round like an effigy for the public to stare at, and end up cast in bronze to stand in the market-place. Then there are changes of names and surnames, divine honours awarded to a nobody, official ceremonies devised to raise even the most criminal of tyrants to the level of the gods. All this is utterly foolish, and more than one Democritus is needed for these absurdities, everyone agrees. Yet from this source spring the deeds of valiant heroes to be lauded to the skies in the writings of so many eloquent men. This same folly creates societies and maintains empires, officialdom, religion, law courts, and councils—in fact the whole of human life is nothing but a sport of folly. See *Praise of Folly* in *Collected Works of Erasmus,* ed. A. Levi (Toronto, 1986), 27: 101–2. The literary appetite for paradox and praise of ignorance was sharpened by a reading of Lucian and Plutarch, among other classical authors. The literary skills of Alberti, Agrippa of Nettesheim, Giambattista Gelli, Ortensio Landi, in the company of More and Erasmus, were much beholden to these ancient texts. One recalls the collaboration of More and Erasmus in translations of Lucian from Greek into Latin. So, too, did the moralizing of the ancient stoics have their influence. When Marcus Aurelius noted in his *Meditations* that "where there are things which appear most worthy of our approbation, we ought to lay them bare and look at their worthlessness and strip them of all words with which they are exalted. For outward show is a wonderful perverter of the reason." The benefits and risks of unmasking social and political pretensions were made the subject of a literature stimulated by the French civil wars that engaged the talents of Montaigne, Estienne Pasquier, Etienne de la Boétie, and others. See P. Burke, *Montaigne* (New York, 1981). pp. 33–35; Kaufman, *"Polytyque Churche,"* pp. 95–96.

16. On Ralph Robinson's translation of the *Utopia,* see J. Binder, "More's 'Utopia' in English: A Note on Translation," *Modern Language Notes* 62 (1947), 270–76. Cf.

also, Robinson's translation of *Utopia,* ed. J. Warrington (London, 1951). On More's Latin stylistics, see M. Delcourt's edition, *L'Utopie* (Paris, 1936), pp. 28–32. On republicanism and its impact on Sidney and other literati of sixteenth-century England, see Norbook, *Poetry and Politics,* pp. 30–31, and M. Axton, *The Queen's Two Bodies: Drama and the Elizabethan Succession* (London, 1977), *passim.* On Sir Walter Raleigh, see Christopher Hill, *Intellectual Origins of the English Revolution* (London, 1972), pp. 181 ff.

17. For original aperçus into the interplay between the intellectually innovative aspects of Renaissance literature and the radical elements of a traditional oral culture, see W. J. Ong, *Interfaces of the Word: Studies in the Evolution of Consciousness and Culture* (Ithaca, 1977), pp. 188 ff. Of course Mikhail Bakhtin's *Rabelais and His World,* trans. H. Iswolsky (Cambridge, Mass., 1968), is the work of a master philosopher of language. See also, A. Hamilton, "Elizabethan Prose Fiction and Some Trends in Recent Criticism," *Renaissance Quarterly* 37 (1984), 21–37. P. Zumthor's *Introduction à la poésie orale* (Paris, 1983), provides an imposing bibliography, as well as brilliant excursions into romance philology. For Italy, see C. Ginzburg, "Folklore, Magia, Religione," in *Storia d'Italia,* ed. R. Romano and C. Vivanti (Turin, 1972), 646 ff.; R. Leydi, "La canzone popolare," in *Storia d'Italia* vol. 2, (1973), 1184 ff.

18. For a discussion of Francis Bacon's views on language, see B. Vickers, *Sir Francis Bacon and Renaissance Prose* (Cambridge, 1968), pp. 39 ff. For Aristotle words were signifiers, but in signifying they tended to become more than simple signifiers. Human consciousness converted them into symbols, so they became symbolic. The purpose of rhetoric was to discover "the means of coming as near such successes as the circumstances of each particular case allow." The principal tool of rhetoric, the enthymene, dealt with the probabilistic and contingent (the fallible), while the syllogism dealt with certainties. See *The Rhetoric and Poetics of Aristotle,* trans. W. Rhys Roberts (New York, 1954), 1357 a–b, 1396a, 1402b. L. Jardine's, "The Place of Dialectic Teaching in Sixteenth-Century Cambridge," *Studies in the Renaissance* 21 (1974), 31 ff., and her *Francis Bacon: Discovery and the Art of Discourse* (Cambridge, 1974), are exceedingly useful in untangling thorny problems in rhetorical studies. See the cautionary remarks of B. Vickers in his "Analogy versus Identity: the Rejection of Occult Symbolism, 1580–1680," in *Occult and Scientific Mentalities in the Renaissance,* ed. B. Vickers (Cambridge, 1984), 102–14.

19. Writings on Shakespeare's rhetoric constitute nothing less than an industry. Particularly useful are B. Vickers, *The Artistry of Shakespeare's Prose* (London, 1968), and his "Shakespeare's Use of Rhetoric," in *A New Companion in Shakespeare Studies,* eds. S. Schoenbaum and K. Muir (Cambridge, 1972), 83–98. The critical tradition pertaining to Shakespeare's *Love's Labour's Lost* is reviewed in great detail by W. Carroll in *The Great Feast of Language in 'Love's Labour's Lost'"* (Princeton, 1976).

20. Keith Thomas, *Man and the Natural World: Changing Attitudes in England 1500–1800* (New York, 1984); see M. Foucault, *The Order of Things: An Archaeology of Human Sciences* (London, 1970), pp. 17–76; Bossy's comments on Foucault are enlightening and appreciative in *Christianity in the West,* pp. 168–72. For some cautionary remarks on Foucault and a higher evaluation of the persistence of humanist rhetoric, see N. Struever, "The Conversable World: Eighteenth-Century Transformations of the Relation of Rhetoric and Truth," *Rhetoric and the Pursuit of Truth* (Los Angeles, 1985), 102–5. For documents pertaining to comparisons between Dante and Petrarch, see *Prosatori latini del Quattrocento,* ed. E. Garin, pp. 798 ff. It should be noted that the tradition of etymological investigation, whereby truth was sought as hidden in words and human language was viewed as accidental to a basic grammar, was extremely sturdy. Language as the confection of philosophy, with vocabulary and

syntax worked out to mirror things in the world of experience, was indeed durable. If we follow the intellectual career of Coluccio Salutati and the genesis of early humanism, we observe that an interest in spelling was grounded in the assumption that words reflected reality in their composition and that incorrect spelling would distort truth. Only late in life did Salutati desist from the energetic effort to penetrate to the core of reality by employing etymological analysis to unlock the truth bound up in words. Difficulties confronting early humanists working toward a conception of the conventionality of language were daunting and should not be underestimated. See Witt, *Hercules at the Crossroads,* pp. 211 ff.

21. Literary movement toward the mimetic worked against activating general propositions about life that might be psychologically fantastic but morally instructive. Instead, the mimetic operated to create the illusion of real life situations in which natural feelings and obligation took precedence over the higher truth. Cf. D. Brewer, *The Poet as Storyteller* (London, 1984), pp. 42–43. In humanist political writing we detect that the literary representation of civic life called for a more comprehensive treatment of attachments to persons and places, as well as a more explicit analysis of the daily emotional and sensual responses to the problematics of human existence. The defense of civic life and its innumerable encounters extended on many fronts because, it would be argued, the complex and wide range of human talents required living in society. These talents could not be readily organized under any one principle or hierarchy. Family, friends, the arts, human affection, and patriotic sentiments must be lent their full literary value. See W. Bouwsma, "Venice and the Political Education of Europe," in *Renaissance Venice,* ed. J. Hale (London, 1973), 445–66, esp. 447.

22. For a critical account of the linkage between *res and verba,* see R. Cardini, *La critica del Landino* (Florence, 1973); cf. also, David Summers' masterful treatment of the changing language of artistic creation and illusion in *Michelangelo and the Language of Art* (Princeton, 1981). E. Cropper, in her review of Summers' book *Art Bulletin* 65 (1983), 157–62, highlights the significance of increased self-consciousness concerning the relationship between *res* and *verba* in the fine arts. For an extended discussion of earlier theories of language, see Gellrich, *Idea of the Book,* pp. 252 ff. Saint Augustine acknowledged the potential for arbitrary response when meditating on language as the most appropriate paradigm for the temporal character of fallen humankind and their world. Saint Thomas Aquinas recognized an enduring disjunction between the linguistic *modus quo* and the transcendent reference of learning. In both writers, however, a discourse of analysis and reference is deflected from a radical departure because the governing structure in which they worked is never unsettled. See in addition to the above citation, T. Reiss, *The Discourse of Modernism* (Ithaca, 1982). Humanists contended that the "reified ontological" vocabulary of scholasticism was unable to permit a pragmatic and flexible response to the claims of human society. This argument, forwarded so effectively by Lorenzo Valla, maintained that in order for a logic or dialectic to possess utility it must be responsive to the linguistic and social criterion of *consuetudo* (usage). See V. Kahn, "Humanism and the Resistance to Theory," in *Literary Theory/Renaissance Texts,* ed. P. Parker and D. Quint (Baltimore, 1986), p. 375.

23. Especially illuminating on the thorny subjects of medieval grammar and hermeneutics, is B. Stock's *The Implications of Literacy: Written Language and Models of Interpretation in the Eleventh and Twelfth Centuries* (Princeton, 1983). R. Howard Bloch's *Etymologies and Genealogies: A Literary Anthropology of the French Middle Ages* (Chicago, 1983), is a daring synthesis of literary theory and anthropology. Very useful for the study of syntax is B. Cerquiglini, *La parole mediévalé: Discours, syntaxe, texte* (Paris, 1981). The many scattered and fugitive papers of R. Hunt have been assembled and published in his *The History of Grammar in the Middle Ages: Collected Papers,* ed. G. Bursill-Hall (Amsterdam, 1980). For a consideration of the

particular bias of the speculative grammarians (modists), see the comment of G. Bursill-Hall, *Speculative Grammars of the Middle Ages: The Doctrine of Partes Orationis of the Modistae* (The Hague-Paris, 1971), p. 38. "Their conception of reality and of human reason led them to maintain that grammar must be 'one', and therefore Robert Kilwardby, one of the immediate predecessors of the Modistae, could argue that grammar can only be a science if it is one for all men; as a result of the intimacy between the reality of things and their conceptualization by the mind, grammar becomes the study of the formulation of these concepts, their actual expression being accidental, and therefore incidental to Modistic grammatical theory. Furthermore, this theory of grammar had the effect of creating the belief that the universality of things as conceived and understood by the universality of human reason could be expressed in the universal language, Latin, which was thus raised to the status of metalanguage. Minor matters such as the vernaculars had perhaps the effect of attesting differences in vocabulary, but these could be dismissed since they could not affect structure."

24. In delivering the annual sermon on Saint Thomas, Valla offended the Roman Dominicans by elevating patriotic models of theology over those of the scholastics. Valla appreciated Aquinas for his spiritual qualities rather than his theology. One of the audience, after listening to Valla's encomium, decided that he was quite mad. See H. Gray, "Valla's Encomium of St. Thomas Aquinas and the Humanist Conception of Christian Antiquity," in *Essays in History and Literature Presented to Stanley Pargelis*, ed. H. Blum (Chicago, 1965), 37–52. S. Camporeale's *Lorenzo Valla, umanesimo e teologia* (Florence, 1972), provides a judicious consideration of Valla's conception of theology, as well as of his method. Cf. also, Mario Fois, *Il pensiero cristiana di Lorenzo Valla nel quadro storico-culturale del suo ambiente* (Rome, 1969); Giovanni di Napoli, *Lorenzo Valla, filosofia e religione nell' umanesimo italiano* (Rome, 1971); Cesare Vasoli, *La dialettica e la retorica dell' Umanesimo 'Invenzione' e 'Metodo' nella cultura del XV e XVI secolo* (Milan, 1968).

25. In a recent article aimed at a synthesis of the consequences of Erasmian humanism, J. McConica states the following: "The most crucial single change was the replacement of medieval grammars with those of humanist grammarians, and the corresponding displacement of logic and dialectic by the early study of grammar and rhetoric; in the latter were found, of course, poetry and history as well as the art of persuasive speech. It was to be an education in virtue as well as knowledge, and the conduct of the child was to be as much a part of discipline as the language it would learn." See "The Fate of Erasmian Humanism," in *Universities, Society, and the Future* (Edinburgh, 1983), pp. 37–61, esp. 41.

26. For a recent discussion of Dante's views on language, see G. Mazzotta, *Dante, Poet of the Desert: History and Allegory in the "Divine Comedy"* (Princeton, 1979). Cf. also, R. Hollander, *Allegory in Dante's Comedy* (Princeton, 1969), pp. 9–70; C. Singleton, *Dante Studies, I: "Commedia," Elements of Structure* (Cambridge, Mass., 1954), pp. 13–70.

27. G. Olson, *Literature as Recreation in the Later Middle Ages* (Ithaca, 1982), pp. 31–36. Quintilian's modest epistemological assertion (*Institutio Oratoria* 2.17, 38–9) is that the orator does not know that what he says is true; rather, he argues *probiliter* or *verisimiliter*. This served to fructify instruction in *ars bene dicendi* (the art of speaking well) by permitting the inclusion of such topics as "sorties" and "dilemma" when arguing "truth seeming." The logical status of these topics was at best dubious, but their rhetorical power was incontestable. See L. Jardine, "Lorenzo Valla and the Intellectual Origins of Humanist Dialectic," *Journal of the History of Philosophy* 15 (1977), 143–64.

28. G. Folena's *La crisi linguistica del Quattrocento e l'Arcadia" di I. Sannazaro* (Florence, 1952), is a treasure trove of erudition on the topic of new linguistic coinage;

cf. esp. pp. 125–88. S. Rizzo's *Il lessico filologico degli umanisti* (Rome, 1973) is also helpful. On the contribution of the Florentine mercantile lexicon to new developments in the vernacular, see C. Bec, *Les marchands écrivains*, pp. 301–30.

29. F. Tateo's *Dialogo interiors e polemica ideologica nel "Secretum" del Petrarca* (Florence, 1965) is a seminal study of the literary tactics of Petrarch in particular and Italian humanists in general. See also, T. Cave's *The Cornicopian Text: Problems of Writing in the French Renaissance* (Oxford, 1978), which treats the reception of humanist rhetoric in the north of Europe in the sixteenth century, especially the themes of the mobility of consciousness and literary strategies for amplification. On the displacement of the Christian examination of conscience from an ecclesiastical context to a private conversation between the author and his spiritual mentor Saint Augustine, see Petrarch's *Secretum*. The conversation takes place in the presence of the allegorical figure Truth (Veritas). The judge, however, remains silent, and in the end no clear notion of truth emerges either for the reader or the anguished author. Cf. T. Greene, "Ritual and Text in the Renaissance," to be published, and *Light in Troy*, pp. 81–103.

30. A knowledge of classical Latin might prove valuable in resolving recalcitrant historical or theological issues if the difficulties could be located in their linguistic formulation. The perplexing and longtime puzzle of the authenticity of the Donation of Constantine was a case in point. See A. Grafton and L. Jardine, *From Humanism to the Humanities* (Cambridge, 1986), pp. 67–71. When Valla used the extended metaphor of "language as coinage," the image connoted *currency,* not alienation, as Marxist critics would argue. It did connote *artificiality,* but this was "an artificiality humanistically understood as both goal and achievement." See N. Struever, *The Language of History in the Renaissance: Rhetoric and Historical Consciousness in Florentine Humanism* (Baltimore, 1970), p. 157. See Lorenzo Valla's critique of Aristotle in the proem to his *Dialecticae disputationes* for not participating in the arena of civic life. L. Valla, *Opere omnia,* ed. E. Garin (Basel, 1540); reprinted, (Turin, 1962), 2: 644.

31. For reflections on Dante, Saint Augustine, and the idea of peace, see A. P. d'Entreves, *Dante as a Political Thinker,* pp. 31 ff. For examples of the many circumstances under which the rituals of peacemaking were invoked, from entries in account books of the Peruzzi Company (*Libro di Commercio*) to the rites of pacification among warring urban factions, see Battaglia, *Grande dizionario della lingua italiana,* 12: 318–19.

32. Aby Warburg and Erwin Panofsky have perceived links between the agitated stylistics of Italian literati and artists. Italian Quattrocento artistic taste was impressed and excited by the tragic restlessness of the antique. Using the expressive power and beauty of the human body, the artist translated the language of the antique into an Italian idiom for portraying agonostic and erotic pathos. See A. Warburg, *Gesammelte Schriften* (Berlin and Leipzig, 1932), 1:175 ff.; E. Panofsky, *Meaning in the Visual Arts* (Garden City, N.Y., 1955), pp. 236–85.

33. V. Branca's *Boccaccio: The Man and His Works,* trans. R. Monges (New York, 1976), is an amplification of his *Boccaccio medievale,* and while it does not avail itself of recent scholarship in Florentine history, it remains an excellent work of literary analysis. On the *Decameron,* see pp. 223–65. The contribution of the *Decameron* to the literature of "civil conversation" is worthy of notice. The characters meeting to escape the plague and while away the time with story telling, conduct an amiable and cultivated exchange of views on crucial topics such as justice, liberality, courtesy and love without becoming narrowly pedagogical. Further, they reason on traditional values so that they undergo serious mutation, yet the characters do not break the tender web of sociability. See A. Tartaro, *Boccaccio* (Palermo, 1981) for an explication of his own critical insights and criticism of others. The transposition of narrative

strategies prompted by classical authors and vernacular achievements to the art of the humanist Latin epistle is illustrated by the letters of Poggio Bracciolini. See especially his letter to Niccolò Niccoli on his visit to the baths of Baden and his letter to Leonardo Bruni Aretino on the condemnation of the righteous and admirable heretic, Jerome of Prague (1416). See *Prosatori latini del Quattrocento,* ed. E. Garin, pp. 218–28, 228–41. Yet another celebrated narrative is Poliziano's account of the death of Lorenzo de' Medici, directed to Jacopo Antiquari (1492), ibid., pp. 886–901.

34. On artist contracts and increased emphasis on skill, see M. Baxandall, *Painting and Experience in Fifteenth-Century Italy* (Oxford, 1972), pp. 14–17. E. Gombrich's review of *The Rare Art Tradition* by J. Alsop in *The New York Review of Books* (2 December 1982), 39–42, packs a lifetime of reflection and sturdy common sense into a few pages devoted to analysis of artistic change in the Renaissance. Gombrich's *Norm and Form: Studies in the Art of the Renaissance* (London, 1960), is a collection of some of his highly informative writings.

35. Cf. M. Baxandall, *Giotto and the Orators* (Oxford, 1971), pp. 140–43. On Alberti, see his *De pictura,* II, 25, ed. C. Grayson (Rome, 1975), p. 41. The earliest classicizing orations may well have been the panegyric composed by the humanist Pier Paolo Vergerio honoring Saint Jerome in Padua (1392–1408). Vergerio belonged to the humanist literary circle of Giovanni di Conversino of Ravenna, Vittorino da Feltre, and Guarino da Verona. These new orations relinquished the form of the traditional *laudes sanctorum,* abandoning their structure, theme, divisions, authorities, and dialectic in favor of the topos of the classical *genus demonstrativum.* The classical orator aimed to "movere" and "delectare," whereas the traditional thematic sermon emphasized teaching (*docere*) and instruction in doctrine. See O'Malley, *Praise and Blame in Renaissance Rome,* pp. 81–115. Hans Baron's historical appreciation of the relationship between the arts and Florentine civic spirit set the stage for a debate among scholars concerning the evaluation of possible causes for the genesis of a classically minded public culture in the early Quattrocento. See *Crisis of the Early Italian Renaissance,* 2d ed, (Princeton, 1966) pp. 120 ff.

36. For the more strictly limited ideals of Giotto, see John White, *Art and Architecture in Italy, 1250–1400* (Baltimore, 1966), pp. 213–23. L. Berti, in his *Masaccio* (State College, Pa., 1967), pp. 17 ff., offers a stimulating comparison of Masaccio and Van Eyck emphasizing the former's insistence on the priority of visual truth over interior fantasy. Cf. also, A. Smart, *The Renaissance and Mannerism in Italy* (London, 1971), pp. 30–31. Coluccio Salutati, the humanist chancellor of Florence, posed this detached and historical view of the religious image: "I think [an ancient Roman's] feelings about his religious images were no different from what we in the full rectitude of our faith feel now about the painted or carved memorials of our Saints and Martyrs. For we perceive these not as Saints and as Gods but rather as images of God and the Saints. It may indeed be that the ignorant vulgar think more and otherwise of them than they should. But one enters into understanding and knowledge of spiritual things through the medium of sensible things, and so if pagan people made images of Fortune with a cornucopia and a rudder—as distributing wealth and controlling human affairs—they did not deviate very much from the truth. So too, when our own artists represent Fortune as a queen turning with her hands a revolving wheel, so long as we apprehend that picture as something made by a man's hand, not something itself divine but a similitude of divine providence, direction and order—and representing indeed not its essential character but rather the winding and turning of mundane affairs—who can reasonably complain?" See M. Baxandall, *Painting and Experience,* pp. 42–43. James Banker presents the results of an investigation into rhetorical handbooks and their instruction in letter writing with an eye toward the social context in his "*Ars Dictaminis* and Rhetorical Textbooks." H. Wieruszowski's important articles on instruction in rhetoric and on a variety of other matters pertaining to

education in thirteenth-century Italy have been collected and published in her *Politics and Culture in Medieval Spain and Italy* (Rome, 1971).

37. E. Panofsky's *Early Netherlandish Painting: Its Origins and Character*, Vol. 1, (Cambridge, Mass., 1958) makes numerous telling comparisons between the art of the North and that of the South. In his *The Life and Art of Albrecht* Dürer (Princeton, 1955), p. 17, Panofsky chronicles Dürer's contact with artists such as Barbari, Bellini, Pollaiuolo, Mantegna, Lorenzo di Credi, and Raphael, as well as with thinkers like Alberti and Leonardo da Vinci. Dürer's Italian experience is, in Panofsky's opinion, not responsible for the tension between the German artist's need for "theoretical rules" (*rechtes Grund*) and his humble, worshipful reverence for the particular. This contact did, however, make the conflict both more articulate and self-conscious. Yet another response of Dürer to his Italian experience has to do with his sojourn in Venice and the letter he wrote to his dear friend and humanist mentor, Willibald Pirckheimer, in which he confided that while in Italy he felt very much the "gentleman," but in Nuremberg he was ever the "parasite." See Gent, *Picture and Poetry*, pp. 14–21; M. Fumaroli, "Genèse de l'épistolographie classique: Rhétorique Humaniste de la lettre, de Pétrarque à Juste Lipse," *Revue d'histoire littéraire de la France* 78 (1978), 891–900. For a further consideration of the comments attributed to Michelangelo comparing the painting of the Flemish with that of the Italian, see Huizinga, *Waning of the Middle Ages*, pp. 264–66. Giorgio Vasari, in the proem to part 2 of his *Lives of the Artists*, introduces the Florentine Quattrocento and the "superb" Masaccio with these notable and measured words: "In this way the artists tried to reproduce *neither more nor less* than what they saw in nature, and as a result their work began to show more careful observation and understanding. This encouraged them to lay down definite rules for perspective and to make their foreshortenings in the exact form of natural relief, proceeding to the observation of light and shade, shadows, and other problems. They endeavoured to compose their pictures with greater regard for real appearances, attempting to make their landscapes more realistic, along with the trees, the grass, the flowers, the air, the clouds, and the other phenomena of nature. They did this so successfully that the arts were brought to the flower of their youth, holding out the promise that in the near future they would enter the golden age." See *Lives*, trans. G. Bull (Harmondsworth, 1965), p. 93.

38. On narrative and the effort of the artist to lend verisimilitude to the complexity and contingency of the visible world, see Patricia Brown, "Painting and History in Renaissance Venice," *Art History* 7 (1984), 264–83. On Giotto, see Bruce Cole, *The Renaissance Artist at Work: From Pisano to Titian* (New York, 1983), pp. 15–30; John White, *The Birth and Rebirth of Pictorial Space* (London, 1957), pp. 57–71; D. Gioseffi, *Giotto architetto* (Milan, 1963), pp. 17–33. Roland Barthes' comments in his *Introduction to the Structural Analysis of Narrative* (Binghamton, N.Y., 1966) on fulfilling the narrative expectations of an audience: ". . . the imitation of life is a contingent quality: the function of narrative is not to 'represent' it is to provide a display which is still an enigma to us, but which can only be of the mimetic order. The 'reality' of a sequence does not lie in the 'natural' succession of the action of which it is composed but in the logic which is revealed in it, is risked and satisfied." A reluctance to display its codes, and the ambition to give the narrative a natural cause of existence is a feature of the displacement of archaic forms and decline of an aristocratic culture in the judgment of K. Grandsden in *Virgil's Iliad: An Essay on Epic Narrative* (Cambridge, 1986), pp. 18–23.

39. For a discussion of the quote from Alberti, see J. Spencer's translation of the artist's treatise, *On Painting* New Haven, 1966), p. 68. Cf. also, *De pictura*, II, 25, ed. C. Grayson (Rome, 1975), p. 45. On Da Vinci, see M. Kemp, *Leonardo da Vinci: The Marvelous Works of Nature and Man* (Cambridge, Mass., 1981), p. 39.

40. See Gent, *Picture and Poetry* pp. 12–24. Cf. also, H. Janson, "The Birth of

Artistic Licence," in *Patronage in the Renaissance,* ed. G. Fitch and S. Sorgel (Princeton, 1981), 344–53. The deeper philosophical issue of the need to utilize fictions in order to acquire certain types of understanding, is treated in detail by Johnston, *Rhetoric of 'Leviathan'* pp. 1–25. This is a problem of great epistemological significance for the writing of history in the sixteenth and seventeen centuries, as it is also today. Hobbes will argue in his translation of Thucydides' *History of the Peloponnesian War* (1628) that the invention of fiction is essential for any genuine causal understanding of historical events. The reason for this, Hobbes proposed, was that thoughts and motives, which were after all decisive causal elements in human affairs, were inaccessible by any direct strategy of access. The use of fictitious speeches or deliberative orations was advocated by the humanist historians in order to convey the "grounds and motives" of actions to the reader. Our knowledge of thought and motive must always remain conjectural, therefore, any device used to explain them must involve an element of fiction or contrivance.

41. Sidney did not argue in his *Defense of Poesie* that truth rests only, or even ultimately, on the "foreconceit" of the poet. It might be well to quote Arthur Kinney's telling observation on this essential matter: ". . . Sidney contends, meaning rests in the complicit judgment of the reader. Sidney makes his point openly when he admires the irony of Erasmus (and Agrippa) and when he scorns readers who are content to believe everything literally—readers content *not* to judge. By the virtue he awards icastic art (divinely revealed or humanly counterfeited) juxtaposed with the fantastic shows of wantonness (unreal because evil in God's and the poet's created universes) Sidney rewakens, without admitting it, the caution of Plato, the cynicism of Sextus. Even when such evil is not present, the inherent conflict between icastic and fantastic representation demands a third response in the reconciliation by the reader in his well knowing: an act of triangulation through which the reader gives the final significance on the inherent disputation of any text using images—on any act of poetic fiction. See A. Kinney, "Rhetoric and Fiction in Elizabethan England," in *Renaissance Eloquence,* p. 391; Sir Philip Sidney, *A Defense of Poetry,* ed. J. Van Dorsten (Oxford, 1966), pp. 32–34.

42. Garin, *Italian Humanism,* p. 34, and his *L'umanesimo italiano,* pp. 34–37. See also, R. Black, *Benedetto Accolti and the Florentine Renaissance* (Cambridge, 1985), pp. 79–84.

43. In characterizing fifteenth-century English literary achievements, Derek Pearsall portrays this as an age of consolidation, "a pedestrian exercise dominated by translation. The paradox for English poetry, however, is that it finds itself poised to receive its full European inheritance at the very moment when the traditions of that inheritance are devitalized and exhausted. . . . What we are witnessing, in fact, is a shift in the role of poetry from a social form to an art-form. For the medieval poet, poetry is an aspect of the general intellectual tradition, a form of discourse not essentially different in kind from other forms of discourse, except in its capacity to give pleasure. This is now changing: poetry, when it is not relegated to base functions, is now becoming the property of a reading élite and the product of a particular kind of elevated being, the Poet. It is difficult to imagine an *Apology for Poetry* in the English Middle Ages, or to imagine the kind of attack on poetry as a form that produced the *Apology.*" See *Old English and Middle English Poetry* (London, 1977), p. 283. On Wyatt and things Italian, see S. Baldi, "Sir Thomas Wyatt and Vellutello," *English Studies Today* 4 (1966), 121–27; D. Guss, "Wyatt's Petrarcanism: An Instance of Creative Imagination in the Renaissance," *Huntington Library Quarterly* 29 (1965), 1–15. On Surrey, see W. Davis, "Contexts in Surrey's Poetry," *English Literary Renaissance* 4 (1974), 40–55. A. Spearing's *Medieval to Renaissance in English Poetry* (Cambridge, 1985), pp. 278–326, furnishes a model synthesis of the literary accomplishments of Wyatt, Surrey and others.

44. For the influence of Ficino on John Colet and his circle in England, see S. Jayne, *John Colet and Marsilio Ficino* (Oxford, 1963). For the impact of Pico on Erasmus, see L. Pusino, "Der Einfluss Picos auf Erasmus," *Zeitschrift für Kulturgeschichte* 46 (1927), 75–96. Cf. also, I. Kaufman, "John Colet and Erasmus' 'Enchiridion' ", *Church History* 46 (1977), 296–372, and his *Augustinian Piety and Catholic Reform: Augustine, Colet and Erasmus* (Macon, Ga., 1982), pp. 121–33.

45. *Earthly Republic*, pp. 189–90. For the complete text, see F. Barbaro, *De re uxoria liber in partes duas*, ed. A. Gnesotto in *Atti e Memorie di R. Accademia di Padova* 32 (1915), pp. 8–103.

46. Garin, *Italian Humanism*, p. 40. See also *L'educazione umanistica in Italia*, ed. E. Garin (Bari, 1959), pp. 115–128.

47. The new styled sermon with its borrowings from classical rhetoric went beyond classical diction, vocabulary, syntax, and figures of speech. Concentrating less on abstract doctrines (the standard matter of the thematic scholastic sermon), the new style featured God's deeds—his *beneficia*. History replaced philosophy and the purpose of the sermon was transformed from an argument and dialectical exercise in proof into a hymn of praise. A religious view was conveyed uncompromisingly positive in its appreciation of man and the word of God. The theme of the dignity of man is much beholden to this new rhetorical development. See J. O'Malley, "Sixteenth-Century Treatises on Preaching," in *Renaissance Eloquence*, 236–52, and his *Praise and Blame in Renaissance Rome*. Vernacular sermons will favor the epideictic genre with emphasis on *elucutio; inventio* and *distositio* will decline in prominence. Finally, scholastic division of the *thema* became old-fashioned as the sermon approached literature with a heightened self-consciousness. See E. Garin, *La cultura filosofica del Rinascimento italiano* (Florence, 1961), pp. 166–82.

48. For a full bibliography and balanced treatment of the humanists' position on this theologically prickly question, see R. Coogan, "The Pharisee against the Hellenist: Edward Lee versus Erasmus," *Renaissance Quarterly* 39 (1986), 476–500. Cf. also, A. Levi, *Pagan Virtue and the Northern Renaissance* (London, 1974), pp. 10–17. Erasmus's Dame Folly refused to "touch on original sin" or to avoid "seeming to agree with the opinion of Plato and Origen who teach that souls sinned before they came into human bodies." See Levi's comments in his Introduction to Praise of Folly, Vol. 27, *Collected Works of Erasmus*, pp. xxii–xxiii.

49. J. Mirollo, *Mannerism and Renaissance Poetry: Concept, Mode, Inner Design* (New Haven, 1984), pp. 3–8. Cf. also, F. Berni, *Rime*, ed. G. Barberi (Turin, 1969), pp. 179–80. Gianfranco Contini's "Introduction to Dante's *Rime*," trans. Y. Freccero in *Dante: A Collection of Critical Essays*, ed. J. Freccero (Englewood Cliffs, N.J., 1965), 28–39, offers a comparison of the poetic stylistics of Dante and Petrarch.

50. For a revue of literary criticism on *res* and *verba*, see H. Boom, *Poetry and Repression: Revisionism from Blake to Stevens* (New Haven, 1976), pp. 21–26. Cf. also, A. Howell, "Res et Verba: Words and Things," *English Literary History* 13 (1946), 131–42. On the grammatical implications, see G. Padley, *Grammatical Theory in Western Europe 1500–1700: The Latin Tradition* (Cambridge, 1976), pp. 135–39. On Vico, see M. Mooney, *Vico in the Tradition of Rhetoric* (Princeton, 1985), chap. 4, "Culture: Wisdom and Eloquence," 170–254.

51. On Malory's *Morte Darthur*, see D. Brewer's introduction to *The Morte Darthur, Part Seven and Eight* (London, 1968). Cf. also, *The Works of Sir Thomas Malory*, ed. E. Vinaver, 2d ed. 1: (Oxford, 1961), introduction, xix–xxxiv. For a succinct and thoughtful account of English prose stylistics, see M. Roston, *Sixteenth-Century English Literature* (New York, 1982), chap. 1, esp. pp. 3–20. Cf. also, J. Carey, "Sixteenth- and Seventeenth-Century Prose," in *English Poetry and Prose, 1540–1674*, ed. C. Ricks, revised ed. (London, 1986), 329–417. E. Vinaver fixes Malory's

prose style as "too straightforward to be archaic," yet "just old enough to allure and mark the age"; *Works of Sir Thomas Malory*, p. lx.

52. Sir Thomas Elyot, *The Boke Named the Gouvernor*, ed. H. Croft (London, 1880), 1. 1. See M. Roston, *Sixteenth-Century English Literature*, p. 15; C. S. Lewis, *English Literature in the Sixteenth Century Excluding Drama* (Oxford, 1954), pp. 273–76. By the term "Gouvernor," Elyot means one who rules under a king as a member of the governing class.

53. Erich Auerbach's parallel *explication* of fifteenth-century literary texts and diplomatic documents makes us attentive to the pompous literary style and array of apostrophes and adverbial phrases they share. He goes on to evoke an image of an entire procession of preparatory clauses, both in text and document, that have the appearance of "a prince or king, who is preceded by heralds, body-guards, court officials and flag bearers." See his *Mimesis: The Representation of Reality in Western Literature*, trans. W. Trask (Princeton, 1968), pp. 242–43. Auerbach's assessments of the high style in the French vernacular can be matched by an analysis of fifteenth-century literary English prose. Vernacular prose was the battleground of matter versus words. Distinction between the plain and aureate manner survived well into the next century. Lord Berners made translations from Froissart's *Cronycles* (1523 and 1525). These translations were replete with the beloved redundancies of the aureate style. It is notable that Lord Berners also translated from Marcus Aurelius's *Meditations* (*The Golden Boke of Marcus Aurelius*). Berners' political vision was shaped by ideals of service, trust, and lordship. His politics and stylistics were conjoined in an almost perfect match between form and content. For him polity was synonymous with lordship and he expressed this idea so: "With divers stones and one cement building raised . . . and of divers men and one lord is composed a common wealth." See James, *Society, Politics and Culture*, p. 274; P. Thomson, *Sir Thomas Wyatt and His Background* (Palo Alto, Ca. 1964), pp. 98–110.

54. For a discussion of the passage from More's own unfinished English version of the *Historia Ricardi Tertii*, see Roston, *Sixteenth-Century English Literature*, p. 18; Carey, "Sixteenth- and Seventeenth-Century Prose," p. 331. C. S. Lewis' comments on More's character sketches as being "pithy and sententious," with a mingling of "charity and severity," are worth recalling, as are his insights into the prose of Malory: "The English Prose Morte," *Essays on Malory* (Oxford, 1963). More's success at reconciling the plain and aureate manners is evident in his *Dialogue concernynge Heresyes & Matters of Religion* (1528): "But nowe I praye you let me knowe youre mynde concernying the burning of the new Testament in Englysh which Tyndal lately translated, & as men say right well, whiche maketh men muche meruayle of the burnyng. It is quod I to me great meruayle that anye good Christen manne hauing any drop of witte in his head, would anye thyng meruayle or complayne of the burnying of that booke yf he knowe the matter. Whiche who so calleth the new Testament, calleth it by a wrong name, excepte they wyll call it Tyndals Testamente or Luthers Testament. For so hadde Tyndall after Luthers counsayl corrupted and chaunged it from the good and wholesome doctrine of Christ to the deuelishe heresyes of their own, that it was cleane a contrarye thyng." In this prose there is repetition but it is controlled, alliteration but subdued, and tautology but balanced. In William Tyndale's *Parable of the Wicked Mammon* (1528), we observe a prose in which the plainness of the colloquial is conjoined with repetition and an appreciation for the rhythms of word order. See Thomson, *Sir Thomas Wyatt*, pp. 99–100.

55. On early Tuscan stylistics, see C. Segre, ed., *Volgarizzamenti del Due e Trecento* (Turin, 1953). For poetry and poetics, see A. Chiaffini, *Tradizione e poesia nella prosa d'arte italiana dalla latinità medievale a G. Boccaccio* (Rome, 1943). On the vernacularization of Latin classics, see F. Maggini, *I primi volgarizzamenti dai*

classici latini (Florence, 1952). On the novella, see L. di Francia, *Novellistica: Dalle origini al Bandello* (Milan, 1924). On the first humanists and their literary background and culture, see R. Witt, "Medieval 'Ars Dictaminis' and the Beginnings of Humanism: A New Construction of the Problem," *Renaissance Quarterly* 35 (1982), 1–35.

56. On religious processions and the need for verisimilitude in their imagery, see D. Arasse, "Entre devotion et culture: Fonctions de l'image religieuse au XVᵉ siècle," in *Faire croire: Modalites de la diffusion et de la réception des messages religieux du XIIᵉ au XVᵉ siècle* (Rome, 1984), 141–60.

57. A fair Roman lady must choose between two suitors: one is noble by birth, the other by deeds. Wishing to offend no one, the lady entertains petitions from both suitors in this arena of discourse. Calling attention to her desire not to give insult to any, yet she must make a choice. Not the well-born suitor but the one who "by means of his virtue to honor doth rise." Moreover, was not the chosen one, says the lady, a most loyal servant of the Roman state? For a treatment of this type of rhetoric in the English context, see James, *Society, Politics and Culture*, pp. 370 ff. On Niccolò Acciaiuoli, see M. Villani, *Cronica*, ed. F. Dragomanni (Florence, 1846), bk. 4, chap. 91. For Boccaccio and Acciaiuoli, see Branca, *Boccaccio* pp. 303–7.

58. For a historical review of the changing usages and extension of the semantic field of key words, see entries in Battaglia, *Grande dizionario della lingua italiana;* M. Cortelazzo and P. Zolli, *Dizionario etimologico delle lingue italiane* (Bologna, 1979–). Of course the fundamental *Vocabolario degli accademici della Crusca* (Florence, 1865–79) is a reference work perhaps unrivaled and indispensable to the present effort.

59. For the word *conversazione* and the range of its usage, from sacred and gaining the benevolence of one's companion to civil, civilized, public, and polite discourse, see Battaglia, *Grande dizionario della lingua italiana,* 723–24. Linkage between politeness and detente in public discourse conduced to social and discursive peace. Rhetorical models were conversational rather than controversial. In literature and the arts, taste and gentility as metaphors and meanings, lexicons and strategies moved from one area of discourse to another. Finally, the magnetic field of the idea of a society distanced from one lent structure by archaic forms of behavior commenced to take shape. Continental and English literature, with their accent on "polite conversation," "polite society," and "polite learning," suggest something of the linguistic dimension of this tilt. A selction from a seventeenth-century English text, *The Art of Complaisance, Or the Means to Oblige in Conversation,* might be cited as an introduction to the mechanisms of politeness: " 'Tis not enough, to gain the esteem and love of all men, that we possess the greatest qualities of mind and body; This rather is necessary, that we expose those great vertues without ostentation, or striving to eclipse the smaller merits of others; Those who act otherwise attract but hate or envy, under the burthen of which they are oft seen to stagger. This Complaisance . . . Is an Art to regulate our words and behaviour, in such a manner as we may engage the love and respect of those with whome we Converse, by distributing our praises and differences, where the quality or merit of the person require it. By a seeming diligence to give our assistance, and by mildly suffering the errors and miscarriages of others." For the above quotation and a sensitive appraisal of polite society, see L. Klein, "The Rise of 'Politeness' in England 1660–1750," (Ph.D. dissertation, Johns Hopkins University, 1984), chap. 2, "The Modes of 'Politeness,' " 28–128, esp. p. 32.

60. For the quote from Matteo Palmieri, see Garin, *Italian Humanism*, p. 67. See also, Baron, *Crisis of the Early Italian Renaissance*, Vol. 1, passim; M. Palmieri, *Libro della vita civile* (Florence, 1529), fols. 69–89; F. Patrizi, *De regno et regis institutione* (Paris, 1567), fols. 187 ff. On Decembrio, see R. Sabbadini, *Classici e umanisti da codici Ambrosiani* (Florence, 1933), pp. 94–103. In the writings of

Lorenzo Valla, perhaps the most gifted and original of the humanists, charity and fortitude become one, having their origins of self-sacrificing and self-gratifying love. Both stem from the same fundamental drive evolving into one or the other according to the depth of vision and magnanimity or strength of the soul of the individual. See Trinkaus, *In Our Image and Likeness,* 1: 160–70, and his "Religious Thought of the Italian Humanists," p. 361.

61. On the word *patience* and its usages, see T. Burrow, *Medieval Writers and Their Work: Middle English Literature and Its Background 1100–1500* (Oxford, 1982), pp. 217–18. For an appraisal of the ways in which the older meanings of this heroic and demanding virtue is subtly modified in sixteenth-century English literary writings, see James, *Society, Politics and Culture,* pp. 387–90. Transformations in Italian usage are recorded in Battaglia, *Grande dizionario della lingua italiana,* 12; 881 ff. On the word *interest* and its changing meaning, see ibid., 8; 230–31. L. McKenzie, in "Interest in Early Modern Political Thought," *History of European Ideas* 2 (1981), 277–96, traces the vocabulary of "interesse" and "interesse proprio," borrowed directly from the language of commerce. Examples are given of the transference of these words to an analysis of political affairs.

62. For the early usage of *grazia,* see M. Cortelazzo and P. Zolli, *Dizionario etimologico,* 2: 62. Other volumes contain entries for other words. Cf. also references in Battaglia, *Grande dizionario della lingua italiana.* W. Trimpi, "The Ancient Hypothesis of Fiction," *Traditio* 27 (1971), 41–55 and "The Quality of Fiction," ibid. 30 (1974), 51–61, presents a masterful account of the enlargement of the moral significance of language as it moves toward a comprehensive multiplicity and away from a rigid philosophical dualism. Early examples of literary Italian, such as poetry contained in the *Ritmo laurenziano* (late twelfth to early thirteenth century), contain praise and exaltation of great clerics and lords in return for gifts and hospitality. Poetic hyperbole controlled by a high order of rhetorical sophistication was exchanged for such evidence of grace as the bestowal of a horse or arms on the troubadour. See *Poeti del Duecento,* ed. G. Contini (Milan-Naples, 1960), 1: 5–6.

63. Cf. M. Becker's review of D. Wilcox's *The Development of Florentine Humanist Historiography* in *Journal of Historical Studies* 1 (1969–70), 198, in which Bruni's *History of Florence* is commended as offering deep insight into a changing political process. Becker observes that Bruni portrayed a crucial change in Florentine government. No longer do speakers advising the signory appear so exclusively as representatives of a corporate constituency, but instead they take their place as individuals prone to orate from a civic point of view. With the advent of the Quattrocento we have the emergence of a very different style of political conduct. Gene Brucker has argued against the position advanced by Becker that the corporate foundations of communal government atrophied in the late fourteenth century. But in his recent work (*The Civic World of Early Renaissance Florence* [Princeton, 1977], p. 11), he moves away from his former position, stating that he agrees with "those scholars who have argued that the corporate foundation of the commune grew weaker in the fourteenth century." (The scholars, however, remain nameless.)

64. R. Goldthwaite, "The Florentine Palace as Domestic Architecture," *American Historical Review* 77 (1972), 977–1017. Alberti's advice was widely circulated in the writings of contemporaries such as Giovanni Rucellai, the Pseudo-Pandolfini and others. See T. Kuehn, *Emancipation in Late Medieval Florence* (New Brunswisk, N.J., 1972), pp. 60–61.

65. Of course Machiavelli's hard-bought observation that men pursue the good either out of ulterior motives or under compulsion of necessity stands: "One can make this generalization about men, they are ungrateful, fickle, liars and deceivers, they shun danger and are greedy for profit; while you treat them well, they are yours.

They would shed their blood for you, risk their property, their lives, their children, so long . . . as danger is remote; but when you are in danger, they turn against you." *The Prince,* trans. G. Bull (Harmondsworth, 1961), p. 96. Machiavelli then goes on to argue that attempts to reach men's higher nature must fail, for they only respond to force and threats: "Men worry less about doing an injury to one who makes himself loved than to one who makes himself feared. The bond of love is one which men, wretched creatures that they are, break when it is to their advantage to do so; fear is strengthened by a dread of punishment which is always effective."

66. Montaigne's reaction to Guicciardini's *History of Italy* conveys something of the problematic and troubled psychology of a sophisticated sixteenth-century reader reluctant to accept such a stark and unheroic version of recent European historical experience: "I have also noted this, that of so many souls and actions that he judges, so many motives and plans, he never refers a single one to *virtue, religion, and conscience, as if these qualities were wholly extinct in the world;* and of all actions, however fair in appearance they may be of themselves, he throws the cause back onto some *vicious motive or some profit.* It is impossible to imagine that among the infinite number of actions that he judges there was not a single one produced by the way of reason. No corruption can have seized men so universally that someone would not escape the contagion. This makes me fear that his taste was a bit corrupted; and it may have happened that he judged others by himself." *Complete Works of Montaigne,* p. 305 (*Essays,* II, 10). See also, M. Phillips, *Francesco Guicciardini: The Historian's Craft* (Toronto, 1977), pp. 30 ff.

67. On the genesis of new ways of conceptualizing politics and public life, see F. Gilbert, "Florentine Political Assumptions in the Period of Savonarola and Soderini," *Journal of the Warburg and Courtauld Institutes* 20 (1957), 187–214. Cf. also, D. Weinstein, *Savonarola and Florentine Prophecy and Patriotism in the Renaissance* (Princeton, 1970). For an analysis of change in the meaning of certain key words, such as *fortuna, necessità, ragione dello stato,* and a battery of others, see Gilbert, *Machiavelli and Guicciardini; passim.*

68. For an informed critique of Foucault and his view that the seventeenth century was the locale for initiation of the demand to renounce "similitudes" in favor of "exact comparisons," see Funkenstein, *Theology and the Scientific Imagination,* pp. 35–42.

69. For a discussion of the language of Hoby's translation of Castiglione, see Carey, "Sixteenth- and Seventeenth-Century Prose," p. 350. It is worth noting that in matters esthetic the Italian vocabulary did not easily find English equivalents. According to the *OED,* the term "fine arts" did not surface in English writing until the mid-eighteenth century. Giorgio Vasari's "arti di disegno" and the French "beaux arts" were converted by English commentators into "polite arts." William Aglionby, in his *Painting Illustrated in Three Dialogues* (London, 1985), has one interlocutor aver that painting was "the admiration of antiquity, and is still the greatest charm of the most polite part of mankind." When questioned about "that glorious epithet," he replied: "I mean chiefly the Italians, to whom none can deny the privilege of having been the civilizers of Europe, since painting, sculpture, architecture, music, gardening, polite conversation and prudent behaviour are, as I may call it, all of the growth of their country and I mean, besides all those in France, Spain, Germany, Low-Countries, and England who are lovers of those arts, and endeavour to promote them in their own nation." In the preface, Aglionby makes a most telling moral judgment as to the utility of painting as a "polite art" for a dissolute gentry: ". . . the loss of time, the ruin of their fortunes, the destruction of their health, the various tragical accidents that attend men who once a day lose their reason, are all things worthy their serious reflection and from which, the love of the Politer Arts would reclaim them." Klein, "Rise of 'Politeness' in England," pp. 86–88.

3. THE COLLOIDAL SOLUTION

1. Contracts, agreements and liabilities to the crown were expressed as debts. The complexities pertaining to property ownership led to the testing of property rights. This involved questions of inheritance and even the handling of routine buying and selling of land by the courts. Law was the language of social obligation. The relation of crown and people was expressed through the law. See E. Ives, *The Common Lawyer of Pre-Reformation England* (Cambridge, 1982), *passim*. I wish to thank Patricia McCune for permitting me to read her unpublished paper, "The Image of the Law and Lawyers in Late Medieval Complaint Literature." Mervyn James's study of the Durham region is exemplary for its evocation of the density of the texture of relations shaped by personal dependence within the framework of good lordship, fidelity, friendship and so forth; see his *Family, Lineage and Civil Society: A Study of Society, Politics and Mentality in the Durham Region 1500–1640* (Oxford, 1974). For bibliography and a general discussion of gentry and aristocracy, see G. Mingay, *The Gentry: The Rise and Fall of the Ruling Class* (London, 1976), pp. 29–34. Cf. also, D. Carpenter, "King, Magnates and Society," *Speculum* 60 (1985), 39–71; J. Lander, *Crown and Nobility 1450–1509* (London, 1976), pp. 31–35; C. Russell, *The Crises of Parliament: English History 1509–1660* (Oxford, 1971), pp. 28–43; P. Williams, *The Tudor Regime* (Oxford, 1979), pp. 2–10.

2. For the remarks of Soranzo, the Venetian ambassador, see *A Companion to Shakespeare Studies,* ed. G. B. Harrison and H. Granville Barker (New York, 1937), pp. 203–4. Miller, in her *Henry VIII and the English Nobility,* pp. 132–61, discusses in detail the topic of the nobility and attendance at war.

3. E. F. Jacob, *The Fifteenth Century* (Oxford, 1961), p. 305. R. Mohl's *The Three Estates in Medieval and Renaissance Literature* (New York, 1933), pp. 109–121, 165–66, 287–93, contains a useful discussion of the theory of the orders. See C. Crowder, "Peace and Justice around 1400: A Sketch," in *Aspects of Late Medieval Government and Society,* ed. J. Rowe (Toronto, 1986), 53–81, in which he discusses Bishop John Stafford's address to parliament at its opening in 1433, with appropriate references to the psalms and the Old Testament heavily freighted with a tripartite vision of a Christian community. Cf. also, S. Chrimes, *English Constitutional Ideas in the Fifteenth Century* (London, 1936); J. Mann, *Chaucer and Medieval Estates Satire* (Cambridge, 1973).

4. For the quotation from *Macbeth* and a discussion of its implications, see Morris, *Political Thought in England,* pp. 107 ff. For a sensitive appraisal of historical consciousness and the English medieval chroniclers, see R. Southern, "The Sense of the Past," *Transactions of the Royal Historical Society,* 5th series, 23 (1973), 246–56. M. Becker, "Individualism in the Early Italian Renaissance," *Studies in the Renaissance* 19 (1972), 273–97, considers the problem of the decline of ceremonial bonds and ritual ties in the fourteenth and fifteenth centuries.

5. J. Catto, "Andres Horn: Law and History in Fourteenth-Century England," in *The Writing of History in the Middle Ages,* ed. R. H. Davis (Oxford, 1981), p. 363. Horn was perhaps the only chronicler in England of his generation to possess in some measure a historical imagination. The antiquarian interest of Horn grew out of his careful search for legal precedents.

6. On court procedures, techniques, and their rituals, see T. Plucknett, *Early English Literature* (Cambridge, 1958), pp. 85 ff. M. Clanchy, "Remembering the Past and the Good Old Law," *History* 55 (1970), 167–76, explores the borderland between legal pleading and minstrelcy. F. Lane and R. Mueller, in their *Money and Banking in Medieval and Renaissance Venice: Coins and Moneys of Account* (Baltimore, 1985), Vol. 1, provide telling comparisons between the rudimentary credit structure and the minimal need for money changers in the less urbanized England of the later Middle Ages, over and against the commercial towns of north and central Italy. They also

summarize the "relations" prepared by secretaries to the Venetian ambassadors resident in England. Dating in the very late fifteenth century (1497–98) and the early sixteenth century, the Venetian observations feature the pervasiveness of extravagance in churches, monasteries, convents, and in the households and wardrobes of feudatories, ecclesiastics, and London merchants. In the earlier "relation" the Venetian observer locates fifty-two goldsmith shops on the Strand alone, "so rich and full of silver vessels, large and small, that in all the shops of Milan, Rome, Venice and Florence put together I do not think there are as many of such grandeur as are to be seen in London." See Lane and Mueller, p. 67; F. Fisher, "The Development of London as a Centre of Conspicuous Consumption in the Sixteenth and Seventeenth Centuries," in *Essays in Economic History,* ed. E. Carus-Wilson (London, 1962), 2: 197–207.

7. One can appreciate the complexities of rendering judgment on the various forms of tuition by reading the serpentine arguments of Thomas More. No one was more critical of the aristocratic retaining system and the brutalization of the young when attached to great households. Yet he defended the education of the young serving in the houses of great prelates, and his own experience endorsed this view. The issue was further complicated by the fact that great ecclesiastics were expected to live in splendor befitting their rank as temporal lords, while at the same time responding to the imperatives of Christian humility and poverty. See *Complete Works of St. Thomas More,* Yale ed., 4: 346. To feast and drink with his entourage of course redounded to the lord's "profit" and "worship." Hospitality and generosity went together. The root of the word "lord" coming from Anglo-Saxon times, signified one who provided his followers with bread. J. Powis, *Aristocracy,* (Oxford, 1984), p. 26. The conflict between recognition of the social value of pageant, generosity, display, and aristocratic lifestyle as essential for sustaining spiritual solidarity, social harmony, and ensuring the benefits of an economy of service was set against an appreciation for a version of nobility and social life less indentured to ritualized and archaic political arrangements. Not only were these tensions felt in secular life, but also among high clergy where largess and hospitality were primary expectations with undeniable social value. Cf. F. Heal, "The Archbishop of Canterbury and the Practices of Hospitality," *Journal of Ecclesiastical History* 33 (1982), 544–63; *Of Prelates and Princes* (Cambridge, 1980). More himself was not unappreciative of the political need for ritual and pageant as vital ingredients in royal policy. Sometimes he was literary and cynical, mocking royal vanity and popular credulity. See Thomas More, *Latin Epigrams,* ed. L. Bradnor and C. Lynch (Chicago, 1953), pp. 205–6.

8. For the "Rules of Robert Grossteste," see *Walter of Henley and Other Treatises on Estate Management and Accounting,* ed. D. Oschinsky (Oxford, 1974). See also, M. Carruthers, "The Gentelesse of Chaucer's Franklin," *Criticism* 23 (1981), 101–11. F. Menant, *Structures féodales et féodalisme dans l'Occident mediteranées (Xe–XIIIe siècles)* (Paris, 1980), pp. 285–92, offers treatment of household service among the Italian nobility from the tenth to the thirteenth century.

9. Chaucer was an esquire of the royal household; for this he gained *gentil* status. Without the security of rents and land he depended on his career in service for a living. Official posts, patronage, and annuities were essential for retaining his position in society. S. Thrupp, *The Merchant Class of Medieval London, 1300–1500* (Chicago, 1948, reprinted Ann Arbor, Mich., 1964), p. 282. On the general subject of knights and squires in the time of Chaucer, see N. Saul, *Knights and Squires: The Gloucestershire Gentry in the Fourteenth Century* (Oxford, 1981). Of course there is Chaucer's own affectionate portrait of the squire in the prologue to the *Canterbury Tales:*

> A lovyere and a lusty bacheler,
> With lokkes crulle as they were leyd in presse.

Of twenty yeer of age he was, I gesse.
Of his stature he was of evene lengthe,
And wonderly delyvere, and of greet strengthe.
And he hadde been somtyme in chyvachie
In Flaundres, in Artoys, and Pycardie,
And born hym weel, as of so litel space,
In hope to stonden in his lady grace,
Embrouded was he, as it were a meede
Al ful of fresshe floures, whyte and reede.
Syngynge he was, or floytynge al the day;
He was as fressh as is the month of May.
Short was his gowne, with sleves longe and syde.
Wel koude he sitte on hors and faire ryde.
He koude songes make and wel endite,
Juste and eek daunce, and weel purtreye and write.
So hoote he lovede that by nyghtertale
He sleep namoore than dooth a nyghtyngale
Curteis he was, lowely, and servysable,
And carf biforn his fader at the table.

10. How easy it was to sin by not giving thanks to God "which all grace sendeth!" How frequent was the use of the word *surquidrie,* that is, *superbia.* Of course one thinks of Chaucer's ending of his *Parson's Tale* with his prose prayer asking for forgiveness of his "enditynges of worldly vanitees" (frivolous composition). Failure to complete *The Canterbury Tales* is emblematic of a literary defeat. On the subject of Chaucer's perspective on knighthood, the argument that he sought to present a satirical picture of the young squire whose humility matched his exquisite appearance and horsemanship has been vigorously challenged by M. Keen, "Chaucer's Knight, the Aristocracy and the Crusades," in *English Court Culture in the Late Middle Ages,* ed. V. Scattergood and J. Sherborne (London, 1983), 45–61.

11. For an informative treatment of the English alliterative tradition with its bleak view of political prospects, see R. Peck, "Willfulness and Wonders: Boethian Tragedy in the Alliterative Morte Arthure," *The Alliterative Tradition in the Fourteenth Century,* ed. B. Levy and P. Szarmach (Kent, Ohio, 1981), 153–82, esp. 153. Cf. also, G. Shepherd, "The Nature of Alliterative Poetry in Late Medieval English," *Proceedings of the British Academy* 56 (1972), 56–76; T. Turville-Petre, *The Alliterative Revival* (Cambridge, 1971); Preface to the critical edition of *The Alliterative 'Morte Arthure'* by V. Krishna (New York, 1976), pp. 1–34, with bibliography, pp. 35–38. The epic model of the fourteenth-century English poet, typical of the alliterative revival, combined heroic sentiment with vibrant realism endowing the work with consistent archaism of manner, spirit, and meter. What better target for the poet who would elevate the romances of the Arthurian legends to the lofty sphere of the heroic? Cf. E. Vinaver, *Works,* by Malory, p. lvii.

12. Research on these topics is of course beyond measure, but see D. Robertson, Jr., *A Preface to Chaucer: Studies in Medieval Perspectives* Princeton, 1963); C. Muscatine, *Chaucer and the French Tradition: A Study in Style and Meaning* (Berkeley, 1964); T. Donaldson, "Chaucer the Pilgrim," in *Chaucer Criticism,* ed. R. Schoeck and J. Taylor (South Bend, Ind., 1971), 1–12; P. Kean, *'The Pearl': An Interpretation* (London, 1967); J. Lawler, *Piers Plowman: An Essay in Criticism* (London, 1962); J. Benson, *Art and Tradition in 'Sir Gawain and the Green Knight'* (New Brunswick, N.J.; 1965).

13. If one compares the humanist funeral oration and the Italian burial ceremony over and against the rituals and monuments of the north of Europe, the differences are not trivial. In Quattrocento Florence and Venice it was the public man, his accomplishments, and the enhancement of civic life that were robust themes, whereas in

England a warrior band mourned the loss of a dead chieftain. The rituals and ceremonies of funeral of a peer, with its pomp and heraldry, served to express with conspicuous extravagance the lost world of the *comitatus* (warrior band). Further, the death of an English peer was a time of crisis in the life of the community over which he had presided. See James, *Society, Politics and Culture*, pp. 176–87, in which full attention is paid to these *rites de passage*. On this subject, and so many others pertaining to the ins and outs of social history, the work of Lawrence Stone is the rock bed. Cf. "The Anatomy of the Elizabethan Aristocracy," *Economic History Review* 18 (1948), 8–16, and of course his *Crisis of the Aristocracy*, pp. 572 ff.

14. See Douglas Gray's judicious remarks on English religious literature of the fourteenth and fifteenth centuries in *Themes and Images in the Medieval English Religious Lyric* (London, 1972), p. 30: ". . . it is not now hard to see that some aspects of the way the inherited tradition had been developed must have made it very difficult for writers to achieve that moderation, that *mesure*, as the English would call it, to which Michelangelo's 'true harmony' is related. In the later Middle Ages, Christian writers sometimes managed to make impressive works from emotional attitudes which were violent, frenzied and even theatrical. It is quite remarkable that so many English lyrics were successful in achieving clarity, simple dignity, and moderation." Cf. also, H. White, *Tudor Book of Saints and Martyrs* (Madison, Wisc., 1963), in which the direction of the literary treatment of religious exempla concerning the lives of holy men and women is discussed in detail. On the subject of Michelangelo, it should be noted that his stern denunciation of the piety of Flemish monks and women was remarked by his contemporary biographer, Francesco da Holanda.

15. On Giovanni di Bologna, see M. Clanchy, *From Memory to Written Record: England 1066–1307* (Cambridge, Mass., 1977), p. 35. See also, chap. 1 of the same volume, where English legal treatises are discussed. K. Levine's *The Social Content of Literacy* (London, 1986), pp. 58 ff., considers the basis for retention of preliterate practices.

16. Italian visitors were struck by the small scale of English urbanization. See Colin Platt, *The English Medieval Town* (London, 1976), p. 15; also the anonymous Italian author, *A Relation or Rather a True Account of the Island of England,* ed. C. Sneyd (London, 1847), with its vivid description of the backwardness of the English urban economy and its archaic banking and credit system—all of this in comparison to the advanced structure of Italian business practices. Poggio Bracciolini's observations based on his long stay in England (1418–22) resulted in a comparative disquisition on the various differences among nobility in the diverse countries of Europe. The English were, in his view, allergic to life in the city and despised trade and merchandising. How different from the nobles of Tuscany! See *Opera omnia* (Basel, 1538), reprinted and ed., R. Fubini (Turin, 1964), pp. 64–83. The idea of derogation took shape in the late fourteenth century and suggests something of the difference between French attitudes toward the social role of nobility and those popular in Tuscany. The *Vieux coustumier de Poictou* (c. 1417) voiced the following judgment: "A noble who practises commerce or manual labour or in other ways lives by a mechanical craft publicly and notoriously like a commoner, not conducting himself as a noble, using or exercising arms and living nobly, shall not enjoy the privilege of a noble." See P. Contamine, "France at the End of the Middle Ages: Who Was Then the Gentleman," in *Gentry and Lesser Nobility in Late Medieval Europe,* ed M. Jones (New York, 1986), p. 204.

17. P. J. Jones's "Florentine Families and Florentine Diaries in the Fourteenth Century," *Papers of the British School at Rome* 24 (1956), 183–205, is the classic account of Florentine record-keeping. C. Klapisch-Zuber's valuable articles have been assembled and republished in *Women, Family and Ritual in Renaissance Italy,* trans. L. Cochrane (Chicago, 1985); pages 78–89 contain a wide-ranging discussion of

Florentine *ricordanze* and their utility for the social historian. Cf. also, Herlihy and Klapisch-Zuber, *Tuscans and Their Families,* for a masterful, statistical analysis of Tuscan family structure. For Genoa, see Diane Hughes, "Urban Growth and Family Structure in Medieval Genoa," *Past & Present* 66 (1975), 3–28. The tilt toward civility, or a civil society, finds expression in certain of the *ricordi* of the late fourteenth and early fifteenth centuries. For example, Giovanni di Pagolo Morelli, in his *Ricordi,* ed. V. Branca (Florence, 1956), pp. 130–31, observed that in bygone times high and formidable towers were built, and wars were waged in the city between feuding families. Now, in the early fifteenth century, such contests are no longer fought with sword but with votes in the council halls (black and white beans). Barna Valorini wrote to his father, Valorino: "Today vendettas are fought in the palace [of the signory] and not with knives." See Brucker, *The Civic World of Early Renaissance Florence,* pp. 29–30.

18. For the quotation from Morelli's *Ricordi,* see C. Klapisch-Zuber, *Women, Family and Ritual,* p. 78. Another typical citation of his cautionary counsel runs thusly: "But above all if you wish to have friends and relatives, try not to have need of them. Put your mind to having ready money and learn to keep it and treat it cautiously, and this will be the best friend and best relative that can be found." See Becker, *Florence in Transition* I: 144–45, for additional examples of advice on practical matters. On the subtleties of the exchange system and transfer of social credit emanating from service, ceremony, and ritual, see P. Bourdieu's *Outline of the Theory of Practice,* trans., R. Nice (Cambridge, 1977). I wish to thank my colleague Diane Hughes for this valuable reference.

19. Velluti judged the historical moment for such a display of extravagant behavior as entirely inappropriate, since the merchants of the city were suffering economic privation in a town ruled by a tyrant. See Velluti, *Cronica domestica,* p. 162. For a helpful survey of materials from Florentine *ricordanze* and the impact of the language of courtesy on merchants and lawyers, see D. Bonamore, *Prolegomeni all'economia politica nella lingua italiana del Quattrocento* (Bologna, 1974), pp. 41 ff.

20. The quotation is in J. Larner, *Italy in the Age of Dante and Petrarch 1216–1380* (London, 1980), p. 72. For detailed information, see A. Schiffini's preface to his edition of *Il libro di buoni costumi, documenti di vita trecentesca* (Florence, 1945). This is the *ricordi* of Paolo di Messer Pace da Certaldo.

21. On books of private memorials and the mode of reckoning blood debts, see J. Hyde, *Society and Politics in Medieval Italy: The Evolution of the Civic Life, 1000– 1350* (New York, 1973), pp. 171–73. The problem of collecting debts from great nobles could indeed lead to serious difficulties. See Bene Bencivenni's pessimistic entry in his *libricciolo di crediti* (1277–96), in which he notes the difficulty of collecting a loan made to the powerful Count Guido Novello of Pisa. Cf. *Nuovi testi fiorentina del Ducento,* ed. A. Castellani (Florence, 1952), p. 368; V. Branca, "Ricordi domestici nel Trecento e nel Quattrocento, " in *Dizionario critico della letteratura italiana* (Turin, 1973), 3: 189–92.

22. On the romantic and tender novella tinctured with irony relating the fate of the famous cavalier, Messer Federigo degli Alberighi (*Decameron* V, 9), for the Lady Giovanna, see Branca, *Boccaccio,* pp. 54–59. G. Mazzotta, in his *The World as Play in Boccaccio's 'Decameron'* (Princeton, 1986), pp. 86–89, considers the general question of the antimony of values of wealth and love.

23. For the quote on Niccoli, see Vespasiano da Bisticci, *Renaissance Princes, Popes and Prelates,* trans. W. George and E. Waters, with an introduction by M. Gilmore (New York, 1963), p. 402. On interior space, the family and the household, see V. Pardo, "Gli spazi del quotidiano: l'abitazione privata," in *Rituale, ceremoniale, etichetti,* 111–26. For a detailed examination of Florentine legislation on the topic of sumptuary laws, see R. Rainey, "Sumptuary Legislation in Renaissance Florence,"

(Ph.D. dissertation, Columbia University, 1985). The comment of the Luccan ambassador to Florence, writing in 1600, does not settle the matter of possible changes in styles of life but is still worth quoting. He records the passing of an older society in these words: ". . . under the Principate [the nobility] has left its old parsimony in private life, and given itself over to courtly living, and thus the larger part . . . disdaining commerce, belts on the sword, and those who persist, reputing [trade] unworthy of their hands, make use of the services of underlings, so that their profits are much diminished, and their expense is increased disproportionately, these men living with such splendor at home and abroad as to be no less than titled lords. . . . " See Litchfield, *Emergence of a Bureaucracy,* pp. 213–14. Litchfield considers in detail the possible transformations of the Florentine patriciate after the fall of the Florentine republic in 1530. By inference the ethos of republicanism worked to temper public display.

24. For Salutati, see DeRosa, *Coluccio Salutati,* pp. 45 ff. The moral requirement that property be divided among the youthful heirs while the father was hale and hearty, rather than exercising patriarchal tyranny, is a commonplace theme in the writing of Italian humanists. This generous ideal underscores the normative vision of the family held together by affective ties. See F. Patrizi, *De regno et regis institutione,* fol. 185v; F. Beroaldo, *Opuscula* (Paris, 1505), sig. B4. Florence, unlike other cities such as Genoa and Venice, did not facilitate the binding of estates with entails (*fedecommessi*) until the sixteenth century. The original form goes back at least to the twelfth century, and it was not until the sixteenth with the principate that the *fedecommesso* was systematically employed to keep property indivisible, as well as rendering it inalienable, by fixing an order of succession. See R. Goldthwaite, *Private Wealth in Renaissance Florence: A Study of Four Families* (Princeton, 1968), pp. 271–75; Litchfield, *Emergence of a Bureaucracy,* pp. 221–26.

25. I wish to thank my colleague, Professor Diane Hughes, for making available to me her soon-to-be published paper, "The Death of Mourning: Controls on Ritual Life in the Italian Commune." See also, her "Sumptuary Laws and Social Relations in Renaissance Italy," in *Disputes and Settlements: Law and Human Relations in the West,* ed. J. Bossy (Cambridge, 1983), 67–98.

26. For a further discussion of Cristoforo Buondelmonti, see R. Weiss's entry in *Dizionario Biografico degli Italiani,* 15: 198–200. For further discussion of archaic burial customs and tribal pomp of ceremony, see the writings of the fifteenth-century humanist Pandolfo Collenuccio, especially his *Compendio de le istorie del regno di Napoli,* ed. A. Saviotti (Bari, 1929), pp. 39–43. Vovelle, in his *La mort et l'Occident,* pp. 7–26, offers an excellent up-to-date introduction to recent scholarship on burial customs and other matters funereal. Giambattista Giraldi Cinzio, in his "An Address to the Reader by the Tragedy *Orbecche,*" comments on the subject of anachronism utilizing evidence pertaining to the changing character of burial practices: "While the historian is obliged to write only of deeds and actions that are true and as they really happened, the poet presents things not as they are but as they should be, that they may serve to instruct his readers about life. And this is why, though the poets write of ancient affairs, they nonetheless seek to harmonize them with their own customs and their own age, introducing things unlike those of ancient times and suitable to their own. This is seen in Virgil's account of Aeneas, for though he came from Troy, and the methods of sacrificing, conducting funeral ceremonies, and arming in Asia were not like those in Italy, yet Virgil has the Trojans sacrifice, bury, and fight according to Italian habits and not even according to the habits of the time before Rome was founded but those of the age of Octavian. And good poets have not merely taken this license, but have named things that did not exist in the time of the men of whom they write, not otherwise than as if in early times customs had been in use that appeared much later, as can be seen in Homer and Virgil. The writers of romances have also

made some use of this method, for the reason that the poet (as I have said) does not write of things as they were or are, but as they should be, in order to give at once profit and delight by satisfying the men of that age in which they write, a thing that is not permitted to those who write histories. . . ." See A. H. Gilbert, *Literary Criticism: Plato to Dryden* (New York, 1940), pp. 270–71.

27. For a review of the essential ideas of Altieri, see C. Klapisch-Zuber, *Women, Family and Ritual,* pp. 145–47. Altieri's *Li nuptiali* is edited by E. Narducci (Rome, 1873). A. Asor-Rosa's "Marco Antonio Altieri," in *Dizionario Biografico degli Italiani,* 2: 560–61, gives extensive bibliography on the life and writings of this Roman humanist.

28. For the quote from Poggio Bracciolini, see J. Pope-Hennessy, *Luca della Robbia* (Ithaca, N.Y., 1980), p. 24. M. Boskobits, *Pittura fiorentina alla vigilia del Rinascimento* (Florence, 1975), p. 7, treats in detail the significance of Poggio's account of the incident of the peasants and the image of Christ. On Petrarch and his distancing from certain rituals and ceremonies of his own times, see the recent analysis of Thomas Greene, *The Vulnerable Text: Essays on Renaissance Literature* (New York, 1986), pp. 18–45.

29. The textured views of Petrarch, Salutati, and other humanists writing on the fine arts and poetry are analyzed with caution by Arasse, "Fonctions de l'image religieuse," 131–46, esp. 134–8; cf. also, Baxandall, *Giotto and the Orators,* pp. 139–44; H. Janson, "The Birth of Artistic License," in *Patronage in the Renaissance,* ed. S. Orgel and G. Fitch (Princeton, 1981), 344–53; Pope-Hennessy, *Luca della Robbia,* pp. 211 ff.; P. Barasch, *Theories of Art from Plato to Winkelmann* (New York, 1985), pp. 115 ff. For prescient comments on Simone Martini and the borderland between things secular and spiritual, see White, *Art and Architecture,* pp. 239–41.

30. R. Goldthwaite's "Local Banking in Renaissance Florence," *Journal of European Economic History* 14 (1985), 5–15, challenges traditional views of the modernity of the city's fiscal institutions. The rate of technical progress of the Florentine banking establishments can be exaggerated. Older guild statutes requiring that accounts be kept in Roman numerals in order to reduce the possibility of fraud were still in force in the early fifteenth century. Only later in that century were accounts kept in arabic numbers. For other examples of the persistence of traditional practices in matters of financial exchange, see Goldthwaite, "Medici Bank," 3–31 and "Organizzazione economica e struttura famigliare," in *I centi dirigenti nella toscana tardo communale* (Florence, 1983), 6–10.

31. For an extended analysis of key words in the Florentine *ricordi,* see C. Varese, *Storia e politica nelle prose del Quattrocento* (Turin, 1961), pp. 100–21. Cf. also, F. Pezza-Rossa, "La memorialista fiorentina tra medioevo e Rinascimento: Rassegna di studi e testi," *Lettere Italiane* 31 (1979), 96–138; C. Bec, "Au debut du XVe siècle: Mentalité et vocabulaire des marchands florentins," *Annales, E.S.C.,* 22 (1967), 1200–26. A primordial sense of occupational identity did not broaden into class consciousness. Social role as an aspect of personality changed almost imperceptively. For example, it took considerable time before the contracts of apprenticeship came to resemble those of wage labor. See R. Goldthwaite, *The Building of Renaissance Florence* (Baltimore, 1981), p. 261. Cf. also, *Letteratura italiana: Produzione e consumo,* ed. A. Asor Rosa (Turin, 1983), for a useful collection of studies.

32. Florentine bankers were reluctant to maintain an exact record of cash movement, and this was related to the need to avoid the appearance of exacting usury in moneylending. Present-day Florentine economic historians have elevated the records of multifarious economic activities such as moneychanging and speculation in the money market into the profession of banking. Cf. C. de la Roncière's *Un changeur florentin du Trecento* (Paris, 1973); Goldthwaite, *Building of Renaissance Florence,* pp. 81 ff. and his "Local Banking," 5–55.

The *oste* could be a protector who regularly received gifts from his dependents. Some were clearly symbolic offerings such as eggs on special feast days, whereas others were unpaid obligations such as cart and carrying services—legacies from the past. Loans to *mezzadri* (tenants on shares) amounted to a considerable total, but when wealthy Florentines listed their liabilities for tax purposes, these so-called loans often did not qualify for exemption. It was no easy matter to distinguish between credit transactions and aid and assistance provided by rich benefactors. See P. J. Jones, "From Manor to Mezzadria: A Tuscan Case Study in the Medieval Origins of Modern Agrarian Society," in *Florentine Studies: Politics and Society in Renaissance Florence,* ed. N. Rubinstein (London, 1965), 223 ff.; Herlihy and Klapisch-Zuber, *Les Toscans et leurs familles* (Paris, 1978), pp. 262–72.

33. L. B. Alberti, *I libri della famiglia,* trans. R. Watkins (Columbia, S.C., 1969), p. 51.

34. Ibid., p. 55. On the gradual evolution of the idea of town planning, see J. Heers, *Family Clans in the Middle Ages,* trans B. Herbert (Amsterdam-New York, 1977), p. 163. See also, L. B. Alberti, *Ten Books on Architecture,* trans. J. Leoni (London, 1965), p. 134.

35. Alberti, *I libri della famiglia,* p. 55. See also, R. Watkins, *Humanism and Liberty: Writings on Freedom from Fifteenth-Century Florence* (Columbia, S.C., 1978), pp. 98–103, in which an analysis and translation of Alberti's dialogue "On Happiness" is provided. The purpose of this brief but remarkable dialogue concerning certain newly captured slaves is not to demonstrate the cruelty of this commerce or the human depravity of the slavers, but rather, to exhibit the response of ordinary mortals subjected to the extreme blows of fortune. Stoicism, while it is a reasonable response to adversity, is much too demanding a philosophy for ordinary mortals. Further, the dialogue demonstrates how precious is freedom. It is not a matter of making choices or taking risks but of having one's roots firmly planted and nurtured in an autonomous and dignified community, that is, the family with its continuities ensconced in town or village. For added material on Alberti, see J. Gadol, *Leon Battista Alberti, Universal Man of the Early Renaissance* (Chicago, 1969), pp. 245 ff.

36. N. Struever provides a sensitive appraisal of Guicciardini's rhetoric in her "Proverbial Signs: Formal Strategies in Guicciardini's Ricordi," *Annali d'Italianistica* 2 (1984), 94–109. See the Introduction by M. Spinella to F. Guicciardini's *Ricordi, diari, memorie* (Rome, 1981). Kenneth Clark, "Leon Battista Alberti, 'On Painting'," *Proceedings of the British Academy* 30 (1944), 3–11, provides a brief but incisive portrayal of Alberti's character and motives.

37. Theology of course could be secular in that it was oriented towards the world (*ad seculum*). At its most radical the proof for the truth of Christianity might be described ethnographically. Montaigne, in his "Apology for Raymond Sebond," offers a vivid instance: "In truth, considering what has come to our knowledge about the course of this terrestrial government, I have often marveled to see, at a very great distance in time and space, the coincidences between a great number of fabulous popular opinions and savage customs and beliefs, which do not seem from any angle to be connected with our natural reason. The human mind is a great worker of miracles; but this correspondence has something or other about it that is still queerer: it is found also in names, in incidents, and in a thousand other things.

For nations were found there that never, so far as we know, had heard anything about us, where circumcision was in credit; where there were states and great governments maintained by women, without men; where our fasts and our Lent were represented, with the addition of abstinence from women. Where our crosses were in credit in various ways: here sepulchers were honored with them; there they applied them, and especially the Saint Andrew's cross, to defend themselves from nocturnal visions, and placed them on children's beds against enchantments; elsewhere they found a wooden one, of great height, worshiped as the god of rain, and that very far inland.

There they found a very clear likeness of our shriving priests; the use of miters, the celibacy of the priests, the art of divining by the entrails of sacrificed animals; abstinence from every kind of flesh and fish in their food; the fashion among the priests of using a special language, and not the vulgar one, when officiating" (II, 12) See *Complete Works of Montaigne,* pp. 431–32. For a treatment of the theme of "a secular theology," see Funkenstein, *Theology and the Scientific Imagination,* pp. 3– 12.

38. For Pietro Pomponazzi's disquisition on the poet's right to feign, see B. Weinberg, *A History of Literary Criticism in the Italian Renaissance* (Chicago, 1961), p. 368. The quotation from Pomponazzi's *De incantationibus* runs as follows: "For the mode of expression in the laws, as Averroes says in his *Poetry,* is similar to that used by the poets; for just as the poets do, they invent fables which, according to the literal meaning of the words, are not possible, but within they contain the truth, as Plato and Aristotle frequently point out. For they tell untruths so that we may arrive at the truth, and so that we may instruct the vulgar crowd which must be led toward good action and away from wicked action." Cf. also, F. Robortello's critical comments on Aristotle's *Poetics* cited by Weinberg, ibid., 1: 391 "Since, then, poetics has as its subject matter fictitious and fictional discourse, it is clear that the function of poetics is to invent in a proper way its fiction and its untruth; to no other art is it more fitting than to this one to intermingle lies. . . . In the lies used by the poetic art, false elements are taken as true, and from them true conclusions are derived." For a recent discussion of the right to fictionalize and its influence on Sidney, Thomas Lodge, and other Tudor "defenses of poetry," see K. Eden, *Poetic and Legal Fiction in the Aristotelian Tradition* (Princeton, 1986), chap. 4, "Image and Imitation: Aristotle's Contribution to a Christian Literary Theory, pp. 112–75.

39. For Chaucer's use of Petrarch, see *Chaucer: Sources and Background,* ed. R. Miller (Oxford, 1977), pp. 136–52. For Chaucer and Boccaccio, see ibid., 314–30. Cf. also, B. Windeatt, *Chaucer's Dream Poetry: Sources and Analogues* (Cambridge, 1982); W. Bryan and G. Dempster, *Sources and Analogues of Chaucer's Canterbury Tales,* 2d ed. (London, 1958). For an excellent bibliography of Chaucer criticism, see *Golden-tree Bibliographies,* ed. A. Baugh 2d ed. (Arlington Heights, Ill. 1977). Boccaccio composed the first redaction of *De casibus illustrium virorum* between 1356 and 1366, offering a definitive civic warning to the reader by providing exempla of princely corruption, violence, and lust. He took the work up again in 1373 contending that he could find no reigning potentate either ecclesiastical or secular worthy of the work's being dedicated to him. The author then excoriated the militant pope occupied with reconquest of church lands by arms, the torpid emperor, the Valois king of France, Edward III of England, and the semibarbaric monarchs of Spain. Boccaccio would select his fellow Florentine, Mainardo Cavalcanti, generous, noble, and steadfast, over and against the degenerate monarchs of his day. Northern European translations of the *De casibus* shied away from such scathing criticism of royalty. Moreover, they repudiated Boccaccio's ultimate political lesson that literati must distance themselves both from the crowd and the equally vulgar popes, emperors, and princes. See P. Ricci's edition of *De casibus* in *Opere di G. Boccaccio* (Milan-Naples, 1965), pp. 794 ff; N. Mann, "Petrarch and Humanism: The Paradox of Posterity," in *Francesco Petrarca, Citizen of the World* (Albany, N.Y., 1980), 287–98.

40. G. Kane, in his *Chaucer* (Oxford, 1984), p. 47, characterizes Chaucer's close and altogether enigmatic literary relationship with Boccaccio thusly: "He took or used more from Boccaccio than from either of the other Italians. He knew Boccaccio's *Filostrato, Filocolo* and *Teseida,* and his three encyclopaedic Latin works, *The Disastrous Careers of Famous Men, Illustrious Women* and *The Genealogy of the*

Pagan Gods. He based the central element of his first venture into moral philosophy, *The Parlement of Foules,* on a Boccaccian passage and its author's commentary. And the plots of his *Knight's Tale* and *Troilus and Criseyde* are Boccaccian. He echoed, in effect quoted, Boccaccio without acknowledgement, countless times. He mastered and very skilfully naturalized in English the distinguished grace and elegance of Boccaccio's youthful style, and plundered the erudition of his later years. For Chaucer Boccaccio's works were a repository of motifs, models of rich and elaborate systems of rhetoric and style, a port of entry into the antique world, a liberal education. J. Mann, in her "Chance and Destiny in Troilus Criseyde and the Knight's Tale," in *The Cambridge Chaucer Companion,* ed. P. Boitani and J. Mann (Cambridge, 1986), 75–92, discusses the significant changes Chaucer made in Boccaccio's narratives to reveal that human efforts were negligible when evaluated against the power of chance. John Lydgate, the monk of Bury St. Edmunds (d. ca. 1449), in translating Boccaccio's *De casibus* (*The Disastrous Careers of Famous Men*), was satisfied to draw up vivid and dreary catalogues of those vices, from cruelty to sloth to lechery, that occasioned the fall of princes. Walter Schirmer, in his *John Lydgate: A Study in the Culture of the Fifteenth Century,* trans. A. Keep (London, 1961), p. 213, indicates the intellectual dilemma of the author of *The Fall of Princes* succinctly: ". . . on the one hand the entire world is portrayed as a fatalistic dream of the fickleness of Fortune and the transitoriness of earthly glory; on the other hand history is seen as a manifestation of the world of divine justice. Lydgate fails to extricate himself from the toils of this contradiction."

41. Auerbach's *Mimesis,* pp. 240–63, offers an unrivaled analysis of fifteenth-century French vernacular rhetoric. P. Zumthor, in his *Le masque et la lumière: La poetique des grands rhetoriquers* (Paris, 1976), argues that the late fifteenth century "rhetoriquers" of Flanders and Burgundy demonstrated many of the moral concerns and intellectual interests, as well as the historical outlook of Italian literati and humanists. Intimidating traditions and their own sense of social insecurity (commoners for the most part serving as court poets) compelled them to adhere to ritualized modes of discourse. They did, however, express their individual visions by exaggerating particular linguistic forms and subverting literary convention. The poets examined are Pierre Gringoire, Jean Lemaire de Belges, Jean Meschinot, Jean Molinet, Jean Robertet, and a battery of others.

42. Huizinga, *Waning of the Middle Ages,* pp. 324–26. It is useful to compare the reaction of the Italian humanist Pier Candido Decembrio to Petrarch's *De remediis utriusque fortunae* with that of Northern European scholastics and literati. Decembrio opines that philosophy cannot provide consolation by mouthing empty words. Poverty, exile, disgrace, and dishonor are real enough, and, as Seneca says, an empty stomach requires something more real than examples taken from books. "The body has need day and night of money, as Horace says, not sententious and grave phrases." Cf. H. Baron, "Franciscan Poverty and Civic Wealth," p. 27, n. 1. Northern European translators and commentators on Petrarch's *De remediis* appreciated the work for extraneous reasons. Petrarch's aim was not to supply an encyclopedia of remedies for accidents of fortune, as his Northern European admirers maintained, but rather it was intended to reduce the psychological impact of favorable events and misfortunes. The moral intent was to reduce false elation as well as the state of melancholy attendant upon both trivial and grave happenings. Also, Petrarch provides the first laic treatise on the dignity and excellence of man made in the image of God. Through the Incarnation humankind has its inestimable reward—the promise of salvation and deification. Finally, Petrarch concludes with a refutation of the principal defects of humans as catalogued so bleakly by Pope Innocent III in his frequently copied tract *De miseria humanae conditionis.* See C. Trinkaus, "The Religious

Thought of the Italian Humanists, and the Reformers: Anticipation or Autonomy?" in *Pursuit of Holiness,* ed. Trinkaus and Oberman, 355–56.

43. D. Brewer, *Chaucer: The Poet as Storyteller* (London, 1984), pp. 43–59. The Florentine reception of the *Decameron* has been meticulously chronicled by V. Branca in his *Boccaccio medievale,* 5th ed. (Florence, 1981), and in his "Per il testo del *Decameron,* "*Studi di Filologia Italiana* 8 (1950), 29–143. The work found enthusiastic and extensive audience among the *mercatores* of the city. Furthermore, the prose masterpiece became the subject of sophisticated literary criticism. Lorenzo de' Medici in his *Comento ad alcuni sonetti d'amore,* in *Scritti scelti,* ed. E. Bigi (Turin, 1965), p. 309, gave this sensitive appraisal of the *Decameron:* "Chi ha letto il Boccaccio, uomo dottissimo e facundissimo, facilmente giudicherà singulare e sola al mondo non solamente la invenzione, ma la copia ed eloquenzia sua. E, considerando l'opera sua del *Decameron,* per la diversità della materia ora grave, ora mediocre ed ora bassa, e contenente tutte le perturbazioni che agli uomini possono accadere d'amore ed odio, timore e speranza, tante nuove astuzie ed ingegni, ed avendo ad esprimere tutte le nature e passioni degli uomini che si truovono al mondo; sanza controversia giudicherà nessuna lingua meglio che la nostra essere atta ad esprimere."

44. See G. Elton's review of R. Marius, *Thomas More: A Biography,* in the *New York Review of Books* (31 January 1985), 29–31, in which the reviewer comments on the tensions in More's character between flesh and spirit. Cf. also, the recent biography by A. Fox, *Thomas More: History and Providence* (New Haven, 1982), pp. 9–49; J. Trapp, "Midwinter," *London Review of Books* (17 November 1983), 15–16.

45. M. Domenichelli, *Wyatt: Il liuto infranto* (Ravenna, n.d.), p. 129. See also, F. Petrarca, *Canzonieri, Trionfi, Rime Varie,* ed. C. Muscetta (Turin, 1958), p. 117. On Wyatt, see P. Thomson, *Sir Thomas Wyatt,* pp. 148–60; Greene, *Light in Troy,* pp. 242–67.

46. Ralph Williams, *Images of Love and Death in Late Medieval and Renaissance Art* (Ann Arbor, Mich., 1976), presents a textured description of the infusion of motifs and contradictions in Petrarchanism. Again, in considering Chaucer's literary relation to Boccaccio, stock should be taken of the fact that the Englishman did not acknowledge his debt to the Tuscan: "Indeed he invented a fiction that the source of his *Troilus and Criseyde,* for which Boccaccio's *Filostrato* had provided the story, was that nonexistent Latin historian of Troy, Lollius; and once, in *The Monk's Tale,* where Chaucer drew on Boccaccio he implied that his source was Petrarch." See Kane, *Chaucer,* p. 47. Chaucer's Clerk mutes the praise accorded Petrarch, "the laurait who rethorike sweete / Enlumyned al Ytaille of poetrie," by adding a eulogy of a professor of canon law. Chaucer's learned Clerk finds Petrarch's tale of Griselda personally disturbing and even criticizes the rhetorical strategy of the introduction. It should also be noted that the three seven-line stanzas Troilus composes in his song, which are the translation of the Petrarchan sonnet, express the feelings of an emotionally disturbed adolescent in the grip of a destructive passion, rather than the spiritual torment of a mature poet. Kane, *Chaucer,* p. 46. Petrarch's method is empirical; he advocates no moral, ideal, or rule applicable to the generality of humankind. Any attempt to abstract a general idea from the sonnet would trivialize the meaning into the tag "love is an indefinable sentiment." Petrarch is not concerned with whether this incomprehensible sentiment is love or not. Troilus raises the philosophical question: Does love exist or not? Not all of these differences can be explained in terms of the alleged immaturity of Troilus. See Thomson, *Sir Thomas Wyatt,* pp. 152–66, in which she deals with the Canticum Troili. For a careful analysis of Chaucer's "misunderstandings" of the Italian text of Petrarch, see E. Wilkins, *The Making of the "Canzoniere" and other Petrarcan Studies* (Rome, 1951), pp. 307 ff.

47. Cf. D. Cernecelli's edition of *Lord Morley's Tryumphes of Fraunces Petrarcke: The First English Translator of the Trionfi* (Cambridge, Mass., 1971); L. Salinger, *Shakespeare and the Tradition of Comedy* (Cambridge, 1974), pp. 249 ff.

48. *Edmund Spenser: The Critical Heritage,* ed. R. Cummings (London, 1971), p. 46. The originality and fruitfulness of the structural invention of the *Faerie Queene* rested in the felicitous combination of medieval allegory and the Italian romance epic. This fusion permitted the poet to range over a medley of experiences such as religious melancholy, false gallantry, frivolous chivalry, the frustrations of love, the pain of self-accusatory passion, sensual temptation, and the blissfulness of true love. Like Ariosto and the Italians, Spenser was able to express shades of feeling and varieties of experience at a historical time when there was no biographical novel. Further, these conditions of the human heart were explored in the company of an audience whose taste required plots freighted with exciting adventures and comic relief. See Lewis, *English Literature in the Sixteenth Century,* pp. 380–93. Lewis's line about Spenser's poem deserves quoting: "I never meet a man who says that he *used* to like the *Faerie Queene*."

49. For a sympathetic appraisal of Browne's equipoise when confronting the pull of earth and heaven and the greatness and littleness of the sons of Adam, see D. Bush, *English Literature in the Earlier Seventeenth Century, 1600–1660* (Oxford, 1962), pp. 353–56. S. Chauduri's *Infirm Glory: Shakespeare and the Renaissance Image of Man* (Oxford, 1981) furnishes literary background and numerous examples from contemporary writings on the motif of the protean nature of humans.

50. P. Sidney, *Miscellaneous Prose,* ed. K. Duncan-Jones and Jan van Drosten (Oxford, 1973), p. 82.

51. It is not *filosofia scholastica* suitable among close friends and in private conversation that is appropriate in the councils of princes, but a *filosofia civilior.* This scholastic or academic philosophy thinks "that everything is suitable to every place." Not so with *filosofia civilior* which is "more practical for statesmen, which knows its stage, adapts itself to the play in hand, and performs its role neatly and appropriately." Finally, this stark advice: "Whatever play is being performed, perform it as best you can, and do not upset it all simply because you can think of another which has more interest." By extension, this is translated into the domain of politics: "So it is in the commonwealth. So it is in the deliberations of monarchs. If you cannot pluck up wrong-headed opinions by the root, if you cannot cure according to your heart's desire vices of long standing, yet you must not on that account desert the commonwealth. You must not abandon the ship in a storm because you cannot control the winds." The reiteration of Morus's speeches is intended to suggest that the high evaluation placed on *filosofia civilior* was part of the author's preoccupation with a view of language having its origin in "temporal *utilitas,* not in some unearthly fixed correlation between things and our signs for them. In advancing this pragmatic or instrumentalist notion of signification, More capitalizes on the fact that Aristotle's own logical writings were traditionally known as the *Organon* ("Tool" or "Instrument". . .). Even dialectic itself, the most abstract of the three "language arts," was contrived with a straightforward view to supplying a practical need in particular historical circumstances." Cf. *The Complete Works of St. Thomas More,* Yale ed., p. lix. The vision of Erasmian humanism moved away from the narrowly didactic toward the practical legislating for the philosopher rather than the saint and substituting the fool for the sinner. See Thomson, *Sir Thomas Wyatt,* pp. 79–86.

52. Cf. R. Sylvester, "*Si Hythlodaeo credimus:* Vision and Revision in Thomas More's *Utopia,*" *Soundings* 51 (1968), 268. For an exploration of the hidden sources of violence in More's character, see F. Manuel, "Thomas More—Reconsideration," *The New Republic* (24 June 1978), 37–41. R. Marius's new biography, *Thomas More,* is a masterful analysis of More's personality and its attendant tensions.

53. T. Hoby, *The Book of the Courtier,* Everyman ed. (London, 1978), p. 3. For the portrayal of politics as a dangerous game, see Polydore Vergil's account of the false oath of fidelity to Henry VI sworn by Edward before York in 1471. If Edward had refused the oath, he would have pleased God but lost his throne. Politics is the domain of contradictory demands and ambiguous motives replete with temptation and inevitable entanglement. When Henry VIII spoke of the Pilgrimage of Grace as "this tragedy," he was commenting on the many ways in which the lives of great men and women resemble a tale where the mighty are cast down partly by hostile fortune and partly as a consequence of their obdurate will. *The "Anglica historia" of Polydore Vergil,* ed. D. Hay, cited and discussed in James's *Society, Politics and Culture,* pp. 262–65. Cf. also, D. Hay, *Polydore Vergil* (Oxford, 1952), pp. 140–44; F. J. Levy, *Tudor Historical Throught* (San Marino, Calif., 1967), pp. 171 ff.; R. Sylvester, "Cavendish's Life of Wolsey: The Artistry of a Tudor Biographer," *Studies in Philology* 57 (1960), 44–71.

54. R. Mulcaster, *Positions,* ed. R. Quick (London, 1888), p. 291. It should be recalled, and often it is not, that the purpose for which the talents of the perfect courtier were honed was, in the final analysis, political. *Il Cortigiano* cannot be reduced to a catalogue of courtly comportment and dissembling. Castiglione's courtier must gain the ear and confidence of the prince so that he may give counsel and exercise political influence. His many accomplishments would be mere frivolities and vanities: courtiership is in no way to be taken in and for itself: "Therefore, I think that the aim of the perfect Courtier, which we have not spoken of up to now, is so to win for himself, by means of the accomplishments ascribed to him by these gentlemen, the favor and mind of the prince whom he serves that he may be able to tell him, and always will tell him, the truth about everything he needs to know, without fear or risk of displeasing him; and that when he sees the mind of his prince inclined to a wrong action, he may dare to oppose him and in a gentle manner avail himself of the favor acquired by his good accomplishments so as to dissuade him of every evil intent and bring him to the path of virtue." See Castiglione's *Book of the Courtier,* trans. C. Singleton (Garden City, N.Y., 1959), bk. 4, 5, p. 289.

55. R. Mulcaster, *First Part of the Elementarie,* ed. E. Campagnac (Oxford, 1925), pp. 13–14. Mulcaster, Spenser's teacher, also announced that "the qualitie of our *monarchie* wil admit trew speaking, wil allow trew writing, in both with the bravest, so that it do please, and be worthie praise, so that it preach peace, and preserve the state." See ibid., p. 273.

56. B. Giamatti gives a shaded analysis of the complexities of Spenser's poetic insights into civilization and its values over and against the descent into bestiality. See Giamatti's *Play of Double Senses: Spenser's "Faerie Queene"* (Englewood Cliffs, N.J., 1975), pp. 4–12. Greenblatt, whose *Renaissance Self-Fashioning* has become so influential in recent years, takes a very harsh stance toward Spenser reducing his poetic vision: "Spenser sees human identity as conferred by loving service to legitimate authority, to the yoked power of God and the state." See p. 222.

57. For a survey of recent literature on the sprawling topic of social control and regulation in sixteenth-century England, along with bibliography, see P. Slack, "Poverty and Social Regulation in Elizabethan England," in *The Reign of Elizabeth I,* ed. C. Haigh (Athens, Ga., 1985), 221–41; 285–88. See also the excellent study of C. Pythian-Adams, "Ceremony and the Citizen: The Community of Coventry, 1450–1550," in *Crisis and Order in English Towns, 1500–1700,* ed. P. Slack (London, 1972), 57–85.

58. For quotations from the plays and prose writings of Ben Jonson, see the *Dictionary of Literary-Rhetorical Conventions of the English Renaissance,* ed. M. Donker and G. Muldron (Westport, Conn. 1982), p. 46. Barber's *Shakespeare's Festive Comedy* is a model for those seeking to use English literary writings to

explicate the changing awareness of archaic social customs and practices. See also, M. Becker, "A Historian's View of Another Pericles," *Michigan Quarterly Review* 15 (1976), 197–211, for a further examination of the use of literary evidence to chart social changes in the sixteenth century. Christopher Marlowe in his prologue to *Tamburlaine the Great* (1587), announced that his purpose was to break with the dominant English stage tradition which he harshly characterized as mere "jigging veins of rhyming mother wits, / And such conceits as clownage keeps in pay." In place of these archaic literary practices, he boldly favors a new form of tragic drama:

> We'll lead you to the stately tent of war,
> Where you shall hear the Scythian Tamburlaine
> Threatening the world with high astounding terms,
> And scourging kingdoms with his conquering swords.

59. Cf. Javitch, "Rival Arts of Conduct," 178–92 and his *Poetry and Courtliness in Renaissance England* (Princeton, 1978), pp. 131 ff.; Briggs, *This Stage-Play World*, pp. 186–89. Sir Philip Sidney in *The Defense of Poesie*, pt. 2, chap. 48, condemns English drama of his day, with the single exception of *Gorboduc*, in these oft-quoted words: "Our tragedies and comedies not without cause cried out against, observing rules neither of honest civility nor skillful poetry, excepting *Gorboduc* (again, I say, of those that I have seen), which notwithstanding, as it is full of stately speeches and well-sounding phrases, climbing to the height of Seneca's style, and as full of notable morality, which it doth most delightfully teach, and so obtain the very end of poesy, yet in truth it is very defectious in the circumstances, which grieves me, because it might not remain as an exact model of all tragedies."

60. For a discussion of the quotations from the writings of Elyot, see Briggs, *This Stage-Play World*, 126–27. For a general treatment of the educational ideals of Elyot and others, see F. Caspari's *Humanism and the Social Order in Tudor England* (Chicago, 1954). For a comparison of these ideals with those of an earlier time (the 1350s), see *Metrical Romances*, ed. H. Weber (Edinburgh, 1810), and *The Middle English Metrical Romances*, ed. C. Hale and W. French (London, 1964). In speaking of versifying, Elyot offers the justification that "the making of verse is not discommended in a nobleman, since the noble Augustus and almost all the old emperors made books in verse." *The Gouvernor*, 1. 10. 3. A cautionary note, however, is sounded when it comes to a reading of Ovid's *Metamorphoses* and the *De fastis*. Both are "right necessary" for an understanding of other poets: "But because there is little learning in them concerning either virtuous manners or policy, I suppose it were better that, as fables and ceremonies happen to come in a lesson, it were declared abundantly by the master, than that in the said two books a long time should be spent and almost lost, which might be better employed on such authors that do minister both eloquence, civil policy, and exhortation to virtue." Yet Elyot cannot be entirely dismissive of such lascivious poets as Ovid and Martial, who although they have written wanton books, have also composed "right commendable and noble sentences." Elyot gives proof of this and then pays historical tribute to the Latin writers able to express themselves "incomparable with more grace and delectation to the reader than our English tongue may yet comprehend."

61. E. Saccone's *"Grazia, Sprezzatura, Affettazione* in the *Courtier,"* in *Castiglione: The Ideal and the Real in Renaissance Culture*, ed. R. Hanning (New Haven, 1983), 45–68, presents a detailed analysis of the changing meaning of words such as *grace, eloquence, isolate,* and so on. Cf. also, G. Hunter's careful study of language and courtly humanism in *John Lyly: The Humanist as Courtier* (London, 1962), pp. 130 ff. Again, Sir Philip Sidney's comments are worth quoting, this time on "courtly and pedantic styles." See *The Defense of Poesie*, pt. 2, chap. 54: "Undoubtedly (at

least to my opinion undoubtedly) I have found in divers small-learned courtiers a more sound style than in some professors of learning; of which I can guess no other cause but that the courtier, following that which by practice he findeth fittest to nature, therein (though he know it not) doth according to art, though not by art; where the other, using art to show art, and not hide art (as in these cases he should do), flieth from nature, and indeed abuseth art." The ethical message of the *Arcadia* was framed to dampen the self-assertiveness of violence in word and deed in competition for glory, and to accept in patience the discipline of obeying a just political order hedged by divinity and secured by religious faith. Recognition of finite and fallen human nature converted ideals of heroic self-sufficiency into an appreciation of human interdependency. The world of happenings do not usually manifest themselves under the aspect of trials and tests demanding heroic intervention. See James, *Society, Politics and Culture*, pp. 388–89.

62. For the poet Skelton's description of the fifteenth-century earl of Northumberland as having "knights and squires at every season when / He called upon them as menial house men," see the citation accompanied by a battery of evidence from contemporary opinion in Stone, *Crisis of the Aristocracy*, pp. 208–17. Rough estimates of the number of offices at the disposal of the crown during the reign of Elizabeth run about 2,500; the number eligible to serve figures between 15,000 to 20,000. Instances can be cited in which individuals arranged for the education of sons by placing them in households of aristocrats. See L. Stone, *An Elizabethan: Sir Horatio Palavicino* (Oxford, 1956), p. 32. By the late sixteenth century, however, such tuition was exceptional: the rise of the grammar school, with its religious and humanist emphasis, challenged, successfully, the aristocratic household with its archaic honor culture. For upper-class lay folk this had become the typical educational environment. See James, *Society, Politics and Culture*, p. 358 and his *Family, Lineage and Civil Society*, pp. 67–107. Of course Stone's *Crisis of the Aristocracy* was first with the most.

63. Buckhurst continues his explanation to the earl: "And when in the country you dwell in you will needes enter in a warr with the inferior therin, we thinke it both justice equity & wisdom to take care that the weaker part be not put doun by the mightier." Fulke Greville's observation that Elizabeth "did not suffer the nobility to be servants one to the another, neither did her gentry weare their liveries as in ages before" must stand for many. See his *The Life of the Renowned Sir Philip Sidney*, ed. N. Smith (Oxford, 1907), p. 189. For Buckhurst's comments and a variety of other contemporary notices, Stone, *op. cit.*, pp. 237 ff. For an assessment of the poetry of John Skelton and its transitional place on the historical map, see the comment of Stanley Fish, *John Skelton's Poetry* (New Haven, 1965), p. 249: "Skelton's poetry gives us neither the old made new nor the new made old, but a statement of the potentiality for disturbance of the unassimilated. It is a poetry which could only have been written between 1498 and 1530, when the intrusive could no longer be ignored as Lydgate had ignored it and before it would become part of a new and difficult stability as it would after 1536." Cf. also, I. Gordon, *John Skelton: Poet Laureate* (Melbourne, 1943), p. 9 for a similar fix on the grappling of the poet with the transitional character of the historical moment.

64. This quotation from Selden, the following ones from Francis Bacon, and that attributed to Sir Walter Raleigh are from Appendix B of J. Hexter's "Storm Over the Gentry," published in *Reappraisals in History*, pp. 153–57. See also, the critical comments of J. Pocock, *The Machiavellian Moment: Florentine Political Thought and the Atlantic Republican Tradition* (Princeton, 1975), pp. 354–60; Q. Skinner, *The Foundations of Modern Political Thought: The Age of Reformation* (Cambridge, 1978), 2: 356 ff.

65. F. Heal's survey of sixteenth- and early seventeenth-century writings on good

lordship, the open household, and conviviality is extremely useful. See "Idea of Hospitality." For a particularly vivid debate on the pros and cons of gregariousness and openhandedness, see *Dialogue Cyvile and Uncyvile* (1579), in *Inedited Tracts*, ed. William Hazlitt (London, 1864), pp. 80–86. See also, L. C. Knights, *Drama and Poetry in the Age of Jonson*, pp. 114 ff.

66. For Bacon's "Of Ceremonies and Respects," see the Everyman edition of his *Essays* (New York, 1906), p. 154. Cf. also, Javitch, *Poetry and Courtliness*, pp. 48–52; F. Whigham, *Ambition and Privilege*, pp. 97–98. On the critical question of "making things up," see Lewis, *English Literature in the Sixteenth Century*, pp. 318 ff. In an earlier time Chaucer did not praise Homer for his "feyninge," but blamed him for lying like a Greek partisan (*Hous of Fame* III, 1477–9). Homer belonged in the same class with Josephus. See C. S. Lewis, *The Discarded Image: An Introduction to Medieval and Renaissance Literature* (Cambridge, 1964), pp. 212–13.

67. See the introduction to G. Willcock's and A. Walker's edition of G. Puttenham's *The Arte of English Poesie* (Cambridge, 1936). Thomas Lodge's assertion in his *Defence of Poetry, Music, and Stage Plays* (1579) is typical of many another pronouncement: "Poetes were the first raysors of cities, prescribers of good lawes, mayntayners of religion, disturbors of the wicked, advancers of the wel disposed, inventors of laws, and lastly the very fot-paths to knowledge and understanding." See *Elizabethan Critical Essays*, ed. G. Smith (Oxford, 1904), 1: 75. William Webbe's comments are in a similar vein; cf. *A Discourse of English Poetrie* (1586) in ibid., pp. 231–34. For a valuable review of arguments by literati concerning the progress toward greater civility and civilization, see A. Ferguson, " 'By Little and Little': The Early Tudor Humanists on the Development of Man," in *Florilegium Historiale: Essays Presented to Wallace K. Ferguson*, eds. Stockdale and Rowe, pp. 126–50.

68. For the quotation of Gabriel Harvey on Spenser, see *Spenser*, ed. Cummings, p. 57. On references to "meere illusion of the mind," see Javitch, *Poetry and Courtliness*, pp. 49 ff. On Peter Heylyn's *Microcosmos: A Little Description of the Great World*, see *Dictionary of Literary-Rhetorical Conventions of the English Renaissance*, p. 204. Erasmus, in *Praise of Folly*, states the matter succinctly: "But to return to my subject. Take those wild men sprung from hard rocks and oak trees—what power brought them together into a civilized society if not flattery? This is all that's meant by the lyre of Amphion and Orpheus. What was it which recalled the Roman mob to harmony in the state when it was plotting violence—a philosopher's speech? Not a bit of it. It was a silly, childish fable made up about the belly and other parts of the body. A similar sort of story told by Themistocles about a fox and a hedgehog had the same effect. No sage's speech could ever have achieved so much as that fictitious white hind of Sertorius, or the ridiculous anecdote invented about the famous Spartan with his two dogs, and the one told by Sertorius about pulling the hairs out of a horse's tail, to say nothing of Minos and Numa, who both ruled the foolish mob by means of fantastic trumped-up tales. It's absurdities like these that sway the huge powerful monster which is the common people. But what society ever took its laws from Plato or Aristotle or the teachings of Socrates?" See *Collected Works of Erasmus*, 27: 101.

69. Thomas Starkey, *A Dialogue between Reginald Pole and Thomas Lupset*, ed. K. Burton (London, 1948), p. 22. For a discussion of this passage in the context of the reception of humanist political thought, see Q. Skinner, *Foundations of Modern Political Thought*, 1: 213–43. Foster Watson's translation and edition of Juan Luis Vives, *On Education* (Cambridge, 1913) presents a thinker whose arguments for studies appropriate to the practical exigencies of daily life was most influential in the sixteenth century.

70. That the study of rhetoric was a postulate of Tudor literati was a thing certain. Furthermore, dedication of their handbooks and treatises to the principal public

figures of the day was de rigueur. Sir Thomas Elyot's *The Gouvernor* is dedicated to Henry VIII; Thomas Wilson's *Arte of Retorique* is dedicated to Lord Dudley ("Lord Lisle, Earle of Warwicke, and Master of the Horse"); Richard Rainolde's *A Booke Called the Foundation of Rhetorike* to Lord Robert Dudley, Master of the House of Privy Councillor; Henry Peacham's *Garden of Eloquence* to Sir John Puckering, Lordkeeper of the Great Seal of England; and, by intent, George Puttenham's *Arte of English Poesie* to Queen Elizabeth. We should also note that Sir Humphrey Gilbert's plan for a university at London, included provision for a teacher of rhetoric and logic who would instruct his students by "Orations made in English, both politique and militare, taking occasions owt of Discowrses of histories." This sketch was entitled, *Queene Elizabethes Achademy*. See B. Vickers, "The Power of Persuasion": Images of the Orator, Elyot to Shakespeare," in *Renaissance Eloquence*, p. 416.

71. For a reference to the appropriate passage from Golding's translation of Ovid, see Kinney, "Rhetoric and Fiction," in *Renaissance Eloquence*, 385–93, esp. p. 386. Medieval readings of Ovid had tended to be more or less indifferent to the integrity of the whole text. Instead they were prone to read intermittently conveying the materials as a series of autonomous episodes. See S. Battaglia, "La tradizione di Ovidio nel Medioevo," in *La coscienza letteraria del Medioevo* (Naples, 1965), 23–30; A. Monteverdi, "Ovidio nel Medioevo," *Atti dell'Accademia Nazionale dei Lincei: Rendiconti delle adunanze solenni* 5 (1958), 697–708.

72. Fulke Greville, Lord Brooke, *Life of the Renowned Sir Philip Sidney*, p. 18. John Lyly's *Euphues: The Anatomy of Wit* (1578), reprinted "corrected and augmented" in the following year, appeared in five editions by 1581 and twelve more before 1640. The sequel to this work, *Euphues and His England* (1580), was reprinted sixteen times before 1640. The author's principal interest in the first and more innovative work was with the moral debate between an individual naturally endowed with wit and his adversary seeking to offer good, moral counsel. Young Euphues, filled with self-love, spurns the advice of Eubulis. Wit enhances the individual's sense of power, and by so doing may in the end make wisdom inaccessible. Only through experience can one travel the rocky trail to the goal of sustaining knowledge: "It is commonly said, yet I do not think it is a common lie, that experience is the mistress of fools, for in my opinion they be most fools that want [need] it." G. K. Hunter, *Lyly and Peele* (London, 1966), pp. 16–17, and his *John Lyly*.

73. On Sidney and his literary experience, especially in Paris at mid-sixteenth century, see A. Hamilton, *Sir Philip Sidney* (Cambridge, 1977), pp. 12–16; Jan van Drosten, "Sidney and Franciscus Junius the Elder," *Huntington Library Quarterly* 41 (1978), 1–13. Gilbert's *Literary Criticism* pp. 404–61, offers numerous references to the writings of Continental critics who contributed to Sidney's esthetic maturation. See also, the excellent notes in G. Gregory Smith's edition of *Elizabethan Critical Essays* (Oxford, 1904), 1: 157 ff.

74. See the wide-ranging and illuminating study of D. Underdown, *Revel, Riot and Rebellion: Popular Politics and Culture 1603–1660* (Oxford, 1986). See also Lawrence Stone's review in the *New York Review of Books* (26 February 1987), pp. 40–41. Stone emphasizes the significance of regional differences. Old social bonds tend to hold in those geographic areas where the manorial court, the nuclear village, and cultivation of open fields persisted. Older forms of associative life were also likely to be on the rise in pastoral areas with their hamlets and scattered farmsteads, and in unregulated settlements. The spread of a market economy, an increase in population, and enclosure of open fields served to generate pressures resulting in the disruption of an archaic society.

75. For the quote and a discussion of its historial significance, see E. Prosser, *Hamlet and Revenge*, 2d ed. (Stanford, 1971), pp. 24–29. For further examples of cultural relativism and an awareness of "multiple semiotic worlds," see Thomas

Greene's introduction to *The Vulnerable Text,* pp. xi–xv. His quotation from Samuel Daniel, Puttenham's contemporary, is worth quoting: "Suffer then the world to inioy that which it knowes, and what it likes. . . . Seeing that whatsoever force of words doth moove, delight, and sway the affections of men, in what Scythian sorte soever it be disposed or uttered, that is true number, measure, eloquence, and the perfection of speach: which I said hath as many shapes as there be tongues or nations in the world." See S. Daniel, "A Defence of Ryme," (1603) in G. Gregory Smith, ed., *Elizabethan Critical Essays,* 2: 363. This is a response to Thomas Campion's urgent case put in favor of classical meters for English poetry.

76. For the quote and discussion of its implications, see J. Burrow, *Medieval Writers and Their Work: Middle English Literature and Its Background 1100–1500* (Oxford, 1982), pp. 119–20. Cf. also, *Elizabethan Critical Essays,* 2: 60–65. It should be noted that the new antiquarianism brought a growing body of patriotic gentlemen in contact with the world of Continental scholarship. See F. Levy's review of William Camden's *Remains concerning Britain,* ed. R. Dunn, in *Renaissance Quarterly* 49 (1986), p. 128. The critic, George Puttenham, advises the reader, proudly, that he had been in attendance at the great courts of Europe in France, Italy, Spain, and at the court of the Hapsburg Holy Roman Emperors. The first editor of Wyatt and Surrey, Richard Tottel, noted with pride in his preface to *Songes and Sonettes* (1557) that their poetry was proof that English verse-makers can do as well as "Latines, Italians and others." For further critical evaluation, see Thomson, *Sir Thomas Wyatt.*

77. On John Selden, see *Table Talk,* ed. F. Pollock (London, 1927), p. 24. Mention has already been made of Barber's *Shakespeare's Festive Comedy,* a classic study often neglected by present-day historians. Barber explores in convincing detail the consciousness of Tudor literati concerning the disjunction between a folk culture and the customs of their own day. R. Weinmann's *Shakespeare and the Popular Tradition in the Theater: Studies in the Social Dimension of Dramatic Form and Function,* ed. R. Schwartz (Baltimore, 1978), is an encyclopedic account of consciousness concerning the distancing from an archaic and folk culture. At this point it might be well to recall the grand final elegy of John of Gaunt, uncle of Richard II, pronounced within an hour of death. The old man speaks of a glorious England:

> This blessèd plot, this earth, this realm, this England,
> This nurse, this teeming womb of royal kings
> Feared by their breed and famous by their birth,
> Renowned for their deeds as far from home
> For Christian service and true chivalry
> As is the sepulchre in stubborn Jewry
> Of the world's ransom, blessèd Mary's son,
> This land of such dear souls, this dear, dear land,
> Dear for her reputation through the world,

(Shakespeare's *King Richard II,* II, i, 50–58). This realm is passing and a new one coming into being—one which John links correctly to his own death. This England:

> Is now leased out, I die pronouncing it,
> Like to a tenement or pelting farm.
> England, bound in with the triumphant sea
> Whose rocky shore beats back the envious siege
> Of watery Neptune, is *now bound in with shame,*
> *With inky blots and rotten parchment bonds,*
> That England that was wont to conquer others
> Hath made a shameful conquest of itself.
> Ah, would the scandal vanish with my life,
> How happy then were my ensuing death! (II, i, 59–68)

Greene, *Vulnerable Text,* pp. 226–27, sees Gaunt as a character cognizant of anachronism and the new England "with inky blots and rotten parchment bonds." Other scholars would not draw the same bold inferences that Greene does from the terms "inky blots" or "rotten parchment bonds." Instead they would associate these expressions as characterizing both legal corruption and the efforts of the king to extract taxes and levies. With important qualifications, however, it can still be suggested that Gaunt does have something of a deepened appreciation for a receding historical moment. See Shakespeare's *King Richard II,* ed. A. Gurr (Cambridge, 1984), pp. 81–83, esp. the appropriate footnotes.

78. For a consideration of the implications of Ben Jonson's responses to the architecture of his day, see W. McClung, *The Country House* (Berkeley, 1977), pp. 65 ff. R. Weinmann, *Shakespeare and the Popular Tradition,* pp. 181, 291 and Barber, *Shakespeare's Festive Comedy,* pp. 79–83, discuss folk themes and self-consciousness concerning their literary use. See also, Thomas Nashe, *Works,* ed. R. McKerrow (London, 1904), p. 334. On Jonson and his conceptions of an ordered society, see that jewel of an essay by H. Maclean, "Ben Jonson's Poems: Notes on the Ordered Society," in *Essays in English Literature from the Renaissance to the Victorian Age,* ed. M. MacLure and F. Watt (Toronto, 1964), 43–68. Jonson was to quarrel with his collaborator, Jones, about the realistic illusionism that served to generate tensions between poetry and theater. See B. King, *Seventeenth-Century English Literature* (New York, 1982), pp. 60–61. The Caroline masque tended to express the meaning of allegory visually rather than through the poetry of language.

79. Ben Jonson, *Works,* 7: 7–45 for *The Sad Shepherd,* esp. p. 16. Against the repulsive witch, Maudlin, stands the mutual love of man and woman: "Marian and the gentle Robinhood / Who are the Croune and Ghirland of the Wood . . . Where should I be but in my Robins armes. / The Sphere which I delight in, so to move?" Anne Barton's *Ben Jonson, Dramatist* (Cambridge, 1984) presents a nuanced portrayal of the tensions evident in the dramatist's later life between his attraction for archaic subjects and rural folklore, which permitted an imaginative return to the golden but lost world of the English oral tradition, over and against the exigencies of commercialized urban drama. On the Jonsonian masque, see *Complete Masques,* ed. S. Orgel (New Haven, 1969), and Orgel's *The Jonsonian Masque* (Cambridge, Mass., 1965).

80. Ben Jonson, *Works,* 8: 638. See also, McClung, *Country House,* pp. 51–65; J. Rathmell, "Jonson, Lord Lisle and Penshurst," *English Literary Renaissance* I (1971), 250–60. Thomas Greene, in his "Ben Jonson and the Centered Self," in *The Vulnerable Text,* p. 199, concludes that as Jonson aged, he became more attentive to the disruption of customary relations. Centrifugal forces acquired greater power weakening the bonds of community, and with this Jonson's sense of a "beleaguered central self became more insistent and more poignant." Other poems in which the great houses are celebrated, include Jonson's "To Sir Robert Wroth," Robert Herrick's "Panegerick to Sir Lewis Pemberton," Thomas Carew's "To My Friend G. N." and Andrew Marvell's "Upon Appleton House."

81. Cf. E. Muir's "The Polity of King Lear," in his *Essays on Literature and Society* (Cambridge, Mass., 1965), 33–48. It is interesting to note that the *OED* marked the first appearance of the word *malcontent* in 1551, as well as the adjective *melancholic* fixed to scholars and lovers as well as villains and cynics. Cf. *New York Review of Books* (12 February 1987), 5–6, and MacDonald, *Mystical Bedlam.* Literary movement away from Shakespeare's comedies brings the audience into close contact with the centrifugal world. The remedy, if there is one, lies in protean changeability. See Greene, *The Vulnerable Text,* p. 205.

82. A. Kernan, "The Plays and the Playwrights," in *The Revels History of Drama in English, 1576–1613* (London, 1975), 3: 387–94. For a critical discussion of George Chapman, see R. Waddington, *The Mind's Empire: Myth and Form in George Chapman's Narrative Poems* (Baltimore, 1974), pp. 22–46.

83. J. Middleton Murray's *Shakespeare* (New York, 1936) contains some of the best criticism of T. S. Eliot's overly literary view of the archaic, psychic building blocks of the tragedy of Prince Hamlet.

84. Scholarly literature on the subject of drama and humanist rhetoric is superabundant, but see J. Altman, *The Tudor Play of Mind: Rhetorical Inquiry and the Development of Elizabethan Drama* (Berkeley, 1972), for a particularly successful synthesis. See also, Greenblatt, *Renaissance Self-Fashioning;* W. King, "John Lyly and Elizabethan Rhetoric," *Studies in Philology* 41 (1955), 149–61; C. De Stasio, "Il linguaggio grammatico di George Peele," *English Miscellany* 15 (1964), 61–87. The degree to which English drama advanced over that of the Continent was in no small measure the result of the fact that the literary benefits of humanist education came to serve the tastes and interests of a popular, commercial entertainment. This happy union furnished a base for dramaturgy not in evidence in either Italy or France. The *Commedia dell'Arte* of the piazza was segregated from the *Commedia erudita* (learned comedy, classical in inspiration) of court and academy. In France this heady mix of popular and learned was seldom in evidence. That prolific playwright Alexander Hardy may have initiated such dramaturgy, but it never was energized. The emergence of the refined theater of Hôtel de Rambouillet scotched that of the vulgar Hôtel de Bourgagne. The popularity of the London theater has been attested to many times. The stinginess and parochialism of the Tudor court in comparison with that of the Valois and princely courts of Italy made a very different type of support essential to the English playwright. It was London in 1600, with a population of 150,000, 5 playhouses, and an audience 20,000 or so per week that gave the playwright employment. See Hunter, *Lily and Peele,* pp. 7–8, 20–21.

85. The vocabulary John Florio believed to be new to English in his translation of Montaigne's *Essays* often had its origins in a broader world of psychological refinement and leisure. Words such as *amusing, effort, emotion,* and *conscientiousness* suggest the domain of the psychological, whereas words such as *comport, entrain,* and *facilitate* indicate refinements of leisure and abstract thought. Sir William Cornwallis (1579–1619), an essayist who, at least chronologically, was second only to Bacon, imbibed more than Montaigne's idiom: he was able to replicate the Frenchman's posture of detachment while conveying a sense of urbanity. This despite the fact that he knew Montaigne's essays only partially, and through translation. Of course these literary lessons would bear their ripest fruit in the essays of Bacon, whose use of language for analytic and practical purpose permitted him to distance himself from moral allegory, as well as from the time-honored theory of the humours. L. Salinger, "The Elizabethan Literary Renaissance," in *The New Pelican Guide to English Literature,* ed. B. Ford, (Penguin Books, revised ed., 1982), 2: 113. On the history of rhetorical training in argumentation on both sides of an issue, see W. Trimpi, *Muses of One Mind: The Literary Analysis of Experience and Its Continuity* (Princeton, 1983), pp. 59–63; 281–327.

86. On the bleak theme of "Death is even in Arcadia," first taken up by painters and then men of letters, see E. Panofsky's essay, "Et in Arcadia Ego: Poussin and the Elegiac Tradition," in *Meaning in the Visual Arts* (Garden City, N.Y., 1955), 295–320.

87. Hallett Smith, *Elizabethan Poetry: A Study in Conventions, Meaning and Expression* (Cambridge, 1952), p. 306 for citation of relevant passage from Plutarch's *Moralia,* 25C. On North's translation, see Salinger, *Elizabethan Literary Renaissance,* p. 113. See also, J. Barish, *Ben Jonson and the Language of Prose Comedy* (Cambridge, Mass., 1960), pp. 78–85. On the literary penchant for the extended paradox and the ironic, see R. Colie, *Paradoxia Epidemica* (Princeton, 1966), pp. 2–40; S. Fish, *Self-Consuming Artifacts* (Berkeley, 1972), pp. 1–4.

88. Smith, *Elizabethan Poetry,* p. 302 for citation of John Milton, *Minor Poems,* ed. M. Hughes, p. 174, 1. 13–14. Cf. also, M. Hughes, "The Christ of 'Paradise Regained' and the Renaissance Heroic Tradition," *Studies in Philology* 25 (1938), 265–74.

89. See L. C. Knights, "Ben Jonson: Public Attitudes and Social Poetry," recently republished in his *Explorations 3* (Pittsburgh, 1976), 81–94, in which an effort is made to define the hard-won consciousness of society expressed in the poetry of Jonson, Donne, and others of that generation. For an appreciation of the pastoral and an evaluation of the stunning contribution to that form by Jacopo Sannazzaro, see Lewis, *English Literature*, pp. 333–35, where he discusses Sir Philip Sidney's debt to the Neapolitan. The thread of the narrative in the prose which alternates with the poetry, while thin, does produce a landscape with a social structure—in a word—a world. In Sidney the claims of love and desire are, even in the sylvan realm of clear streams and shady glens, pitted against the harsh restraints of law. M. Corti, in his *Metodi e fantasmi* (Milan, 1969), pp. 281–304, provides a critical base for discussing Sannazzaro's *Arcadia.*

90. See Gent, *Picture and Poetry*, pp. 5–18. For a further treatment of the importation of such conceptual terms as *sculptural, pictorial, one view composition,* and so on, see M. Barasch, *Theories of Art: From Plato to Winckelmann* (New York, 1985), pp. 112–15, and of course E. Panofsky, *Galileo as a Critic of Art* (The Hague, 1954), *passim.*

91. On the playwright Webster, see T. Bogard, *The Tragic Satire of John Webster* (Berkeley, 1955), pp. 144 ff. The changing character of the romance comedy is discussed in the introduction to the Arden edition of Shakespeare's *Cymbeline*, by J. Nosworth (London, 1955), pp. xlviii–lxxxiv. The classic account is of course N. Frye's *A Natural Perspective: The Development of Shakespearean Comedy and Romance* (New York, 1965).

92. Keith Thomas's reading of the climate of social and political thought in the time of Hobbes is bracing and masterful; see his "The Social Origins of Hobbes Political Thought," in *Hobbes Studies,* ed. K. Brown (Oxford, 1965), 185–236. Cf. also, J. Wallace, "John Dryden's Plays and the Conception of a Heroic Society," in *Culture and Politics from Puritanism to the Enlightenment,* ed. P. Zagorin (Los Angeles, 1980), 115–34.

93. Socrates was called upon, in Plato's Cratylus, to arbitrate in the debate between Cratylus and Hermogenes. The former, a follower of Socrates, had stoutly maintained that right names attached to things to the point of being identical. Against this Hermogenes contended that names were nothing but signifiers having no natural relation to what they signified. The ironic Socrates was most illusive, refusing to make a judgment, acknowledging that after much study his puzzlement was even greater than before he had begun to investigate this conundrum. He urged the debaters to seek solitude in the countryside, think hard, and when the truth was discovered, return and enlighten him. See E. Heller, "Notes on Language, Its Deconstruction and On Translation," in *Realism in European Literature,* ed. N. Boyle and M. Swales (Cambridge, 1986), 3–4. On the Greeks and cultural and scientific change, see E. Hussey, *The Presocratics* (London, 1977), p. 117; F. Lloyd, *Early Greek Science: Thales to Aristotle* (New York, 1974). M. Screech, in his *Rabelais* (Ithaca, 1979), pp. 377–97, provides a concise and cogent summary of the impact of Italian humanist dialogues and treatises pertaining to language theory upon sixteenth-century Northern European literati. The contribution of the Italians to the debate was fundamental with the *Cratylus* appearing in Ficino's *Opera omnia* of Plato. Agostino Nifo's frequently reprinted edition of Aristotle's *De interpretatione* was also a basic text in the discussion of the language problem.

A case can be made for a more radical sense of anachronism in Renaissance Italy than in classical antiquity. Umberto Eco, in his *Theory of Semiotics* (Bloomington, Ind., 1976), pp. 80 ff., argues very effectively about the inability of key ancient authors to control anachronism. With relatively few exceptions, ancient theorists discounted the risk of mingling literary styles in favor of syncretic assimilation. Further, it was very rare for a classical author to single out an error of anachronistic reading. Greene, in *The Vulnerable Text,* pp. 218–22, summarizes classical thought on the topic of anachronism, comparing it with the mounting Italian literary self-consciousness. The weakness of the sense of anachronism in Greek civilization as compared with the stronger and more durable manifestations, first in Italy and then in the north of Europe, may be a topic worth further consideration. Also, while the idea of progress took hold in fifth-century B.C. Athens and was widely accepted by an educated public, after this time the influence of major philosophical schools was hostile to this notion and it lost much of its attraction. It would seem that the requirement of contrast between an archaic and civil society served as a stimulus for galvanizing this idea, but unlike the experience in Western Europe where the pattern of change was commensurate with the Greek experience, the idea failed to take root. See E. Dodds, *The Ancient Concept of Progress and Other Essays on Greek Literature and Belief* (Oxford, 1973; reprint ed., 1983), pp. 1–26.

94. On the ability to tolerate disequilibrium while pursuing "variety" as a rhetorical goal, see Cave's *Cornucopian Text,* pp. 322 ff. (This is a work not to be missed for those interested in the literary affinity for *copia* of sixteenth-century literati and humanist teachers of rhetoric.) For the introduction of poetic imitation as endeavoring to portray "la vita vivente della realtà" (the organic life of reality), see the influential writings of Giambattista Giraldi Cinzio and Guilio Cammillo, as well as the popularization of their ideas by Francesco Patrizi and Tasso in Garin, *L'umanesimo italiano,* pp. 187–89, with bibliography. The significance of the acceptance of limits was, in the judgment of the historian of science, Anneliese Maier, crucial for seventeenth-century science. Only by renouncing absolute rigor and absolute measurement, were the exact sciences rendered possible. For a nuanced discussion of her work, see Funkenstein, *Theology and the Scientific Imagination,* pp. 70, 122, 144–45, 308–13, 354, 361.

95. On Catherine de' Medici and her preference for a reclining Venus rather than an effigy of rotting flesh, see E. Kantorowicz, *The King's Two Bodies: A Study in Mediaeval Political Theology* (Princeton, 1957), p. 431, E. Panofsky's *Tomb Sculpture: Its Changing Aspects from Ancient Egypt to Bernini* (New York, 1964), offers vivid illustrations of humanist influence on tomb sculpture. Cf. esp. pp. 74–96.

Epilogue: The Fragile Construct

1. B. Migliorini, *The Italian Language,* rev. and ed. T. Griffith (London, 1984), esp. chap. 2, "From Latin to Italian," pp. 35–55.

2. Gilbert's discussion of key words such as *ragione, fortuna, necessità,* and so on is exemplary. See his *Machiavelli and Guicciardini,* pp. 37–44.

3. For a discussion of developments in the fine arts pertaining to Bernini, see Panofsky, *Tomb Sculpture,* (New York, 1964), pp. 63–65.

4. Auerbach, *Mimesis,* pp. 375–76.

5. Ibid, p. 311.

6. On Descartes and the concept of method, see the very useful survey by V. Kahn, "Humanism and the Resistance to Theory," in *Literary Theory/Renaissance Texts,* ed. P. Parker and D. Quint (Baltimore, 1986), 375–88.

7. B. Williams, *Descartes: The Project of Pure Enquiry* (Atlantic Highlands, N.J., 1978), p. 26.

8. Ibid., p. 27.

9. P. Bénichou, *Man and Ethics: Studies in French Classicism,* trans. E. Hughes (New York, 1971), pp. 102 ff., provides a sensitive analysis of the volatile mix of archaic, heroic ideals with restraint of political authority.

Index